MW01059154

Talin Suciyan completed her PhD at Ludwig Maximilian University in Munich where she is currently an assistant professor (Akademische Raetin Auf Zeit) at the Institute of Near and Middle Eastern Studies.

'This study fills a historiographical vacuum. The subjects broached in this work until now constituted a white page, doubtless because the Turkish academic environment was not interested in conducting a study of this nature. The wealth and the originality of the sources is unique, and keeps a good balance between the interventionism of the Turkish state and the internal problems of Armenian society. Highly recommended.'

Raymond Kevorkian, author of *The Armenian Genocide:*
A Complete History (I.B.Tauris, 2011)

THE ARMENIANS IN MODERN TURKEY

Post-Genocide Society, Politics and History

TALIN SUCIYAN

I.B. TAURIS

LONDON · NEW YORK

Published in 2016 by
I.B.Tauris & Co. Ltd
London • New York
www.ibtauris.com

Library of Ottoman Studies 48

ISBN: 978 1 78453 171 3
eISBN: 978 0 85772 972 9

A full CIP record for this book is available from the British Library
A full CIP record is available from the Library of Congress

Library of Congress Catalog Card Number: available

Edited by Dr Burcu Gursel

Typeset in Garamond Three by OKS Prepress Services, Chennai, India
Printed and bound by CPI Group (UK) Ltd, Croydon, CR0 4YY

Dedicated to the beloved memory of Varujan Köseyan

CONTENTS

ACKNOWLEDGEMENTS

This book owes much to the support of various institutions. During the first year of my study, I was awarded the Südosteuropa Gesellschaft scholarship for conducting archival research in Yerevan – the first step into my research. I thank Südosteuropa Gesellschaft for their support. In 2012–13, I was the recipient of a scholarship offered by the Armenian General Benevolent Union (AGBU), which supported my research during my six months on leave. I am grateful to AGBU for granting me a scholarship for two consecutive years. This book is a revised and extended version of my dissertation, *Surviving the Ordinary: The Armenians in Turkey, 1930s to 1950*, which was submitted in partial fulfilment of the requirements for the degree of Doctor of Philosophy in the subject of Ottoman and Turkish Studies at Ludwig-Maximilian University, Institute of Near and Middle Eastern Studies.

However, without financial and moral support from my parents, Hasmik and Hamparsum Suciyan, this work would have taken far longer to complete. I am grateful to them for having supported my decisions even when we disagreed, and feel privileged to have such parents. Having had restricted options in life, they always strive to give the best and the most they can. I thank them for their love and support throughout this intellectually and emotionally challenging period.

I dedicate this study to the memory of the late Varujan Köseyan, who collected and stored Armenian newspapers and other publications at Surp P'rgich' Armenian Hospital, thus bequeathing a priceless source of information to future generations, historians among them. This study would not have been possible without that newspaper archive. I was honoured by Köseyan's friendship and trust during the last two years of his life, and learned very much from him.

In addition to Varujan Köseyan, a group of friends and colleagues supported my work both with their enthusiasm and by providing me access to personal or institutional archives. I thank Meline Pehlivanian, Christl Catanzaro, Varteni Mosditchian, Yeliz Soytemel, Ara Sanjian, Ara Sarafian, Ari Sitas, Dimitri Theodoridis, Haçik Gazer, Helmut Thiess, Hrach Bayadyan, Kevork Kirkoryan, Marc Mamigonian, Mihran Dabag, Boğaç Ergene, Aret Kantian, Martin Kühn, Sevan Değirmenciyan, Taner Akçam, Vahé Tachjian, Wolfgang Schmitt-Garibian and Yavuz Aykan. I owe special thanks to Vartan Matiossian, who proofread the dissertation and made some very valuable comments and contributions, and to Marc Mamigonian for his feedback on the book manuscript. I am grateful to Tomasz Hoskins at I.B.Tauris for taking this project on and to Sara Magness for seeing it through to its completion. I had the good fortune to work with Burcu Gürsel, who edited this book and offered substantial suggestions in my rethinking of 'the habitus'. I thank her wholeheartedly.

One of the most exciting parts of this work was the oral interviews I conducted. My extended family in Canada supported me by contacting Armenians from Istanbul and Asia Minor in Montreal, and facilitated my meetings with them. I thank all the interviewees and cherish the grateful memory of my late aunt Evdoksi Parseghyan (1926–2013), who was very patient with me throughout our sessions. I feel beholden to everyone who accepted my invitation to join my endeavour in oral history.

The main body of this work was written in Yeşilköy (Ayastefanos), in a house that met its own share of the Republican destiny awaiting residences whose owners and inhabitants had to leave Turkey in the 1950s. My cousin's family had been the last tenants, of 30 years, of the house where I spent the summer of 2012 with my cousin Setrak Mendikyan, writing my thesis. The history of its handover, first to the state and then to third persons, exemplifies a common practice that continues to this day and deserves scholarly attention. Nonetheless, I had the good fortune to enjoy its unique atmosphere, silence and tranquility, all of which helped me better concentrate on my work. The writing process involved multiple layers of difficulty, especially when it came to the sections involving my own family on both sides. I thank Setrak for his patience and support throughout those difficult times.

A group of women friends both in Istanbul and in Munich made my life so much easier and helped me throughout the rather troubling period toward the end this study, some by reading and commenting on it, others by taking me out after long hours of work and never leaving me in a state of burnout. I extend my heartfelt thanks to them all.

I am not sure whether I would have attempted to undertake this work had Aret Gıcır not encouraged me in this decision and thus lit the first spark for this project. Both my first advisor, Christoph K. Neumann, and my second advisor Hans-Lukas Kieser from the University of Zurich always made themselves available to read and comment on my work. I thank them for their input, comments and support.

PREFACE

One of the most difficult problems in working with Armenian sources is their worldwide dispersion. In my first year of research, I worked for one month at the Armenian National Library. I then discovered the storage in the Surp P'rgich' Armenian Hospital, where almost all Istanbul newspapers published after 1927, as well as magazines, yearbooks and other printed documents were deposited. This storage area was supposed to become a library, the collection having been put together by Varujan Köseyan, the author of a book devoted to the 150th anniversary of the Armenian Surp P'rgich' Hospital. According to Köseyan's account, he rescued the collection right before disposal or recycling and stored it in a room; I was able to work there during my semester breaks for three years. Without that collection, I could not have written this book. I am very grateful to him, as all historians interested in the post-1923 period and Armenians all over the world should be, for saving this collection. Moreover, I had the privilege of enjoying his friendship and tried to record our talks as much as possible, since he was staying at the hospital's nursing home. I would like to pay my special and heartfelt respects to Varujan Köseyan's beloved memory. After his death in 2011, Arsen Yarman allowed me to continue and finish my research under what remained unfavourable working conditions. Because the room was extremely dusty, I could not stay inside any longer than an hour at a time during my last months of research. I am glad to see that my research contributed to the restoration of that storage room and that by now it has become a well-organised library with its own researchers. The Armenian Teachers' Association's library in Istanbul also had some valuable primary sources, such as the minutes of the General National

[Armenian] Assembly meetings and collections of private yearbooks, as well a remarkably helpful staff. In addition, I was able to locate the collection of *Nor Or* (which was missing in Surp P'rgich') at the *Agos* office.

During my two visits to the United States in 2011 and 2012, I worked at the library of the National Association for Armenian Studies and Research (NAASR) in Boston, at the Armenian Research Centre of the University of Michigan-Dearborn, and at the Zohrab Centre in New York. I am thankful to Ara Sanjian, Marc Mamigonian and colleagues in Zohrab Centre and *Agos* for providing material and enabling me to work in libraries and archives. The research and teaching fellows at the Armenian Teachers' Association and Surp P'rgich' Armenian Hospital were always ready to offer assistance. Last but not least, friends at Aras Publications helped me with my research by sending books or scanning material. I owe them special thanks.

In 2012, I discovered another important archive of Armenian newspapers at the Istanbul University Library, but the fees would require substantial financial means for a researcher to finish a work of this scope.

The Bavarian State Library is also an important source of some very rare Armenian newspapers and yearbooks, as well as books. Wolfgang Schmitt-Garibian and Helmut Thiess, two librarians at the Bavarian State Library, were always ready to help with the Armenian language sources of the Library and taught me a lot about sources that had previously been unknown to me. I am thankful for their assistance.

Most of the material analysed in this book, including oral history interviews, is in Armenian, and some in Turkish. I am responsible for all possible shortcomings in their translation.

In the footnotes, I used the dates as well as the issue numbers of the newspapers that I consulted, with the exception of some of the *Nor Lur* issues after the 1930s, for which the dates are still noted.

TRANSLITERATION SYSTEM[1]

Vernacular	Romanization	Vernacular	Romanization
Upper case letters		*Lower case letters*	
Ա	A	ա	a
Բ	B [P] (see Note 1)	բ	b [p] (see Note 1)
Գ	G [K] (see Note 1)	գ	g [k] (see Note 1)
Դ	D [T] (see Note 1)	դ	d [t] (see Note 1)
Ե	{ E / Y (see Note 2)	ե	{ e / y (see Note 2)
Զ	Z	զ	z
Է	Ē	է	ē
Ը	Ě	ը	ě
Թ	T'	թ	t'
Ժ	Zh (see Note 3)	ժ	zh (see Note 3)
Ի	I	ի	i
Լ	L	լ	l
Խ	Kh	խ	kh
Ծ	Ts [Dz] (see Notes 1, 3)	ծ	ts [dz] (see Notes 1, 3)
Կ	K [G] (see Note 1)	կ	k [g] (see Note 1)
Հ	H	հ	h
Ձ	Dz [Ts] (see Notes 1, 3)	ձ	dz [ts] (see Notes 1, 3)
Ղ	Gh (see Note 3)	ղ	gh (see Note 3)
Ճ	Ch [J] (see Note 1)	ճ	ch [j] (see Note 1)
Մ	M	մ	m
Յ	{ Y / H (see Note 4)	յ	{ y / h (see Note 4)

'Ն	N	ն	n
Շ	Sh (see Note 3)	շ	sh (see Note 3)
Ո	O	ո	o
Չ	Chʻ	չ	chʻ
Պ	P [B] (see Note 1)	պ	p [b] (see Note 1)
Ջ	J [Ch] (see Note 1)	ջ	j [ch] (see Note 1)
Ռ	Ṛ	ռ	ṛ
Ս	S	ս	s
Վ	V	վ	v
Տ	T [D] (see Note 1)	տ	t [d] (see Note 1)
Ր	R	ր	r
Ց	Tsʻ	ց	tsʻ
Ւ	W	ւ	w
Ու	U	ու	u
Փ	Pʻ	փ	pʻ
Ք	Kʻ	ք	kʻ
Եւ	Ew (see Note 5)	եւ	ew (see Note 5)
Եվ	Ev (see Note 6)	եվ	ev (see Note 6)
Օ	Ō	օ	ō
Ֆ	F	ֆ	f

Notes

1. The table is based on the phonetic values of Classical and East Armenian. The variant phonetic values of West Armenian are included in brackets but are intended solely for use in preparing references from West Armenian forms of name when this may be desirable.
2. This value is used only when the letter is in initial position of a name and followed by a vowel, in Classical orthography.
3. The soft sign (prime) is placed between the two letters representing two different sounds when the combination might otherwise be read as a digraph (e.g., Դժնունի Dʹznuni).
4. This value is used only when the letter is in initial position of a word or of a stem in a compound, in Classical orthography.
5. Romanization for letters in Classical orthography, sometimes appears as ու.
6. Romanization for letters in Reformed orthography, sometimes appears as ու.

NOTE ON TRANSLITERATION

The transliteration follows the Library of Congress's transliteration table, found at http://www.loc.gov/catdir/cpso/romanization/armenian.pdf. I have used the Western Armenian transliteration system throughout this book, including names and titles in Eastern Armenian.

I did not transliterate names that already had an established orthography, such as Toros Azadyan, Kevork Arslanyan, Zabel Yesayan, Kevork the VIth, Hayganuş Mark, Puzant Yeghiayan or Echmiadzin. For Armenian surnames, I used *–yan* for Armenians living in Turkey and Armenia, and for all others, *–ian*. As for institutions, I used their own transliterations, e.g. Karagözyan Orphanage. In the case of the book on the history of the orphanage, however, I transliterated it as *Hushamadean Karagēōzyan Orpanots'i*.

I did not transliterate the names of cities, such as Kayseri, Everek, etc. Whenever city names or village names appeared in Armenian, I wrote the Turkish names as well.

Armenian newspapers consulted in this study (such as *Marmara*, *Nor Lur*, *Nor Or*, *Aysor* and *Tebi Luys*) offered their own Latin transliteration (which I too have adopted) under the Armenian title on the front page.

In some books (for instance, by Aras Publishing), the publisher's transliteration is available; I included them in the footnotes in order to facilitate the work of future researchers.

LIST OF ABBREVIATIONS

AGBU: Armenian General Benevolent Union
ANR: Armenian National Relief
ANCA: Armenian National Council of America
ARF: Armenian Revolutionary Federation
CUP: Committee of Union and Progress
GDPF: General Directorate of Pious Foundations (*Vakıflar Genel Müdürlüğü*)
GNA: General National {Armenian} Assembly
NER: Near East Relief
STS: Single Trustee System (*Tek Mütevelli Sistemi*)

The 'perfect crime' does not consist in killing the victim or the witnesses . . .
but rather in obtaining the silence of the witnesses, the deafness of the
judges, and the inconsistency (insanity) of the testimony.

Jean-François Lyotard
The Differend: Phrases in Dispute

INTRODUCTION

The epigraph of this study spells out the import of the contradictions and dilemmas I faced throughout my research in a dusty storage room, where nearly complete sets of Armenian publications in Turkey after 1927 were kept. With the exception of a couple of researchers, hardly anyone was interested in them. I have been to many Armenian libraries around the world, where I have always asked how many people typically come for research – the answer was always the same. The Nubarian Library in Paris felt surreal: 40,000 books, photographs, magazines, personal archives … In Boston, in New York, and elsewhere: libraries, archives of newspapers, of oral interviews conducted with survivors throughout the 1980s. How many hundreds of publications based on these oral accounts might have seen the light of day? Such questions are inspired by the fact that there is a direct connection between the use of sources and denial: Sources have very little to say, if anything at all, when their very existence is denied.

In this book, I attempt to write a post-genocide history of the vestiges of Armenian existence in Turkey – the geography of genocide and denial. The crime has continued to be reproduced by denial, while victims and witnesses have continued to live side by side with the perpetrators. The testimonies of both victim and witness were silenced and denied; as the perfection of the crime proves, memories and testimonies were inverted. Thus, this book mainly deals with the history of denial and strives to make the sources on the Armenian experience speak out. However, under the heavy burden of institutionalised denial, one may very well ask, 'What do they say?' and, more importantly, 'How do they say it?' or 'To whom do they speak?' I can only write about the sources I have consulted, which are in no way monolithic: In some cases, they speak out directly despite being surrounded by institutionalised denial. In others, they speak, but only implicitly. One can easily see that Armenian sources are rather innovative in the art of insinuation. At times, Armenian sources themselves become part of the denial, for a lack of alternatives for existence. However, one of the most important questions has remained unanswered throughout my research and writing process: What is the meaning of speaking when no one is there to listen? Armenian sources are implicitly or explicitly expressive about the problems of Armenians, offering solutions, trying to sort out a way to establish reasonable survival conditions. However, their efforts go unheard by the majority.

I am aware of the limits of history writing as well as my own limits in writing about something that has always been very difficult or even impossible to express.[1] Hence, this study seeks to understand what it means to be born into and live within a post-genocidal context, where language/s, words or memory/ies are all besieged by the absolute denial of genocide. The language, the words, and the memories to which I refer in this book are mainly Western Armenian – a language on the verge of disappearance,[2] and, in fact, one that has become the very language of silence. Thus, the impossibility of trying to put the catastrophe into words is coupled with the ongoing extinction of the language. Writing this book, in Heidrun Friese's evocation of Jean-Luc Nancy, is an attempt to 'bring silence [and voices] "into presence"':[3]

> To write, then, does not mean to write a history of silence, or to attempt to make speak those voices which in the speech of concepts and their sentences have been silenced, or to seize the thread of speech that has comfortably established itself within noisy silence of forgetting. Writing, the work and the gestures of writing mean to move within this painful calamity, these places of differences, the thresholds of language, to bring these silences and voices 'into presence'.[4]

In this book, I endeavour to write a socio-political history of the Armenian community in Turkey during the post-World War II period (especially 1945–50), as based mainly on Armenian-language sources.

The community, or more accurately, communities – comprised of Armenian Apostolics, Armenian Catholics and Armenian Protestants – cannot be demarcated by clear lines. Some sources, like the yearbooks of the Armenian Hospital of Surp P'rgich', may, in certain ways, also be considered Armenian Apostolic, but remain accessible to Armenians in general. Hrant Güzelyan, for instance, was a Protestant Armenian who used to serve all Armenian communities; his memoirs cannot be considered exclusively within the context of Protestant Armenians.[5]

Besides probing the abovementioned issues, this study asks: From the Ottoman *millet* to *Turkish citizens*, what were the ways in which Armenians perpetuated their socio-political existence in the structures and fields of denial in post-genocide Turkey? The attempt at understanding state policies and societal relations in a post-genocidal context of denial opens up an entirely new perspective, especially through the use of Armenian-language newspapers, almanacs, memoirs, magazines and oral history sources, which reveal the social habitus of post-genocide Turkey from the perspective of Armenians remaining in Istanbul, Asia Minor and the eastern provinces. The context of denial during the immediate post-genocide period is a pivotal point of departure in this book, since the imperial legacy of the nineteenth- and early- twentieth-century Ottoman Empire, combined with the Genocide, has created unique socio-political structures in the Republic of Turkey. The structural and administrative continuities between the Ottoman Empire and Turkey deserve particular attention. I will dwell on these continuities and their role in reproducing denial in the first chapter of this book. Similarly, the Single Party period in Turkey should also be read in this context, by putting the institutionalisation of denial at its core, and by using sources from other communities, in order to discover the intertwinement of denialist mechanisms. Consequently, this book is not only about the history of the Armenians remaining in Turkey; it is also a history of Turkey based on Armenian sources.

Sources

The daily and weekly newspapers published in Istanbul in 1945–50 constitute the main sources for this book. Editorials, commentaries and news items in various newspapers concerning the inner dynamics of the Armenian community are analysed in order to understand their socio-political context. I also often felt the need to look at pre- and post-genocide sources, such as the memoirs of patriarchs, so as to tease out the social context of the remaining Armenians in Turkey and to show the social dynamics of the community, including tensions between Armenians coming from the provinces and the local Armenians of Istanbul. In order to depict the background of the period under study, I also consulted newspapers from the 1930s, such as *Nor Luys*, *Ngar*, *Panper* and *Nor Lur*, while for the particular postwar period I scanned *Nor Or* (1945–6), *Nor Lur* (1945–9), *Marmara* (1944–50), *Aysor* (1947–8), *Tebi Luys* (1950) and *Paros* (1950). In addition, I perused the sections of *Jamanak* of 1941–4 that proved relevant to the specific topics in question. I could not scan *all* Armenian magazines and newspapers of the period because of the density of the extant material.

The reference work I consulted to gauge the scope of Armenian publications of Istanbul in the post-1923 period up until 1950 was *Hay Barperagan Mamuli Madenakidut'yun* (1794–1967) (*Bibliography of Armenian Periodical Press*, 1794–1967), which was published in Yerevan in 1970, and which lists 71 periodicals that appeared in 1923–50 in Istanbul.[6] Another list in the same source cites titles by place of publication and includes 94 periodicals published in Turkey in 1924–50.[7] The numerical difference indicates probable mistakes in both lists, since Istanbul was the only place mentioned in the book for all publications during this period. In any case, the number of Armenian periodicals was still high during the first decades of the Republic. Among these publications were monthly and weekly magazines, almanacs, children's magazines and daily newspapers.

While working with the daily and weekly newspapers, I came to understand that the mission of Armenian newspapers was manifold. First and foremost, newspapers were the only instruments for intellectuals to express their ideas, albeit under strict constraints. Their existence was most valuable in the absence of other democratic mechanisms for expression and for Armenian political representation. Second, Armenian newspapers mostly functioned as representatives of various segments of the community. Their political stance was often for or against the Patriarchate, particularly in the period 1944–50, and remained more or less the same at times of heightened (state-organised or other) anti-Armenian campaigns. Third, Armenian newspapers in Turkey were venues for the transmission of historical knowledge, since the teaching of Armenian history was banned. All Armenian newspapers began publishing series of articles on Armenian institutional, religious, economic, social, or cultural history at one time or another. I found an astonishing amount of biographical and institutional information in newspapers, mostly as an introduction to the Armenian contribution from the early Ottoman period to the twentieth century. Fourth, they either translated or sometimes transliterated almost all articles related to Armenians in the Turkish press. Therefore, by reading the Armenian press, one could follow the Turkish press with regard to Armenian-related issues. Fifth, Armenian newspapers were a source of information on worldwide Armenian communities. This was an important mission, since all Armenians had relatives in other parts of the world. Sixth, the Armenian community in Istanbul and elsewhere followed Soviet Armenia mainly through the Armenian press, which constituted a bridge between all of these communities. Seventh, Armenian newspapers played an important role in the search for relatives lost after 1915. Advertisements of 'Looking For' ('*Gě P'ndṛuî*') continue to appear to this day. 'Looking For' advertisements (among others) intended to inform individuals about letters from abroad and to reveal close communal relations. Newspapers would print the names of people for whom letters had arrived so that they may be received. Furthermore, newspapers supported literature, providing an opportunity to produce and publish in Armenian, as was the case for many novels that were first published serially and later as books.[8] The works of prominent Armenian authors that had previously been published elsewhere were also serialised in newspapers.

A brief summary of the history of the newspapers examined in this study is in order. Published in 1924–54, *Nor Lur* was a daily newspaper in the 1930s and a biweekly during the second half of the 1940s.[9] A special book published on the occasion of the 40th anniversary of *Jamanak* stated that *Nor Lur* was in tight competition with *Jamanak*.[10] While doing archival research, I realised that *Nor Lur* had ceased publication after May 1944 and resumed in February 1945. Although the reason for this interruption is unknown, I noticed that it shrank in size once it resumed publication, while its content seemed different than the *Nor Lur* of the 1930s, this time including more commentaries and editorials than news items, probably due to change in periodicity. It featured long articles by editor-in-chief Vahan Toşikyan (Istanbul

1880–1954) and his wife, Hayganuş Mark, the famous Armenian writer and publisher of the banned feminist magazine *Hay Gin* (*Armenian Woman*).[11] According to Step'anyan, Vahan Toşikyan worked in journalism for over 50 years. He first worked in *Manzume-i Efkar* and then for *Jamanak* and *Verchin Lur*,[12] and then, as the editor-in-chief of *Arshaluys* and *Artsakank'* in Izmir (1907–9).[13] In 1922 he returned to Istanbul, working again for *Jamanak* and *Verchin Lur*. He then began publishing *Verchin Lur* as *Nor Lur*, which lasted for 30 years,[14] and which maintained a pro-Patriarchate position during the patriarchal election crisis in 1944–50.

There is conflicting information on the year of first publication for the newspaper *Marmara*. A subscription receipt dated 1925 confirming payment for a subscription in 1923–4 bears the original print titles *Azadamard* and *Jagadamard*, over which the title *Marmara* was written by hand.[15] It appears that the receipts for the old newspapers had been reused for the new one, which indicates that these three newspapers were connected. Both *Azadamard* and *Jagadamard* (its new name after resuming publication in the armistice period) had been newspapers of the Armenian Revolutionary Federation (1909–15, 1918–24). *Hay Barperagan Mamuli Madenkidut'yun* states that *Marmara*, founded by Suren Şamlıyan (Kıncılar 1899/1900–Geneva 1951) and published under Bedros Zobyan starting in 1924, was to be the new title for *Jagadamard*.[16] *Marmara Daily* resumed publication in 1940 with editor-in-chief Suren Şamlıyan, and still exists today.[17] Kevork Kirkoryan kindly provided biographical information about Suren Şamlıyan: according to his unpublished research, Şamlıyan was born in Kıncılar (Geyve), near Adapazarı, in 1899 or 1900. Karnig Step'anyan's *Biographical Dictionary* (*Gensakragan Pararan*) notes that he attended an Armenian school in Istanbul, then worked for *Arevelyan Mamul* and *Joghovurti Ts'ayn* in 1918–20, as well as for Turkish newspapers (*Akşam, Vakıt, Cumhuriyet*).[18] He was the editor-in-chief of *Marmara*. Apparently, this *Marmara* was the one published before 1940, since Step'anyan's biographical account follows chronological order. In 1928, he started to publish the short-lived *Shep'or* and *Sharjum*, and then worked for *Daily Express* and *Daily Mail* as well. He left Turkey with his family and settled in Brussels, where he published *Belgo-Türk*. Upon his return, he began to publish *Marmara* in 1940, translated a series of novels and other books into Armenian,[19] and wrote the novel *Dardaneli Baderazmě*.[20] His newspaper opposed *locum tenens* Archbishop Kevork Arslanyan during the crisis of 1944–50.

The newspaper *Jamanak*, founded by editor Misak Koçunyan (1863–1913) and published by the Koçunyan family since 1908,[21] was one of the most widely circulated dailies in Istanbul,[22] and the oldest among them. As many Armenian columnists or journalists in Turkey had worked for *Jamanak* at some point in their careers, it was regarded as a professional training field for Armenian journalists.

A newspaper I discuss extensively in the third chapter of this book, *Nor Or*, started publication as a weekly in July 1945 and became a daily newspaper within a year. According to *Hay Barperagan Mamuli Madenakidut'yun* (*Bibliography of Armenian Periodical Press*), several newspapers were published by the same title in Istanbul and elsewhere.[23] The same source mentions that Avedis Aliksanyan (Istanbul 1910–Paris 1984)[24] was the editor-in-chief of *Nor Or* in 1945–6.[25] As far as I understand from the biographies of the publishers and editorial writers of *Nor Or*, its editors-in-chief were Avedis Aliksanyan, Sarkis Keçyan (pen name S. K. Zanku, Istanbul 1917–Paris 2004)[26] and Aram Pehlivanyan (pen name A. Şavarş; his Turkish alias in the Turkish Communist Party was Ahmet Saydan, Istanbul 1917–Leipzig 1979).[27] Aliksanyan published *Badger* with Ara Koçunyan before *Nor Or*.[28] The latter was definitely one of the most (if not *the* most) outspoken Armenian newspapers published in the post-1923 era. It was banned in December 1946 under Martial Law. The group around *Nor Or*, the first generation of post-genocide Armenian intellectuals, was dispersed around the world by the end of the 1940s as a result of state persecution. Thus, the Armenian community remaining in Turkey after 1915 lost its intellectuals once again within 35 years. In the post-genocidal period the state was still persecuting and imprisoning Armenian intellectuals, thereby attesting to the line of continuity between the Ottoman Empire and the Republic of Turkey in terms of state policies of severing relations between Armenian intellectuals and their community.

After the ban of *Nor Or*, *Aysor* started publication in 1947 and continued as a weekly until 1948 again under the editor-in-chief Avedis Aliksanyan. Pakarat Tevyan commented in his *Erchanig Darekirk' 1948* that *Aysor* followed the literary life of Europe and the US, publishing works by new writers and poets.[29]

Tebi Luys was published by Rupen Maşoyan (Istanbul 1928–99) and Yervant Gobelyan (Istanbul 1923–2010) – two important names in the history of the Armenian publishing world in Istanbul. Maşoyan contributed to *Hantes Mışaguyti* (published by Getronagan alumni), *Jamanak*, *Agos* and *Nor Tar*, among others, and taught at Getronagan High School.[30] Gobelyan was the author of numerous books including *Yerani Te*[31] (1948), *Khıcangarner*[32] (1968) and *Memleketini Özleyen Yengeç* (1998),[33] and established the Tebi Luys publishing house in 1948. He also founded the weekly *Luys* and then published *Tebi Luys* until its termination due to financial problems. In 1953–4 he worked for the daily *Ayk* in Beirut[34] and, on his return to Istanbul, for *Marmara* until 1957, only to go back to Beirut until 1965 and join the weekly *Sp'iwřk'*. During the last 15 years of his life, he worked for the Armenian–Turkish weekly *Agos*. The weekly *Tebi Luys* predominantly published literary pieces, poetry and commentaries on the arts in Istanbul, Soviet Armenia and the diasporan communities. Although according to *Hay Barperagan Mamuli Madenakidut'yun*, *Tebi Luys* started publication in 1948,[35] the date does not seem to be accurate, as the ninth issue was dated 29 April 1950 (which puts the start of publication in March 1950).[36] The confusion may stem from the fact that there was a homonymous publishing house established in 1948, but the newspaper itself did not exist. The newspaper had to cease publication due to financial problems in June 1951, but resumed within a year.[37]

Another weekly, *Paros*, started publication in 1949 under Takvor Acun and in the midst of the patriarchal election crisis and the ensuing polarisation of the Armenian community. *Paros* was a common title for Armenian periodicals around the world. *Hay Barperagan Mamuli Madenakidut'yun* mentions many, but not the one published in Istanbul. According to Pakarat Tevyan's almanac, *Paros* was briefly published as a daily; it ceased publication after five years, in 1954.[38]

After newspapers, yearbooks, which could be published by institutions or by individuals, constitute the second important group of sources. One of the most well-known yearbook publishers was Teotig[39] and his *Amēnun Darēts'oyts'ĕ* (*Everyone's Almanac*). This book examines *Türk Ermeni Hastanesi Salnamesi/Ēntartsag Darēkirk' Surp P'rgich' Hiwantanots'i (1932, 1937, 1938, 39, 42, 44, 45, 46, 47, 48, 49)* and *Erchanig Darēkirk' (Happy Almanac, 1944, 45, 46, 47, 48, 49, 50, 51, 52, 53, 54, 57, 58)*, published by Pakarat Tevyan.[40] Both almanacs covered a wide range of topics every year including new Armenian publications and literature, new laws, the Armenian press, biographical

information, history, art and statistical data on both Turkey and
Armenians. It is remarkable that Server R. İskit, who published various
volumes on printing in Turkey and worked at the Directorate General of
the Press (*Matbuat Umum Müdürlüğü*), did not mention any of these
sources in the section 'Special Annuals' (*'Hususi Salnameler'*) in his book,
Türkiye'de Neşriyat Hareketleri Tarihine Bakış.[41] Another publication
that is worthy of mention along with almanacs is the special edition
devoted to the 15th anniversary (1938) of the Republic of Turkey by
Toros Azadyan (T. Azad)[42] and Mardiros Koç (M. Koç).[43] This special
edition includes some very important statistical data about the
Armenian population in the provinces. A third important group of
sources is the memoirs by prominent public intellectuals of the time
such as Toros Azadyan, Hrant Güzelyan (or Küçükgüzelyan), Agop
Arslanyan, William Saroyan and Dr Hayk Açıkgöz.

Personal files, such as Aram Pehlivanyan's archives (currently in the
custody of his daughter Meline Pehlivanian in Berlin), and oral
interviews recorded in various places also constitute primary sources for
this study. I have held interviews on recent history with Varujan
Köseyan (Edincik 1920–Istanbul 2011), Civan and Hayguhi Çakır
(both born in Ordu, living in Montreal), Evdoksi Suciyan Parsehyan
(born in Istanbul, deceased in Montreal), Baghdik and Shushan
Hagopyan (born in Istanbul, living in Montreal), A. K. (born in Vakıf–
Hatay, living in Berlin), K. B. (born in Diyarbekir–Lice, living in
Berlin), Ara Toşikyan (born in Istanbul, living in Montreal), Ara
Garmiryan (born in Istanbul, living in Montreal), N. D. (born in
Malatya, living in Istanbul), A. B. (born in Kütahya, living in Munich)
and K. A. (born in Sivas, living in Munich). Open-ended questions were
asked in the course of oral interviews on recent history, mostly starting
with the family background of the interviewee and then moving on to
his or her own experiences.

Armenians in the diaspora founded compatriotic associations that
published voluminous books on the history, ethnography, geography,
population and economy of their cities of origin throughout the last
several decades. Among these books we can cite *Armenian History of Aintab*
(1953),[44] *Tiwtsaznagan Urfan Ew Ir Hayortinerĕ* (1955),[45] *Badmut'iwn
Darōni Ashkharhi* (1956),[46] *Kharpert Ew Anor Osgeghēn Tashdĕ* (1959),[47]
Badmut'iwn Baghnadan (1966),[48] *Badmut'iwn Hayots' Arapgiri* (1969),[49]
Badmakirk' Chmshgadzaki (1971),[50] *Badmut'iwn Zeyt'uni 1409–1921*

(1996),[51] *Badmakirk' Hushamadean Sepasdio Ew Kavaṛi Hayut'ean* (2 volumes, 1974 and 1983)[52] and *Bolis Ew Ir Terĕ* (1965–88).[53] These works, not all of which were available for consultation for this book, usually contain rather short chapters on the mid-twentieth century.

The minutes of the Armenian National Assembly of 1950 and the reports of its committees on the Patriarchate crisis in 1944–50 allowed me to both verify my other sources and reach a deeper and more comprehensive understanding of the legal situation until the 1950s. Along the same lines, the memoirs of Toros Azadyan, who represented the Patriarchate during the trial held in Beirut, helped me to better understand the position of the Patriarchate.[54] The correspondence of the Catholicos of All Armenians Kevork VI with the Patriarchate in Istanbul, with the Catholicosate of Cilicia in Beirut and with religious leaders elsewhere about the Patriarchal crisis in Istanbul constitutes a rich source on the international and inter-communal cross-border power relations behind the crisis.[55]

The Prime Ministry Archives on the Republican period were also helpful in understanding the official Turkish position regarding the Armenian press and Armenian communities in general.

The Rationale for this Book

Modern Turkish history has been defined by the selective use of sources and the exclusion of other categories of materials. Had oral and written records of Kurds, Armenians, Rums, Assyrians or other groups been addressed in Ottoman and Turkish historiographies, we would have had a very different kind of history writing.[56] The core of official Turkish historiography has mainly been based on Ottoman and Turkish-language state documents, memoirs of state officials and certain consular reports, while remaining oblivious to troubling areas of history. As Hans-Lukas Kieser accurately states in the introduction to his *Der Verpasste Friede/Iskalanmış Barış*, Armenians and Kurds, as well as the entire Christian heritage of Anatolia, have simply been left outside official Turkish historiography; without these key elements, the history of Turkey resembles a history of Germany without Jews, or of California without Native Americans.[57] Nevertheless, it was not only the history of the eastern provinces, but also the history of the westernmost parts of Asia Minor that was erased or fabricated by Turkish official historiography. It is only recently that alternative sources are being heard, though they remain in the margins of the public sphere in Turkey.[58] However, if the choice of not using the sources of the other can be considered as one kind of denial (through dismissal and silencing), another is in fact using these sources in a denialist context. A genocidal turn is a radical moment in history that not only establishes the future of the country or region in which it takes place but also determines, through its repercussions over generations, the lives of the survivors everywhere. Therefore, any use of these sources that disregards the multifarious effects of this decisive turning point in history would fail to contextualise the sources themselves.

Another kind of history writing began to take shape in recent decades, mostly abroad and by a handful of scholars including Taner Akçam, Seyhan Bayraktar, İsmail Beşikçi, Hamid Bozarslan, David Gaunt, Dilek Güven, Hilmer Kaiser, Hans-Lukas Kieser, Janet Klein, Eric Jan Zürcher and recently Uğur Üngör and Mehmet Polatel, whose work shed light on the history of Ottoman Rums, Armenians, Assyrians and Kurds. Armenian historians and scholars including Kevork Pamukciyan, Hrant Der Andreasyan, Richard Hovannisian, Anahide Ter Minassian, Vahakn Dadrian, Raymond Kevorkian, Stephan Astourian, Marc Nichanian, Vahé Tachjian, Arus Yumul, Ara Sarafian and Kevork Bardakjian have made important contributions to research on historical continuity, making available some valuable Armenian and Armeno-Turkish sources such as memoirs, novels, newspapers, letters, statistical data and records of Armenian patriarchate, most of which had been inaccessible to historians who work in Western languages or in Turkish. While this was a development outside Turkey, it made an impact on knowledge production within Turkey as well. Since the mid-1990s, a more critical approach to the history of the early twentieth century and onwards has been developing in Turkish academia. Some of the policies against the remaining non-Muslim communities in Turkey, with peaks like the 6–7 September 1955 pogroms, the Wealth Tax of 1942, the expulsion of Greek nationals in 1964, the mass murder and genocidal policies in Dersim in 1938[59] and the expulsion of Jews from Thrace in 1934, constitute areas in which Turkish academic literature has become increasingly substantial in the past two decades.

However, when studying these critical peaks, one should keep in mind the more invisible, rumbling social and political context, the

8eproduce.

everyday reality in which these events take place. This book aims at understanding this ordinary, banal reality of the post-genocidal habitus and its impact on the lives of Armenians both in Istanbul and in the provinces. Daily repercussions of denial must be discussed and understood in a wider context of history writing. I always feel perplexed when teaching the history of nineteenth- and twentieth-century Ottoman Empire and Turkey: Is it possible to talk about these periods without mentioning the mass atrocities and the genocidal turn in the last period of the Empire? Here, I must disclose that teaching in Germany has made my work somewhat easier, since no one born and raised in Germany would envisage a history of Germany in the twentieth century without the Holocaust. However, the same is not taken for granted when it comes to Ottoman and Turkish history. The debates that have taken place since the 1970s and 1980s in German and European historiography, as well as in social sciences, could not really make their way into Ottoman and Turkish history writing either in Turkey or elsewhere. I do not mean to minimise critical historiography in Turkey; however, the concept of denial, in all its its practical and theoretical mechanisms, still awaits exploration.

I have to confess that I was overwhelmed by Armenian-language sources of both the Republican and the Ottoman era, which usually remain invisible to mainstream scholars of Turkey, partly because these sources are linguistically and physically inaccessible to them. This apparent invisibility also serves the reproduction of official historiography and the avoidance of the minefields of history in general.

In my book, I delineate Turkey's socio-political context by focusing on discussions in Armenian publications. Second, I aim to understand the inner dynamics of the Armenian community in Istanbul and to a certain extent in the provinces as well. What were the conditions, regulations and social structures, both in and outside Istanbul, which became constitutive to post-genocide society formation in Turkey? How did the lives of Armenians change with the problems arising after 1923, and what were the reactions of the Armenian opinion makers to these problems?

The Main Reasons for Choosing this Period

My decision to choose this specific period was mandated by my sources, the most important reason for emphasising the period 1944–50 being the Patriarchal election crisis starting with the sudden death of Patriarch Mesrob Naroyan (1875 Hartert– Muş/Daron–Istanbul 1944) in mid-1944.[60] The crisis began with the conflict over the testament of the Patriarch, continued with the Patriarchal election debates, and lasted until the end of 1950, splitting almost all community institutions as well as the Armenian newspapers into two camps: for or against the *locus tenens* in office, Archbishop Kevork Arslanyan (Agn/Eğin 1867–Istanbul 1951).[61] The Holy See of Echmiadzin (based in Soviet Armenia), the Catholicosate of Cilicia in Lebanon, the Armenian communities outside Turkey, the Turkish government and the Armenian community of Istanbul were all involved in this crisis. The Patriarchal election or non-election turned into an international conflict in every sense. A parallel international crisis concerned the territorial claims pushed forward by the USSR government and the Armenian political organisations at the San Francisco Conference. Immigration calls from the USSR to Armenians, as well as the reactions of Turkish public intellectuals to these calls, played an important role in placing the remaining Armenians in Turkey in the middle of international postwar politics. In the complete absence of any administrative and representative body in the Armenian community of Turkey, the task of countering and responding to all anti-Armenian allegations fell on Armenian public figures. Furthermore, starting from 1940 and continuing until the postwar period, one of the most difficult issues that the Armenian community in and outside Istanbul had to deal with was the accusation that Armenians constituted a 'fifth column'. Consequently, Armenian newspapers either found themselves in the position of political actors or were at least regarded as such, which endangered their very existence and freedom, if not the lives of the authors involved. Finally, yet another reason for my decision to focus on this particular period was the fate of the first post-genocide intellectuals and their activities, especially around the newspaper *Nor Or*.

In 1944, two interrelated trends prevailed in Turkey: court cases against the Turkish Communist Party and its members, as well as organised attacks on allegedly leftist publishing houses and newspapers, on the one hand, and on the other, anti-Soviet propaganda, which was to continue well after the end of the war. Simultaneously, Turkey was aware of the danger in aiding Hitler's government via exports of such a strategic metal as chromite ore. In his book based on the archives of the Foreign Relations of United States, *Summer of '42: A Study of German–Armenian*

Relations During the Second World War, Levon Thomassian writes that it was acknowledged that Turkey prolonged the war with its supply of strategic materials to the enemy.[62] In April 1944, German negotiators approached Ankara to renew their trade agreement, which was due to expire in a month.[63] Upon the harsh letters sent by US and British Ambassadors to the Turkish Foreign Minister, which threatened to blockade Turkey if it concluded new trade agreements with Germany for commodities of war,[64] Ankara ceased within six days its shipments of chromite ore to Germany and all other Axis powers.[65] State representatives' public praise of fascist leaders and the Republican People's Party (CHP)'s encouragement of racist ideas among intellectuals and scientific circles highlighted Turkey's position on the *wrong* side by the end of the war. Therefore, the period toward the end of the war was marked by attempts at distancing Kemalist nationalism from the fascist and racist elements that were widespread and continuous from the Young Turk to the Republican elites. One of the best examples for the attempt at distancing is the book published by the Ministry of Education (*Maarif Vekaleti*) by the title *Racism, Turanism (Irkçılık Turancılık)*.[66] The volume includes speeches by the so-called Chief of the Nation (*Milli Şef*) İsmet İnönü, and such prominent opinion makers as Falih Rıfkı Atay, Hüseyin Cahit Yalçın, Burhan Belge, Refik Halid Karay, Necmeddin Sadak, Peyami Safa, Asım Us, Ahmet Emin Yalman, Nadir Nadi and Zekeriya Sertel. They all underscore in their contributions that Kemalism deliberately excluded racism, Turkism and Panturkism. With this publication, the Ministry of Education and, by extension, the state, worked hand in hand with opinion makers to announce that they had shelved ideals of Turkism, racism and Panturkism, as well as racist anthropological surveys. Almost all such articles were written in May 1944, when the famous Racism–Turanism lawsuit against racist Turanists was filed, and racist–Turanist ideologues were driven outside the political scene, if briefly. The lawsuit was one of the most important court cases in Republican history, and was resolved on 29 March 1945, when ten out of the 23 defendants were found guilty. However, they were all to be freed in two years. The timing of the publication, the dates of articles chosen for the book and the court case all overlapped to create a solid image of the newly assumed antiracism and anti-Turanism.

On 2 February 1945, Turkey declared war against the Axis Powers, which was the precondition (to be fulfilled before 1 March) for participation in the San Francisco Conference.[67] However, the San Francisco Conference posed another unexpected challenge for Turkey, namely, the territorial claims of Armenian political organisations in the diaspora.

As is well known, in July 1946, a new governmental election took place in Turkey with the participation of the CHP, the DP and other smaller parties, thus putting an end to the single-party years, at least ostensibly.

How did Armenians deal with the changing international and national conjunctures? What kind of social and political challenges did these changes pose? In order to understand the kind of society we are dealing with, I have collected as much information as possible on the demographic, social, political and cultural field of Armenians remaining in Turkey after 1915, especially during the first decades of the Republic.

This book demonstrates that the legal, political, cultural, economic and physical violence of the last decade of the Ottoman Empire, which arrived at a radical turning point in 1915, left a lasting imprint on state and society formation in the Republic of Turkey. Law making, education, history writing, societal organisations, state politics, cultural life, demographics, strategies and methods of conflict resolution have all been affected by this historical turn. I show that all the policies undertaken against Armenians in 1915–23 continued to be implemented throughout the first decades of the Republic. There were not all that many Armenians left to exile, but those who did remain had to contend with post-genocidal denialist policies in tacit agreement. I call this the post-genocidal habitus of denial.

Extant material demonstrates that the process of becoming diaspora did not end after 1923, but continued throughout the following decades both in the form of perpetual exodus from the provinces to Istanbul or elsewhere and through the loss of institutional and legal basis as a community. The denialist habitus and the process of becoming diaspora are inextricably intertwined. Anti-Armenian campaigns, practices of daily racism and persistent targeting of Armenians (in Turkey and elsewhere) are components of the same habitus. The Patriarchal election crisis in 1944–50 saw the crystallization of such issues as the loss of legal structures, political representation, the role of the press, the assumption of authority and the exercise of power, as well as the loss of institutional structures and reference points.

The first chapter of this book, 'Social Conditions of Armenians Remaining in Istanbul and in the Provinces', depicts the historical background in Istanbul and provinces, and positions Armenians within the early Republican social and political scene. While showing the social impact of state policies, I reconstruct a social history based on day-to-day experiences with the use of news items, memoirs and oral historical accounts. In this chapter, I elaborate on the concept of post-genocidal habitus by underlining the continual interplay between official and social practices. During and even after the first decades of the Republic, perpetrators of harassment, blunt discrimination, or even public physical attacks against Armenians in schools, other state institutions, or the street, were not expected to face legal consequences. The eradication of a sizable population from the country and the state denial of genocide led to a series of other policies that perpetuated the process by liquidating their properties, silencing and marginalising the survivors, and normalising all forms of violence against them. Thus, the first chapter reveals the banality of denial on both the social and the official level. In the last section of the first chapter, I show the international support behind that banality. Furthermore, I draw a line of continuity between the Ottoman Empire and the Republic of Turkey by demonstrating how international mechanisms facilitated denial and its institutionalisation during the post-genocide period.

The second chapter, 'The Legal Context', deals with the new legal framework in which the Armenian community in Turkey found itself after 1923, as well as the issues arising throughout the Single Party years, while emphasising the period that concerns this book: the Single Trustee System (STS) and its impact on the society as a whole, including legal problems, the issue of representation, community administrative systems and the eradication of representative institutional mechanisms. The sources reveal the process of undermining the legal basis of Armenian society, leaving its legal issues to *de facto* practices instead of binding legal mechanisms.

The third chapter, 'State Surveillance and Anti-Armenian Campaigns', shows how Armenian publications, not only in Istanbul but also around the world, were closely scrutinised, banned, and, in the case of foreign origin, prohibited to enter Turkey. Anti-Armenian campaigns are closely related to state scrutiny because during the Single Party years, especially since the mid-1930s, the difference between the government/

state and the press was notoriously minimised; editor-*cum*-parliamentarians acted as state or party agents, directly influencing Armenian sociopolitical life with their columns, or even their attitude. Here I demonstrate the interaction between the Armenian and the Turkish press, the response by Armenian editors and public intellectuals to anti-Armenian campaigns, and the consequences of this struggle for the Armenian press and society as a whole. One of the most important themes of the anti-Armenian campaigns after 1945 was the issue of territorial claims presented in the San Francisco Conference by the Armenian political organisations. Territorial claims were further pushed forward by Stalin, along with immigration calls to all Armenians to relocate to Soviet Armenia. These developments became the main pretexts for reproducing anti-Armenianism in Turkey. Looking at the Single Party period and the post-World War II period under the light of Armenian sources, one can see a rather different picture than the myth of liberalisation starting in 1946.

The fourth chapter, 'The Patriarchal Election Crisis, 1944–50', which also defines the time period of my study as a whole, attempts to understand the election crisis of the Patriarchate of Istanbul in the context of changing power relations during the postwar international scene as well as the changing nature of the conflicts between the Holy See of Echmiadzin, the Holy See of Cilicia, the Patriarchate of Jerusalem and various Armenian dioceses. This conflict evolved into an international crisis between Armenian diasporan communities and played an important part in shaping a new set of relations between the newly restructured Holy See of Echmiadzin and patriarchates and dioceses around the world. Undoubtedly, the issue was even more complicated for Armenians living in Turkey, since the Turkish government was also involved in the crisis at various levels. The tensions between the other diasporan communities and the one in Istanbul, as well as between Patriarchates, Catholicosates and states created the first international crisis for Armenians during the Republican era.

Theoretical Approaches: Habitus and Diaspora

Habitus

In this book I make use of two theoretical tools to understand the history of Turkey and to structure my argument: habitus[68] and diaspora. I adopt the concept of habitus first and foremost in order to explain the fields and structures in which social practices and state–society interactions, in the widest sense, take place and become ordinary – a process that, as I have found in my research, relates intimately to autobiographical knowledge. Although biographical or autobiographical knowledge is a term more typically used in the research on memory or amnesia in the field of psychology,[69] I prefer to use the term as knowledge based in experience and transmitted from one generation to the next. Literature on families, or *Familienforschung* as it is called in Germany, has contributed greatly to this field of research.[70] While this line of inquiry has developed in the context of Holocaust research, the same has not yet taken place in Turkey. Family histories – stories handed down from the elderly, the history of inhabited places, daily practices and the person's own experience – are at the core of this knowledge. The transmission of this knowledge from one generation to the next plays an important role in turning it into a way of life without even recognising its merits as a tool. It was this knowledge, embedded in denial and yet uninterrupted over generations, that I came to understand in my examination of my sources and in my interviews of oral history.

The individuals I interviewed were born and raised in Turkey; some have left and the others still live there. The intersection point of these oral histories was a kind of autobiographical knowledge similar to what I knew from my own 'sociation'. Loïc Wacquant defines sociation as 'categories of judgement and action, coming from society [. . .] shared by all those who were subjected to similar social conditions and conditionings',[71] which in fact points to the preconditions of socialisation. It is precisely this world of practices and sociations that I myself was born into and grew up in that I came to understand throughout this research. Moreover, all the other sources used in this book reveal a world of written or printed documents that evidences a set of created values, daily practices, and mechanisms denying the experience of the survivor. In other words, denial has been established as the core mechanism of sociation and individuation, at the expense of the survivor with all his or her being, including his or her experiences, language, told or untold histories, and knowledge. The people I interviewed opened up a new space in which I could trace the similarities both in their experience and in the *way* they related to their own experiences. My interviewee's experiences, which proved quite difficult to relate at certain points, as well as the fact that they regarded these experiences as a regular, ordinary part of their lives, led me to Pierre Bourdieu's concept of 'habitus', first and foremost because the theory of habitus is a theory developed out of practices: 'It is to account for the actual logic of practice [. . .] that I have put forth a theory of practice, as the product of practical sense.'[72] The habitus allows for a wider and deeper understanding of practices that have become regularities: by structuring the regular and the ordinary, habitus *structures the structure*: 'Habitus as a structuring and structured structure, engages in practices and thoughts.'[73] Thus, practices and thoughts create a world of regularities, which is itself ultimately a structured world, the outcome of a certain sociation.

Wacquant, whose work expands on Bourdieu's legacy, points out that habitus 'is an old philosophical notion, originating in the thought of Aristotle and of the medieval Scholastics, that was retrieved and reworked after the 1960s by sociologist Pierre Bourdieu to forge a dispositional theory of action.'[74] While Norbert Elias uses the term habitus in his *Über den Prozess der Zivilisation* in 1937, Bourdieu began to develop this theory in the 1970s. According to Wacquant,

> it is in the work of Pierre Bourdieu, who was steeped in these philosophical debates, that one finds a thorough socio-logical revamping of the concept designed to transcend the opposition between objectivism and subjectivism: habitus is a mediating notion that helps us revoke the common-sense duality between the individual and the social by capturing 'the internalization of externality and the externalization of internality,' that is, the way society becomes deposited in persons in the form of lasting dispositions, or trained capacities and structured propensities to think, to feel and to act in determinate ways. [. . .] Habitus supplies at once a principle of sociation and individuation: sociation because our categories of judgment and action, coming from society, are shared by all those who were subjected to similar social conditions and conditionings (thus one can speak of a masculine habitus, a national habitus, a bourgeois habitus, etc.); individuation because each person, by having a unique trajectory and location in the world, internalizes a matchless combination of schemata. Because it is both structured (by past social milieus) and

structuring (of present representations and actions), habitus
operates as the 'unchosen principle of all choices' guiding actions
that assume the systematic character of strategies even as they are
not the result of strategic intention and are objectively
'orchestrated without being the product of the organizing
activity of a conductor'.[75]

Reading the 'internalisation of externality' and the 'externalisation of
internality' as part of both sociation and individuation, it becomes
possible to understand the production of autobiographical knowledge
and the basis of the production of everyday life. The individual is both
structured by the habitus and has agency in it. Bourdieu assigns a
systematic character to strategies of choices, even if they are not the
result of a strategic intention, or perhaps, even if the individual is not
fully aware of the results of the choices s/he makes. This does not
minimise the role of the individual as an agent: Bourdieu states clearly
that human actions are not instantaneous reactions to immediate
stimuli; they are embedded in the history of the given relationship.[76]
Bourdieu's definition indicates a set of regularities and norms of
sociation that produce a meaning through which social life is structured
in a certain historical context. Combining this social aspect with agency,
I see two parallel but asymmetrical processes developing throughout
the post-1923 period. On the one hand, we see the creation of and
international support for fields of power – such as state law enforcement,
socio-economic fields and cultural–political fields – that prioritise rules
of agency and representation for one group at the expense of others.
In other words, certain structures and kinds of individual agency in
Turkish society were prioritised and readily mobilised against others,
and this kind of privileged agency was itself rooted in the practices of
everyday life. On the other hand, this prioritised institutional and
individual agency operated by way of the institutional and individual
eradication of the other, i.e. the non-Muslim and non-Turkish
population, and specifically for this study, Armenians. In Bourdieu's
terms, this is a response to a relation, which is itself embedded in history.
    Regarding the external conditions (the society and state structures
I live in) and the internal conditions (the community and family
structures I have been part of), I came to understand that this change
into new sets of practices was embedded in denial: language, history,

annihilation and survival were all denied on various levels. Yet there was no theory as such to comprehensively formulate the denial in all its social dimensions. There was a world constructed with practices over generations, of which I too was a part, but this practice did not find its well-deserved place in knowledge production systems in the form of a theory. Thus, the abstraction that should have been made out of catastrophic experiences and practices over generations was left unrealised. This study is an attempt in that direction. By catastrophic experiences and practices I am referring to having a family in which grandparents were killed or lost, various stories of kidnapping were normalised, relatives were known to be converted, and property and assets were lost through confiscation policies. In our families, the norm was to use different names in different places (at home and outside), including strange surnames issued through the Surname Law, which was aimed at disconnecting Armenians (as well as other non-Muslim, non-Turkish groups) from their family line by giving them surnames that had very little, if anything, to do with their group identities. Our families had been coerced to work in certain professions or areas and not in others, by way of either *de facto* or *de jure* restrictions, or by virtue of living in exclusive districts or even buildings where other non-Muslims lived. Our families were used to refraining from speaking their mother tongue in certain places, having developed a set of strategies to hide their own existence – I use the word 'existence,' since I think by utilising all these strategies, one hides not only his or her identity, but also becomes invisible in society at large, and visible or in fact existent in its own community alone, both spaces having been defined by the denialist habitus. Thus, there has been no way to exist without being part of denial.

However, even under these preconditions of existence, the denial of the descendants of survivors and the denial of the descendants of perpetrators should not be considered on equal footing. While both reproduce denial, the descendants of perpetrators continue perpetration through denial, whereas the descendants of victims continue to be victimised through that denial even if they must partake in it as a way of life. As an abstraction of all the material I have analysed in my book, I am offering a term to define the structures structuring the structure: *the post-genocidal habitus of denial*. Here, the 'post' in post-genocidal does not mean that genocide has come to an end; on the contrary, the catastrophe of genocide is endless and irreversible. However, it has to be acknowledged that the character of physical violence and the attendant policies deserve special consideration in the period of the 'crystallisation' of these policies. Therefore, 'post' stands for the period of crystallisation in which exclusive genocidal policies were implemented and the denial of the catastrophe, in abstracted and encapsulated form, turned into the habitus spanning the decades leading to the present.

Habitus reveals itself only in relation to definite situations; it is only *in relation to* certain structures that habitus produces given discourses or practices.[77] Hence, it has the capacity to create a completely different result as well. I interpret, for instance, Armenian intellectuals' struggle for equality, namely the generation of *Nor Or*, which was born and raised in denialism, as an example of this aspect of habitus. Their struggle with this habitus created a different result, which was in turn subjected to denialism, that is violently forbidden: the members were imprisoned or exiled, and lost contact with the community they were born into, while their works have been forgotten for decades.

In my book I argue that not only general institutional impact, but also the differences created by institutions, were internalised by individuals and reproduced over generations, thus strengthening this habitus. 'Difference' duly appears in one of the definitions of habitus: 'Habitus is thus at the basis of strategies of reproduction that tend to maintain separations, distances and relations of order(ing), hence, concurring in practice (although not consciously or deliberately) in reproducing the entire system of differences constitutive of the social order.'[78] Race, culture, education, language, and socio-economic conditions can be readily instrumentalised for the sake of creating systems of differences. The internalisation of a system of differences and exclusions might be understood in the context of participation in social and institutional structures. However, in a geography of genocide, all internalisation acquires sharper meanings and forms. One can thus argue that the state's claim of equality for all citizens during the post-1923 period was nothing more than a discursive tool to undermine the claiming of rights by Armenians (and other non-Muslims and non Turks); it was *de facto* a method of reproducing differences under the cover of equality.

For the case in hand, habitus encompasses, operates through and structures all state policies and socialised subjectivities,[79] in the 'field' (in Bourdieu's terms) of the law (consisting of the Settlement Law, the

Law of Pious Foundations (*Vakıf*), the denial of the recognition of rights guaranteed by the Treaty of Lausanne by *de facto* prohibiting the opening of Armenian schools in the provinces, juridical practices such as confiscations of *Vakıf* properties, and court cases on 'denigrating Turkishness'), in the academic field (selective and directed knowledge production, exclusive support for denialist topics, arguments or methods and inaccessible archives), and in the social field (practices including harassment, discrimination and racism on a daily basis on the streets, in schools, by neighbours or by colleagues). Therefore, the post-genocidal habitus of denial generates a world-view and a world of practices.

Bourdieu has been criticised for his formulation of agency, his emphasis on the role of history in the individual's sociation and the impact of social conditions on the reproduction of habitus.[80] However, Steinmetz argues that Bourdieu clearly warned against modelling social practice on rule-following and against reducing social agents to mere 'bearers of the structures'.[81] The collaboration of agents and the reproduction of the habitus of denial are prerequisites in social relations: social acceptability and prestige, the construction of a valid career, regular economic income, participation in the state mechanisms, etc. Whereas these were the benefits for the majority of society in Turkey, for the non-Muslims and non-Turks the same habitus *offered* a space of inexistence and invisibility, or, as for instance in the case of Armenian parliamentarians, a space defined strictly by the denialist habitus. The reproduction of denialism was implicit in the 'deal,' a precondition, a matter of tacit agreement, or in Bourdieu's terms, a matter of 'common sense':

> One of the fundamental effects of the orchestration of habitus is the production of a commonsense world endowed with the *objectivity* secured by consensus on the meaning [*sens*] of practices and the world, in other words the harmonization of agents' experiences and the continuous reinforcement that each of them receives from the expression, individual or collective (in festivals, for example), improvised or programmed (commonplaces, sayings), of similar or identical experiences.[82]

Improvised or programmed, collective or individual, similar or identical experiences find their place in the overlaps between official policies and social responses, which, I argue, cannot be considered coincidental, since genocide is a crime of *commission* and not *omission*.[83] Hence, the more ordinary people become part of such a crime by profiting from it, the easier it is to reproduce denial. Nor does the profit have to be only material. The state as well as the constitution and structure of society changed radically and decisively during the last decade of the Ottoman Empire. Class, culture, architecture, the economy, daily life, and even nature and all other areas of life were affected for decades to come. As a result, denial has become an ordinary part of life and a profound characteristic of the state, or, what Bourdieu has called in his definition of the concept of habitus, a 'history turned into nature, i.e. denied as such'[84] – that is (not the intrinsic but) the ordinary, the usual, 'the way it ought to be'.

While academic denialist material is overwhelming in quantity, a recent example demonstrates the relevance of the habitus, in the form of denied history, as a tool to maintain knowledge production. There are not many scholars who analyse the history of Turkey through the concept of habitus. In her recently published book based on her dissertation, *Yenilgiden Sonra Doğu Batı ile Yaşamayı Nasıl Öğrendi*, Ayşe Zarakol applies the theory of habitus to Turkey in a comparison between Turkey (1918–39), Japan (1945–74) and Russia (1990–2007).[85] She refers to the habitus not as a social theory but rather as a tool to analyse different perceptions in international relations. The author discusses the habitus mostly in the context of the state and international actors, almost without reference to the social environment, with the exception of the designation 'Turks'.[86] While society does appear as a concept in the definition of the habitus, the role of society in its reproduction and the way these mechanisms operate in Turkey are left unexplained.[87]

A discussion on the concept follows in the second chapter of the book in terms of 'the impact of the stained national identity'.[88] Zarakol argues that the three countries, which were previously empires, had two characteristics common to their habitus: an identity 'stained' or marred (*lekelenme*) by 'backwardness' throughout the process of modern nation state formation and a consciousness overshadowed by a greater past.[89] Although Zarakol indeed argues that incidents affecting the establishment of the state also play an important role in the national habitus, what distinguishes the Ottoman Empire from Japan and Russia is the 'trauma caused by the Christians of the Empire' who 'stabbed the Empire in the back'[90] – a definitive distinction, but one left inexplicably (and unexplained) in scare quotes. Zarakol consistently keeps count of the losses of the sovereign empire, which must explain the paranoia pervading 'Turkish thought' (*'Türk düşüncesi'*).[91] Thus for Zarakol, neither genocide, exile, deportations, nor confiscations, nor any other such policies played a role in that habitus, although they took place precisely during the establishment process of the Republic. It is more than ironic that the cover features the ruins of Ani, the former medieval capital of Armenian Bagratuni Kingdom, and that the book starts with the reactions in Turkey to Orhan Pamuk's Nobel Prize. In fact, her report on his discussion of these issues is itself obscurantist and denialist.[92] Here I suggest that, ironically, it is Bourdieu's definition, of history turning into nature and being denied as such, that becomes visible in the cover, structure, and the presentation of the book itself. The book thus starts with a discussion that in fact defines its own context, i.e. the post-genocidal habitus, which includes the scholarly manipulation of sources.

Although it is not always easy to deploy sociological theories in the field of history, Steinmetz argues that Bourdieu's theory, with its key concepts, is inherently historical: 'In fact, *both* social reproduction and social change are at the very heart of Bourdieu's project. Bourdieu's main theoretical concepts – habitus, field, cultural and symbolic capital – are all inherently historical. Indeed, for Bourdieu, "every social object is historical".'[93] On the role of history in the creation of a certain habitus, Bourdieu himself writes:

> the habitus, the product of history, produces individual and collective practices, and hence history, in accordance with the schemes engendered by history. The system of dispositions – a past which survives in the present and tends to perpetuate itself into the future by making itself present in practices structured according to its principles, an internal law relaying the continuous exercise of the law of external necessities (irreducible to immediate conjunctural constraints) – is the principle of the continuity and regularity which objectivism discerns in the social world without being able to give them a rational basis.[94]

Here Bourdieu points out an important aspect of durability of habitus, which seems to be less rational and therefore probably more difficult to comprehend. Once habitus is historically set, even if the external conditions change, habitus continues to reproduce itself. We might presume that, for a change to occur in habitus, there needs to be a situation of crisis, a historically registered breaking point – a radical change in power relations, a redefinition of fields and sociations. The period 1915–23 can be called, in Bourdieu's terms, a time of 'crisis' in which the routine adjustment of subjective and objective structures are brutally disrupted.[95] In Ermakoff's words,

> times of crisis are times of disjuncture. Practices do not produce their anticipated effects. Dispositions inherited from the past are dysfunctional out of phase and disconnected from situational challenges or imperatives. They have lost their relevance. As a result actors are at odds with the world that is emerging before their eyes.[96]

While the post-1923 period was marked by a radical institutionalisation of denial on which I elaborate in the first chapter, the pre-1915 period had been a period of a different set of rules for sociation, of official and social representation, of mechanisms of administration, political collaboration, and conceptualisations of participation in Empire, as well as a host of other differences which I do not discuss in this book. It is, nonetheless, important to underscore the profundity of these historical differences and changes without idealisation, before analysing post-genocidal structures and practices embedded in denial.

While in the case at hand, in the history of Turkey, various moments of crisis came to pass including the territorial claims of the USSR and Armenian organisations during the San Francisco Conference after World War II, none of them challenged the set of values and norms or the fields of power relations set in 1915/16–23, which are mostly due to the larger set of values and norms accepted by the international world. Thus, any historical change to transform the denialist habitus in this case would have to rely on multi-layered power relations. However, Bourdieu also states, 'Habitus is not the fate that some people read into it. Being the product of history, it is an *open system of dispositions* that is constantly subjected to experiences, and therefore constantly affected by them in a way that either reinforces or modifies its structures. Habitus is durable but not eternal!'[97] When applied to a context of genocide and denial, the theory of habitus offers a possibility of change or transformation; however, considering the requisite stretches of time, as well as the diffuse and rooted mechanisms of state and society formation, the transformation may require a set of crises in different realms, i.e. in the economic, political, and social spheres, that would change and restructure daily life. In other words, the habitus over generations must prove itself obsolete or unable to reproduce. Although agents of habitus have the potential to change the social and institutional set of practices and sociations by recognising this habitus and decisively addressing its mechanisms, its value systems and regularised practices, they still need a meaningful reason to make this choice. A comparison between Germany post-1945 and Turkey post-1915 would be crucial for future research in defining the contrast between the recognition of genocide in the former and denial in the latter, in understanding the post-genocidal habitus of denial and in socially, institutionally, economically and politically charting a habitus of recognition. If, in the case of Germany, a new set of norms and values has been established over the decades, it is also the result of a crisis and a series of struggles that brought about the transformation.[98]

Diaspora

A second argument in theorising the post-1923 period on the grounds of the evidence provided in this study concerns the process of becoming diaspora. Both the physical conditions of continuing exile and state-induced settlement policies forced Armenians out of Asia Minor and northern Mesopotamia, by hindering the reproduction of their culture and language, by dismissing the rights granted by the Treaty of Lausanne (for instance the reopening of any Armenian schools in the provinces),[99] by decreeing resettlement due to security reasons (that is, labelling the remaining Armenians either as foreigners,[100] or as an internal enemy), by destroying their religious and cultural monuments, and by building antagonistic social pressure. Masses of Armenians continued to move to Istanbul through the Republican era or to Syria in the 1920s and 1930s. Throughout this book, one may follow the line of structural and social eradication of the Armenians remaining in Turkey. This in turn created a diaspora community throughout the Republican era. The first three decades are thus of crucial importance in understanding the process of becoming diaspora in Turkey.

The discussions around the legal and social conditions of the remaining Armenians in Turkey are mostly shaped by a legal terminology within the understanding of the nation state, namely, the terminology of 'minority'. However, as Akçam and Kurt have pointed out, the issues related to Christians and Jews remaining in Turkey cannot be regarded as mere 'minority' issues, because the Turkish Republic was established on the annihilation of the same groups, which are today regarded as 'minorities'.[101] Here, again, clarification regarding the terminology is called for. 'Minority' as a concept refers rather to a juridical category that renders invisible the history of the genocide and of various exiles, thereby legitimising the result. Secondly, the term minority reproduces a series of concepts related to nation state structures, offering a framework of regularity in which the majority is 'the nation' and the minority is the 'other'. Nonetheless, both categories are in fact imagined and, more importantly, as is shown in this book, the structures of the administration of non-Muslims inherited from the Empire do not always correspond to the mechanisms of the nation state. Furthermore, the term 'minority' indicates a rather limited area of study, since it refers to 'a small group' as opposed to the majority, while it should be just the opposite: Anything related to the 'minority' is first and foremost about the majority. Another problem with the terminology emerges once we want to create a general category of groups that in one way or another became subjects of discriminatory policies or daily racism – that is, the category of non-Muslims. The fact remains that none of the non-Muslim groups in the Ottoman Empire had identical rights or the same socio-political or juridical background. Therefore I choose to refer to the groups with their names, without trying to create a generic umbrella group. In this book, I will refer mostly to Armenians, as I have more extensively used their sources. This does not mean that other groups were not affected by the same policies; in some cases they were and in others they were not. However, I do not have the requisite material for each and every group and am not convinced that a generic group can be created since, at the very least, the juridical backgrounds carrying over from the Ottoman Empire vary widely.

The formation of the Armenian diaspora after 1915 is a result of genocide. Therefore, there is no categorical difference between Armenian survivors, be they in Malatya or in Ordu or in Glendale, or between an Armenian from Diyarbekir living in San Francisco and an Armenian from Diyarbekir living in Istanbul. Their way of life and the issues they have to deal with in their daily life are certainly different, but their reason for not living in their hometowns remains the same. Secondly, the institutional and legal eradication throughout the first decades of the Republic has created a new reality for Armenians in Turkey. They have by and large lost their organisational and representative rights. The legal and social basis on which to remain in Asia Minor and in Northern Mesopotamia has been radically extirpated. The first chapter deals with this process. The second and fifth chapters, in turn, investigate the process of becoming diaspora, the loss of acquired rights, and the transformation into mere members of a 'minority community', as well as the forceful confrontation with the reality that they were neither a constitutive part of the state nor of the society, and that, therefore, their agency as a *millet* was no longer relevant.

The Armenians remaining in Turkey have not used 'diaspora' as an alternative term. Nonetheless, the founder of the academic journal *Diaspora*, Khachig Tölölyan, regards the Armenians of Istanbul even before 1915 as diaspora:

> In each post-Genocide diasporic community there was varying but, on the whole, impressive level of commitment to rebuilding institutions that had existed in the prosperous old diasporic communities of the great imperial centres, especially Istanbul. [...] It is worth noting that what was for a couple of centuries the largest and most important Armenian diasporic community, that of Istanbul, rarely thought of itself as diasporic; except when persecuted by the Turkish state, it regarded itself as 'at home' in an ancient, superbly organised and institutionally saturated community [*hamaynk*] that was accommodated by the composite society of Istanbul.[102]

It must be emphasised that the Armenians in Constantinople constituted a well-organised diaspora community up until the nineteenth century. The existence of institutions such as hospitals, churches, schools and *vaqf*s, and the advanced level of intellectual production such as periodicals, newspapers and books prove the *living knowledge* of Armenians in Constantinople. Here I am using the concept of Mihran Dabag, *'diaspora als gelebtes Wissen'*.[103] According to Dabag, diaspora is a form of collectivisation, '*Vergemeinschaftungsform*', which requires durability.[104] The Armenian Patriarchate and the structures stemming from it can be regarded as the components of this requirement. On the other hand, as Raymond Kevorkian points out in his voluminous book, *Ermeniler*, the Patriarchate turned into a point of reference for Armenians in the Ottoman Empire only after the mid-eighteenth century: 'It was not until mid-eighteenth century that the Patriarchate in Istanbul gained hierarchical superiority over the Catholicosates of Cilicia and Aghtamar, prelacies in the provinces, and the Patriarchate in Jerusalem.'[105]

The authority and the presence of the representatives of the Patriarchate in the provinces were rather limited until the mid-nineteenth century, and the Patriarchate remained under the pressure of the Armenian financial aristocracy.[106] As Kevorkian has shown, the Patriarchate gained its authority throughout the centuries and, as such, its existence did not automatically turn Istanbul into a 'home' for all Ottoman Armenians, especially given the fact that Istanbul has never been part of the historical Armenian kingdoms.

Ulf Björklund defines the Armenian community in Turkey as a 'classical hostage diaspora'. Since he himself does not offer any historical periodisation, I assume that his definition refers to the post-1915 or post-1923 period: 'The position of the Bolsahayutiun (Armenians of Constantinople) resembles that of the classic hostage diaspora; their basic predicament is that of being in the land of the enemy. This is, I think, a view shared by most Armenians, whether insiders or outsiders.'[107]

Diaspora literature has come to refer to Jewish and Armenian communities all over the world.[108] Nonetheless, defining Armenians remaining in Turkey as a diaspora does not always prove easy. Public intellectuals or scholars from Istanbul are reluctant to call 'diaspora' the Armenians of Istanbul and Turkey as a whole. Melissa Bilal, for instance, finds 'problematic to call the Armenians in Turkey as "diaspora"'.[109] The editor-in-chief of the Armenian daily newspaper *Nor Marmara*, Rober Haddeciyan, proclaims: 'The Armenians of Istanbul do not belong to *Spiurk* [Diaspora]. *Spiurk* is made up of people who have left their homeland. We have not.'[110] The late Hrant Dink, editor-in-chief of *Agos*, used to make a distinction between the Armenians living elsewhere and those living in Turkey in his various articles and statements. In the first article of the series that he wrote on Armenian identity, he stated that whether or not Armenians in Turkey were considered to be part of the diaspora, any discussion that took place in the diaspora on Armenian identity was important for all Armenians.[111] In late February 2004, Dink wrote another article where he clearly stated that despite the fact that there was historically no difference between other Armenians living in the diaspora and the Armenians in Turkey, there was a distinction between the two, mainly the fact that Armenians in Turkey were still living with Turks, which led to a healing of the identity traumas; their coexistence proved that there was a possibility to normalise the relations.[112] A week later, instead of a headline, there was an article signed by *Agos*, which stated that the newspaper was neither the spokesman of Armenia nor of the diaspora.[113] This piece was a response to the racist attacks to the newspaper and to Dink's person after the publication of the series. Nonetheless, Dink's articles show that he imagined Armenians in Turkey as a third party, as in: Armenians in the diaspora, Armenia, and Armenians in Turkey.

Dink himself was born in Malatya and left for Istanbul with his family. Today, there are almost no Armenians in Asia Minor or in Northern Mesopotamia, at least no surviving Armenian social and cultural life. The stories of the continuing exile of Armenians throughout the post-1923 era still remain to be written and are not as vivid as they were half a century ago. Furthermore, the denialist habitus of Turkey, through both public intellectuals and state policies, has turned the concept of 'diaspora' into a smear, thus dehumanising and demonising the victims, the survivors and their offspring.

The concept of 'home' also lies at the centre of these debates. How shall the concept of home be defined for the post-genocide third or fourth generation Ottoman Armenians? The Republic of Armenia? Very unlikely. Marseilles, Paris, Glendale, New York? Bilal argues that, for Armenians living in Istanbul, 'belonging' and 'displacement' with regard to the same place define the minority experience in Turkey.[114] She points out the need for opening up a space for questioning 'displacement' in the 'homeland' within the context of minority experiences.[115] I agree with her argument in general, but not with her concept of minority, for the reasons I have explained above. Furthermore, to what extent 'homeland' could have remained a homeland for survivors is another question that should be considered for the Armenians in Turkey. My suggestion therefore is to build a more comprehensive conceptualisation of the diaspora that includes the social, legal, institutional, cultural and economic experiences of Armenians remaining in Turkey after 1923. Based on the material provided in this book, it is difficult to assume that the survivor generation felt at home in Istanbul or even in the provinces. How different has Istanbul been from any other city hosting survivors? It may be argued that the difference lies in the existence of the Patriarchate in Istanbul. The Monastery of the Armenian Patriarchate in Jerusalem hosted survivors from Aintab, Marash and other places, while Jerusalem had long remained under Ottoman rule. However, such points do not invalidate the fact that Armenian survivors living in Jerusalem have constituted an important diaspora community.

I suggest that the concept of diaspora should not simply be understood as a self-identification or as an identity category, but rather as an analytical tool to make sense of the post-genocide conditions of Armenians remaining in Turkey, just like other communities established after 1915 in Syria, Lebanon, Cyprus, the United States, or elsewhere.

This book demonstrates that, in the first three decades of Turkey, the remaining Armenians had to make considerable effort to distance themselves from communities of Armenian survivors in other places. The claims of property, the claims to return, and the political organisation of survivors played an important role in the demonisation process of these communities by the Kemalist state. Therefore, the distancing of the Armenian community in Istanbul from the rest of the Armenian communities in the world and from the Republic of Armenia, as well as the dehumanisation of the diaspora, result from Kemalist constructs. Akçam and Kurt cite a series of examples from the statements of public opinion makers and state officials right after the signing of the Treaty of Lausanne, especially towards Armenians who wanted to return and claim their property rights.[116] This anti-Armenian attitude reproduced itself throughout the 1930s and 1940s in a variety of ways. The third and fourth chapters of this book show continuing anti-Armenianism on the levels of both the state and society in various contexts. Armenians who became citizens of other states and who could claim their rights in Turkey have been continuously dehumanised and demonised. This trend amounts to the violation of the personal lives of people and has alienated them from their own lives to such a degree that, while almost every Armenian family in Istanbul has some relatives in other diaspora communities, they often approach the term 'diaspora' with outright reservation or as a concept with negative connotations, to say the least.[117]

Consequently, I see two parallel processes during the post-1923 period: The first is the ongoing flow of the Armenians from the provinces, which indicates a continuing process of becoming diaspora in its widest sense. The second is the eradication of the institutional and social life in the provinces – the closing of schools, choirs, orphanages, churches, monasteries, etc. – and the undermining of the legal structures of the community as whole, all of which point to an extremely fragile diaspora community confined to Istanbul.

A short excerpt from Hagop Mnts'uri (1886–1978) may help us understand that Istanbul was not always regarded as 'home'. Mntsuri had come to Istanbul from his village, Armdan, in 1914 to have a tonsillectomy and had to stay because he missed his ship back. World War I broke out and he was drafted with the mobilisation order. He could never go back to his village. When the deportations began in 1915, he sent several telegrams to his family, only to find out that were 'deported to an unknown place'. He never heard from his wife, his parents, or his four children again. Mntsuri lived in Istanbul until the end of his life and wrote hundreds of articles, chronicles and seven books. In the section 'I' ('*Ben*') in his *Memoirs of Istanbul, 1897–1940* (*Istanbul Anıları*), he writes, 'What business do I have in this city? [...] Vicissitudes have thrown me here. If I had been able to decide, I would have never left our mountain pastures and lyrical riverbanks. I am a hostage and remain condemned to live as a hostage here [in Istanbul].'[118]

CHAPTER 1

SOCIAL CONDITIONS OF ARMENIANS REMAINING IN ISTANBUL AND IN THE PROVINCES

Historical Background

Within the ongoing debate around the ruptures and continuities from the Ottoman Empire to the Republic of Turkey, new historical material has become available thanks to recent research on the Ottoman Empire in the nineteenth century. I begin this chapter with an overview of the historical background – the set of conditions, structures and practices – which I consider to be decisive in the period. For instance, the confiscation of property and law-making mechanisms during the final period of the Ottoman Empire and the mechanisms legitimising post-genocide processes reveal a most important area of study, namely the economic order of the post-1923 period.[1] The more we find out about the structures and practices of the transition period form the flourishing literature, the better we are able to understand the nature of the continuities and ruptures.

Published in the mid-1980s, Erik Jan Zürcher's book, *Turkey: A Modern History*, started to reveal such lines of continuity. The biographical survey at the end of his book is an especially fruitful starting point in tracking the careers of some of the prominent figures throughout the last decades of the nineteenth and first half of the twentieth century.[2] Taner Akçam too argues that the roots of Turkey's current problems can be found in its Ottoman heritage.[3] However, my aim here is, rather than to go into the details of this discussion, to draw attention to one aspect emphasised by Akçam, namely, '[the] "[c]ontinuity of mentality" which survived the empire-to-republic transition, and which fundamentally explains the behavioural worlds of both ruler and ruled in the Turkish Republic'.[4]

The policies concerning the eastern provinces and secondary literature on institutional and structural continuities from the nineteenth century onwards must be interpreted in conjunction, not only because the series of policies continued well into the post-1923 period, but also because the main group that I deal with, Armenians, constituted the local population of the region. The question of continuity must thus be pursued in secondary literature in the context of centre–periphery relations.

The eastern provinces did not constitute a popular topic within centre–periphery relations until recently. In *The Ottoman Empire 1700–1922*, Donald Quataert provides a detailed account of changes in the state apparatus and practices throughout the nineteenth century,[5] devoting a section subtitled 'Centre–Province Relations' to this issue. However, under this subtitle he elaborates only on the 1840s with regard to Damascus and Nablus, whereas one of the most important processes was taking place in the eastern provinces. Nor does Quataert dwell on the Ottoman legacy of the first two decades of the twentieth century. Şerif Mardin, a sociologist who has worked extensively on the modernisation processes of the Ottoman Empire and the Turkish Republic,[6] examines centre–periphery relations in his study of Ottoman state structures and their functions. Mardin considers two important turning points in relation to centre–periphery relations during the early Republican period: the Sheikh Said revolt in 1925 in the east and the Menemen incident in the west.[7] According to Mardin, the suppression of the Sheikh Said revolt took place in a context of 'nightmarish fissions before and during the War of Independence', while the Menemen incident was regarded as yet another treason of the periphery against the centre: 'The province, the primary locus of the periphery was once more identified with treason against the secularist aims of the Republic.'[8] As Cihangir Gündoğdu and Vural Genç also reveal in their recent book, the absence of state sovereignty in the eastern provinces in the nineteenth and the twentieth centuries were decisive in the policy making of the state in terms of centre–periphery relations; the authors argue that the intended solutions especially after the Tanzimat period are worthy of scrutiny.[9] The line of continuity in the approach of the state can be clearly traced both in the language used before and after 1923 and, in practice,[10] through the *layiha*s.[11]

While the problematisation of the absence of control in the context of the eastern provinces made an important contribution to the literature, a second aspect – the nature of centre–periphery relations in relation to the different groups in the nineteenth century and afterwards – also deserves scrutiny. Acording to Martin van Bruinessen, one can assume that there were simultaneous tendencies of both centralisation and decentralisation.[12] The problem that was formulated in the second half of the nineteenth century as the 'Eastern Question' was a multi-layered issue of the execution of power. Both the agreements with the Kurdish tribal chiefs in 1840s and the administrative changes undertaken thereafter – such as *Vilayet Reformu* (1864, Reform of the Provinces), *Arazi Kanunnamesi* (The Land Code, 1858),[13] and the change in administrative structures – can be regarded as a process of colonisation in the widest sense. Hans-Lukas Kieser refers to the process of negotiations with Kurdish tribal chiefs as a process of 'internal conquest' (*binneneroberung / iç sömürgeleştirme*).[14] In their study of the *layiha*s, Cihangir Gündoğdu and Vural Genç provide valuable data as well as analyses regarding the centre–periphery relations for the region of Dersim, a region populated densely with Armenians, as well as Alewis and Kurds. The authors regard *Arazi Kanunnamesi* and *Vilayet Reformu* as policies that aimed to strengthen the power of the Sultan as the head of the Empire and to undermine the influence of local power centres.[15] Drawing on Ussama Makdisi's work, where he asserts that '[i]n an age of Western-dominated modernity, every nation creates its own Orient. Nineteenth century Ottoman Empire was no exception',[16] they argue that Dersim was the 'East' of the Ottoman ruling elite.[17] As an example, they point to a *layiha* by Mikdad Mithad Bedirhan, where he refers to Dersim as the '*vahşi Afrika akvamı*' ('savage African tribes') of the Ottoman world and suggests such measures as those of the British colonists in Sudan.[18] The authors assert that, as in the case of North Africa and the Arab provinces, the Ottoman elite created its own pre-modern discourse in Dersim.[19]

Although the past decade has seen a considerable amount of publications on the Ottoman Empire and colonialism, especially on the

Arab Provinces,[20] the literature hardly ever considers the policies dealing with the requests of Armenians in the context of the colonial exertion of power during the same period, i.e. during the second half of the nineteenth and beginning of the twentieth centuries. Lawyer and parliamentarian Krikor Zohrab's article 'Pnagch'ut'iwn' ('Population') on the demography and tailoring of the borders of the provinces starting in the 1880s contains some interesting pieces of data.[21] Zohrab assumes that the restructuring of the smaller *vilayet*s and the inherent demographic engineering, as with the Rums and Bulgarians in Rumelia, aimed at turning the Armenians into a minority in the eastern provinces.[22] As for the period before the shaping of the provinces, drawing upon the official reports or petitions (*takrir*) which were received from the provinces and submitted to the government by the Patriarchate, Masayuki Ueno investigates the local problems in the provinces and their repercussions in Istanbul.[23] According to the minutes of the Armenian National Assembly in 1849–69, 539 *takrir*s were evaluated involving complaints to the government, the majority of them coming from the eastern provinces.[24] For the most part, the *takrir*s were about violence against Armenians (210), complaints against local officials (122), and problems related to tax collection (76).[25] Although the response of the Patriarchate was limited until 1860, Ueno states that newspapers started to bring the issues of the eastern provinces to the attention of the Istanbul Armenians.[26] The issue remained on the community agenda; after the election of Khrimyan as Patriarch, he placed the issue of 'oppression in the provinces' on the agenda of the Assembly itself, as well as referring to the problem in his talks.[27] Thus, starting from 1840s, there are reports of complaints from the provinces, which reportedly increased from the 1860s to the 1870s as observed by newspapers. We can thus assume that the issues related to violence against Armenians, including the security of life and property, were not tackled. The complaints did not receive satisfactory answers or solutions and, during the Hamidian period, they were followed by massacres. In my opinion, more research is needed on two points: centre–periphery relations in the context of Armenian administration within the Ottoman Empire, i.e. correspondences between the Armenian Patriarchates and Catholicosates, as well as the nature of parallel relations, the Ottoman administration of Kurdish–Armenian relations at the beginning of the nineteenth century.

As Ueno shows, the Armenian populations' requests in the eastern provinces added yet another layer to centre–periphery problems in the nineteenth and the early twentieth centuries, which I read as a period of constant efforts to bring a peaceful solution to the various sets of problems that were later brought under the umbrella of the formulation 'the Eastern problem'. The state decisively took a genocidal turn, after which not only were all the efforts in vain, but also the entire context itself changed. Consequently, the troublesome centre–periphery relations of the nineteenth century carried over to the post-1923 period, with the additional heavy burden of the genocidal turn. Regarding the policies during the post-1923 period, Mardin has pointed out that the periphery remained under close scrutiny in 1923–46, since it was considered an area of potential dissatisfaction:[28]

> The official stand of the Republic was to dismiss the checkerboard structure of Anatolia by passing it under silence. The generations that were socialized into the ideology of the Republic were thus ready to dismiss local religious and ethnic groups as irrelevant survivals from the dark ages of Turkey. Whenever encountered they treated them as such.[29]

Silence, dismissal and the view on 'local religious and ethnic groups as irrelevant survivals from the dark ages' have direct implications for the last period of the Empire, and therefore connote genocidal policies and denialism, in a gentler formulation. Non-Muslims still remained in Asia Minor and Northern Mesopotamia after 1915; their very existence had to be denied or erased, where possible, by various local or central policies. From the perspective of the state, non-Muslims in Istanbul could at least be kept under strict control, whereas those remaining in Asia Minor and Northern Mesopotamia eventually had to be ousted.

In contrast to decades of scholarship that disregarded and omitted the issues and policies related to eastern provinces, Ottomanists and historians of the Turkish Republic from younger generations consider this topic of utmost importance. Hans-Lukas Kieser too underscores the importance of the passage from the nineteenth century to the twentieth:

> No other state of the nineteenth and twentieth century has changed the ethnic map of the land under its authority in such a

calculated and systematic way. No other state went so far as to use all modern tools of its times – such as the military, the telegraph, the press and the railway – within a territory that is proclaimed 'national', by annihilating the physical and cultural existence of a whole group of people.[30]

This violent turn in the state and administration mechanisms, law making and social practices, especially after 1908, has been omitted for quite a long time from historiography, and its imprint on the state and society was also ignored until recently. The differences of the use and organisation of power in the context of the state and the government is a topic for research in its own right;[31] I maintain, however, that the policies regarding Armenians and the eastern provinces in particular during the Republican period can be useful sources in unravelling the continuity in the mentality and the organisational practices of the state. We may thus suggest that the Republican state took over the legacy of the centre–periphery tension, but this time in a post-genocidal context.

In his memoirs, Patriarch Zaven Der Yeghiayan records an administrative meeting at the Board of Governors (*Meclis-i İdare*) that took place in 1911, when he was the religious leader of the province (*vilayet*) of Diyarbekir. He writes that, before the meeting started, he entered the office of the Governor (*vali*) and saw Ali Ulvi and Principal Clerk (*Mektubci*) Muhtar Bey, who stopped talking as soon as they saw him. After some moments of silence, Governor Galib Pasha asked Der Yeghiayan why Armenians kept complaining about the Ottoman government. Der Yeghiayan took out the articles published in the provincial newspaper *Diarbekir* – the editor-in-chief was the *Mektubci* himself – and showed the headlines to Galib Pasha. There was an article in the newspaper about 'foreigners and Christians' explaining how one should deal with foreigners when they wanted to establish churches, schools or other charity organisations. Der Yeghiayan stated that Armenians were natives of this land and not newcomers, that, 'as subjects and citizens', Armenians had never had any problem with Turkish sovereignty, that they had always paid their taxes and participated in the administration, and that they had sent their children to the army for the defence of the country:[32] '[So, I now] ask you gentlemen, what right does the Central Government have to put us on the same footing as foreigners? This is the problem. We have been expressing our unhappiness about this all along.' The Governor responded: 'If this is the reason for your unhappiness, you are right.' According to Der Yeghiayan, 'Galib Pasha granted that we had the right to be dissatisfied, but the Turkish government never sincerely accepted this right.' Der Yeghiayan's account is important because it reflects a governmental mindset prevailing not only in the provinces, but probably also in the capital. Furthermore, as the date in question comes, not after, but before 1915, the account provides important insight into the pre-genocide social and official conditions of the Empire, even before the Balkan Wars.

After 1915, and especially during the Armistice period, thousands of Armenian survivors went to Istanbul looking for shelter and protection. These immigration waves continued intermittently throughout the Republican era. However, the idea of collecting the remaining Armenians from Asia Minor at a designated place was expressed as early as November 1922, when nearly panic-stricken non-Muslims were leaving the country. Zaven Patriarch Der Yeghiayan wrote in his memoirs that he told the representative of the Ankara government in Istanbul, Refet Bele:

Patriarch – The Turkish government looks upon us with suspicion and is bothered by our presence. We, in turn, are troubled by [the government's] suspicions and its resultant attitude toward us. We wish that a corner of this country would be designated for us, naturally with a somewhat different administrative structure than the rest. After all we are not Greeks, and we could not be exchanged against the Muslims of Greece; no European country wants to receive us, and they are under no obligation to do so.
Refet Pasha – Where do you want [to be assigned to live]?
Patriarch – It is not for us to decide. Let the state decide where.
Refet Pasha – If, for example, we were to choose the Province of Brusa ... Aren't there Muslims there, too?
Patriarch – For six centuries we have lived with Muslims, and we are still living with them. We would never demand that they be removed.
Refet Pasha – This is a complicated problem.
Hamamjian – It is possible to expand Armenia's borders to give these people a place to live.
Refet Pasha – You can go all the way to Moscow and settle there![33]

Hagop Hamamjian was the *charge d'affaires* of the Armenian community at that time and Harutyun Mosdichian was the head of the General National Assembly.[34] Although Refet Bele did not reject the idea of gathering the remaining Armenians in one definite place, the conversation changed track following Hamamjian's question. One should also keep in mind that the period was a turning point both for Armenians and Turks, as the Lausanne Treaty was not yet signed and there was great pressure on the Patriarchate, with each Armenian leader making his own proposal to secure his life. Patriarch Der Yeghiayan considered his decision to take Hamamjian to the meeting 'unfortunate'.[35]

The secret parliamentary hearings of March 1923 reveal the mentality of the future Republic and the intention of creating a strict zone of control in Istanbul. Dr Rıza Nur, who took part in the negotiations in Lausanne and reported to the parliament, was greatly disturbed by the presence of stateless peoples like Armenians, Chaldeans and Assyrians in Lausanne, along with all other states that positioned themselves against the Turkish delegation.[36] In his speech, he insisted that one of the most difficult and important issues was that of 'minorities' and Christians:[37]

> There will be no minorities left. Only Istanbul will be an exception. [Voices: Armenians]. However, how many Armenians are there? [Voices: Jews]. There are thirty thousand Jews in Istanbul. They have not created problems. [... Noises.] Jews, as everybody knows, are people who go where one moves them. [*Museviler malum, nereye çekilirse oraya giden insanlardır*].[38]

According to Rıza Nur, the Rum issue had been solved through the population exchange. Even the Rums who had come to Istanbul from the provinces were subjected to it.[39] The next issue, concerning the Patriarchate, had also been sorted out. Rıza Nur expressed the view that the Turkish delegation actually required the Orthodox Patriarchate and its community to leave the country altogether:

> Today the Patriarchate has nothing more than its religious mission. It will not be able to conduct legal duties or whatever it does [*muhakeme bilmem ne*],[40] and we will be able to expel it in the case where it deals with any kind of political issue. [...] Today he

[the Patriarch] is nothing more than an ordinary village priest [*köy papazı*]. He no longer has an official title. [...] He is like a priest in our paw, in Istanbul and excluded from everything else – this is the most befitting description [*en güzel bir tariftir*]. Hence, this issue is sorted out.[41]

The parliamentarians were not satisfied with Nur's explanations and asked whether the title of patriarchate was going to remain. He replied, 'Gentlemen (*Efendiler*), after losing all of its capacity, it does not have any power. It will remain helplessly in our paw.'[42] Regarding the Armenians, Rıza Nur was again very clear, telling the members of parliament that 'Turkey cannot be a home (*yurt*) for them.'[43]

Rıza Nur's ideas and statements regarding leftover non-Muslims in Turkey reveal an official attitude. His words about the Ecumenical Orthodox Patriarchate could easily be prescribed to the position of the Armenian Patriarchate as well, although the authority of the former was much stronger than that of the latter. The process of undermining communal rights for the remaining non-Muslim communities, specifically those received throughout the nineteenth century with the *Nizamname*s, had already been formulated by early 1923. Without going into detailed textual analysis, it suffices to say that the language used in this speech was bluntly racist. However, the comments of fellow parliamentarians were also in line with Rıza Nur's. By reading the minutes of the secret hearings, it is possible to gauge the degree of normalised racism, the internalised and institutionalised hostility of parliamentarians, and the parliament's stance against non-Muslims.

As was the case during the Hamidian massacres of 1894–7,[44] after 1915, Armenians considered Istanbul to be safer than the cities of Asia Minor and the eastern provinces. One of the aims of the early Republican Kemalist elite was the evacuation of the remaining non-Muslims from Asia Minor. Therefore, the same stance was adopted towards the Rums as well. The Rums of Istanbul and those on two islands – Bozcaada (Tenedos) and Gökçeada (Imvros) – were allowed to remain when the population exchange took place in 1922. However, later in the Republican era, systematic policies aimed at the expulsion of Rums from the islands.[45] In the end, Istanbul would remain the only place with any Rum population. In 1925, the Ministry of Interior decided to forfeit the right to travel for non-Muslims.[46] Based on a circular note of the government dated 2 February 1925, the governorate of Üsküdar forbade the travel of non-Muslims in the areas of Kartal, Maltepe and Pendik to Istanbul,[47] which meant that they needed to ask for permission from Ankara to be able to go to work on a daily basis.[48] The travel area accessible to non-Muslims, as specified by the Ministry of Interior, extended from Gebze to Çatalca, which is tantamount to the city limits of Istanbul at the time. The restrictions on travel based on the Travel Regulations (*Seyr-ü Sefer Talimatnamesi*) became a reason for the cabinet to issue a resolution to prohibit Armenian construction workers and taskmasters from Anatolia from working in road construction in Istanbul.[49] In 1928, the Governor of Istanbul allowed non-Muslims to spend their summer a little farther, in Kilyos, Polonezköy and Yakacık.[50] These examples demonstrate the importance of Istanbul as a strict control zone, or, in fact, a panopticon in which each and every move of the non-Muslims were closely followed.[51] The panopticon was originally developed as a control mechanism for prisons; in this case, the whole city has turned into a prison where the inhabitants are not only controlled by the police or the security forces, but also by all other means, such as their neighbours, their acquaintances, their grocers, etc. Therefore, travelling became a serious matter for local administrators. Regardless of where non-Muslims were travelling from – which specific neighbourhood in Istanbul did not really matter – their travel to Istanbul was strictly controlled. In 1929, another decree for the security of military zones allowed non-Muslims to travel only to Bursa, Tuzla, Yalova or Çeşme in May–September.[52]

However, Armenians continued to relocate to Istanbul from the provinces for a variety of reasons. State policies forced remaining Armenians to migrate to Istanbul throughout the post-1923 period, especially by disallowing the re-opening of Armenian schools in Asia Minor and northern Mesopotamia. As an example of the obstruction of the (re)opening of Armenian schools in the provinces, I can cite an important oral account from Malatya; according to the account, the person who told N. D. that it was impossible to open the Armenian schools in that city was none other than İsmet İnönü, then President. According to N. D. (born in Malatya, 1957):

İnönü's mother was from Malatya. So he came to Malatya to visit his family members for *Bayram*. My father and my uncle Asadur went to convey their *Bayram* greetings as representatives of the

[Armenian} community in Malatya. İnönü made them wait for hours. They waited for such a long time that their families got worried at home. They went to the police station to report that their men had gone to greet İnönü but never came back. [. . .] After long hours of waiting, İnönü received them and asked them about their life in Malatya. He asked how many people we were, whether we were comfortable or not, and what he could do for us. My father and Asadur said that, first of all, we wanted our school to be reopened and the church to function. İnönü replied, 'I'll tell you straight away: there is no chance for the school to be opened. But I can help you with the church.'⁵³

According to N. D., this event took place toward the end of the 1940s. İnönü's straightforward answer represented the official stance of the state. There are various other failed attempts to open the schools in the provinces that will be discussed later in this chapter. Such systematic institutional obstruction was one of the most important reasons for the Armenians remaining in the provinces to migrate to Istanbul in the 1950s, especially after the opening of Surp Haç Tıbrevank (Surp Khach Tbrevank') boarding school in 1953. This example, among others in this book, confirms the special status of Istanbul in the eyes of the state.

Perpetual Exodus

N. D. described the systematic attacks on the Armenians who managed to return to their homes after 1915, prior to the foundation of the Republic. According to his account, armed gangs raided and plundered Armenian houses and terrorised the dwellers. The next day, they visited the same places with their weapons and introduced themselves as 'Ateşoğlu Yıldırım' – a person or organisation previously unknown to the community. Whoever filed a complaint to the police about them was beaten up and sent back home – which in effect perpetuated 1915 in a concerted attempt to force Armenians out of their homes:

According to my mother's account, my father went to government officials he did business with [. . .] and asked for guns in order to protect himself and his family at a time when one Armenian house or another was raided every other night. My mother told me that

my father had good relations with these government officials. [. . .]
In response, he was told: 'Do not be afraid, Mr Behçet, we are the
Ateşoğlu Yıldırım. Why should we come to your house?' I heard
this from my mother. This was what my grandfather told her. The
officials he talked to said that they would also go to Kayseri and
Sivas, which means that the same was also happening in Kayseri
and Sivas. I heard the same story from many people in Malatya.[54]

Here was one of the most systematic post-genocide state policies, and
perhaps the least known, adopted to oust returning (post-1915) Armenians
away from Asia Minor and northern Mesopotamia. I have tried to follow
this line of inquiry and conduct other oral historical studies. However, the
person whom N.D. had previously contacted, and who had a similar story,
did not respond to his calls: on the same day an elderly Armenian woman
was killed in her house in the Samatya district of Istanbul and found with a
cross-shaped cut on her body, while another woman was severely beaten up
in the same district. Although I could not continue my research at that
time, Vahé Tachjian's work drew my attention to the description of such
organised attacks in Arshag Alboyadjian's book on Malatya, *Badmut'iwn
Malatio Hayots'*.[55] According to this source, in 1923, the attacks of *Ateşoğlu
Yıldırım* or *Yıldırım Ateş* intensified; houses were marked with stars and
their inhabitants were asked to leave within ten days.[56] Two Armenians
signed a letter to Mustafa Kemal on behalf of 35 Armenians of Malatya
in November 1923.[57] They sought the right to a secure life in their
homes and asked whether they were required to leave Turkey. If so, they
wanted to be officially informed and not be subjected to constant raids.
The signatories were invited to leave Turkey, and the letter did not
improve the situation.[58]

Raymond H. Kevorkian's work provides a detailed account of
Armenians remaining in or returning to Asia Minor and northern
Mesopotamia, as based on the Ecumenical and Armenian Patriarchates'
and eyewitness accounts such as Yervant Odyan's. In total, 255,000
Rums and Armenians were able to return by early 1919.[59] However, not
all of them could stay.

The exodus of Armenians to Istanbul from the provinces was a
scorching controversy during the first decades of the Republic. The
community hosted thousands of people in Istanbul who were in need of
shelter, work and food, among innumerable other things. The Patriarch

and the community organisations tried to find ways to administer the situation with their own means. However, orphanages and many of the shelters for survivors had to be closed or relocated from Turkey after 1923. In 1918, *kaght'agayan*s and orphanages were completely full.[60] After the Armistice of Mudros, Armenian exiles were transported by train from Aleppo to Istanbul. The number of exiles, according to Patriarch Zaven Der Yeghiayan, was around 35,000.[61] He wrote in his memoirs that the community formed three bodies to address the situation: The first was a committee to take care of the orphans, the Committee for Orphan Relief (*Orpakhnam*); the second, the Society for Exiles (*Darakrelots' Engerut'iwn*), and the third, the Armenian Red Cross.[62] The latter two organisations merged on 28 February 1919, to form the Armenian National Relief (*Hay Azkayin Khnamadarut'iwn*).[63] According to Patriarch Yeghiayan's memoirs, this organisation had branches in all Istanbul districts and opened centres for the exiles and survivors. However, noticing that the situation worsened and the donations were insufficient, the Armenian National Assembly introduced a special Tax for the Fatherland. According to Der Yeghiayan, 'The needs of destitute and homeless co-nationals would be met with the tax revenue until they could resettle on their native land; hence, the Fatherland Tax ...'.[64] Varujan Köseyan mentions 12 orphanages in his book on the history of Surp P'rgich' Armenian Hospital. According to his data, those orphanages depended on community financial support for six years.[65] Patriarch Der Yeghiayan put the number of orphanages at 15 and the number of survivors – arriving in Istanbul mainly from the areas between Amasya and Merzifon, and on the route Istanbul–İznik–Konya, until the evacuation of Cilicia – at 35,000.[66] This number rose dramatically by 1920. A year after the armistice, the number of orphans was 100,000, while another 100,000 women and children were estimated to be held as captives.[67] According to Der Yeghiayan's memoirs, the orphanages under the supervision of the Armenian National Relief were: Kuleli Central Orphanage (1,000 children), Orphanage of Beylerbeyi (250 children),[68] Yedikule Orphanage, within the complex of Surp P'rgich' Hospital (300, many of whom had trachoma or other illnesses), Beşiktaş Orphanage for Girls (100), Kumkapı Orphanage for Girls (100), Üsküdar Orphanage for Girls within the American College of Üsküdar complex (100), Hasköy Orphanage for Girls (130), Arnavutköy Orphanage for Girls (100 young women brought in from Turkish houses), Balat Orphanage for Girls (100),

Kuruçeşme Orphanage for Girls (50), Makriköy Orphanage (80), Armenian Catholic Orphanages of Sisters of the Immaculate Conception in Pera and in Samatya (more than 500). According to Yeghiayan, Tbrots'asēr Association took care of hundreds of orphans. These orphanages were moved to Salonica, Marseilles and Paris in 1922. Another agricultural orphanage was settled in Armash (near Bahçecik), with 60 children. A British charitable organisation, the Lord Mayor's Fund, ran two more orphanages that were later transferred to Corfu. A second orphanage in Makriköy run by a Swiss Armenian organisation was transferred to Switzerland and then closed.[69] The reason that the names mentioned in Der Yeghiayan's memoirs and in Köseyan's book do not match might be that after 1923 some of these orphanages had to be moved to other locations, and Köseyan may have referred to the later period. By 1921, since the financial situation of the community had not improved, the Near East Relief started to help financially.[70]

After the arrival of Refet Bele in Istanbul in November 1922, the pressure on Patriarch Zaven increased.[71] He became *persona non grata* in Mustafa Kemal's circle and was forced to leave Istanbul and his post on 10 December 1922. Consequently, the orphanages in Istanbul were relocated to Greece,[72] while those in Harput, Sivas, Kayseri,[73] and Diyarbekir were transferred to Aleppo after 1922.[74] In 1923, when the Rum population of Asia Minor was expelled, Armenians from Yalova, Bandırma, Kütahya and Eskişehir too were deported with them, first to Thrace and then to Greece.[75] Armenians remaining outside Istanbul were also threatened. Varujan Köseyan's account of how his family had left Edincik demonstrates the continuing exile of Armenians, especially during the expulsion of the Rums, during the so-called population exchange:

They forced us to leave along with the Rums. We came to Bandırma in 1923. Some of the people on the harbour went to Greece, some came to Istanbul. I once heard people at home say that our neighbours in Edincik threatened against returning and claiming our properties. They said, if you do so, we will shoot you in the leg and leave you disabled, making you beg for money all your life.[76]

The orphanages and *kaght'agayan*s in Istanbul remained one of the most important socio-economic issues of the community during the first decades of the Republic. Armaveni Miroğlu's article on the issue of exiles and orphans provides important factual data: As of 31 August 1923 there were 6,385 *kaght'agan*s in 13 *kaght'agayan* in Istanbul, and the number of these refugees rose to 7,036 in 1924.[77] The Karagözyan Orphanage had 124 children in the academic year 1922–3. However, the Kuleli Orphanage was evacuated in 1922 and 125 orphans found shelter in Karagözyan for approximately ten days.[78] An article published in 1933 in the weekly *Panper* states that over 500 orphans had found shelter, care and education in Karagözyan throughout the previous two decades.[79] Karagözyan was originally an orphanage and workshop, and was then turned into an orphanage and elementary school, while providing training in shoemaking, bricklaying and ironworking in its workshops.[80]

A detailed report entitled 'National Relief' was presented to the community administration and published in the Surp P'rgich' Yearbook of 1932. According to this report, there were 600 orphans and children of *kaght'agan*s studying in nine community schools.[81] Hence, the National Relief (*Azkayin Khnamadarut'iwn*) dealt with the combined issue of orphans and *kaght'agan*s.[82] There were only two orphanages left in Istanbul in 1939, with 500 *kaght'agan*s and more than 200 orphans.[83] According to *Nor Lur*, there were 120 orphans at the Karagözyan orphanage in 1947,[84] whereas according to *Paros*, 1,000 students had already passed through Karagözyan in 1950.[85] Medical care and pharmaceutical resources were also provided. Kalfayan Orphanage, which was established in 1866 in Istanbul by 'nun' Srpuhi Kalfayan (Palu 1822–Istanbul 1899),[86] has remained active as an orphanage to this day.[87] These centres and orphanages were not the only institutions providing care to Armenians from the provinces. There were also trade schools (*arhesdanots'*) for girls and women who would have to work for a living. Numerous articles were dedicated to this issue in almost all Armenian newspapers published in Istanbul throughout the first two decades of the Republican era.

The poverty levels of the community increased significantly after 1938, following the passage of the Foundation Law of Turkey and the introduction of the Single Trustee System. During the same period, Karagözyan and the Scutari/Üsküdar Orphanage of Tutelage (*Sgiwdari Khnamadaragan Orpanots'*) had to merge their orphanages and finances in order to be able to continue their work. According to Toros Azadyan's account, there were 70–90 orphans in the orphanage of Üsküdar, and 400–500 *kaght'agan*s in two *kaght'agan* centres.[88] In the official letter of merger of the two orphanages, there is also a reference to the situation of Armenians from the provinces:

> Taking care of the *kaght'agans (kaght'agan)* is part of the work of caring for the orphans. However, the latter should remain within minimum budget, as the work in this respect is almost in the process of dissolution. A competent body is still needed to take care of 400–500 *kaght'agans* who are not yet self-sufficient.[89]

While such was the situation in Istanbul, in the provinces Armenians were variously and continually threatened and forced to leave. Based on American consular archives, Dilek Güven finds that Armenians were prohibited from leaving Sivas in 1928–9. At the same time, they were deprived of work and earning power. Under these circumstances, many of them applied for a special permission to leave the country.[90] Soner Cagaptay provides a detailed account of a series of attacks including two homicides – murders of a Catholic Armenian priest Yusuf Emirhanyan in Diyarbekir and an Orthodox priest in Mardin – which played an important role in the exodus of Armenians.[91] After these cases the Catholic mission in Elazığ was constrained to cease activities, while the priests on duty (two Armenian, one French and one German) left for Beirut.[92] Around the same time, the Armenian Protestant Church in Harput was bombed and set on fire, while another Assyrian priest in Diyarbekir was attacked.[93]

As one can see in this overwhelming body of evidence, the laws and legal measures of the time had the specific objective of severing relations between the land and the people. According to Murat Bebiroğlu, the Settlement Law of 1934 also played an important role in the migration process. Bebiroğlu interviewed a person who was forced to leave Yozgat and migrate to Istanbul at that time, who said that the law affected their situation and was used as a pretext for their forced migration.[94] Dilek Güven provides a detailed account of the impact of the Settlement Law where she makes a reference to the archives of the US Embassy on the expulsion of Jews from Thrace and İzmir: '"the voluntary" migration of aforementioned minority groups [Jews] – and also Christian groups like Armenians in Anatolia – was actually the result of planned exclusion'.[95] Furthermore, Güven provides detailed statistical data on Armenian migration in 1929–34. According to the same sources, even before the enactment of the Settlement Law, there had occurred another wave of forced migration: around 600 Armenians left their homes for Istanbul.[96] Moreover, agents of the Turkish government encouraged Christians in the provinces, especially in Diyarbakır and Harput, to leave.[97] Güven puts the number of Armenians migrating to Syria in 18 months in 1929–30 at 6,373,[98] whereas Cagaptay states that the number of people who left Turkey for Syria varies. According to American diplomats, the number was 10,000–20,000,[99] whereas British diplomats in 1930 estimated the number of emigrants to be 2,000–4,000.[100]

In the meantime, the Armenians who were unable to sustain their lives in Istanbul, especially those in shelters, were looking for means to return to their villages or to immigrate. Tensions arose between the *kaght'agan*s and the community administration because of the impossibility of establishing a life in the shelters. The state as an actor was almost non-existent, and in the cases where it intervened, it only acted at the expense of the *kaght'agan*s. In 1934, another Istanbul-based newspaper, *Ngar*, published a story describing how Armenian *kaght'-agan*s from the provinces found themselves financially insecure in Istanbul and, having no source of income, preferred to return to their villages.[101] In a news item published in March 1934, *Ngar* reported that the number of Armenian *kaght'agan*s in Istanbul was 750.[102] It is not clear whether they were newcomers or already existing *kaght'agan*s. There is a lot more to say about the situation of the community in Istanbul, the troubles in dealing with orphans, women and continuing migration from the provinces. The problem concerning the *kaght'agan*s, orphans and women was not a simple statistical matter: it had serious socio-political consequences, and Armenian newspapers are a rich source on these issues. For instance, *Panper*[103] published two lengthy articles on *kaght'agan* centres in April and May 1933. One of them was about the Samatya centre, which had served as a shelter since 1920, according to a news item.[104] Armaveni Miroğlu has also confirmed that Nunyan Makruhyan Armenian School in Samatya had been used as a *kaght'agan* centre since 1920, all its rooms and halls fully occupied.[105] The Surp P'rgich' Yearbook of 1932 stated that there were 800 people in the Samatya and Ortaköy *kaght'agan* centres and that, as soon as they left, newcomers would fill their places.[106] However, these figures did not include the *kaght'agan*s who went from the provinces to Istanbul to stay with relatives. The report included in the Yearbook of 1932 makes little mention of the social issues around the *kaght'agan* centres. The press published various series of articles that provided factual data and described the physical conditions and socio-economic problems. With all the windows covered with paper, each and every corner of the buildings was filled with *kaght'agans* of all ages. According to the news, there were 268 people at the time, 120 of them aged 11 or younger.[107] Some had lived in the centre for up to ten years. There were workshops in this centre too; a woman from Kayseri was reported to be weaving a rug. A new wave of *kaght'agans* arrived at the beginning of April 1933 from the village of Bebek in Yozgat, with a total of 28 families or 147 people.[108] *Ngar* gave the number of the Burunkışla *kaght'agans* as 350 and stated that the Minister of Interior sent back home the people who were on their way to Istanbul in order to stop population flow.[109] Although the minister made a statement advising *kaght'agans* to go back, the issue of *kaght'agans* remained unsolved. There are more than 20 reports on the issue published in Vahan Toşikyan's *Nor Lur* during 1935. One of the two centres in Samatya, a building rented for newcomers from Yozgat (Burunkışla), was shut down that year. The process of evacuation was exceedingly troublesome. People staying there protested continuously against the evacuation, claiming that they were hungry, lacked money or jobs, and had nowhere to go.[110] The relief organisation (*Khnamadarut'iwn*), on the other hand, was in a financial crisis and, according to these reports, could no longer pay the monthly rent for this place. Time and again, the inhabitants of the centre wrote petitions to the central administration of the Armenian National Relief (ANR), pleading to stay there. Most likely prompted by the organised migrations to Soviet Armenia in 1933–6, they approached the organisation again and asked the relief agency to send them to Yerevan, as no answer was forthcoming.[111]

When their attempt failed, once again they asked the administration to give them money to return to their homes in the provinces.[112] All their requests were denied. In the end, they went to the Governor's office in Istanbul and complained about the ANR. From that moment onwards, government officials were also involved in the question. They ran talks with the ANR administration and were told that the administration could not afford to keep another building for emigrants. The remaining *kaght'agans* could either be transferred to the other building in Samatya or to the Ortaköy centre.[113] *Nor Lur* reported on 16 November 1935 that, after the evacuation of the second Samatya centre, the Governor's office had inspected both Ortaköy and Samatya *kaght'agan* centres, and found out that the latter was overcrowded.[114] According to another news item, there were 320 people in Samatya.[115]

The newspaper also reported on an evacuation that took place in Üsküdar, publishing an open letter to the editor-in-chief under the signature 'Resident of the District'. According to this letter, an Armenian *kaght'agan* family was living in a shack owned by the Armenian Surp P'rgich' Hospital on Arapzade Street, in Üsküdar. One evening, Mr Goganyan, in charge of the properties of the hospital, had come with the police and evicted the family by force. They found shelter in the house of their Turkish neighbour. The author of the letter found the eviction to be a breach of the law, and added that the place was not even a house for rent; it had been empty for three or four years before the family was accommodated there.[116]

The situation of the ANR was also delicate. Articles published in *Nor Lur* encouraged people to help the community to deal with the orphans and the Armenians coming from the provinces. People waited for days in front of the ANR, insisting that they were hungry. The ANR administration asked for help from Surp P'rgich' Hospital to take eight to ten disabled and orphans, since it was no longer able to deal with the given situation.[117] According to yet another report, the relief administration failed to honour the request of the priest of Kayseri to shelter two orphans on the grounds that the orphanages should be united first; they would then see what they could do.[118] The yearbook of Surp P'rgich' Hospital of 1939 provides more information on the issue of orphans/ *kaght'agan* children: there were 535 *kaght'agan* students in 'dire straits' (*'kaght'agan garod usanoghner'*);[119] 150 people were living outside *kaght'agan* centres,[120] most likely with financial support of community organisations. The same information had already been published in the yearbook of 1938; thus the numbers must have either been copied or arrived at separately.[121] However, both yearbooks make clear, albeit without detailed information, that the *kaght'agan* centres were still open, given that they had a designated budget.

There is no question that it was extremely difficult to cope with the socio-political consequences of *kaght'agan*s in Istanbul. According to press reports, the relief organisation and the Armenian Hospital were not able to meet the needs of the people coming from the provinces, which in turn gave rise to serious issues between these provincial Armenians and the administrative bodies of the community in Istanbul. Reading these news items, one gets the impression that the members of the Armenian administration tried to avoid direct contact with the newcomers due to fear of violence in some cases. The *kaght'agan* centres were closed by the end of the 1930s. However, Armenians continued to leave the provinces for Istanbul.

A. B. (born in Kütahya, 1945), an Armenian woman from a family exiled from Halvori (a village of Dersim), who then resettled in a village of Kütahya, Ayvalılı, and who currently lives in Munich, Germany, told me that even settling in Istanbul did not resolve their predicament. Her family was forcefully converted to Islam in Kütahya and were not allowed to meet with their relatives, who were exiled and resettled in other villages of Kütahya. Thus, she was born as a Muslim Turk. All family members had Turkish names and surnames. Only elderly people could secretly speak in Armenian. After 6–7 September 1955, the family decided to move to Istanbul, possibly for security reasons.[122] They settled in Gedikpaşa, where many deported Armenians from Dersim also lived. As soon as they settled in Istanbul, their mother told them that they were Armenian Christians.

> No one helped us. [...] We were hungry, so I had to work; as soon as we came to Istanbul I started to work. [...] I could not speak Armenian. There were so many Armenians living in Gedikpaşa; all of Gedikpaşa was full of Armenians. None of them offered to teach me Armenian. [...] We could not relate to the Armenians of Istanbul. No one told me that I should go to school. I never went to school, I was illiterate, and my younger brother went to a Turkish school in Istanbul.[123]

She got engaged at the same age of 15 to an Armenian from Dersim whom she did not know. A few years later, A. B. came to work with her family in Germany, where she continues to live today.

Armenians coming from the provinces remained at the bottom of all power hierarchies. In the case of A. B., like that of many other forcefully Islamised Armenians, another layer of exclusion was palpable. Many Armenians from the provinces left Turkey in 1960s and 1970s.

The Armenian Existence in Istanbul and in the Provinces

Concerning the Armenian population of the provinces, we find some detailed statistical data in the 82-page booklet, *The Gift* [*Armağan*], published by Toros Azadyan and Mardiros Koçunyan (editor-in-chief of the daily *Jamanak*) on the 15th anniversary of the foundation of the Republic.[124] In the Republican archives can be found a letter (and a summary of the booklet in Turkish) sent by the authors to Prime Minister Celal Bayar on 31 October 1938.[125] The booklet devotes three pages to Hatay since it was published a year before the annexation of the Sancak of Alexandretta.[126] The Turkish summary of the booklet sent to the Prime Minister was seven pages long, of which one and a half were devoted to the issue of Hatay and three and a half dealt with the 'national struggle of liberation, war of independence, and legendary victories of the Turkish army'.[127] The booklet offers a list of cities with Armenian inhabitants, with information on the population in each area, including the number of Armenians in the city centre and in the villages of the province, the occupations of Armenians (even, in some cases, the occupations of women), and community organisations in the cities, such as functioning churches:

> 1-Kayseri: 2,280 (both female and male), in Everek 900, Aziliye (Pınar Başı) 20, Bünyan ten. There are 3,470 Armenians in the province (*vilayet*). Five per cent of the active population are shopkeepers, 35 per cent craftsmen, such as carpet sellers, scrap dealers (*hurdacı*), ironsmiths, stone masons, butchers, pastrami-sausage (*pastirma-sucuk*) sellers, roof masters, construction workers, cutlers, millers, painters, etc. 60–70 women work in the local cotton (field). Priest Haygazun Garabetyan holds regular masses at Surp Lusaworich' church of Kayseri. The trustee of the church, until 15 May 19[3?]8, was Jivan Ashĕkyan, the lawyer.[128] After he settled in Istanbul, according to clause 2762, Evkaf decided to take over the management of the foundation until the community elects a new trustee.[129] Everek also has a church, Surp T'oros, which is open. The trustee is Arshag Sēmizyan. Priest Eghishê T'akworyan executes religious duties.
> 2-Yozgat: There are approximately 1,200 Armenians in the city and the district of Boğazlıyan altogether. 20 per cent are craftsmen, while most of the rest are ironsmiths.

3-Sıvas: More than 1,000 Armenians live in the city and its towns (such as Zara, Derdene, Kangal, Gürün, Şarkışla, etc.). 25 per cent are peasants and unqualified workers. The rest are craftsmen (ironsmiths, coppersmiths, roofers, construction workers, pantoffle [slipper] maker/ seller, millers, scrap dealers)

4-Tokat: 900 Armenians inhabit this city, all townships included. 20 per cent are ordinary workers; most of them are peasants, vine growers, shepherds, millers, roofers, *yazmacı*s [kerchief makers].

5-Kastemuni: Approximately 2,000 Armenians live in the city of Kastemuni and the surrounding towns (Taşköpri, etc.). 40 per cent of the active population are craftsmen (threaders, scrap dealers, tinsmith.), 35 per cent workers, 20 per cent sieve-makers, 5 per cent shopkeepers and petty merchants.

6-Amasya: There are only around 800 female and male Armenians, including the townships (Merzifun, Gümüş Hacı Köy, etc.). Five per cent are traders and shopkeepers, 40 per cent vine growers, gardeners, fruit sellers, etc., 20 per cent peasants and shepherds, and the rest craftsmen (shoemakers, jewellers, *yazmacı*s, roofers, millers, construction workers etc.)

7-Samsun: There are more than 500 Armenians within the city and Ordu and its surroundings. Most of them are craftsmen and tradesmen, while the rest are peasants. The priest of Ordu is Kēōrk Sahagyan. The church is open and the Holy Mass is celebrated.

8-Kharpert: Altogether, there are approximately 1,500 Armenians, including Armenian Catholics. Ten per cent are tradesmen and shopkeepers, 25 per cent stock farmers, oil sellers and grocers, 55 per cent are craftsmen (coppersmiths, roofers, cobblers, millers, tailors, bricklayers, etc.), while the rest are ironsmiths.

9-Malatya: There are approximately 1,600 Armenians in this *vilayet* including its townships (Agn, Arapgir, Divrig etc.). They work as herdsmen, grocers, ironsmiths, carpet makers, threaders, etc.

10-Diyarbakır:[130] There are a thousand Armenians in the whole *vilayet* (the figure includes Maronite, Assyrian and Coptic Christians). Ten per cent are working as grocers or shopkeepers, 40 per cent are craftsmen (bricklayers, jewellers, fruit sellers, construction workers, stonemasons, roofers, etc.) and the rest are peasants. Armenians in Diyarbakır have a priest who is in charge of religious affairs.

11-Konya: There are approximately 600 Armenians in the city centre
and in Ereğli and Aksaray. Ten per cent are artisans, five per cent are
small retailers and wheat-traders, 40 per cent are peasants,
shoemakers, coppersmiths, carters etc. The rest are regular workers
and farmers. In Konya, there is a dentist by the name of Osdan
Giwlistanyan. In Ereğli, Dr Simon Bey Terzioghlu enjoys wide
public appreciation. His brother Melkon works as an intermediary.
12- Adana–Mersin: In this area there are approximately 30
Armenians, male and female. They work as peasants and
craftsmen.[131]

In lieu of a conclusion, the booklet states that there were 4,500
Armenians living in different parts of the country: 'They all live in peace
and harmony with the Republican administration.'[132] The editors of the
booklet provide this information by using 'various documents', since
they had no access to official records.[133] Since the Patriarchate in
Istanbul received reports from the Armenian priests in the provinces,
these detailed demographic data were probably based on the reports.
In the yearbook of Surp P'rgich' Armenian Hospital of 1932, there is a
similar list of villages and demographic details on Armenians living in
the provinces. One example demonstrates the similarity: 'Burun Kışla –
Armenians earn their living by agriculture and cattle breeding. Their
figures are the following: male 147, married/ widowed women 138, girls
135, grand total 553. They have a church named Surp T'oros. 205
children have been baptised.'[134] This list and the detailed two-page
report on Kayseri and its surroundings were provided by the deputy
religious leader of Kayseri, Fr Serovpē Burmayan. According to
Burmayan, there were 775 males, 818 females, 822 boys and 702 girls,
with a total of 3,157 people in the villages of Kayseri and Yozgat.[135]
Apparently, Azadyan and Koçunyan consulted these sources while
preparing Armağan. Azadyan was the editor of the yearbooks of the
Armenian Hospital, and therefore had access to the data. On the other
hand, it is surprising to see how little information they used from this very
rich database. The information about the entire Armenian population of
the provinces is summarised in two pages of Armağan, whereas the
Yearbook of 1932 devoted the same number of pages to demographic data
on just the region around Kayseri and Yozgat. It is reasonable to assume
that Koçunyan and Azadyan did not want to give much space to the

Armenian presence in the provinces in *Armağan*, and prepared a draft account to minimise attention. Nevertheless, even though the figures provided in this booklet still need to be verified, the information does convey a general picture of the existence of Armenians, their professions and living conditions. For instance, according to the memoirs of Güzelyan, there were 2,000 Armenians living in and around Sivas in 1941,[136] whereas the abovementioned booklet puts the number of the Armenian population in Sivas and its surroundings at 'more than 1,000 people'.[137] This example shows the difficulty of the verification of actual numbers. In all likelihood, the numbers were higher rather than lower. I have included this schema of demographic information in order to show that the community still continued to collect data about the survivors in the provinces, although I had never previously come across it.

Kaspar Basmajian, who visited Arapgir in 1954, wrote a chapter on the Republican period in another history book on Arapgir, *Badmut'iwn Hayots' Arapgiri*. According to Basmajian, the Armenian population of Arapgir at the time consisted of 350 people, i.e. 30 families. Armenians from Arapgir were constantly migrating to Istanbul and Malatya. A total of 410 families had already settled in Istanbul, while ten families took residence in Malatya.[138] It is also possible to find information about the fate of Armenian neighbourhoods in the 1950s in the memoirs of Basmajian. Most of the monumental buildings, like churches, girls' schools, and the religious centre had been confiscated by the state and used as Turkish schools.[139] According to Basmajian, other houses and pieces of land that remained behind had all been confiscated and sold to Turkish people, while some were bought back by Armenians.

In 1938, the same year of the publication of *Armağan*, President Mustafa Kemal signed an order to move Armenians from Efkere, away from the military stations in the region – a decision approved by the Chief of General Staff and the Interior Ministry.[140] While Efkere had been an important centre for Armenians in Kayseri (Gesaria) before 1915,[141] Kayseri and Everek–Fenese remained one of the few cities to still have a priest in the 1940s according to the yearbook of the Armenian Hospital.[142] The priest of Kayseri, Haygazun Garabedyan,[143] who had already been serving in Kayseri for eight years in 1945, told the Armenian newspaper *Marmara* during his visit to Istanbul that there were a total of 400 families (2,300 Armenians) in Kayseri, and 20–25,000 Armenians in Anatolia.[144] *Nor Lur* reported a wedding ceremony from Kayseri in April 1947;

according to the special correspondent, nine people from Sivas visited Kayseri on 16 March 1947 in order to experience a 'traditional religious Armenian wedding'. The priest, Haygazun Garabedyan, fulfilled their request. The report noted that the visitors were originally from Tavra,[145] but had been living in Sivas and working in the mills.[146] This incident shows that local communities remaining in Asia Minor had at least irregular contacts based on communal needs and tried to maintain the rituals of the Armenian Church so as to preserve their identity. In late May 1947, Priest Haygazun wrote to *Marmara* on the occasion of its intervention in the auctioning of Armenian properties in Kayseri, which I discuss in the following pages of this book. Priest Haygazun thanked the newspaper for its intervention and reported that 450 Armenian families lived in poverty; 95 per cent did not own houses and rented places while working in the fields, while ten elderly people lived in a house in the courtyard of the church to which it belonged.[147] In 1950, *Marmara* reported on the visits of the priest of Everek, T'oros Ch'algjyan, to the provinces. According to these reports, there were 170 Armenian families in Malatya, 115 families in Arapgir, and three or four families in some villages.[148] During his stay in Arapgir, Fr T'oros had conducted 55 marriages and 126 baptisms.[149] Furthermore, according to the same article, there were six Armenian families in Divrighi, two in Armutagh (Armutak), three in Hodr (Odur) and six in Khrnavul (Harnavul).[150] There is a long list of the Armenian population of Arapgir identified by name at the end of the news item.

As for the overall Armenian population of Turkey, *Marmara* published the demographic breakdown of Armenians living all over the world in 1946, according to which the population in Turkey was 120,000.[151] Three years later, *Nor Lur* estimated the Armenian population in Turkey to be 100,000.[152] The book prepared for the 160th anniversary of Surp P'rgich' Armenian Hospital includes a document drawn up by the administration of the hospital in 1950, which puts the number of Armenians in Turkey at 60,000.[153]

It was not easy to keep track of the circumstances of Armenians scattered around the country. After 1950, Patriarch Karekin Khachaduryan (Haçaduryan) established the position of itinerant priest for the provinces. However, it was not always a desirable duty.[154] Priest Şavarş Balımyan from Zara (in the province of Sivas), who had grown up in the Karagözyan orphanage in the 1930s, took up this position with pleasure, and travelled across the country throughout the 1960s in order to deliver religious services to Armenians and develop relations with the communities that had lost all connections to Istanbul.

Considering that, to this day, there has been no way of finding out the exact number of the Armenian population of Turkey, these demographic data at least give a general idea about the Armenian presence in the first decades of the Republic. There is no doubt that numbers decreased in following decades.

The Destruction of the Cultural Heritage

Armenian newspapers published news of the systematic confiscations of the properties of pious foundations and subsequent legal trials. Therefore, it is relatively easier to trace that history than the story of the destruction of Armenian material culture in the provinces. One of the oral histories and two newspaper reports provide some information about the processes involved. It is probable that more information is available in newspapers I have not seen; however, based on the material that I have consulted, I have doubts that such information would be as systematic as the reports from Istanbul. One has to bear in mind that it was a challenge for the newspapers to establish relations with Armenians in the provinces. The priests serving in the provinces usually wrote reports or articles that found their way to the Armenian press. According to the Surp P'rgich' Armenian Hospital yearbooks of 1948–9, there were Armenian priests in four Anatolian cities only: Ordu, Diyarbakır, Kayseri and Everek–Fenese.[155]

According to an account by Civan Çakır, who was born in 1924 and lived in Ordu until 1949, there were 72 Armenian families in the city in 1918. These families, including his mother's family, had managed to return to their hometown after 1915. He reported that, in the 1940s, 10–15 Armenian families were left in Ordu. The church demolished in 1939 on the grounds that the Erzincan earthquake had caused severe damage to the building:

[In fact] the church was not affected by the earthquake, but they wanted to get rid of it; therefore, they fabricated a report stating that it was damaged and demolished it. Before then, my father used to sing in the church and I also used to go to there. [...]

There was also a priest, Der Kevork [Sahagyan, mentioned in *Armağan*] I guess, who at the same time worked as a roof maker. [...] He left in 1949 too, first for Istanbul and then for Argentina, where he died.[156]

Civan Çakır left Ordu in 1949 for Istanbul and then Canada, where he lives today.

In 1947, the government took steps to sell three Armenian churches with all their properties, up to 300 in total.[157] These were the Armenian church in Talas (Türab district) including the school land, the Armenian church in Muncusun (Kayseri) and the Armenian church in the 'High School Square' including the school nearby.[158] According to a report in *Marmara*, the local newspaper of Kayseri announced on 24 April 1947 that Armenian churches would be sold at a public auction two weeks later, on 7 May.[159] Upon this news the editor-in-chief of *Marmara* called its correspondent in Ankara, Mekki Seyid Enes, and asked him to inform the Prime Minister's office about this unlawful practice. According to the report, the deputy of Prime Minister Mümtaz Ökmen interfered and stopped the auction. On 6 May, Şükrü Sökmensüer, Minister of Interior, declared that the announcement of the auction had been an error.[160]

The main church in Sivas, which was no longer in use and instead occupied by the military, according to a news item in the local paper *Ülke* and translated in *Marmara*, was demolished in 1950. The report stated that 'no harm was done to the environs during the dynamite explosion'.[161] This is clear proof that the main Armenian church in Sivas, after being occupied for years by the military, was literally destroyed with explosives. The official reason for the destruction was the poor state of the building.[162] According to *Marmara*, the community in Sivas had applied to the Patriarchate in Istanbul five to six months before so as to have the renovation completed and to house a permanent priest in Sivas. However, it is not clear how any renovation would have been possible while the church was under military occupation. Furthermore, the land of the church was to be sold at an auction on 28 March.[163] According to *Ülke*, the technical council reporting to the Governor's office in Sivas and the respective municipality made an investigation and decided 'to take necessary measures in order to prevent any possible damage'. This news item shows that a number of actors bore responsibility for the destruction. The headline in *Marmara* blamed the deputy Armenian Patriarch rather than the state or its institutions for the destruction: 'The Armenian Church in Sivas Collapsed Due to Archbishop Arslanyan's Incompetence.'[164] As we can see here, the word 'destruction' was not even used. The newspaper held the Armenian community, and more specifically, the Armenian leadership, responsible for the destruction of the church. On the other hand, in the same breath, *Ülke* mentioned the Governor, the municipality and the military – in other words, all local official authorities. It thus seems clear that the main issue was the explanation of the event and not the destruction itself. Apparently, this case was part of *Marmara*'s anti-Arslanyan campaign. The fifth chapter of this book deals with this conflict in detail. *Marmara*'s headline on 20 March 1950 was, 'The Issue of the Sivas Church Has Been Resolved.'[165] One wonders what the solution was if the church had already been destroyed. According to the report, the auction of the land and of the church ruins was postponed after news items on its destruction appeared in *Marmara*.[166] The newspaper regarded this as a solution. However, another piece of news published on 26 March proves that the issue was not yet resolved. According to this article, the Governor of Sivas declared that the destroyed church was registered as abandoned property (*emval-i metruke*) and the community could not prove that it belonged to them.[167] As absurd as all this may sound – that an Armenian newspaper was reporting the destruction of a church in this way, that the church was put on auction or that the community could not prove that the church belonged to them – all such elements are constitutive parts of the post-genocidal habitus of denial that turns this story of absurdity into a normality. As explained earlier in this book, Armenian newspapers themselves sometimes become part of this habitus, writing creatively around these issues that otherwise could not have been aired at all.

I conducted oral interviews with an Armenian, K. A., who was born in 1938 in Sivas and who had lived there until he came to Germany as a worker in 1960. K. A. said that he witnessed the explosion of the church first-hand. As he was walking on the street, a passer-by fell on him because of the explosion. The church had not been used by the community for a long time; at least he had never been there as it was occupied by the military for as long has he could remember.[168]

The Armenian church in Tokat met a similar fate. According to Agop Arslanyan's account, the church was destroyed in the 1940s. Deprived of a priest or a church, the community gathered in clandestine fashion in Arslanyan's house, which was periodically stoned when the liturgy became audible in the street. Thus, a state policy of destroying churches fuelled, in turn, racist attacks on houses. However, another account from Diyarbekir indicates that there were also attacks on churches, especially when there was a community inside. Garabet Demircioğlu, an Armenian from Diyarbekir who was most probably born at the end of the 1960s, recounts: 'We used to go to church, the Surp Giragos Church. Our mothers used to hold our hands tightly on the way. While we were inside, there was always a sound accompanying the mass: the stones thrown at the door. [...] One day, that wooden door could not stand anymore and crashed. It was replaced by another, of iron.'[169]

The destruction of Armenian cultural heritage continued in the provinces. The Monastery on Akhtamar Island was similarly dynamited and largely destroyed in 1951. It was just a coincidence that novelist Yaşar Kemal witnessed some of this destruction in his initial years as a journalist and successfully intervened through the connections of his editor-in-chief of *Cumhuriyet*, Nadir Nadi.[170] The church of the Holy Cross on the Akhtamar Island is the only remaining section of the seminary today.

The destruction of a church or the stoning of a house where communities met – the former as state policy and the latter as an instance of mundane racism – indicates consistency between official and social practices. The motivation behind the destruction and the attacks seems to be the prevention of the members of the community from convening, reproducing their cultural life and performing religious ceremonies, while the ultimate goal or consequence is forced displacement and the destruction of the attachment between a people and their homeland. Uğur Üngör and Mehmet Polatel's analysis holds true: the object of destruction and appropriation was similar to that of the Young Turk policies, which aimed not only at the appropriation of property but, more importantly, at the physical removal of a people.[171]

Ordinary Cases: Concubines, Converts and Kidnapped Armenian Women in the Provinces

Another social reality for Armenians living in the provinces was the all-too-common phenomenon of converts, concubines and kidnapped women.

I do not intend to dwell on the details of the phenomenon itself, which remains a subject for further research in its own right. I rather emphasise here the banality of these cases in order to draw attention to another aspect of a post-genocidal society: These women were direct victims, in high numbers, of the genocidal practices that started in 1915. Important research by Vahé Tachjian,[172] Ara Sarafian,[173] Katherine Derderian,[174] Raymond Kevorkian[175] and Taner Akçam[176] sheds light on the issue. Tachjian has mentioned that one in three families must have had such an incident in their background.[177] My family, whose fate I discuss at the end of this section, was one such family.

The topic of Armenian women has received much attention in Turkey, especially after the publication of Fethiye Çetin's book, *Anneannem*, which relates the story of the discovery of the Armenian identity and roots of the author's grandmother. One of the first books on this issue, entitled *Tamama*, was published in 1993, and recounts the life of a child of a Pontic family living in Espiye, on the shore of the Black Sea. Exiled with her family in 1916, she had lost her parents by the time she reached Sivas. During the death march, with deportees dying one after the other, the people seemed to grow numb to the sight of death. After two years of walking, she decided to stay with a Turkish soldier's family – or so she related in her own story. No one knew of her Rum roots until she descended into a state of dementia, when she suddenly started to speak in Pontic Greek. Tamama's case demonstrates the extent to which concubinage, kidnapping and rape were all normalised. In his memoirs, Güzelyan too discussed Armenian women who were kidnapped during 1915 as ordinary occurrences among families in rural areas. Civan Çakır from Ordu recounts:

> Yes, we knew about them. For instance, Fuat's mother. We knew that his mother was Armenian. His mom, I guess from Merzifon, married a Georgian. When he [Fuat] finished high school and wanted to attend military college, he was not accepted because they found out about the Armenian origin of his mother. He was very upset. He married an Armenian woman. I know five women who were married and had children like this. [...] They were taken by the pashas during the deportation [*sevkiyat*].[178]

The women Çakır mentions were converts, and yet it was still known that they were Armenians. Güzelyan too mentions Armenian converts in

Zara.[179] In Agop Arslanyan's memoirs, both converted women and men are mentioned.[180] Although the numbers are not clear, there are at least two more oral historical accounts published in Turkish books.[181] This banality also revealed itself during my own research, especially when, in the course of my oral interviews, the fate of Armenian women came up and was expressed as an ordinary occurrence, a banality – which should give us an idea of just how common it must have been.

In *Islam, Nationalism and Secularism in Modern Turkey: Who is a Turk?*, Soner Cagaptay cites a note from the archives of British Foreign Office on the topic of concubines: 'It is true that there exists a large numbers of Armenian women in Turkish houses in the capacity of servants and concubines, but their Armenian children (who are brought up as Moslems [*sic*]) have become absorbed in the Turkish population, and their existence is not officially admitted. I doubt whether in the whole of Turkey outside of Constantinople there are even 10,000 Armenians living as such.'[182] The numbers, however, were much higher than stated in this note.

The case was no different in my family. The cousins of my grandmother, İskuhi Bozoyan Oskanoğlu (Erzurum 1915–Istanbul 1999), were exiled from Erzurum to Mosul. After six months of walking, Nvart Pnjoian (my grandmother's niece, born in 1896 in Erzurum) married Abdalla al Dagistani, a soldier in Mosul who was born into the Ajamatov family in Daghestan, who was a mechanical engineer and who had studied and lived in Germany for 13 years. After the 1917 Revolution, he could not go back to Daghestan and thus ended up in Mosul as an officer of the German Army. I received this information from Nvart Pnjoian's grandson, W. Y., who lived with his family in Mosul until the summer of 2014, who speaks fluent Armenian, and is a Sunni Muslim. The marriage part of this story remains unclear to me. While the family version, as my mother told me, is that Nvart was sold to Abdalla al Dagistani, according to W. Y.'s account, the marriage was rather part of a deal in which Nvart could bring the remaining family members with her.[183]

My own family's story, strange as it may sound, was considered an ordinary part of our lives, and thus intimately connects my family history to the banality of the issue. The reason for never questioning this history was this banality itself. I remember asking my mother from time to time what our relationship to W. Y. and his family was. However, these questions never challenged the ordinary nature of things. I have since heard similar stories from my friends as well. This banality, that such a reality existed pervasively enough in society, and that it existed as a normal part of life, constitutes an important aspect of post-genocidal society – the common and ordinary knowledge and silences of public opinion.

Furthermore, as I will show below, the kidnapping of Armenian girls did not come to an end as a practice in the provinces, but continued to pose such an important threat to Armenian families that it was an actual reason to move to Istanbul in the first decades after 1923. Many Armenian girls were unable to attend local Turkish schools because of the danger of kidnapping. Another interviewee, K. B., born in 1951 in Lice, gave an example of the gendered dimension of the troubling conditions in the provinces:

> We came to Diyarbakır in 1958. We no longer had the good fortune to continue living in Lice. My two sisters had to wear the chador to be able to visit their acquaintances in another neighbourhood. Otherwise, they could not. There were lots of Armenians living in Diyarbakır who had come from the villages in the region.[184]

According to his memoirs, *Tebi Gakhaghan*, Keōrk Halajian came across Armenian women who had been kidnapped as well as men who had kidnapped Armenian girls at almost every stop from Istanbul to Harput during the years 1925–8. I will quote only one example from among many – that of Usta Torig:

> He is an old man, originally from Erzurum. He kept his Armenian name and does not hide his ethnicity. [...] He lost everything he had during the exile and is the only survivor from his family. [...] One day he heard that his daughter was in Diyarbekir. He went there from Mardin only to find that his daughter married to a Turk. [... He said,] 'Despite the fact that I could not rescue my daughter I saved the lives of more than 50 Armenians girls. [...] I will stay here, since there are orphans to take care of.'[185]

Post-Genocide Habitus: Denial in Social and Official Practices

Agop Arslanyan's book depicts certain episodes of racist violence, which give an idea about the social conditions in Tokat, especially the animadversion toward the Armenians on the part of Muslim immigrants from the Balkans. For instance, during an Armenian funeral, these *kaght'agan* families' children threw stones at them while singing, 'In-in-in-infidel, snap his neck with a cleaver, put him in the cauldron and roast him like turkey, in-in-in-infidel!' (*Ge ge ge ge gavur, boynunu satırla vur, kazana koy hindi gibi kavur, ge ge ge ge gavur*).' Arslanyan writes, 'Our funeral was accompanied by this song and the stones. The coffin stood in the middle and we hid behind the trees.'[186] According to Arslanyan, the situation further deteriorated when an Armenian woman tried to stop the children, who in turn threw even more stones at the community members. In the end, an Alewi *dede* who happened to pass through intervened with his pistol, and the children had to escape. Another act of violence took place when Arslanyan's mother visited the ruins of an Armenian church to pray. A middle-aged man cursed, shouted fiercely at her and urinated on the ruins.[187] Yet another example concerns the conflict between Armenians and the children of immigrants. Agop and his brother Kevork were stopped on the street by Muslim immigrant children, who ordered them to spit on the cross, and beat them severely when they refused.[188] Arslanyan also wrote about the Jews living in Tokat: whenever the Rabbi was seen on the street, the children started to harass him by saying 'Jewish germ swallows all / Jewish lice, our stray dog' ('*Yahudi illeti, yutar bütün milleti / Yahudi yaka biti, bizim sokağın iti*').[189]

Similar observations about Diyarbekir can be found in Garabet Demircioğlu's account as well, which presents the situation after the 1940s – most probably in the early 1970s. Demircioğlu, who was imprisoned and brutally tortured after the *coup d'état* of 1980, describes his childhood in Diyarbekir:

Like any other Anatolian Armenian, all our grandparents were 'remnants of the sword.' The rest were either in exile or leading the lives of immigrants. My grandmother, who witnessed the killing of her brothers and sisters and all her family, used to tell us the stories of the survivors who made their way to Kamışlı and Aleppo in Syria. My aunts were in Syria too. [...] My uncle used to live in France. [...]

We could not speak Armenian anywhere except in the house, and we could not say our names. I always thought that if I successfully hid these two things, nobody would know that I was an Armenian. So I thought that everything depended on my success in hiding, but it did not. They always figured it out, or rather always kept track of who was an infidel or *fille* [the Kurdish word for infidel]. I attended an elementary school named after Süleyman Nazif.[190] Children of other districts would corner me and the other Armenian children, bring their index fingers together and raise them, asking, 'Are you a Muslim?' or they would make a cross with both index fingers and ask, 'Or are you a *fille*?' Most of the time they would not even wait to hear that ominous answer and would start spitting in our faces and beating us. In those days, I most often heard about my own existence as a sacrifice to be exchanged for a place in heaven. 'If I kill 7 *fille*, I will go to heaven!' I lived whole my life as a potential *fille* [through whom the murderer could] ascend to heaven.[191]

The similarity between the two accounts, one from Tokat in the 1940s and the other from Diyarbekır, probably from the late 1960s, is striking. The stereotypes built around infidels continued to play an important role in the process of 'othering' and the use of violence against the other, although these processes were not only part of discrimination policies within society, but also embedded in the history of the genocide; they continued to banalise the deep evil within society by reproducing hatred, violence and the politics of exclusion within the social realm.

Education was vital for Armenian communities after the first half of the nineteenth century and especially in the beginning of the twentieth century; therefore, Republican elites purposefully prohibited the reopening of Armenian schools. As has been previously pointed out, one of the most important reasons for the continual flow of people to Istanbul was the absence of Armenian schools in the provinces and the consistent policy of thwarting any opportunity to teach Armenian or to express Armenian culture in the provinces. In the mid 1950s, Güzelyan went to Kayseri to gather Armenian children with the hope of bringing them to Istanbul and giving them the opportunity to attend Armenian schools. The priest of Kayseri, Der Haygazun, with whom he discussed such prospects, related that they 'made several appeals to Ankara, saying that there are Armenians; there are churches and school buildings, but no, Armenians are not allowed to have schools, although, according to the Treaty of Lausanne, it was the duty of the government to provide buildings for the education of Armenians in rural areas.'[192] From the 1950s onwards, the community made a considerable effort to gather Armenian children from the provinces. This effort was first directed at boys and, after a while, at girls in smaller numbers. The establishment of Tbrevank Boarding School in 1953 was instrumental in this respect. Through the efforts of Hrant Güzelyan, this collective initiative lasted until the 1980s. In the eyes of Armenian community leaders, not attending Armenian schools ultimately amounted to assimilation.[193] On the other hand, bringing Armenian children from the provinces to Istanbul meant that the families of these children would have to move to Istanbul too, which in turn played an important role in the evacuation of the provinces.

While Armenians in Istanbul were worried about the assimilation of the survivors living in the provinces, according to Kēōrk Halajian's memoirs, *Tebi Gakhaghan*, the representative of Diyarbekir, Şeref Bey, also followed the facts regarding the assimilation of Armenians in Diyarbekir:[194] '[Turkifying the Armenians] might have been very difficult had their connection with the outside world not been cut. They have neither schools here, nor Armenian literature. Intellectuals have already left; 80 per cent of those who are left behind are illiterate. The elderly die, and the younger generation is educated in Turkish schools.'[195]

It is clear from Şeref Bey's account that the prohibition on the opening of Armenian schools in the provinces is part of a larger project: assimilation or displacement from the provinces. He further recounts the measures taken against Armenians: 'All their letters, both sent and received, are checked by censors. Armenian newspapers are strictly prohibited here. Even those published in Istanbul are not known here. In any case they are not given the time and opportunity to be interested in that kind of luxury.'[196] According to Halajian, Şeref Bey emphasised the importance of promoting mixed marriages, which would facilitate the melting-pot process.[197]

Civan Çakır's wife, Hayguhi Çakır, also from Ordu, tells the story of her sister and her sister's daughter, who had the good fortune, despite being Armenian, of attending a Turkish school, but not of getting the grades they deserved: 'In middle school, teachers used to give Turkish students good grades, because it was obvious that *we* would not work and have a career. This was taken for granted. My sister and my sister's daughter experienced this [discrimination] too.'[198] All evidence points to the fact that, for Armenians in the provinces, access to education was limited. Girls faced the constant threat of being kidnapped once they were sent to school; there were no Armenian schools to attend, and in Turkish schools discrimination was common. Beside the absence of schools, religious needs too were unmet in many cities in the provinces, which, coupled with the community's concern that the remaining Armenians in the provinces would be assimilated in the long run, shaped plans to bring Armenians to Istanbul.

Another day-to-day experience during this period was the existence of legal cases under the law that criminalised 'denigrating Turkishness'. Elçin Macar notes that he has encountered many cases against non-Muslims under this article,[199] while Cemil Koçak draws attention to these cases – 421 cases in 1926–42 filed against non-Muslims under the law against denigrating Turkishness.[200] Koçak points out that there is little information on the details of these cases or files, and that there must be a connection between them and the 'Citizen, Speak Turkish' campaigns that were intermittently launched during this period to prevent non-Muslims from speaking their own language in public.[201] He also comments on the arbitrariness in filing a case against a non-Muslim based on denigrating Turkishness, emphasising that any kind of simple criticism may have ended up in court.[202] Koçak wonders whether personal conflicts, competitions, or enmities turned into legal cases, admittedly answering in the affirmative, even in the absence of archival sources to prove this argument.[203]

Oral historical accounts are very rich sources on the problem of personal enmities resulting in arbitrary charges of 'denigrating Turkishness', since those who faced such accusations are still alive. Indeed, one can easily sense from the interviewees that these cases turned into a social phenomenon of sorts. Baghdik Hagopyan's wife, Shushan Hagopyan, illustrates just how easily such cases were filed: 'It was an alibi for everything. Neighbours would have quarrels within the same building and this would end up in [charges or lawsuits of] "denigrating Turkishness".'[204] Armenian newspapers are full of news items about such and other criminal cases filed against non-Muslims. Ara Garmiryan similarly notes, regarding cases of denigrating Turkishness, that they 'were cause for trouble. Slander and reality could not be differentiated.

Every single reason for any personal enmity could easily turn into a case as soon as someone articulated the phrase "denigrating Turkishness".'[205]

Civan Çakır told me that, either in 1942, before his obligatory military service, or later in 1945, while he was on the boat returning to Ordu from a sports competition in Fatsa, the son of a local journalist purposefully touched him, turned around and slapped him for no apparent reason. I asked him whether the person might have slapped him in order to provoke him to say something to denigrate Turkishness. Çakır replied that some such incident had happened to his father when he was working in a field that was going to be confiscated by the state. People asked him why he cultivated it anyway. The ensuing discussion became grounds for a case in 'denigrating Turkishness', and resulted in the six-month imprisonment of Çakır's father. This event took place in 1934 or 1935, when Civan Çakır was ten years old. Çakır said the prison was the Rum church.[206] Cemil Koçak provides the full list of cases that he found in the Prime Ministry Archives of 1926–52. However, neither Çakır's nor any other case from Ordu could be found on this list.[207] As Koçak argues, this instance manifests that not all records could be found in those archives. Çakır's experiences suffice to demonstrate how easy it was to file cases of denigrating Turkishness, as well as the kind of habitus reigning in the post-genocide period. In 1949, a story in an Armenian newspaper cited yet another example: A court case on illicit sex between Rezzan and Hovhannēs resulted in the imprisonment of Hovhannēs. During the ruling, his sister Madlen angrily shouted at the police officers and was arrested for denigrating Turkishness.[208]

Another episode related to these cases was relayed by Evdoksi Parsehyan and concerns the 'Citizen, Speak Turkish' campaigns. I asked her whether she remembered these campaigns. She replied: 'Unfortunately, I do. I was afraid to speak Turkish on the street, because my Turkish was not good enough. So I chose not to speak, to remain silent.'[209] And silent she remained although neither she nor her immediate circle had been harassed. Nor was she alone in her choice: from the perspective of the perpetrators of these campaigns, her decision represents the ideal outcome – she was literally afraid to open her month in public spaces. Aram Pehlivanyan's article on the first page of *Nor Or* on 1 September 1946 raised precisely this issue:[210] 'Civil Courage' discusses Armenians who feared to speak in Armenian or read Armenian newspapers on the boat or in other public spaces. Pehlivanyan advocated the right to speak one's native language and stated that it was already granted to Armenians living in Turkey:

> Often, [hostile] remarks are made on public transportation and boats; people are even beaten up just because they committed 'the crime/sin' of speaking in their mother tongue. [. . .] In order not to be subjected to daily harassment, they choose to keep silent and not to speak in their mother tongue, at least in public spaces.[211]

Rifat N. Bali provides other examples of violence in an article published in *Birgün*; for example, this incident from an article written by Cihad Baban:[212]

> We saw some youngsters from Boyacıköy severely beating up a man on a Bosphorus ferry. We heard that the man being beaten up was a creditor [. . .] On the day before, he had asked back for his money from these youngsters, and now they beat him up for not speaking in Turkish. In those days, such incidents happened one after the other. We heard that a woman speaking to her husband – she was a foreigner who knew no Turkish – was raped.[213]

In this incident, as in legal cases of denigrating Turkishness, an area of licence was opened to cover up personal aggressions with official practices – one of the most important and persistent characteristics of the post-genocide habitus. The 'Citizen, Speak Turkish' campaign, launched in 1928 by the Law School Student Association (*Dar-ül-fünun Hukuk Fakültesi Talebe Cemiyeti*), had already been gaining support in the government and among public opinion makers for at least three years. İsmet İnönü gave a speech in the Turkish Hearths (*Türk Ocakları*, a supporting organisation of the 'Citizen, Speak Turkish' campaign), which later became the *Turkish Historical Association*, emphasising the importance of 'discarding elements opposing Turks and Turkishness'.[214] Around the same time, Necmeddin Sadak referred to minorities as 'one of the problems' (*meselelerden biri*') of the Republic and dwelled on the impossibility of accepting them as citizens unless they spoke in Turkish.[215] In July 1925, the municipality of Bursa issued a resolution obligating city-dwellers to speak only in Turkish; two Jews who spoke in Spanish were fined.[216] *Türk Ocağı* launched a similar campaign in Izmir in August 1925.[217] Thus, when 'Citizen, Speak Turkish' was established as a campaign, public opinion makers, alongside local and national politicians, had long prepared the society. The campaign was easily turned into an instrument of harassment and assault on non-Muslims members of society, whatever the underlying personal disagreement, just as in the cases of 'denigrating Turkishness'. Thus, when Aram Pehlivanyan wrote about civil courage in 1946, he was referring to a history of more than 20 years.

As can be seen in these cases, 'Citizen, Speak Turkish' was, rather than a campaign to speak in Turkish – which would have been problematic enough – a campaign to silence, to make people invisible in the public realm. These campaigns should be contextualised within the post-genocidal habitus of denial, since they aimed to make socially invisible the remaining non-Muslims in general and Armenians in particular. The violence unfolding as a result of these campaigns seeks to not only establish the silencing of the 'unwanted' but also create and reproduce a value system in which it is disgraceful to be Armenian or Jewish or foreign.

Another interesting instance from the provinces was the court case against the publisher of a local official newspaper (*Vilayet Gazetesi*)[218] of Isparta. In its 5 February 1947 issue, the newspaper published a short piece on its front page signed by a certain 'MUTLU'.[219] The title of the piece was 'Pari Siragan'.[220] Writing of the past, the author recounts that when he had to learn Armenian at the age of 23, he wanted to know his teacher's political views. His teacher was neither a member of the Hunchakian Party nor Tashnakts'utiwn, but a member of Pari Siragan (in Van), on which I could not find any information. It appears that MUTLU was from Van, which he defined as 'the centre of Armenian society and culture'.[221] This very sentence was grounds for a letter of protest from Van–Erciş under the signature of one 'İzzet Davaoğlu and his friends'. On 3 March 1947 a file was submitted to the Prime Minister.[222] Three days later, *Marmara* reported the incident, which had already turned into a legal case at the Isparta court, and noted that the case was based on 'harming Turkish nationalistic feelings' and insulting Turkish history. The prosecutor's argument further relied on a telegram (mostly illegible, but present in the file in the Prime Ministry Archives) from Van–Erciş asking the author why he felt the need to learn Armenian and praise Pari Siragan. I could find no other news piece following up on the case, neither in the papers nor in the Prime Ministry Archives. However, extant evidence suffices to show how easily a lawsuit could be filed, even against a local official newspaper, just because it referred to the existence of Armenians in a certain place. More importantly, it was crucial to garner support from the people of Van, which demonstrates, once again, the consistency of official and social practices. Even if the telegrams were just a fabrication, there was a need to establish a link between official and social practice to claim broader legitimacy.

In this section, I have demonstrated the consistency between official and social practices: Genocide denial was the catalyst of official practices, discourses, and laws on the one hand, and the creation of mechanisms that legitimised oppressive social practices on the other – all of which became even more visible during the years of Wealth Tax and the *Yirmi Kura Askerlik*.

Social Consequences of The *Yirmi Kura Askerlik* (Random Draft of Non-Muslims) and Other Practices During World War II

Various aspects and experiences of the *Yirmi Kura Askerlik* were revealed throughout oral historical accounts I have compiled. Zaven Biberyan's novel, *Mrchiwnneru Verchaloysĕ* (translated into Turkish under the title of *Babam Aşkale'ye Gitmedi*), masterfully depicts the period in which *Yirmi Kura Askerlik* labour battalions – the random draft of non-Muslim men into the military – was implemented, followed by the Wealth Tax in the next year. Sources differ on the exact age of the men who were drafted: Dilek Güven puts the age span at 25–45,[223] whereas Ayşe Hür states the respective birth-year range as 1896–1913,[224] and Rıfat N. Bali as 1894–1913.[225] My grandfather, Haçik Suciyan, who was born in 1895, was also drafted. More importantly, these men were drafted regardless of whether they had ever served in the military; thus, sometimes their military service amounted to three to four years in the form of forced labour. This practice had been widely known since World War I years.[226] The issue of Labour Battalions (*Amele Taburu*) was raised even during the Lausanne negotiations. Reporting on the negotiations to the Parliament in March 1923, Rıza Nur mentioned that the representatives of European states raised the issue of *Amele Taburları* in the context of exempting non-Muslims from obligatory military service. The European powers required that Turkey not require obligatory military service from non-Muslims, arguing that it would lead to *Amele Taburları*. Rıza Nur related the conversation thusly: '[They said] You would establish *Amele Tabur*s, send them back, and slaughter them. We said, no, we would not slaughter them.'[227]

The details of *Yirmi Kura Askerlik* per se lie outside the scope of this study, as it is extensively covered by the existing literature.[228] My focus here is on how Armenians in the provinces experienced the *Yirmi Kura Askerlik*, as well as their social consequences, which are rarely addressed. An unintended aspect of this extraordinary type of military service was that it enabled people such as Güzelyan, Köseyan, Koçunyan, Biberyan, Yervant Gobelyan,[229] Haygazun Kalustyan,[230] and others to get in touch with the communities that were left over or hidden in the provinces. These men were conscripted in various places during their military service. At least in the case of Güzelyan and Köseyan, we know that they came across Armenians almost everywhere. Discussing his years in the military, Köseyan says that he met the Armenian community in Adana/Ceyhan that started to organise holy masses on Sundays. He contributed his first articles to the daily *Jamanak* from Adana.[231] In his memoirs, Hrant Güzelyan too recounts his encounters with Armenians in various cities in the provinces during his military service after 1941:

> Travelling in the provinces was suspect in those days. There was always the same question: 'Where are you going? Why are you going? Whom are you visiting?' Poor people, they did not have churches, schools, or any opportunity to get together. They were always under control and, on top of that, [they experienced] the shame of being born Armenians.[232]

In the same vein, Civan Çakır relates his experience of the *Yirmi Kura Askerlik*:

> I joined the *Yirmi Kura Askerlik* group ten months later. [. . .] I was taken to the military in March 1942. [. . .] We were mixed with the people of *Yirmi Kura Askerlik* ('*Yirmi Kura*'); we were road labourers. My military service lasted three and a half years. We had a roof over our heads for no more than six months. [. . .] One day, there was an earthquake, and I formally asked for permission to

pay a visit home, because Ordu had also been hit by the earthquake. I got the permission. But then I had to walk 55 km under the rain. As there was no road whatsoever at that time, I had to walk in the mud from morning till evening to arrive in Adana. I stayed there for a month and a half. From Adana we were sent to Hassa, on the border with Syria. When I got back, I heard that 130 Armenians had escaped to Syria, writing Good-bye ['*Mnak' Parov'*] on their tents. We only had four–five officers in charge of us, so they could not do anything. There were no landmines at that time either, although they had to pass the river. Two people died and 130 people crossed the border to Syria. This should be in 1943 or 1944, after the Wealth Tax.[233]

Çakır adds that, while he was working as a forced labourer, his father was charged with a Wealth Tax of around 700 liras, which they paid off by selling the last piece of their land that had been confiscated by the state in 1915 and only been partly returned to his family.[234] Even disabled Armenians were forcefully drafted into the *Yirmi Kura Askerlik*, as Agop Arslanyan notes. Semerci Maksut from Tokat, who was deaf, was badly tortured before being drafted into the military, and never returned.[235]

The editor-in-chief of *Jamanak* at the time, Ara Koçunyan (also conscripted to this military service), estimated the number of drafted Christian men as 20,000.[236] The *Yirmi Kura Askerlik* made an extremely negative impact on the social life of the Armenian community, and yet rarely finds a place in historiography. For instance, in the field of sports, the Nor Şişli Sports Club (*Nor Şişli Spor Klübü*) ceased its activities because all its active members had been called to military service.[237] Varujan Köseyan, also drafted, told me about yet another social repercussion of the *Yirmi Kura Askerlik*: the church choirs suddenly lost many of their members.[238] Evdoksi Suciyan Parsehyan (born in Istanbul, 1927) repeated the same outcome regarding the church choirs: 'We established a special choir of women, since there were no men left. And the church in Yeşilköy was occupied by soldiers. That's why we used to go to the church in Bakırköy. We were all women. [...] There were only two men on the altar who were very old and therefore exempted from military service.'[239] As to why the church was occupied, her answer was that the Armenian church in Yeşilköy was used as a military warehouse.[240] She could not remember the exact duration of the occupation, although she said it was at least for one year. Beside the church and private houses in Yeşilköy, the Surp P'rgich' Armenian Hospital also hosted Turkish troops. The annual report of the hospital notes that the section used by the military was partitioned with a wooden fence in order to avoid 'unwanted incidents',[241] while the *Hushamadean Surp P'rgich' Hiwanatanots'i* states that the occupation lasted from 1941 to 1950 and ended with the newly elected administration.[242] The occupation did not limit itself to the hospital, but extended over to the properties of the Hospital, such as the apartment buildings by the names Vuçino and Yardım, and Yusufyan Han.[243] In 1947, *Nor Lur* reported that the Armenian church of Surp Nshan in Pendik was occupied by the military until *locum tenens* Kevork Arslanyan claimed the church back from the authorities.[244] The occupation of the churches can be seen not only as a preventive measure of the state to store ammunition in an emergency situation, but also as the obstruction of congregation via the occupation of a community centre, i.e. a church complex that includes rooms, halls, and other spaces. Considering the fact that there were no other gathering places for the community, the occupation of such premises was intended to hinder the right to gather.

My grandfather, Haçik Suciyan (Istanbul 1895–1966), was also drafted during the *Yirmi Kura Askerlik*. The way he submitted himself to the officials partly illustrates the habitus in which Armenians lived. According to my aunt Evdoksi Parsehyan,

> On his last evening, he ran into the village security officer on his way and the officer said, 'Oh, Müsü Haçik, where are you going?,' obviously just to greet my father. 'Tomorrow I'll come and sign up,' he responded hastily. He thought that the security officer was looking for him, although he was not. The next day my sister and I took him to the train station, crying. He was sent to Kütahya.[245]

Evdoksi Parsehyan told me how her father's forced military service affected her educational life. Due to the loss of family income in the absence of a working father, she could not continue her education.[246] A similar case is Arslanyan's in Tokat: After his father and his uncles were drafted during the *Yirmi Kura Askerlik*, Arslanyan, a good student, had to quit school and start working at the age of nine or ten, since otherwise the family could not have subsisted.[247] Thus, the *Yirmi Kura Askerlik* not only affected the drafted non-Muslim men and their families, but also the educational life and future prospects of the children.

Another aspect of World War II, as far as non-Muslims were concerned, can be seen in a practice carried out by government authorities in Yeşilköy: the occupation of large residences by the military. My grandparents' house was among those occupied in 1943. According to Evdoksi Parsehyan's account, her mother Bercuhi shut down all the doors to hinder the entrance of the soldiers, but they got in through the windows.

> We were not at home when they came. [...] Once we were back home, we saw military vehicles in front of our house. My mom said that she did everything she could to stop them, but they entered through the window. We had to give them two rooms. One of them was for a military veterinarian and the other for a doctor with their soldiers in assist. We spent the winter with them in the same house. [...] Not only ours, but many houses in Yeşilköy were occupied. Our neighbour's house across the street, Mintanciyan's house, and the house of a Jewish merchant were occupied too. Not all Christians' houses, but many, were occupied. The military stayed through the winter and left in May. I guess they were coming from Hadımköy and returned in the end. [...] We were lucky though, as ours were both captains (*yüzbaşı*). [...] In some of the houses, they remained for years. One of the houses was turned into a military policemen base (*inzibatlık*) and remained thus for many years.[248]

In my oral interview with Ara Garmiryan (born in Istanbul, 1920), I asked him whether he knew anything about occupied houses. He said he had heard about such cases in Yeşilköy. When I further asked why he thought that the occupied houses belonged only to non-Muslims, he laughed and said: 'Do you think this question makes sense? Had they asked Muslims, they would have picked a fight. Armenians would feel crushed.'[249]

The Sancak of Alexandretta

The Sancak deserves a separate section, since the conditions there were different than in any other province. Armenians continued to live in the

Sancak, under French rule, until 1939. When Toros Azadyan and Mardiros Koçunyan devoted a special section to the Sancak in their book *Armağan*,[250] they knew what a delicate issue for the Republic of Turkey it was. They dedicated a total of four pages to Hatay, with the second part entitled 'Armenians in Hatay'. The booklet explained, 'Today there are 30,000 Armenians living in Hatay, enjoying all their citizenship rights, and sincerely embracing the progress of the country. In the last elections in the Sancak, the number of Armenians who had the right to vote was 5,504.'[251]

The history of the region is indeed complex: As opposed to in Turkey, in the Sancak of Alexandretta, Armenian political parties were active and rivalries between them consequential. Annexation meant yet another exodus for a group of Armenians, namely the members of Tashnakts'utiwn. As one of my interviewees, A. K., born in Musa Dağ in 1953, recounts:

> Until the annexation [to Turkey], Tashnaks, Hunchaks, Ramgavars and Communists were all very well-organised in Hatay. In 1937, in the parliament of the Sancak of Antakya during the transitional autonomous Republic, there was even a parliamentarian representing Musa Dagh: Movses Der Kaloustyan.[252] He was from the Tashnak party. Hunchaks were poorer, yet well-organised. When annexation discussions grew, Movses led the Tashnaks out of Hatay. Hunchaks remained there, thinking that one day they would immigrate to Armenia. My father and my uncle played an important role in this process. Tatyos Babek's grandfather, whose name was also Tatyos, was an important figure too. He was appointed head of the six villages. The state decided to turn the village of Hidir Bey into the centre [of these six villages]. The appointed administrator (T. B.) was a member of the Hunchak Party whereas his father was a Tashnak. The state found the best candidate. This person was full of love for Atatürk and Ismet Pasha. In the 1980s, he wrote about his love in the newspapers *Kulis*[253] and *Marmara*.[254]

In 1939, the Ministry of Interior prepared a special report on Armenians who had left the Sancak. The report was submitted to the President, the Chief of General Staff, the Ministry of Foreign Affairs and the Chief of Police. The very detailed three-page report has five chapters. In the first, there is a list of the reasons for the immigration of Armenians, including the high unemployment rate in Sancak, the poor government of the autonomous state of Hatay and fears related to the past, among others. Part two discusses the destination of Armenians. The third part is rather sophisticated and very detailed, and explains the concerns of the Turkish government, especially regarding the areas where Armenians were settled. The report makes it clear that the Armenians' departure did not suffice for the government, which constantly received information about the location of their new settlements, whether the area of settlement would create geopolitical threats to Turkey, how many Armenians lived in which areas in Lebanon or in Syria, in what kind of businesses they were active, and what kind of organisations were in place to help immigrants, etc. For instance, the following passage reveals the strategic importance of the new settlement areas: 'In the northern part of Latakia, the area of Bayir–Bucak–Türmen, there is not even a single empty or deserted lot. Therefore, any attempt to settle Armenians in this area would mean that the aim is to create a concentration of Armenians near the border and to diminish the Turkish majority in the area.'[255]

The state thus paid special attention not only to the annexation of the Sancak of Alexandretta, but also to the Armenians who left the Sancak. It is very interesting to see in the documents that both Armenian existence in general and their nonexistence – including their existence in another country, in this case Syria and Lebanon – mattered to Turkey, and this vigilance in turn affected Armenians. As will be seen, the omission of the annexation to Turkey was even a reason to shut down an Armenian newspaper. The fact that Armenians were still active in politics in the region, as seen in the election results mentioned in the footnotes, posed a disturbing challenge to the Republican elite and opinion makers throughout the process of annexation. The publishers' decision to devote a separate section to the Sancak becomes more meaningful in this light. Its multicultural population, and its Armenian population in particular, turned the politics around the region into a very sensitive issue. Only a couple of years after the annexation, in 1941, the *Yirmi Kura Askerlik* (labour battalions) was to be implemented there too. According to A. K., who belongs to one of the families remaining in the region of the Sancak:

Yirmi Kura Askerlik was a name given to this practice in other places. We called it 'the Group of nine,' since nine groups of men were sent from our village. My father and his acquaintances went to Kandıra. Both my father and the new priest, Der Ghewont, went there. They made them carry coal and load it on the German ships. [. . .] Apart from that, all those in Kandıra were Armenians, my father used to say. Upon his arrival in Istanbul, he went to the office of *Jamanak*. In 1945–1950, he wrote articles about the developments in the Sancak.[256]

A. K.'s account of his childhood and of Reşat, the General Director of Pious Foundations (*Vakıflar Genel Müdürü*) in Hatay, provides a sketch of the situation in the area after the annexation. Reşat was there to take care of the so-called 'abandoned' lands, since the annexation of the area had driven a considerable number of Armenians from the region and from their land ownership.

The best house of the village was given to Reşat and was turned into the headquarters. Reşat settled in this house too. He was the head of GDPF in Hatay and always wore an officer's uniform. His main duty was to generate income from the abandoned lands. [. . .] He had a military uniform, khaki coloured boots up to his knees, a fur cap on his head, a horsewhip in his hand. Sometimes, he would pass by our door. People would shout 'Reşat is coming' and I would run away at once. [. . .] He was a scary man. He had a gun on his belt. No one could complain about him, yet no one would invite him to his house either. He never drank our coffee. You were not supposed to show him the newspaper you were reading.[257]

However, Reşat was not just a scary figure, according to A. K.'s account. His sexual abuse of both children and their parents in Vakıf, the only Armenian village left in Musa Dağ, greatly upset the villagers and their relationships:

He would give jobs to the children of the poor, for example, to put up this wall, to cut down those trees, to cultivate this land, and so on. Two thirds of the lands were abandoned anyway . . . GDPF had the best portion of the lands. He would have fun with the children at night. He would abuse a father and one of his children. Everyone knew what Reşat did. Honest people who did not need money were very afraid of him. One of the adults that Reşat had abused later took over his position.[258]

The Sancak, its annexation, the historical significance of the region for Armenians due to the legacy of the Musa Dağ resistance, all had a role to play in the discourse of annexation and racism fuelled against Armenians at the time. Thus, the Sancak had special status in the eyes of the government because of its past and its demographic profile. Zaven Biberyan's article 'Enough Is Enough' ('*Al Gĕ Pawē*') touches upon the issue of Hatay and the hatred reproduced by the newspapers against the Armenians:

We still remember the time when Hatay was annexed to Turkey. Not a day passed by without an anti-Armenian article published in the newspapers. If a man by the name of Margos would kill a woman in China, this would have repercussions in Hatay, and the language would be one of hatred and anger towards the Armenians of Hatay.[259]

Since the Sancak of Alexandretta was Syrian territory until 1938, the Catholicosate of the Great House of Cilicia, which had been resettled in Antelias, near Beirut, was responsible for the Armenian community living in Musa Dağ. The priest of the Sancak was also appointed by the Catholicosate and retained its position after the annexation. When the priest visited Istanbul in 1947, a brief on his visit stated that Father Ghewont Kartunyan lived in the village of Vakıf as the priest of Surp Asduadzadzin Church, and that he was the leader of 500 Armenians living in the area.[260]

Nor were demographic issues a small matter for the state. A document from the Prime Ministry Archives in Istanbul shows that the government continued to monitor the demographic situation closely, especially with regard to non-Muslims. A report prepared by the General Directorate of Statistics reveals that, after the 1927 census, the government required another report on the population of 'non-Turks'[261] and non-Muslims in 1930, this time from the Police Department.[262] As the results of the two differed considerably, Prime Minister İsmet İnönü required a third report on the population of both groups from the General Director of Statistics. The reporter verified that he had personally met the people who gathered that information and discovered that the Police Department utilised birth registers that were considered unreliable, since some deaths and births, as well as some of the newcomers, were not registered. The report consists of two sections, the first of which concerns non-Turks, specified as 'racial nationalities'.[263] Data-gathering relied on spoken language, that is mother tongue, as the main criterion. The reporter tries, unsuccessfully, to find out whether there was a real increase in the population of different nationalities living in the country at that time. Regarding non-Muslims, the reporter states that the religious categorisations of the Police Department were inaccurate, since categories such as Slavic, Molokan,[264] or Bulgarian were grouped as religions. By contrast, the Orthodox faith could not be found in the Police Department's report. The reporter thus emphasises that the results of the census were not comparable to those presented by the Police Department. In conclusion, he calls for a census to identify the actual figures on the ground. At the time of the 1934 pogroms in Thrace against the Jewish population and during the ensuing exodus, the daily *Cumhuriyet* reported on two issues in a single article: a new wave of 50,000 Muslim immigrants arriving in Turkey, their settlement[265] and citizenship procedures, and the measures taken to reorganise birth and death registers. According to the article, through the new regulations of late February 1934, new births and deaths would be carefully registered, and the number of personnel duly increased.[266] The second census of the Republican period, as is known, was conducted in 1935.

Another interesting piece of information regarding demographic matters is the resolution of 25 August 1949 of the Council of Ministers which annulled the Turkish citizenship of 250 people who had either left the Sancak for Syria and Lebanon without using their right to plebiscite, or changed nationalities without obtaining permission.[267]

The Establishment and Institutionalisation of Denial

So far I have aimed at drawing a picture of the Armenian presence in Istanbul and in the provinces by underscoring the overlaps in social and official practices, which, in my view, constitute the post-genocide denialist habitus. I have pointed to the constraints on the right to practice certain professions, travel, cultural expression and religion: Non-Muslims in general and Armenians in particular remained the target of state policies of economic destruction. The Wealth Tax, the annihilation of man power in forced labour camps through the *Yirmi Kura Askerlik*, social pressure faced by Armenians on a daily basis, and the normality or banality of kidnapping women were all constitutive parts of this habitus. Daily racist attacks against the remaining non-Muslims were common both in the provinces and in Istanbul, and unchecked due to the absence of legal consequences for racist crimes until the present day:[268] While 'denigrating Turkishness' was a crime, denigrating any other identity was not. State policies have left room for the reproduction of racist attacks by not considering them a crime. Over the decades, denial – and not only of genocide – has become systematic practice and the main pillar for the machinery of state sovereignty, official ideology, society formation, and the cultural and economic policies of the state. As I will show in the following pages of this book, state denial meant complete silence about all of the practices mentioned above. Not only the genocide, but also the policies that followed, such as the *Wealth Tax* or the *Yirmi Kura Askerlik*, have remained taboo subjects for decades, only to be recently thematised, but not yet acknowledged and condemned as racist state policies or considered a cause for reparations.

Discussions of genocide denial should place its beginning at the level of the state and its consistent policies that were already producing cultural material outcomes as early as 1916. Based on such material, denial continued to be reproduced throughout the following hundred years. Talat's talk in the CUP congress of 1917[269] and the Ottoman State Report that has been published both in French and in Ottoman[270] were to become the main documents on which denial would be constructed in the following years. The discourse of 'stabbing the Empire in the back' was established based on this narrative and the photographs in which Armenians appeared armed with many weapons. Correspondence and statements of prominent Armenian leaders were selectively presented, the content of the education in Armenian schools was problematised, literary pieces were 'translated' as evidence and theoretical background for the hostility of Armenians against the Ottoman Empire. Furthermore, the history of political parties and the activities or passivity of patriarchs were all tracked in order to bolster the image of Armenians as an 'internal enemy' who could not be persuaded of peace, and who therefore had to be exiled in order to protect the Empire. Despite the fact that the book was translated into French a year after its Ottoman publication, to my knowledge these books have still not been subjected to critical reading in a bilingual comparative framework. These books and their content have been published and reproduced in various forms, but their content as the milestones of denialism remain unproblematised, which should itself be understood within the same decades-old denialist habitus of knowledge production.

In *A Shameful Act: The Armenian Genocide and the Question of Turkish Responsibility*, Taner Akçam provides a detailed account of the discussions that took place in the parliament in 1918 regarding what had happened to Armenians and Rums,[271] how the trials proceeded and how all attempts at bringing war crime suspects to justice failed in the end, with many moving on with their political careers after 1923.[272] Although after 1920 Britain continued to demand punishment for those responsible for the massacres, they too eventually abdicated their demand.[273] Soon afterwards, as early as 1926, the parliament decided to provide aid to the families of the political leadership that had organised and committed genocide, i.e. the CUP leaders.[274] In 1943, Talât's remains were relocated to Turkey and reinterred.

In 'The Roots of American Genocide Denial', Donald Bloxham argues that American diplomacy became fertile ground for denial due to opportunistic foreign policy.[275] It is well known that, before 1923, the US-based Near East Relief (NER) was a vital humanitarian aid organisation for the survivors. However, as Bloxham points out, the activity of NER and the interests of the US government did not always overlap. For instance, after the great fire of Smyrna in 1922, American High Commissioner Mark L. Bristol still advised NER not to take orphans out of Anatolia.[276] NER representatives began to see Bristol as an obstacle to the fulfilment of their function, yet Washington kept backing Bristol.[277] He even went on to say, 'The Greeks and Armenian merchants [. . .] have been the leeches in this part of the world sucking the life blood out of the country for centuries.'[278] Bristol not only supported but also reproduced the idea that the non-Muslims of the Ottoman Empire 'were foreigners and in a generation or two would become Turkish citizens like foreigners become citizens of the United States'.[279] Charles H. Sherrill, Ambassador of the United States in

Turkey (1932–3) and successor to Joseph C. Grew, wrote that 'Turks needed re-Turkification – a purification from all the base metals that made up the Ottoman amalgam.'[280] According to Bloxham, these ideas were very much favoured by the CUP cadres and Kemalists.[281] He further shows how US ambassadors' instruments were then implemented in Republican methods of denial:

> Sophistry was a vital tool, and Bristol employed it liberally. [...] After the 1921–2 war Bristol told anyone who would listen that Christian refugees 'had themselves committed outrages upon the Turks.' [...] In his focus upon Christian crimes, however, Bristol blurred past and present events. [...] Grew copied the technique. [...] With the rhetoric of Turkey as the 'underdog,' Bristol and Grew were doing exactly what prominent Turkish nationalists, many of whom had been implicated in the massacres of 1915–16, were themselves beginning to do: using the history of post-1918 war of independence to present retrospectively the prior world conflict as a defensive, anti-imperialist war, the killing of Armenians as an act of resistance against an internal aggressor.[282]

Moreover, Bloxham argues that genocide denial had been accepted and furthered by the American government before the term 'genocide' was even coined.[283] Taner Akçam and Ümit Kurt's recent work, *Kanunların Ruhu*, sheds light on American policy and its implementation. For instance, in August 1923, when a number of Ottoman Armenians who possessed US passports tried to enter Turkey, they were immediately arrested and sent back. Bristol advised his government not to give passports to people with this particular background.[284] The same study also reveals the position of the American government. According to the US Department of State archives, the American government made it clear that it had no intention of protecting the property rights of Ottoman citizens who acquired US citizenship.[285] By 1929, the French government acted along the same lines: during the negotiations between Turkey and France on Armenians living in Syria and Lebanon, France decided to disregard the claims on properties that belonged to Armenians living in these countries.[286]

Steeped in such international endorsement of denial, Turkish Republican governments reproduced and institutionalised it. According to Hilmar Kaiser, the grounds on which to deny the Armenian genocide were laid as early as the summer of 1915 by the propaganda material put together by the Directorate of Public Security in the Ottoman Ministry of Interior.[287] The same method had been used in 1914 by Ottoman officials and by the 'Special Organisation' to destroy the Zionist settlements and communities in Palestine.[288] Kaiser traces the trajectory of denial through the writings of the CUP leaders and prominent figures. In addition to Talat's writings, posthumously published first in 1921 and then in 1946, and Cemal's memoirs,[289] we have the memoirs of Ali Munif, who later became the representative of Adana (until 1950) and wrote to minimise his role and distort historical facts.[290] Likewise, the deputy of Izmir, Mustafa Reşat (1939–43), who later worked at the Agricultural Bank (until 1950), published his two-volume memoirs in 1946 as based on Ottoman propaganda publications of World War I and Ottoman statistics.[291] Kaiser shows how Mustafa Reşat exculpated himself and the Turkish state through his autobiographical account, although he himself had prepared the black lists of Armenian intellectuals and interrogated them. Ahmet Esat Uras – again a name favoured by Kemalists – who remained active in politics until the 1950s and was a permanent and active member of the Turkish Historical Association, wrote a massive volume on Ottoman Armenians. Published in 1950,[292] his work became a reference book thereafter and was translated into English in 1988.[293] Kaiser clearly articulates the continuity of the cadres and the mentality of denial:

> The biographies of the deniers under discussion here show that no fundamental break in the structure of administrative personnel occurred during the transition from the CUP controlled Ottoman governments to the establishment of the 'nationalist' governments under Mustafa Kemal Pasha. In the ideological sphere, it appears that in regard to Armenians the continuities are even stronger. The old elite continued to rule the country as before, pursuing their nationalist ideals.[294]

Moreover, Halil Menteşe, the Minister of Foreign Affairs of the CUP government, also published his memoirs in *Cumhuriyet* (1946).[295] The fact that most of the accounts mentioned in Kaiser's article were published or reprinted in the 1940s hints at the intellectual field of post-genocide Turkey in that decade. The establishment and activities of the Turkish Historical Association in the 1930s should be considered in this context. This continuity, however, is not limited to individuals and was systematically reinforced by the institutionalisation of denial as well as imperial structures and mentalities. The history of the 1930s was marked by the authoritarianism of the single party and the institutionalisation of Kemalist nationalism. The Turkish Hearth Historical Committee (*Türk Ocağı Tarih Heyeti*), an organisation under the Turkish Hearths (*Türk Ocakları*),[296] was transformed into the Committee for the Inquiry of Turkish History (*Türk Tarihi Tetkik Cemiyeti*), which then became the Turkish Historical Association (*Türk Tarih Kurumu*).[297] The famous 'Turkish Historical Thesis', bringing together the Asian history of Turks with the Kemalist ideals, was developed during those years. The first Turkish Historical Congress was held in 1931, as well as the First Turkish Language Congress. Other related events followed suit: the Institute for the History of the Turkish Reform (*İnkılap Tarihi Enstitüsü*) was established in Istanbul University (1933); the Surname Law was adopted in 1934, when the Settlement Law (*İskân Kanunu*) was passed; the Jewish population in Thrace was exiled, the Regulations on Private Schols (*Hususi Mektepler Talimatnamesi*) brought foreign and community schools under strict supervision, and were mandated to have Turkish deputy principals starting in 1937. Meanwhile, the racist tone of Kemalism was strengthened by pseudo-scientific research, including the *Turkish Journal of Anthropology* (*Türk Antropoloji Mecmuası*, 1925–39).[298] Afet İnan's thesis, which was published in 1946 by the Turkish Historical Association under the title of *Türkiye Halkının Antoropolojik Tarihi ve Türkiye Tarihi*, traces the political evolution of the Turkish population by chronologically examining skeletons.[299] All of this is to be understood in the framework of creating a society and a state in which denial was established starting with one's own name and surname, and perpetuated through the education system and the processes of socialisation, acculturation and politicisation. It is relevant that İsmail Beşikçi points to a speech by Hitler on the occasion of his 50th birthday celebrations, to which Mustafa Kemal too was invited. A high ranking delegation from Turkey attended the events, while Turkish newspapers published enthusiastic news items and articles on this occasion. In his speech (20 April 1939), Hitler proclaimed, 'the first student [*talebe*] of Mustafa Kemal was Mussolini, and I am the second.'[300]

The study of the structures and tools utilised by the Republican state brings into relief a systematic effort to reproduce imperial structures within the structures of the nation state, especially when it comes to the problem of *control*. If one of the ways to deal with the lack of control in the Ottoman Empire was the institution of *Aşiret Mektebi* (the recruitment of children from the provinces to the capital in order to create a group with a defined profile for the long-term promotion of state interests in the provinces),[301] another was the Republican assignment of Turkish deputy principals and teachers to non-Muslim schools. Moreover, boarding schools were planned especially for the eastern provinces, which were by then mostly populated by Kurds.[302] Thanks to recent research on Dersim, we know more, for instance, on Sıdıka Avar, who was noted for her ambitions in establishing Kemalist principles (broadly defined) in the provinces. Minister of Interior Şükrü Kaya's letter (4 June 1937) reveals the extent of this project by outlining the steps taken in the name of reform: The opening of boarding schools far from Dersim, for boys and girls from the age of five; their arranged marriage and resettlement on their inherited (*'miras kalan'*) family property; the building of 'Turkish homes' (*'birer Türk Yuvası'*) and the irrevocable establishment of 'Turkish culture in Dersim' (*'Türk Kültürünün Dersim'de...'*).[303] In this statement, it is made clear that the boarding schools in the provinces were actually part of the machinery of eradication and the establishment of denial over generations. Sıdıka Avar, herself an agent of the denialist habitus, of 'structuring the structure', worked at the Jewish school and the American College in İzmir at the beginning of her career.[304] Although documents demonstrate the policies for establishing a hegemonic 'Turkish culture' in the sense of a 'Turkification', the experience and the result of these policies show that this process is rather one of de-identification, in which a person loses all references to his or her own grandparents, socialisation, culture and history, but cannot fully become part of the society, culture and politics of the imposed system. The state continues to track the 'race' of the families over generations and reminds them of their 'real' identity when necessary, as demonstrated by the ongoing 'race code' discussions.[305] Another Turkish teacher and deputy principal, Emin Keşmer, who worked in schools for non-Muslims, recounts that his letter of teaching appointment called him an officer of *'tedvir'*: not only a teacher but also an administrator[306] – a wording he found surprising.[307] The appointment of

Turkish deputy principals has functioned as a control mechanism to this day. Betraying suspicion about the loyalty of non-Muslims towards the Turkish state, this policy aims, as does the education system in general, at creating future intermediaries with whom the state might communicate on the level of community administration.[308]

The administrative and institutional measures for establishing the field of state sovereignty during the post-1923 period were heavily 'inspired' by the Empire's knowledge reservoir. For instance, the Settlement Law of 1934 too had its roots in Ottoman imperial policies: demographic engineering was a consistently implemented policy in 1913–18, if not before.[309] The institution of *General Inspectorship*, another practice embedded in the state policies of the nineteenth century, was reintroduced in 1927. As Cemil Koçak explains, the existence of this institution was one of the examples pointing to the continuity of the institutional administrative and political mentality from the Ottoman Empire to the Republic of Turkey.[310] Koçak also draws lines of continuity between the General Inspectorships and the policy of State of Emergency Governorate (*Olağanüstü Hal Valiliği*, OHAL) after the 1980s,[311] and underscores two important character-istics of the General Inspectorships: the 'public order'[312] and the reform mission.[313] While it is not entirely clear what the public order or the reform mission meant, they still share a connotation: the absence of central administrative control over some regions of the country. General Inspectorships oversaw a wide range of duties and issues, as listed in a meeting in 1936: security, smuggling, border control, development of villages, political issues and demographic policies.[314] Janet Klein has drawn yet another line of continuity to a later period of the Republic, the 1980s, namely the 'village guard' ('*korucu*') system, which directly takes after the Hamidiye light cavalry.[315] All these policies aimed at gaining strict control over various segments of the population.

One of the most important missing links and in fact intransigent characteristics of Kemalism is the constant and institutionalised denial of the events in 1915/16–23. While there are numerous analyses of Kemalism explaining its modernising or Westernising mission, its component of denial or, more accurately, institutionalisation of denial, is often left unformulated as such. In this regard, I agree with Erik Jan Zürcher's argument that Kemalism 'remained a flexible concept and people with widely differing worldviews have been able to call themselves Kemalist'.[316] Furthermore, it was considered necessary for the creation of national history in the framework of a nation-building process. However, this very flexibility of Kemalism in the first decades and also later periods of the Republic served to actively deny the fact that Turkey was a post-genocide state and that Turkish society was a post-genocide society. Therefore, I prefer reading this flexibility in the context of habitus: '[T]he theory of practice as practice posits that objects of knowledge are *constructed* and not passively recorded; against intellectualist idealism it reminds us the principle of this construction is found in the socially constituted system of structured and structuring dispositions acquired in practice and constantly aimed at practical functions.'[317] Hence, I read Kemalism as an officially constituted system of a 'structured and structuring' set of principles that reproduced mechanisms and practices in which denial maintained its pivotal role, perpetuating itself through a variety of practical functions, in different periods and in different forms.

The incorporation of various layers of society in denialist structures through employment as civil servants and teachers (as shown above) was especially instrumental in the realisation of the habitus. The education system, land and property ownership, demographic engineering, the destruction of cultural heritage, sexual abuse and kidnapping, administrative units (General Inspectorships, etc.), legal, military and fiscal regulations, 'Citizen, Speak Turkish' and other social campaigns all coalesced to create, over the span of several decades, a normalised social habitus with an intrinsic history of racism and denialism.

CHAPTER 2

THE LEGAL CONTEXT

The Eradication of the Legal Basis of Armenian Community Administration: The Armenian Constitution/*Nizamname*

The legal issues of 'non-Moslem minorities [*sic*]', as specified in the Treaty of Lausanne,[1] effectively concerned only Armenians, Rums and Jews, thus eradicating the space in which any other non-Muslims could claim their rights. In this chapter, I explain and analyse the further eradication of the legal foundation of the Armenian community in the period starting in 1923, although the administrative problems of the community were rooted in the genocide and continued with various state interventions since 1915. After the murder or exile of the members of the General National Assembly, the community administration faced the problem of figuring out *de facto* solutions as needed.[2]

In 1925, the state requested that community representatives issue official statements abdicating the communal rights acknowledged by the Treaty of Lausanne. The adoption of the new civil code legitimised this breach of international commitment.[3] The rights in question were enshrined in article 41, clauses 1 and 2 of the treaty,[4] which organise the family and private law of communities, allowing them to observe their own regulations according to their traditions. The Surp P'rgich' yearbook of 1946 provides a detailed account of this process where the administration of the Armenian community, the Religious Committee, prominent community figures and religious officials submitted an affidavit to the government whereby they gave up the right to administer individual and family affairs according to their own traditions, on the grounds that the Swiss civil code, which was to be applied as of 5 October 1926, fully met the needs of individuals and families on the basis of secular principles.[5]

A similar situation arose in the case of the Civil–Political Assembly (*Cismani Meclis / K'aghak'agan Zhoghov*), which was the constitutional unit of the Armenian National Central Assembly established in 1847 by an imperial edict, i.e. *berat*. This edict authorised the Armenian community to elect two separate and independent councils, one for civil–political and the other for religious matters. The imperial document was read to the Patriarch and the *amiras* on 7 May 1847 in the palace of Âli Efendi, Ottoman Minister of Foreign Affairs. According to Hagop Barsoumian:[6]

> This edict instructed the General Assembly, in which the clergy, *amiras* and merchants [*esnafs*] participated, to elect a Spiritual [Religious] Assembly consisting of 14 clerical members, all from Istanbul, and a Supreme Civil Assembly comprised of twenty lay members. The Supreme Civil Assembly, which included nine *amiras* and ten *esnafs*, elected Hagop Grdjigian its *loghthete* (also called *loghofet* or *löfet*) – a kind of executive director, who acted both as its chairman and executive secretary. [...] The Supreme Civil Council was empowered with jurisdiction over secular education, finances and justice, while the Spiritual [Religious] Assembly dealt with religious education, dogma and the ordination of clergy. This system continued until the adoption of a constitution in 1860.[7]

The Armenian Constitution (*Nizamname/Sahmanatrut'iwn*) was not considered a constitution because it only regulated the affairs of a *millet* and not a state, as Arus Yumul points out; it was a constitutional text only in so far as it regulated the entire administrative structure of the community.[8] Yumul's article on the Armenian Constitution/*Nizamname* describes its process of preparation and implementation as based on Armenian sources. Relying on studies by Alboyacıyan[9] and Berberyan,[10] she argues that since the edict of 7 May 1847 allowed the election of members of the Religious and Civil Assemblies, religious and civil–political affairs were separated to a certain degree.[11] The General National Assembly was going to elect both the patriarchs and the members of these assemblies. In 1860, Armenians prepared a text for a constitution. On the order of Ali Pasha, the Sublime Porte heralded new regulations for community administration and the General Assembly approved that this text be put into effect. The Porte finally authorised the text in 1863 after various modifications. According to this *Nizamname*, the General National Assembly (GNA) (*Azkayin Ĕnthanur Zhoghov* in Armenian, *Meclis-i Umumi* in Ottoman) consisted of 140 people: 20 clergymen, 40 representatives from the provinces and 80 elected by local church communities (article 57).[12] Two main bodies, the Civil–Political[13] and Religious Assemblies, remained intact. These two could unite and form the Integrated Assembly (*Khaṛn Zhoghov*, article 23).[14] The members of both Assemblies were elected by the General National Assembly (article 60).[15]

The official report of the investigation committee formed by the end of 1950 states that in 1931, the previous GNA had authorised one of its committees (*Adenabedats' Zhoghov*, Chairmen Committee) to decide on behalf of the GNA in the case of extraordinary circumstances preventing or obstructing the convening of the GNA.[16] It was implied that, before 1931, the normal functioning of national administration mechanisms had met with difficulties during the Republican period – as also indicated in the minutes of the GNA meeting in 1926, which were sent to Antelias during the patriarchal election crisis of 1945–51: the Catholicos of Cilicia was responsible for listening to both sides of the conflict and suggesting a solution to the Catholicos of Holy Echmiadzin. Toros Azadyan's summary of the minutes and Patriarchal *locum tenens* Kevork Arslanyan's report were both published in Azadyan's book, *Lipananean Husher* (*Memoirs of Lebanon*). Given the scarcity of first-hand sources regarding GNA meetings and the lacuna in Patriarch Naroyan's personal notes on the administrative mechanism of the community in 1927–44, this source is enlightening, also because it provides information on the meeting held during the first term of Archbishop Kevork Arslanyan as Patriarchal *locum tenens*, before the patriarchal elections of 1927. According to the minutes, the participants decided to solve the problem of the missing members of the GNA before the patriarchal election. Consequently, local elections were organised and the GNA was revamped with 30 newly elected laymen and five clergymen.[17] According to *Nor Lur*, the Civil Assembly met for the last time with its eight members to make crucial decisions on 12 September 1934.[18]

Subsequent consultations with the governor and representatives of government aimed to 'adjust' the administration of Armenians in keeping with the notion that Turkey was a secular state and thus must form the basis of community administration as well.[19] In fact, as will be shown throughout this chapter, the main aim of these state policies was to find a way to undermine the Constitution/*Nizamname* by bereaving the community of its legal basis, and more importantly, by reducing the patriarch to a mere religious function stripped of any relation to the social, economic and political life of the community. Murat Bebiroğlu has argued that Patriarch Naroyan was forced to accept this role.[20] There is indeed evidence to support Bebiroğlu's claim. According to the abovementioned article in *Nor Lur*, the Patriarch was obligated to consent under pressure by Vahan Surēnyan, head of administration:[21] Naroyan was invited to Surēnyan's house where he was threatened and asked to leave his position as community leader and become a mere religious representative.[22] As a result, he was no longer allowed to be the head of community administration, and the activity of the Civil–Political Assembly would cease.[23] According to the agreement with the governor, the Civil–Political Assembly of the GNA was to be replaced with a National Administrative Committee (*Azkayin Varch'agan Zhoghov*) formed after an election among local representatives.[24] The negotiations were verbal, and the Armenian party had already presented a list of 30 candidates to the governor, 10 of whom would be elected for the Administrative Committee.[25] This list consisted of prominent Armenians, whose prominence was measured in accordance with their good relations with the government and their position within the community, and who were otherwise randomly chosen by the administration.[26] As of yet, no secondary source verifies this information; however, since the mechanisms already failed to function properly, this may have been the way to create a *de facto* solution to pressing administrative problems. In the meantime, the article in *Nor Lur* implies that the Civil–Political Assembly had long been unable to meet. Furthermore, it is not clear exactly when the last meeting of the General National Assembly was held. Many newspapers noted that the national administrative mechanisms had not been functioning since the days of Patriarch Mesrob Naroyan;[27] likewise, the minutes of the GNA held on 2 December 1950 to elect the new patriarch also mention the difficulties in holding a GNA meeting and cite the last date as '193_', (with the last digit left unprinted).[28] Toros Azadyan's *Lipananean Husher* represents the official position of the Patriarchate and is therefore important. Azadyan was sent to Beirut as the representative of *locum tenens* Arslanyan to discuss the patriarchal crisis with the Catholicosate of Cilicia established in Antelias. His book includes a short excerpt from Patriarch Naroyan's diary of 1939: 'Religious and educational life is not getting any better. The Religious and Administrative Assemblies have ceased their activities. I am alone; I only count on the mercy of God.'[29]

Regarding the changes in administrative mechanisms, the above-mentioned issue of *Nor Lur* features an article translated from *Cumhuriyet* on the Armenian community's success in adapting its administration to the secular principles of the Republican state.[30] The former administrative structure of the community is called '*köhne*', i.e. obsolete, and the new Administrative Committee welcomed.[31] A note added to the news item in *Nor Lur* provides hints about the pressure exerted on community leaders: the Republican Peoples Party's new head of the Istanbul branch, Dr Cemal [Tunca], requested a summary of the Armenian national administration system, including the role and authority of the Patriarch. Vahan Surēnyan, the representative of the Administrative Committee, presented such a report, after which Dr Cemal asked him to continue the negotiations with the governor of Istanbul.[32] Taking this incident into consideration, Bebiroğlu's claim that the decision for change was due to pressures from outside the community seems relevant.[33] More specifically, it is obvious that there was a state intervention to bypass the Armenian *Nizamname*. An article translated from *Milliyet* on 15 September 1934 informs the Armenian reader that the Civil–Political Assembly dissolved itself after the presentation of the new list of candidates to the governor.[34] In the Armenian newspapers of the day, there were debates concerning the adaptation of the community administration to the needs of secular Republican administration. However, the article in *Nor Luys* argues clearly against the idea that solely the clergy administered Armenian community affairs; on the contrary, civil elected committees had influenced religious affairs since the 1840s and no practice contradicted the secular ideals of the Republic.[35]

The next day, *Nor Lur* already mentions that, with this decision, the Armenian Constitution/*Nizamname* was *de facto* no longer in force, since the changes had already adjusted the administration of the Armenian community to the secular ideals of the republic and aimed at the dissolution of the constitutional organisation, i.e. the Civil–Political Assembly.[36] The language of the article is ambiguous:[37] On the one hand, it lauds the Armenian community for being as secular as the Turkish state; on the other, the editor complains that the community, i.e. the GNA, had been excluded from the decision-making process.[38] The reason for this ambiguity was actually that, if the *Nizamname* were no longer relevant, the question would be moot as to which rules were relevant and how the community administration would function. On the other hand, the functioning of the Religious Assembly had its own problems. *Locum tenens* Arslanyan abolished the Religious Assembly, as justified by the resignation of some of its members, and appointed a new Religious Assembly – a procedure considered unacceptable. However, the election of new members for the Religious Assembly depended upon the GNA, which had ceased activities. *Nor Lur* published the list of the ten members of the Religious Assembly, without mentioning how that committee had been formed. According to the *Nizamname*, the Religious Assembly should have 14 people (article 25).[39] Another lengthy article in *Nor Lur* states clearly that, although there was talk in various newspapers about the National Constitution/*Nizamname* and its rules, none of its institutions were in place.[40] The author observes that there was a *de facto* situation and everything should be considered accordingly, and no longer according to the *Nizamname*.[41]

Conversely, *Marmara* argues in August 1947 that according to the *Nizamname*, the Administration should not have remained on duty for more than two years and yet had stayed rooted for many. Moreover, Şamlıyan believes that there was no difference between the Administration and the Religious Assembly when it came to their legitimacy.[42] On 27 June 1949, *Marmara* published a comprehensive official statement by the Administrative Committee, signed by Vartan Akgül and Levon Papazyan, on its front page.[43] This statement makes clear how complicated the situation was – 'The Administration was elected according to internal rules and the rules of the state'[44] – thus making no mention of the Constitution/*Nizamname*, which means that this Administration was elected, not according to the *Nizamname* but most probably as per the agreement of September 1934. Although lawfully elected, the Administrative Committee could not function properly. 'With the thought that only a new Administrative Committee would bring an end to the period of the former, we remained on duty, which was our debt of conscience',[45] the declaration states, but it acknowledges that, despite 'dictatorial interventions' against the 'traditional and legitimate right of existence, the committee decided to maintain its lawful existence'.[46] The reference was to the dissolution of the Religious Assembly by Archbishop Arslanyan, who declared it illegitimate (although it was the same Assembly that had appointed him *locum tenens*) and who formed another Religious Assembly.[47] As can be gleaned from other news items, the same Committee continued negotiations with the GDPF. In the same statement, the Administrative Committee announced that, 'under the guidance of our republican–democratic government, patriarchal elections will be held with the participation of legally recognised bodies'.[48] This public statement cannot be found in the issues of *Nor Lur* of the same day or after; however, according to another news item that *Marmara* cites from *Jamanak*, it appears that, independently from the Administrative Committee, Archbishop Arslanyan had formed a consultative body to help him decide how to administer the properties of the community. This means that there were, *de facto*, two groups, the Administrative Committee and the consultative body, which did not cooperate and apparently did not even acknowledge each other's legitimacy.[49]

The situation was described accurately by *Paros*, which states that the religious and social mechanism of the community had gradually weakened after 1923, and become reduced to a status of non-sovereignty.[50] This is an important diagnosis, since it points out the fact that the community no longer controlled its own affairs, but was rather controlled by the state, which, unlike the Ottoman Empire, did not recognise the existing structures of the community. As a result of the undermining of the Armenian communal rights derived from the Constitution/*Nizamname*, the community lost one of its most important administrative bodies. The Civil–Political Assembly, which was in charge of socio-political affairs of the community, *de facto* ceased activities.[51] The General National Assembly meetings or elections could not be held either. Moreover, in 1950 *Tebi Luys* emphasised an important aspect of the Law of Associations (*Cemiyetler Kanunu*), which was ratified in 1938,[52] and which prohibited the establishment of any association on the basis of race. The law mentions 'race' (*ırk*) which apparently encompasses communities. *Tebi Luys* argues that, with the passing of this law, it was not possible to establish an 'Armenian Teachers' Union' or an 'Armenian Writers Union of Turkey', or the like.[53] Only after 1946 could the alumni associations be established and bring fresh breath to the social life of the community. On the other hand, in 1938, the changes in the Law of Pious Foundations (*Vakıflar Kanunu*)[54] and the introduction of the Single Trustee System (STS) rendered any other electoral system dysfunctional.

The Single Trustee System and Its Repercussions

What STS meant was that the government managed the foundation administrators' appointment or removal from office. The earliest list of Single Trustees that I could find is from 1941. According to this list, there were four female (including one nun) and ten male STs.[55] The Armenian newspapers reported on the appointments, dismissals, constant non-appointments and problems arising as a result of the STS in general. According to *Marmara*, the Single Trustee of Samatya, Arusyak Torkomyan, was dismissed from her position in June 1947 without justification.[56] *Nor Lur* reports that the contents of the safe of the Samatya Foundation were confiscated by the GDPF and the salaries of the church staff went unpaid. The news adds that the GDPF already ran the administration of Beyoğlu and Kadıköy.[57]

The STS was put into force despite the fact that communities reacted quickly and made all possible efforts to prevent it as early as in 1937, when rumours about the preparation of this system began, by sending their representatives to Ankara in order to explain its inadequacies.[58] However, objections went unheeded. In October 1948, *Marmara* published two telegrams sent by Archbishop Kevork Arslanyan to Faik Ahmet Baruçtu, which note that representatives of the Armenian community went to Ankara to express their ideas on issues related to the Single Trustee System.[59] According to a lengthy analysis by Dr K. Şahnazaryan in the same newspaper, they asked to put an end to the situation created by the *locum tenens* through mechanisms of checks and balances.[60] In these telegrams, Arslanyan did not recognise the legitimacy of those representatives. The report of the Investigation Committee of the GNA (publ. 1951) states that, on one hand, the STS debilitated communal administrative mechanisms and, on the other, the number of the Administrative Committee members decreased due to deaths or resignations.[61] To continue negotiations and put an end to the STS, the Administrative Committee compiled a list of 21 people who received the highest votes during the GNA elections and invited seven to contribute to the Administrative Committee. According to the Investigation Committee report, only three accepted. This practice was not new: the same chain of events had occurred during the Mōsdich'yan administration in 1923–5, when it proved impossible to call a meeting of the GNA.[62]

It seems that even as the Administrative Committee negotiated with the state, it obtained permission to call the GNA for a meeting on 12 September 1948 to make preparations for the patriarchal election. However, the meeting was cancelled as a result of an intervention on the part of Arslanyan, who argued that the patriarchal election preparations could only be led by the Patriarchate, represented by his person.[63]

The changes introduced into the Law of Pious Foundations in 1935 and the introduction of the STS deeply affected the Armenian administration. According to Varujan Köseyan, due to these newly introduced systems, the election of the administration of the Hospital Surp P'rgich', which was normally held every two years, could not take place. The administration that had been appointed by the Civil–Political Assembly for only two years ended up remaining in office from 1933 to 1949 – a decision made by the Administrative Committee and the Patriarch together.[64] In September 1934, the administrative system of the Armenian community underwent structural changes, as has already been pointed out. According to Köseyan, many churches and schools administered by the STS were in a dire straits: Surp Kēōrk Church in Galata and Getronagan High School; Surp Errortut'iwn Church and St Harut'iwn Church in Beyoğlu, and Ēsayan High School; Surp Kēōrk Church in Samatya and Sahakyan High School; the Armenian cemetery in Balıklı; Surp Hovhannēs Church in Gedikpaşa and Mesrobyan Elementary School.[65] Concerned with the newly introduced laws, the community administration and Patriarch Naroyan took note of the fact that the hospital was a very important institution with numerous properties, and made concessions from regular community administration so that the hospital could survive. Indeed, the administration had had to manage the difficult years of the Wealth Tax, the *Yirmi Kura Askerlik* and World War II, as well as the occupation of the hospital and its properties by the military.

The STS remained in place until 1949, when the election system was re-introduced. However, even after the restoration of the old regulation, the impact of the STS could be traced in the newspapers. For instance, the hospital of the Catholic Armenian community, Surp Hagop, had to be closed due to the poor administration of the Single Trustee, a sick man in his seventies.[66] *Marmara* reprinted a story published in *Son Saat*, expressing how astonishing it was to see the closure of a hospital standing in the best location of the city with a hundred properties. The community worked day and night to hold regular elections and reopen the hospital.[67] Eleven days later, the Catholic community too held elections and the administration of the Foundation of Surp Hagop Hospital was established as a result of an election process.[68] After the decision by both Catholicoses in Antelias and Echmiadzin regarding the patriarchal election crisis of Istanbul, Armenian newspapers started to publish news (in October 1949) on the upcoming elections for members of the administrative bodies of foundations on the local level.[69] Around the same time, *Cumhuriyet* reported that, following Armenian Catholics, Rums and Jews too were getting ready for foundation elections.[70]

Evidently, throughout the 11 previous years (1938–49), the community foundations had been severely affected by the STS Trustees appointed from among people with no notion of administering a foundation and with no ties to the community. The income of the foundations became extremely irregular. The state not only tampered with the internal administrative bodies of the communities, but also visibly prepared the ground on which to cause rifts within the communities. Elçin Macar's book and article offer valuable information on this issue.[71] Although the government was in charge of appointing an administrator to each foundation, when problems arose, the Ministry of Foreign Affairs – it is remarkable that this particular ministry took action – intervened by leaving appointments in limbo: no administrator and administration was designated for the foundations in question.[72]

Armenian newspapers discussed the legal issues of the community at length. In the absence of any other legal entity, newspapers were the only public forum for community issues. Two letters sent to the Prime Minister by the Greek newspaper *Metepolitefsis* and the Armenian Catholic community reveal the problems caused by the STS.[73] The first complained in 1941 about the corruption of the Single Trustees and advised that a control mechanism be devised by the respective communities. The second letter, written in 1943, was yet another complaint about the results of non-appointment of trustees, which caused manifold problems for four years. Both letters were submitted to the Prime Minister in 1943 with a document signed by the General Directorate of Pious Foundations, which explained the impossibility of creating such control mechanisms and asked for permission to solve the 'real' problem. In apparent reaction to the complaints, the government assigned a commission of experts from the Ministry of Foreign Affairs, the General Directorate of Pious Foundations and the Ministry of Interior to prepare a report. The ensuing report stated clearly that non-Muslim pious foundations could not be treated in the same way as the Muslim *vaqf*s. Moreover, for bureaucratic reasons the STS could not be properly applied; the best way was to either put in force the old regulations or to make the necessary changes that had been targeted but not achieved through the STS. This undated report mentions that, despite the fact that the STS had been in place for five years, there still remained foundations that had not been held financially accountable.[74] Thus, the report was most probably prepared in 1943.

It is not a coincidence that the institutions of non-Muslim communities were targets of state intervention during the massive process of the institutionalisation of Kemalism and its control mechanisms in the 1930s. Schools, administrative bodies and, most importantly, the *Vaqf*s were at the heart of these interventions in non-Muslim communities. The issue of the GDPF and the *36 Beyannamesi* (1936 Memorandum) should be considered separately in this context. Persistent court cases in the 1930s concerning Sanasaryan Han, Yusufyan Han and the land of Pangaltı cemetery (among others), all due to the bypassing of the *Nizanname*s, have to be analysed in the framework of a strategy to undermine the structure, the financial means, the legal basis and thus the very existence of non-Muslim communities. The Armenian *Nizamname* of 1863 was the only text that defined the administrative and legal structures of the Armenian *millet* in a sophisticated manner. Therefore, undermining the *Nizamname* meant creating a *de facto* reality with no other option than the enforcement of spontaneous regulations as needed. This in turn left the door open for the state to manoeuvre ambiguously and arbitrarily. I will not go further into the GDPF except to emphasise that the court cases mentioned above and the *36 Beyannamesi* should be studied in detail, in the framework of the structural and legal rupture of the communities. These processes aimed at gaining control over the finances of the communities, thereby weakening, if not destroying in the long run, both community institutions and the communities as a whole.

In 1945, an editorial of *Nor Or* criticised the Single Trustee System:

> Previously, we had local organisations in which representatives were elected by the residents of a given area in a one-step electoral system with both secret and open vote. This system had the power to counterbalance the elected bodies, and in turn these bodies were responsible for the churches and the administration of properties owned by the foundation of the church. [...] However, the foundation law, introducing the 'single trustee' (*tek mütevelli*) system, put an end to this liberal mechanism. In this [new] system, the General Directorate of Pious Foundations [*Vakıflar Genel Müdürlüğü – GDPF*] appoints one responsible person. This person is omnipotent in all matters related to church and administration of its properties. S/he does not have to consult the community or its leaders. S/he is not accountable to the Armenian community. S/he is only responsible before the GDPF and before her/his conscience. The limits of his/her responsibilities are so ambiguous and general [...] Moreover, s/he has the right to cash a certain amount of money from the revenues collected from the properties of the church in cases involving orphanages, poor elementary schools, and people in need.[75]

As it may be surmised, on the one hand, the STS was a way to control all finances of the communities and, on the other, it created chaos within the communities by neglecting to appoint trustees, by appointing inappropriate trustees, or by leaving decisions to the trustee's arbitrary judgment. As the *Nor Or* editorial suggests, the most important aspect of this practice was that it broke the link between the community and the administration by intervening in and abolishing the participatory systems established in the Ottoman Empire during the nineteenth century.

In early March 1947, on the eve of the declaration of the Truman Doctrine, a positive attitude toward Armenians suddenly manifested itself in Ankara. Suren Şamlıyan, who participated in a journalists' meeting in

Ankara, reported on discussions about the Armenians. According to his account, Ahmet Emin Yalman,[76] who had recently returned from the United States, offered that although a group of Armenians were conducting anti-Turkish propaganda, many pro-Turkish Armenians had sent him letters that he was willing to publish. In quick succession, Prime Minister Recep Peker declared that they were about to make some 'radical changes' to bring minorities together under the 'umbrella of democracy' and 'put an end to all kinds of discrimination'.[77] Şamlıyan approached Recep Peker and pointed out that former Prime Minister Şükrü Saraçoğlu had promised to amend the Single Trustee System and thoroughly change the Law of Pious Foundations. Peker confirmed that experts were working on the issue, and that it was not forgotten.[78]

Ten days after the announcement of the Truman Doctrine, *Marmara* reported enthusiastically on the 'new law on minorities':[79] the STS was to be tackled and election mechanisms reformed; the problems in minority schools caused by the appointment of a Turkish deputy principle by the Ministry of National Education would be addressed, and the community as a whole would be reformed in groundbreaking ways. *Marmara* was consistent with its firm belief that the government was eager and ready to solve the problems of non-Muslims, and that Suren Şamlıyan's visits to Ankara played a crucial role in the process of improving the legal and social conditions of the community. This stance was obvious in the headlines and the news content. For instance, the title of the news on 22 March was 'The New Regulation on Minorities Reaches the National Assembly'.[80] It can be gleaned from the piece, however, that the regulation was not yet in the National Assembly; it was going to be discussed in the Assembly *soon*. There was neither a set date nor a publishable draft. Nevertheless, *Marmara* heralded that the STS had already become history, that the Administration should take all necessary actions to facilitate the upcoming changes.

As opposed to *Marmara*, *Nor Lur* was rather suspicious of the news on the regulation and its nature. It was not clear for the newspaper what the address to 'the administration' meant. Furthermore, *Nor Lur*, along with *Jamanak*, considered the existing administrative bodies of the community obsolete and advocated the establishment of a new administrative system headed by the Patriarch.[81]

Yet, Suren Şamlıyan and his daily *Marmara* were not the only enthusiastic spokesperson or outlet. *Tasvir*, which was bluntly anti-Armenian, used the argument of 'the change of policy towards minorities' as a weapon to threaten Armenians in Turkey in relation to the activities of American Armenians. *Nor Lur* translated an article arguing that the activism of American Armenians would lead to the discomfort of Armenians living in Turkey, during a period when the government was about to change its policies.[82] Cihad Baban, a leading editor-in-chief *cum* parliamentarian from the Democratic Party, was vehemently against any legal improvement.[83] The argument that the government was ready to undertake reforms to improve the situation of Armenians if only Armenian American activities ceased meant that both *Tasvir* and the government – as well as subsequent governments – found it reasonable to punish fellow citizens for activities carried out by foreign citizens in the country.

Although Hilmi Uran, the general secretary of the CHP, confirmed the upcoming changes in the STS and community administration, according to *Marmara*,[84] the STS remained in place until 1949. The issue of community administration structures remained unresolved and continued to trigger conflicts within the community, as well as between the state and the community.

Marmara was further encouraged by the retirement of Fahri Kiper, head of the General Directorate of Pious Foundations (GDPF). Kiper had reportedly said that, as long as he was the head of GDPF, he would never undertake any changes in the Foundation Law.[85] *Marmara* rooted for his retirement, arguing that his absence would facilitate change. Thus, according to Şamlıyan, it was Kiper's personal choice whether or not to undertake any changes in the law. Upon his retirement, Şamlıyan wrote a series of articles referring to the first press meetings in Ankara (where he was present) and the contradictory situations on the issue of the GDPF law during these meetings.[86] Şamlıyan made it clear in this series (under his pen name Prof Nargizyan) that not everything was as rose-coloured in those meetings as he had claimed. At the time he could not include the negotiations between the government and the community administration, and yet, according to him, it was Kiper who resisted the orders of Saraçoğlu.[87] Moreover, Kiper was not alone in his sabotaging act. According to Şamlıyan, Armenian newspapers, which criticised the current administration or considered it inappropriate, constituted the basis for Kiper's bid to resist reforms in the GDPF. Thus, Şamlıyan blamed other Armenian newspapers, at least *Nor Lur* directly,[88] and probably *Nor Or* indirectly, as well as Kiper, the state representative.[89] These pieces on discordance and conflict within the community were closely followed and duly taken advantage of by the state. Interesting details can be found in this series of four pieces published in July 1947. For instance, Şamlıyan describes the manner in which Kiper talked to him:

> The head of GDPF, with whom we held a number of meetings, always spoke to us with a smile. Furthermore, he expressed special sympathy towards Armenians and mentioned his Armenian neighbours and friends. He also confessed that the Law of Foundations for Muslim foundations was not applicable to non-Muslim foundations and promised to undertake changes according to the Prime Minister's orders.[90]

Şamlıyan's attitude here mirrors that of the sovereign proponent of denial, which is to trivialise and downplay the impact of the STS. In the same article, Şamlıyan also points out that Saraçoğlu angrily asked Armenian journalists why they had not raised the issue any earlier. Reportedly, Saraçoğlu knew nothing about the troubles caused by the STS.[91] In the second part of the series,[92] Şamlıyan published a letter originally written on 5 March 1945 by Kevork Çobangil, a lawyer, addressing the GDPF about the issues between this entity and the Armenian community foundations, including confiscations of properties of the foundations like Sanasaryan Han and the general disadvantages of the STS. Below, I provide a detailed account of this unique letter, since it shows the nature of communication between state institutions and prominent figures of the community. The scarcity of this kind of source, revealing both personal and official relations between two parties, brings its significance into relief.

According to the letter, Çobangil visited Fahri Kiper in December 1945. As I understand from his characterisation, their meeting was not official:

> You have listened with your unique tact to the problems of Armenian communities concerning the foundations, and to my suggestions for a solution. [...] As I was not prepared in advance, I expressed my willingness to present my ideas about the issue in

written form. Encouraged by your consent and despite the fact that
I am somewhat late, I dare to write you today so as to present my
explanations [on the issue].[93]

Thus, Kiper was not actually expecting a letter or a written document
from Çobangil, who acted on his own initiative, most probably because
nothing had changed in the STS in the preceding three or four months.
According to the information provided in Çobangil's letter, he had
worked with Fahri Kiper as a financial inspector (*Maliye Müfettişi*) when
he was a member of *Mülkiye Heyet-i Teftişiyesi*. He expressed his gratitude
for this former duty and the prestige he acquired through this
position.[94] Çobangil writes:

> Whenever we struggle financially [...] and are unable to pay the
> five per cent counterpoise fee, it [GDPF] never makes us feel
> uncomfortable; [on the contrary] it treats us as a merciful father
> would. Our community will forever remember your careful
> intervention to secure the 15,000 [liras] granted to our Hospital
> by the solicitous government. Your name has an indelible place in
> our hearts. However, despite all this, we have come across some
> frustrating cases.[95]

After his long introduction, Çobangil comes to the point: the Law for
Pious Foundations is far from meeting the needs of the community. In the
third part of this series, Çobangil's letter returns to the confiscation of
Sanasaryan Han, arguing that it was unlawful and that the community
needed its income to finance the care of destitute children.[96] He then raises
the issue of the expropriation of the church of Surp Lusaworich' in Taksim,
along with the cemetery in Pangalti.[97] Çobangil also points to the Wealth
Tax of 1942, levied upon Surp Errortut'iwn Church at an amount of
150,000. Apparently, this tax was paid through the sale of some of the
foundation properties, which was in fact prohibited by paragraph 9 of the
Law of Foundations itself, according to Çobangil's analysis.[98] The same
law, in paragraph 40, established that the GDPF should protect the
foundations in case of discordance or juridical processes concerning
Appendant Foundations (*mülhak vakıflar*).[99] Çobangil argues that a list of
the properties belonging to *mülhak vakıflar* had been submitted to the
GDPF upon request in 1912.[100]

The taxes of these properties had been paid by the hospital and by the respective churches:

> Thus, the GDPF knew about these properties and knew that they belonged to the Hospital and to the churches. Instead of helping them, it filed lawsuits against them in the courts, claiming the right to own them. Fortunately, the courts and the courts of appeal understood the nature of the issue and decided with fairness.[101]

Çobangil's letter proceeds with the issue of the STS, especially the two Single Trustees appointed to the Surp P'rgich' Church in Galata and Surp Errortut'iwn Church in Beyoğlu (Ohannes Şahinkaya and Tavit Yılmaz, respectively). According to Çobangil, these two trustees had established a system of terror and stolen thousands from the community: 'Unfortunately, the GDPF never controlled the acts of the Single Trustees and did not draw attention to the rising voices of opposition from the community.'[102] According to Çobangil, some of the Single Trustees continued to form administrative bodies from previously elected people, and yet others appointed a group of people to the administration. The members of the foundation administration considered themselves staff of the GDPF and thus did not feel accountable to the community at all.[103] It would appear that when Çobangil and Kiper met in December 1945, Kiper asked whether it was meaningful to reform the STS with a group of up to three trustees, and Çobangil replied that that would not change anything.[104]

Furthermore, Kiper asked whether the creation of companies and the transformation of all foundations into associations (*cemiyet*) to subject them to the Law of Associations (*Cemiyetler Kanunu*) would help. Çobangil's response was again unfavorable, since the two bodies and their functions were entirely different, and this would have created even more complications as each foundation had a school, church and properties. Being subject to *Cemiyetler Kanunu* would require creating *cemiyets* for each and every body, i.e. school, church, properties, etc. However, this was not a novel suggestion, as it had already been made during the Surenyan Administration, in 1937.[105] In the Yearbook of the Armenian Hospital of 1939, there is a discussion of the whole issue of *Cemiyetler Kanunu*, *Vakıflar Kanunu*, the STS and the Armenian *Nizamname*.[106] That suggestion was yet another attempt at undermining the *Nizamname*. Çobangil's suggestion was to return to the old regulation, i.e. the regulation before the STS. Kiper expressed his doubts based on the fact that the old regulation would allow the intervention of the Patriarchate, which was merely a religious institution whose special attributions had been nullified by the Treaty of Lausanne.[107] Çobangil replied that the intervention did not affect his sphere and had nothing to do with the authority of the Patriarchate regarding the foundations. He referred to the regulations (abolished in 1916[108] and restored in 1918[109]) that were all in force.[110] The document that Çobangil referred to was the *Badriarkarani Ganonakir* (Patriarchate Bylaws),[111] which defines the Patriarchate's functioning mechanisms. Çobangil gave the example of the election of the *locum tenens* of the Patriarch after the death of Patriarch Naroyan in 1944 to prove that the bylaws were in force and that the Patriarchate still based the legitimacy of its actions on the bylaws.[112]

In the fourth part of his series, Şamlıyan reports on a conversation that took place while he was in Ankara for the press meeting, where he elicited Fahreddin (Fahri) Kiper's opinion on Çobangil's letter: 'I read Mr Çobangil's letter. I found some very interesting points that were unknown to me. Unfortunately, I will not be able to put it into effect given political issues involved and that I am not allowed to deal with them.'[113] Şamlıyan insisted on his question: 'What will be your response to it?' The answer was: 'I will not answer, since I should not have officially received such a letter in the first place.'[114]

The letter is an important document on the nature of the relations between the Armenian community and the GDPF. It makes clear that the GDPF offered all kinds of compromises to avoid returning to the previous regulation based on the Patriarchate bylaws, which were still in force. Knowing this, the state insisted on suggesting new ways to undermine and erode the existing legal structures (turning foundations into companies was one of them), while the STS was already in place and fulfilled its function of structural eradication. Such measures reveal the state's resistance to recognising the legal structures and rights of the community, as well as its reliance on distortion and loopholes to undermine the system as a whole. Indeed, this stance met with some measure of favourable response in the community as well. The extended deadlocks, ambiguities and new problems forced opinion makers of the community to seek solutions. Thus, the argument that the state did not know the problems of non-Muslim foundations does not obtain, since we here see intense contact and at least one detailed briefing, which most probably was not the only one that the GDPF received from the Armenian and other communities.

In February 1948, *Marmara* published reports from the Armenian daily newspapers *Arev* (Cairo), *Yeprad* and *Arevelk* (both in Aleppo) on the community in Istanbul. These included news regarding the Single Trustee System and related injustices or issues. The editors-in-chief of these newspapers followed their colleagues in Istanbul and were aware of the problems of the community. They also mentioned the absence of a central communal organisation. *Arevelk* noted, 'They put you through the wringer if you dare to advocate [your] rights or communal interests. This is sundown for the intellectual life of the rich and vivid capital of yesteryear, leaving only a pale beam of light.'[115] In late 1948, *Marmara* again reported, through its Ankara correspondent, Mekki Seyid Esen, the tidings that the STS was going to be abolished at the end of May 1949. However, this time it included a very brief footnote indicating that it had corroborated the news with *Cumhuriyet* and *Yeni Sabah*.

The STS period came to an end with the new regulation in the Law for Foundations.[116] However, throughout 1948–9 the Armenian community in Istanbul was deeply polarised because of the patriarchal crisis. The problems engendered by the STS became entangled with the patriarchal election crisis. For instance, right before the abolishment of the STS, *Marmara* reported a protest in the Gedikpaşa community against the Single Trustee who had apparently objected to a religious ceremony held by Archpriest Hmayak Bahtiyaryan on the grounds that he was one of the five priests who opposed *locum tenens* Kevork Arslanyan, who, in turn, had cancelled their ecclesiastic privileges. Upon the appointed trustee's veto, the Gedikpaşa community penned an open letter of protest and sent it to *Marmara*, which published it in facsimile.[117] Protests took place in various towns, usually related to the patriarchal election crisis. I will dwell upon this issue separately, but the abolition of the STS remained an important turning point within the larger legal dilemma of proper administration in the community.

The process of returning to the election structure was not automatic. Local administrative bodies were elected by their communities in December 1949. However, the new regulation, which had been in force since June 1949, was not immediately put into practice. In February 1950, along with other pieces regarding the non-implementation of the law, *Marmara* translated an article from *Son Saat* criticising the delay.[118]

Marmara published another story in March, claiming that Archbishop Kevork Arslanyan had actually requested the GDPF to hand over the administration of the foundation to the Patriarchate, and arguing that the jurisdiction of religious institutions by the Patriarchate caused the delay.[119] According to another piece in *Marmara*, Tokatlıyan and the 72 pieces of property that belonged to the same foundation were handed over to the elected local body on 17 March 1950.[120]

A booklet on the activities of the foundation and the church in Beyoglu, *Bēyoghlui Egeghetseats Ew Anonts' Ent'aga Hasdadut'eants' Madagararut'ean K'aramea Deghegakir 1950–1953*, states that the elections were held on 25 December 1949. However, the elected administration headed by Dr Andre Vahram could not obtain any of the documents or records belonging to the Church either from the STS or from previous periods.[121] The administration requested that the GDPF return the properties belonging to the foundation of the church, but others tried to prolong this process. This deadlock could only be resolved through the governor's intervention.[122] Furthermore, when the newly elected administration asked for the money collected throughout the direct administration of the GDPF, it turned out that the amount was much less than expected.[123]

Dr H. Peştimalciyan wrote a similar report, but one of success, on the administration of Surp P'rgich' Armenian Hospital in 1933–49: they did everything to stop the GDPF from implementing STS in their foundation and were eventually successful, since the administration was recognised by the GDPF. Thus, there were cases of exceptions to STS as well.[124]

In 'A Case Study in the Sociology of Assimilation I: Trapped in Ambivalence', Zygmunt Baumann sheds light on the kind of interaction and coercion that the state sought with members of the Armenian community, as illustrated in this first section of this chapter:

> The modern state meant the disempowerment of communal self management and the dismantling of local or corporative mechanisms of self-perpetuation: by the same token, the modern state sapped the social foundations of communal and corporative traditions and forms of life. Self reproduction of communally grounded forms of life either became impossible or at least met with formidable obstacles.[125]

Baumann argues that ambivalence and assimilation are interrelated in the newly emerging power structures of the nation state and draws attention to the dominant group's practice of inviting individuals from stigmatised groups to desist their loyalty to the group of origin.[126] This invitation by the dominant, according to Baumann, puts them in a position of arbitrating power, a force entitled to set exams and to mark performance.[127] As Baumann argues in the context of Jews in the process of German unification of 1871, 'Equality before the law meant, after all, the sapping of communal autonomy, discreditation of communal authority, undermining the centrifugal influences of communal and corporative elites; it was an indispensable part of the process which lead to the institution of modern state power with its monopoly of law-making and coercion.'[128] Likewise, the Single Trustee System was one of the practices targeting the community administration system in order to eradicate its legal basis. Thus, it controlled the subject on the community level, with all its administrative, financial and social organisations, by creating arbitrary practices on the one hand and undermining their participatory community structures on the other, all within an argument of equality. As I have shown, the breaches of the *Nizamname* and the administrative mechanisms especially were based on the argument that the Republican state was secular and established on egalitarian principles. The eradication of legal and administrative structures from Empire to Republic was thus legitimised by the self-proclaimed egalitarianism and secularism of the nation state, while the Armenian administration, with all its mechanisms, was required to adapt itself to the new *de facto* conditions that breached its current legislations – which in turn meant the loss of its erstwhile communal rights and mechanisms.

The Claim of Equality

In the absence of committees to organise socio-political life, the community had no representative to respond to the incessant questioning by Turkish journalists and opinion makers, who most often also belonged to the political elite. Placing these issues at the core, Zaven Biberyan's articles in the second half of the 1940s were hot potatoes.[129] 'Enough is Enough', his most famous article, which appeared in *Nor Lur* on 5 January 1946, asks, 'Are we equal citizens of Turkish Republic or people with a temporary residency permit? Are we free and equal citizens or people whom they (journalists) have the right to talk about condescendingly, often with a domineering and threatening tone?'[130] While pointing out the absence of political representation for Armenians in the public realm, Biberyan also differentiates between the Ottoman Empire and the Republican era. In the former, Armenian parliamentarians had the right to represent Armenians, while in the Republic, the representative of Afyonkarahisar, Berç Keresteciyan (Türker), an Armenian, did not represent the Armenian community, but only the voters from Afyonkarahisar. Biberyan underscores the fact that the Armenian community did not have an administrative or representative body to deal with political questions.

Representation issues created manifold problems. When called for, the editors-in-chief of Armenian newspapers came to be regarded or perceived as representatives throughout the Republican period. This created an illusory role for the editors and put them in a fragile and structurally unfair position unlike that of the often governmentally employed editors-in-chief of Turkish newspapers. Armenian newspapers appeared in their own language and thus had a rather restricted readership relative to *Cumhuriyet*, *Son Posta* and *Vakıt*, among others.

Nonetheless, as in the case of Keresteciyan, editors of Armenian newspapers, who were somehow considered to be representatives, could in turn assume manipulative power, as can be seen in the case of *Marmara*. The editor, Suren Şamlıyan, was invited to the monthly press meetings in Ankara starting in September 1945. As I understand from his articles in *Marmara*, the editor-in-chief of *Jamanak* also participated in those meetings. Şamlıyan wrote enthusiastically in *Marmara* on his second visit (4–12 October 1945) to Ankara, where he sat next to the Prime Minister and had a chance to chat with certain Turkish editors-in-chief. He himself believed in the representative role he played in Ankara. According to his reports, he met Prime Minister Şükrü Saraçoğlu and raised such issues as the Single Trustee System, the Law of Pious Foundations, the abolition of income tax for Armenian schools, etc. Saraçoğlu was reportedly very receptive and happy to have heard about these problems. He even seemed disappointed about the issue of taxation and asked why the community had not brought these issues to his attention before.[131] Şamlıyan also met Nedim Veysel İlkin, press representative, and Fahri Kiper, head of GDPF.[132] His articles were not informative, but rather impressionistic, and sometimes full of other participants' jokes. Although he did not achieve any tangible result, one can sense a general feeling of being welcomed and accepted by 'his excellency', and an ensuing satisfaction.[133] Şamlıyan felt the need to write that, after the foundation of the Republic, Istanbul was no longer the heart of the country; in order to understand the issues concerning the country, one must go to Ankara.[134] He thus shifted his attention from the imperial capital to the Republican (considered superior, as exemplified by his respect for the location where the meetings were held, 'Anadolu Klübü', and its modern infrastructure),[135] although Armenians had no role there as notables, parliamentarians or elites, and despite the fact that the existence of the remaining Armenians in general was, at the very least, a matter of discomfort for the Republican elite. It was therefore understandable that Şamlıyan felt himself to be an outsider, but a privileged one for having been twice invited to present the issues of the communities before 'his excellency'.

The internalised superiority of the other vis-à-vis the internalised inferiority of the self marks the entire series on his impressions of Ankara. It is against this background that Şamlıyan, talking to other editor-in-chief *cum* parliamentarians, expressed his willingness to be considered a leading community representative:

> It is very unfortunate that the administrations throughout the period of Patriarch Naroyan [1927−44] did not establish direct ties with the highest echelons of the state; their passive stance allowed some adventurers to manipulate this area. [...] The same thing happened during the period of Archbishop Arslanyan; his visits did not change anything, either, and served only to strengthen the status quo. Under these circumstances, the duty of defending the interests of the community fell on the shoulders of the press. *Marmara* took this responsibility on with great pleasure.[136]

This constitutes a mission statement that was, and has remained to this day, destined to fail. Şamlıyan presumed that the problems of the community came from the absence of real contact with the government. Therefore, in his view, his participation in the Ankara meetings could in fact change things and perhaps help solve community problems.

In numerous articles, Şamlıyan expressed his belief in solving problems through negotiations with the government. One of these articles was written after the Greek religious representatives visited Ankara. Şamlıyan argues that, whereas the Greek community presented its problems in Ankara and found solutions, Armenians failed to do the same; their problems were still outstanding. He claims that there is no problem without a solution and that the government is very welcoming to any legitimate request.[137] As far as Şamlıyan is concerned, his personal contact with the Prime Minister made it possible for an Armenian play to be put on stage in Istanbul and the Armenian schools' income tax to be discontinued.[138] However, looking at the Surp P'rgich' Yearbook of 1947, one can see that four Armenian theatre groups, all created in 1946–7 (Stüdyo, Eridasartats', Mnagyan, Arpi), were already actively putting various plays on stage, which means that Şamlıyan may very well have exaggerated his role in this cultural endeavour.[139] At the same time, after the legislation changes of June 1946, which legalised alumni organisations, three alumni associations were established in the Armenian community of Istanbul, namely Mkhitaryan, Ěsayan and Getronagan.[140]

After the journalists' monthly meeting in September 1945, Şamlıyan reportedly had a conversation on the train with Asım Us, who was also a parliamentarian *cum* editor-in-chief of *Vakıt*. Curiously, Us here acts as a spokesperson for Prime Minister Şükrü Saraçoğlu: 'Prime Minister Saraçoğlu is very happy with the explanation [Şamlıyan] gave. [...] The government is ready to undertake any measures to solve the shortcomings.'[141] In the first place, his comment confirms the hierarchy between Asım Us and Suren Şamlıyan. Asım Us spoke in his capacity as parliamentarian, an agent of decision-making processes. Secondly, the power relation between the two is rooted, not only in his position as CHP representative, but also in the imperial baggage of Republican Turkey.[142] Thus, neither *Vakıt* nor Asım Us as a person could be conceived of as outside the core of the state.

The *Nor Or* circle's approach to community problems was quite different from Şamlıyan's. As one of the publications advocating the rights of the community, and as the most consistently critical one, *Nor Or* (July 1945–December 1946) is an especially important source. The paper was launched by the first generation of Republican Armenian intellectuals, most of whom were born in the early 1920s and became

involved in socialist–communist politics. Although not a member of the
Nor Or team, Dr Hayk Açıkgöz was another socialist, an Armenian from
Samsun studying medicine at Istanbul University. He writes in his
memoirs that in 1941 they had a separate group of approximately ten
Armenian socialist students who gathered independently as a reading
group.[143] He was first introduced to brothers Vartan and Jak İhmalyan in
that group. In 1944, Aram Pehlivanyan (Üsküdar 1917[144]–Leipzig
1979), Dr Hayk Açıkgöz (Samsun/Havza 1918–Leipzig 2001), Krikor
Sarafyan[145] and Reşat Fuat Baraner, among others, were picked up by the
police in a wave of arrests of anti-fascists.[146] After eight and a half months
of imprisonment,[147] Pehlivanyan (pen name A. Şavarş) was set free and
launched *Nor Or* (*New Day*) with Avedis Aliksanyan and Sarkis Keçyan
(pen name S. K. Zanku, Istanbul 1917–Paris 2004). Quite a few of the
Nor Or editors and columnists were also artists, including Zaven Biberyan
(Istanbul 1921–84, journalist, novelist, translator, politician), who
became one of the best Armenian novelists of the Republican period;
Vartan İhmalyan (Konya 1913–Moscow 1987, engineer, amateur theatre
director);[148] Jak İhmalyan (Istanbul 1922–Moscow 1978, painter); Aram
Pehlivanyan (politician, publisher, poet); Sarkis Keçyan–Zanku (pub-
lisher, poet).[149] This generation has since been referred to as the
Generation of *Nor Or* (*Nor Oryan Serunt*).[150] From its conception in July
1945, *Nor Or* was an activist newspaper with libertarian principles.
It started as a weekly, and turned into a daily in a year, ultimately lasting
until December 1946, when it was closed down by a Martial Law decision.
Aram Pehlivanyan, who was an active member of the Turkish Socialist
Labourers and Peasants Party, and of the 'Democratic Front', was arrested
once again. According to his short autobiographical account, Pehlivanyan
was actively involved in the foundation of the first independent trade
unions (of tobacco, shoe, textile and construction industry workers).[151]

The editorial of the first issue of *Nor Or* argued that liberal virtues
were gaining acceptance in the international arena and that the pre-war
mentality should be overcome.[152] The rallying points in the editorials or
columns were equality, citizenship rights, the difference between the
constitution of the country and the implementation of the constitution,
the right to get organised, the need for a democratic electoral system for
the community, the right to have trade unions and workers' rights,
among others. *Nor Or* published articles on the strikes in the US mining
sector and their repercussions in society and the economy.[153]

Aram Pehlivanyan's article in *Nor Or* points out the difference between having and enjoying rights. According to Pehlivanyan, in one of these meetings of September 1945, the Prime Minister promised to allow the Armenian press to enjoy some of their rights, which already existed but could not be put into practice.[154] The Prime Minister thus effectively accepted that some people were more equal than others. *Nor Or* underscored and problematised the fact that having equal rights as citizens did not mean enjoying them in full. In another article, Pehlivanyan writes:

> God knows how many times we have stated in these columns, and now we shout at all those ignorant people yet another time [...], 'no, no, sir, in this country, people who belong to minorities do not enjoy complete equality and are deprived of many of their rights that have already been acquired.' It is not possible to cover this reality or deceive anyone by saying the opposite. It is true that the Constitution excludes any inequality among citizens. However, in practice, it is also true that there is discrimination against not only the Constitution, but also liberal values and human rights. A change of mentality is needed in this country in order to enable the Armenians, Greeks and Jews to live in harmony with their own national values as equal citizens.[155]

On the eve of the first parliamentary elections with two parties in July 1946, *Nor Or* published articles of a very critical tone. An editorial published on 29 June argues that the CHP became a dictatorial power, while evidently the reforms were already internalised by the people and no longer in need of protection. The same article draws a distinct line between the CHP as a party, which introduced and protected the reform movement, and its policy regarding the minorities, especially the Armenian community. The CHP and the closely associated press harassed Armenians in every possible way, segregating society into citizens and vassals. Most importantly, the editorial mentioned that the atmosphere of relative freedom could not be appreciated since it was granted by the CHP and not obtained by the people. The authors were well aware of the fact that, whatever freedom there was, was a result of the international conjuncture and could easily be taken back. The editor claims that there were certain laws in place that functioned like the sword of Damocles on liberal values. According to *Nor Or*, the only hope was in the newly flourishing socialist parties and the idea of internationalism. Socialism could heal the wounds opened by the CHP.[156] A week later, another article, this time by Zaven Biberyan, tackled the main issues of the country by way of criticising the CHP:

> Today we see clearly that the system, the mentality and the way the CHP operates have been crushed altogether. [. . .] We witness the situation with our own eyes; Anatolia, the village, the peasants, work and the worker, the economic situation of the country, the social mechanisms that are about to crumble. [. . .] Unfortunately [the CHP] has been viewing the people from the ivory tower [. . .] To this day, the CHP's authoritarian mentality has remained in place and bestows only bits of freedom.[157]

According to Biberyan, three main things should change in society: the condition of the peasants and workers, work for little pay, and the attitude against non-Muslims.[158]

Right before the elections, on 20 July 1946, *Nor Or* became a daily newspaper. The issue of representation was again on the agenda, this time in the context of elections. *Nor Or* pointed out why Armenians should not vote for Berç Keresteciyan, who was previously a CHP parliamentarian from Afyonkarahisar, and now the CHP's Istanbul candidate. A prominent, elite political persona both during the last decades of the Ottoman Empire and the first decades of the Republic, Keresteciyan played an important role in Patriarch Zaven Der Yeghiayan's resignation (according to the latter's memoirs), and was indeed one of the most influential figures to exert pressure in that direction in 1922. A propos, *Nor Or* published an editorial by the title 'Who is this person?'[159]

> Who is this person? The former representative of Afyonkarahisar, [. . .] Berç Türker, never uttered a word in the parliament about Armenians' living conditions throughout his political life as a parliamentarian. He voted for the Wealth Tax; he remained completely indifferent when 70-year-old people were sent to Aşkale [. . .] Don't vote for those who sent our fathers and brothers to Aşkale; don't vote for those who deny us our rights. [. . .] He remained completely indifferent when our clothes and beds were

auctioned, and even our houses and shacks were sold in order to pay our brethren's and fathers' tax debts. He remained completely indifferent when we were stripped of our citizenship rights. One should not forget that all this was done by the CHP and that he was standing next to them.[160]

In the end, the editorial re-emphasises that one should not be deceived by an Armenian name, because 'as long as an Armenian is not seeking a solution to your troubles and pains, as long as he is not advocating your rights in the parliament, his Armenianness means nothing'.[161] This important piece reveals the double-edged problems of the community: In the case of Keresteciyan, under the circumstances, his Armenian identity meant automatic representation, although there was no official mechanism as such – he had nothing to do with community affairs and was either uninterested or in no position to improve the legal situation of the community. For the Republican elite, on the other hand, Keresteciyan was a good showcase.

Thus, Armenian editors-in-chiefs had to deal with existing legal issues on the one hand and raise awareness on national-level high politics on the other. *Nor Lur* published the list of candidates of Istanbul from both parties, first the CHP candidates and then the DP. It also ran a short article stating that Berç Keresteciyan Türker was asking for Istanbul-Armenian votes.[162] In turn, the newspaper commented that 'Türker would definitely be a solution to our pains.'[163] *Nor Lur* warned the Armenian community of possible riots, advising them to be responsible and not allow anyone to create rumours that Armenians provoked any disturbance.[164] The newspaper also devoted its columns to İsmet İnönü's election speech on the radio where he promoted himself and 'the glorious party' under his leadership.[165]

As a result of a particularly corrupt election,[166] the CHP remained in power, but Berç Keresteciyan Türker could not enter the parliament, whereas Dr Krikor Keşişyan from the CHP did.[167] Right after the elections, *Nor Or* launched the publication of a series of articles on the administrative affairs of the community. For instance, 'Responsibility' argues for taking responsibility as individuals and as a community in order to regulate community affairs: 'The Armenian community is responsible for its affairs and yet has no right to administer its own affairs. Undoubtedly the biggest share of the responsibility for the said situation falls on the ruling single party.'[168] Then, on 3 August, the editorial took up the role of the Armenian press and Armenian administrators, emphasising the manipulative nature of the visits to Ankara and the ensuing speculations: 'Whenever our editors-in-chief pay a visit to Ankara and meet the Prime Minister, they return like victorious commanders and start [...] a shouting match against one other about how to rescue national interests. However, nothing changes.'[169] On 11 August, another editorial tried to persuade the reader that it was the right time to struggle for a participatory community administration in the broader post-World War II context: 'Thanks to their efforts, Greek national representatives succeeded in achieving some kind of improvement in the Single Trustee System for their community. Those who speak on behalf of the community and have the honour of working for their community have to fulfil the requirements of their position. This duty requires responsibility.'[170] The editorial pushed the issue of community administration and argued that the GNA and the Administration were obsolete models; new models should be based on community participation, given the fact that the international power relations were changing.[171] The issue continued on 13 August with another editorial, 'Och' Ok'' ('No One'). In closing, the article repeatedly argues that 'No one has the right to talk on behalf of the Armenians of Turkey.'[172] A week later, Aram Pehlivanyan wrote another editorial on community administration, this time underscoring the government policy towards minorities: 'First and foremost, the government should change its attitude towards non-Muslim communities. Otherwise, it is impossible to improve the current situation.'[173]

While keeping scathing issues alive, as well as the idea of struggle for rights and equality, *Nor Or* was sceptical towards the second party and the enthusiasm expressed for its 'libertarian' principles. Aram Pehlivanyan writes in 'There is Nothing New for Us':[174]

A remarkable revolution towards liberalism has taken place in our country. Single party domination has been brought to an end. The rights to gather, to think freely, and to express ideas – at least partly – have been acknowledged. Citizens are entitled to vote in a single-round election system. [...] All these are very nice. However, neither the representatives of the Turkish press who take themselves to be the preachers of liberal values, nor the political figures of the country [...], have ever uttered a word about the most basic, disregarded rights of the citizens of minorities. Indubitably, there is nothing new for us.[175]

Similarly, in October 1946, Avedis Aliksanyan wrote a three-part editorial, bluntly stating that the Democratic Party and its libertarianism was never a reason for joy in *Nor Or*, since the founders were the very same people who had served the CHP for decades and shared its principles. It was therefore unlikely that they would ever struggle against it.[176]

Aram Pehlivanyan and the people around *Nor Or* were aware of the nexus of state policies regarding non-Muslims, in particular Armenians, and the problems of community administration. As already shown, *Nor Or* always insisted that this was a community matter, but one that could not be solved without a change in state policy. The same idea was expressed in September 1946 in an editorial written by Pehlivanyan, where he emphasises the role of the Armenian press and claims that *Nor Or* would offer criticism but never react like the other Armenian press to issues concerning community administration.[177] Pehlivanyan and *Nor Or* in general advocated a radical change in the structure of community organisations and demanded the abolition of all existing, obsolete administrative structures: '*Nor Or* will never accept any of the institutions of our community unless they are elected by the community and are responsible and balanced.'[178] This brief article, like many other articles published in *Nor Or*, still remains relevant for Armenians as well as other groups in reflecting a crucial aspect of their habitus – namely, the normalised process of stripping away communal rights and the ambiguities created by consistent state policies to control the administrative and financial means of the communities. *Nor Or* was also very sensitive to world politics, the end of fascism in Europe and the decolonisation processes, in addition to the problems of the Armenian community. Although we lack information on its circulation, *Nor Or* was the only Armenian-language newspaper banned by martial law (December 1946).

In March 1947, representatives of the Rum community visited Ankara, which was echoed in *Marmara* as 'receiving new rights'.[179] A few days later, the head of the administration of the Armenian community, Vahan Papazyan, wrote that 'the new rights could not apply solely to the Rum community'.[180] The next day, Prime Minister Peker declared in his speech at Istanbul University that 'Anti-Jewish attitudes, which mainly flourished under the fascist Nazi regime, are unacceptable, and we condemn them. [...] We should also get rid of its possible old or new traces within our society. [...] Minorities should be equal, not only before the law, but also within the society.' Peker dwelled on the terrors of racism and the insult communism posed to 'immaculate nationalism'.[181] At the end of his speech, the chief physician of the Rum Hospital, Dr Panayot Yağcıoğlu, stated his firm belief in Turkish nationalism and greeted Peker on behalf of his compatriots.[182] The change in the government's discourse could easily be traced in this article. The *Yirmi Kura Askerlik*, the Wealth Tax, economic and political alliances with the Nazi government, and open racist remarks were no longer favourable, at least on the level of Prime Ministers' speeches. In the context of the Truman Doctrine, Peker's speech was very strategic, but on the other hand, there is an honest tone in the speech, since he accepted that non-Muslims were not only unequal before the law, but also unequal in society. But Yağcıoğlu's comment was still the most striking in demonstrating his assumed role of admiring the absolute superior from the position of an inferior subject.

In July–August 1947, upon the illness of *locum tenens* Kevork Arslanyan, discussions arose within the community regarding adminis-tration issues. *Jamanak* offered to appoint a delegate, Vahram Gesar, to take over all the problems of the community.[183] Zaven Biberyan's article on the issue again emphasises representation: 'Armenians of Istanbul have no voice.'[184] *Nor Lur* criticised *Marmara* for attorney Step'an Gülbenkyan's statement in which he declared that the Armenian *Nizamname* was still in force. *Nor Lur* argued that, despite the fact that the Constitution/*Nizamname* was a valuable document, the reality on the ground differed from the regulations and rights under its guarantee:

An organisation with a hundred years of tradition behind it ceased to exist; the national committee had to discontinue its meetings; the civil–secular assembly [which also handled political issues], which was part of the national administration, disappeared from the public arena; the Patriarch was alone or had been isolated within the four walls of the Patriarchate; consequently, all the bodies which were part of the national administration ceased their activities; the huge Sanasaryan Han was almost lost because of the non-existence of administration. Neither the General Assembly nor the Patriarch, neither the Administration nor anyone else raised their voices against it.[185]

A week later, Vartan Gomikyan's article in *Aysor* offered the solution of forming a central administrative body consisting of single trustees.[186] This approach was criticised by a certain Irazeg in the same newspaper.[187] In the following issue of *Aysor*, Zaven Biberyan underscored in another article the fact that the community needed an organisational mechanism to meet its needs under the threat of extinction and that it was futile to deal with offers of a solution that continued to reproduce state preferences and exclude the communities' participation in administration.[188] According to Biberyan, there was no other meaningful mechanism than introducing electoral systems. A few days later, an editorial in *Nor Lur* questioned Irazeg's criticism based on the fact that the community administration itself was non-existent and that, therefore, the Patriarch himself was the only *de facto* actor.[189] Biberyan wrote another critique of Gomikyan's suggestion in October. Gomikyan had tried to legitimise his proposal by saying that the situation of the pious foundations was worse in some districts than in others; there were more people in need and with no recourse. Therefore, a council of single trustees might solve the financial issues of the poorer districts by pooling their resources. In reply, Biberyan argued that the problem could not be reduced to the financial issues of some districts; rather, a radical solution must be found. According to Biberyan, this suggestion would give single trustees more legitimacy than ever and hinder a definitive solution.[190]

Nor Lur was not hopeful either about the new regulations for non-Muslims. Ara Sarkisyan argued in a column that *Nor Lur* duly waited for the new regulation to understand whether or not it would solve the problems of the communities; discussing a law that had not yet been issued would only consume time and ink.[191] On the other hand, Sarkisyan maintained that the Patriarchate should appoint some trustworthy prominent people to administer the financial issues, since the community had no control whatsoever over its own finances.[192] For *Nor Lur* as well, it was the Patriarchate that should have continued to act on behalf of the community, not the community itself. Here too, a quick and pragmatic solution was being offered, bypassing all existing legal regulations of the community. In November 1947, *Marmara* again heralded the news that a new regulation for the minorities was on its way.[193] According to their Ankara reporter, this time the government was working on the Ottoman documents in order to produce fair regulations. *Marmara* also stated that the community administration sent an official letter to the government (the specific ministry or governmental institution remains unclear) on 26 August 1947, requesting the application of all existing regulations to sustain the accountability of every community institution.[194] *Nor Lur* responded to this article by blaming *Marmara* for spreading new lies regarding administrative issues and provoking Turkish newspapers to write that the *locum tenens* had a stroke and was no longer able to fulfil his duties.[195] Moreover, in response to *Marmara*, *Nor Lur* argued that the creation of a mechanism of balance – to countervail the Single Trustee System, which remained outside the community's control – was not the priority. Rather, getting rid of the GDPF law and reconstituting the mechanisms of the community should be prioritised.[196]

A certain A. H. asked the following existential question in *Aysor* with regard to the situation of the community organisations at the end of 1947:

> We, Armenians of Istanbul, what do we look like? What do we look like as a community of 50,000 people? What kind of religious administration do we have? What kind of secular administration do we have? [...] What does it mean to be an Armenian intellectual of Istanbul? [...] I beg your pardon, but I do not know any period in history where 50,000 of us have come together and yet do not look like anything.[197]

Nor Lur, *Marmara* and *Aysor* wrote extensively on the administrative problems of the community in the first days and weeks of 1948. *Marmara* enthusiastically informed its readers of the 'details' of the new law regulating the legal issues of minorities.[198] *Nor Lur* published a series during the first three months of the year on the issues of the community, on the level of both districts and institutions (i.e. the Patriarchate, Surp P'rgich' Hospital, schools).[199] In turn, *Aysor* participated in the discussion of community administration, which had come to a deadlock. *Aysor* discussed in its editorial the latest news in *Marmara* and *Jamanak*, and claimed that, despite their 'good news', there was no change in the current situation:

> Do we have a national administration? If yes, where is it, what is it doing, what are its plans, and why does it prefer to remain behind the curtains as opposed to appearing bravely in the public realm to advocate our rights? If the administration were to resign, then who will constitute a new administration, and how? The Administration that applied to Ankara seems to exist only as a formality. Why does it not introduce itself to the community? Why does it not explain its long silence? [...] How to trust an administration of shadows? How to trust them and let them decide our destiny?[200]

Tebi Luys, published by Rupen Maşoyan and Yervant Gobelyan, also featured a series of articles on these issues in June 1950. In the first article, the focus is on the importance of enjoying equal citizenship rights along with ethnic, cultural and religious differences. The article argues that these differences could not be changed; however, Armenians served the country like all other citizens and thus had the right to be equal citizens as members of a minority group. According to the article, Hamdullah Suphi Tanrıöver,[201] a parliamentarian from the Democratic Party, argued that non-Muslims should not have a national character and that their schools and newspapers should be shut down.[202] Another piece of information in the same article hints at the general public opinion concerning non-Muslims: *Hürriyet* published a reader's answers to its questionnaire. Bearing in mind that the answer or the entire questionnaire might be fabricated, the comment published in *Hürriyet* still carries significance. The reader supposedly suggests that the abandoned properties of non-Muslims should be sold at cheap prices.[203] Although the two examples given in the same article of *Tebi Luys* seem unrelated – the former is about the removal of national administrative systems of non-Muslims and the latter deals with the confiscation of their properties – they illustrate the same structure of absolute supremacy, whether of a regular citizen responding to a questionnaire or of a statesman like Hamdullah Suphi. In this environment, nothing could be more normal than offering to sell the abandoned properties of non-Muslims. The next article in the same series of *Tebi Luys* points to the same supremacy by arguing that minorities were made to regard themselves as inferior subjects.[204] When the US Navy visited Istanbul, many shops displayed 'Welcome' signs in English to show that they knew the language: 'The big difference between "Citizen, Speak Turkish" and "Welcome" makes clear the humiliating, condescending tone. It was the attitude of regarding minorities as their subjects that led them to explode so easily.'[205]

As can be seen, despite the efforts of opinion makers at claiming the representation of the Armenian community in Turkey after the eradication of its legal administrative basis, the state continued to play a significant role in designating those opinion makers in the first place. It is clear that the Armenian press was struggling against the eradication, although the reaction was by no means monolithic. In the process, discourses of 'secularism, citizenship rights and egalitarianism' came to be instrumentalised in forcing the communities to accept de facto interim solutions that would eventually aggravate their problems. In fact, one of the main targets of the discourse of secularism and equal citizenship rights was the Nizamnames and the legal basis they provided to communities. To this day, nothing has replaced them in the way of responding to the needs of the communities.

CHAPTER 3

STATE SURVEILLANCE AND ANTI-ARMENIAN CAMPAIGNS

State Surveillance of the Armenian Press in Turkey and Around the World

Surveillance of the Armenian press in Turkey and the community as a whole was part and parcel of the post-genocide habitus, where any historical approach toward Armenians in Turkey or elsewhere was considered a threat to the perpetuation of the entire denialist construct. Secondly, the isolation of the Armenians remaining in Turkey from other diasporas was intrinsic to this habitus, as was the expectation that the Armenians remaining in Turkey express themselves in line with the Turkish official position. As will be shown in this chapter, the Armenians remaining in Turkey were required to advocate for the official position of Turkey: that Armenians were very happy to live in Turkey, that the territorial claim did not represent their wishes, and that they had nothing to do with those other Armenians abroad. Third, Soviet Armenia's immigration call, conjoined with territorial claims, revived the fifth column accusation against Armenians and gave rise to an international crisis that pushed the Armenian community into international politics without any of the requisite tools.

In this section of the chapter, I first dwell on the prohibition of Armenian publications throughout the 1930s and 1940s and take a close look at the debates in Armenian newspapers concerning articles reprinted from Turkish and international newspapers. The reports by the Armenian translator and the Head of Press shed light on the relationship between the Armenian press and the government, as well as the inner dynamics of the community as they play out in editorials, commentaries and news items.

In the absence of civil representation, the Armenian press became *de facto* responsible for issuing political statements – a position that, as I have already shown, often threatened the very existence and freedom of newspapers and their editors under the massive censorship of the state. Throughout the first half of the twentieth century, journalism, the publication of newspapers and printing were prestigious professions among Armenians in Istanbul because they remained legally accessible, unlike a long list of other professions from which the state excluded non-Muslims.[1] A striking example of pressures exerted on the press can be found in the case of the newspaper *Aztarar*, as related by Ara Koçunyan:

> Atatürk said, from his sickbed, 'Do not make me put on my boots again.' Upon this statement, the French had to leave and Hatay was annexed to the motherland.[2] This news found its place on the front page of all Turkish newspapers in seven columns [. . .], except for *Aztarar*, which published only a small news item of a couple of lines buried in domestic news. This myopic attitude dug *Aztarar*'s grave. Muhiddin Üstündağ, then governor, invited Manuk Aslanyan [editor-in-chief of *Aztarar*] and asked him whether he was not happy about the annexation [of Hatay]. M. Aslanyan understood, of course, that he had dropped a brick; he apologised and promised to write an editorial the next day. He did write the editorial, but a couple of days later *Aztarar* was closed anyway.[3]

The practice of the shutting down or prohibiting newspapers continued well after the Law on the Maintenance of Order (*Takrir-i Sükun*) was annulled in 1929.[4] Mustafa Yılmaz and Yasemin Doğaner have written three extensive articles where they have compiled numerous documents in the Prime Ministry Archives on censorship and the prohibition of publications from the mid-nineteenth century to Republican Turkey.[5] Their articles include decisions on the prohibition of the entry of foreign publications into Turkey, which the state regarded as somewhat harmful. I will refer to those documents in a different context. Yılmaz and Doğaner provide a long history and list of prohibitions, even though they attempt to justify the practice. In fact, while reading their articles, one cannot help wondering what the real mission of *Takrir-i Sükun* was, given that even after this law the press still remained under strict state control. According to Server İskit, there was no censorship during the Republican era,[6] although he then cites the *Takrir-i Sükun* Law and argues that 'the revolution/reform [*inkılap*]' had to take some measures from time to time. The reasons for these measures are well explained in Mustafa Kemal's *Nutuk*.[7] In June 1934, the duties of the Directorate General of the Press (*Matbuat Umum Müdürlüğü*) were amended and described in detail under the Law on the Institution and Duties of the Directorate General of the Press (*Matbuat Umum Müdürlüğü Teşkilatına ve Vazifelerine Dair Kanun*), which aimed at exercising control over publications both within and outside Turkey.[8]

Given the strict control of the press, the abovementioned incident involving *Aztarar* does not seem unusual. *Hay Gin* (*Armenian Woman*) was banned by the state in the early 1930s, but the reasons remain unexplained to this day.[9] The case of *Nor Or*, which was last published (as were some Turkish newspapers and magazines) on 15 December 1946, right before the ban by Martial Law order, was no different.[10] To my knowledge, *Nor Or* was the only non-Turkish language newspaper to be completely banned.

Although not by Martial Law, various Greek newspapers were shut down throughout the Republican years as well.[11] Mustafa Yılmaz cites some 144 publications prohibited by cabinet decision in 1923–45.[12] Newspapers, magazines, or books were prohibited by cabinet decision and the presidential confirmation by İnönü. For instance, in 1949, *Sovedagan Hayastan* (*Soviet Armenia*), a magazine published in Yerevan for the Armenians of the diaspora, and *1920–1945 Soviet Armenia,* an album published in France, were banned. The ban on the delivery of these publications into Turkey also mandated the collection of copies already existing in the country.[13] The same was the case for Kevork Mesrop's book, *Mufassal Ermeni Tarihi*, printed in Sofia by Masis Publishing House in 1937–8 and 1941.[14] The banning order was issued in July 1944.[15] Although the archives are not forthcoming in revealing the mechanisms for collecting the existing copies, the following oral historical account provides hints regarding the book bans:

> We didn't have the right to keep Armenian books at school. That is, it wasn't possible to keep books published before 1923 or

outside of Turkey. The administration didn't know where to keep
them. First they were hidden up in the Surp Haç bell – they snake
them right up the bell tower. Then the church administration
started to become afraid. So they brought them back down to the
school again, and then the school administration started to get
afraid. Finally, because they just didn't know what else to do with
the books, they had to throw them straight into Tbrevank's
heating boiler: I was there, right in front of it, and that moment
will always remain before my eyes. [. . .] The Patriarch's library too
was going to be relocated in Tbrevank; that's what he said in his
will, but for the same reason, it couldn't be done.[16]

An incident of book burning appears in yet another oral historical
account by A. K.:

In ninth grade I took responsibility for the Armenian library. [. . .]
There, I found the bylaws of the Hnçak party. When Margosyan
came to Istanbul in 1967, there used to be a Hagop Aprahamyan
printing house. This man's press was shut down, and handed over
to the Teacher's Association. And then apparently there used to be
this bookstore too. Two trucks full of books arrived at Tbrevank.
It's us who brought those books in – that book-burning in the
boiler ended up taking care of our laundry. But the books had been
sorted beforehand based on the bans in Turkey – most of them
were sent to Badriarkaran [the Patriarchate]. Some were just
thrown out.[17]

In both cases books become 'problems' that schools and other
institutions cannot easily figure out how to handle and can only solve
by way of complete destruction – a process of self-destruction, in fact, in
which the community itself was forced to become complicit as a result of
their obligatory participation in the habitus of denial.

The prohibition was put into effect according to paragraph 51 of the
Press Code (*Matbuat Kanunu*).[18] Several Armenian publications from
Paris were banned in 1928–34: the newspaper *Haraç*, published by the
committee of the Armenian Revolutionary Federation (1928);[19] Simon
Viraçyan's (Simon Vratzian) book *Hayastani Hanrabedut'iwn* (*Ermenistan
Sabık Cümhuriyetinin tarihçesi* [*sic*], 1928; banned in 1934),[20] and *Troşak*,

the central organ of the ARF (1934).[21] Several Armenian newspapers published in Istanbul (*Nor Lur*, *Arevelk* and *Jamanak*) and the Greek newspaper *Apoyevmatini* were banned on 7 August 1938 on the grounds that they all published unfavourable opinions on the government.[22] The prohibition decision stated that these publications included mischievous (*muzır*) articles. Only the resolution concerning *Troşak* was marked as secret or private (*mahrem*). Publications banned in Turkey included *Haraç* (Paris), *Aztak* (Beirut), *Nor Or* (Athens), *Husaper* (Cairo) and *Mşak* (Fresno) in 1931;[23] *Hayrenik* (Boston) in 1933;[24] *Mardgost* (*Mardgots*) (Paris) in 1933;[25] *Aramast* (Athens)[26] and *Baykar* (Boston) in 1934;[27] and *Arev* (Cairo) in 1936.[28] A news item published in *Baykar* on Serbest Fırka in 1930 was translated into Turkish.[29]

It is indeed surprising to see the Turkish government following the Armenian press so closely and applying bans on publications from abroad. According to the documents in the Prime Ministry Archives, the newspaper *Aztarar* of Istanbul was constrained to temporarily cease publication in 1937 on the argument that it posed a threat to internal and foreign state policy.[30] Not only the Armenian press, but publications related to Armenians, especially on the Armenian Genocide, were also prohibited, such as Franz Werfel's *The Forty Days of Musa Dagh* in 1935.[31] The government was also occasionally briefed about the content of certain items. For instance, a report was prepared in 1937 concerning articles on Dersim in *The Truth* (a magazine) and in *Haraç*. Both articles had been translated along with a short news item from *Arev* (Cairo).[32] *Sevğili Ermenistan* (*My Beloved Armenia*), a book published in Chicago by Marie S. Banker (who was said to have graduated from the American College in Izmir),[33] was banned in Turkey in 1937 due to harmful content.[34] In 1939, Masheh Seropyan's (Mushegh Seropian) book, *The Armenian Question*, published in Beirut in Armenian, was also banned.[35]

Of special interest is the source of the accurate translation of Armenian articles into Turkish, which were attached to the state reports I found in the Prime Ministry Archives in Istanbul. Most of the documents do not mention the name of the translator. The note 'Translator for Armenian' ('*Ermenice tercümanı*') at the end of the translation nonetheless does not disclose any names. On the translation of the news item in *Nor Lur* and *Arevelk* about the construction of Ataturk's Pavilion in the Armenian Hospital, the translator's name appears as Halit Gökmen (1937).[36] The translator in some of the documents appears to be Mithat Akdora, on whom there are two articles by the editor-in-chief of *Marmara*, Suren Şamlıyan.[37] According to the first, Akdora was from Üsküdar and attended the Garabedyan Armenian School (closed in 1945). Suren Şamlıyan noted that Akdora's Armenian was perfect and that, though not a regular translator, he was interested in the biographies of Armenian authors and Armenian society. Akdora was in charge of the Armenian department (*Ermeni Masası*) under Vedat Nedim Tör, who had been arrested during a wave of anti-communist hunts (1927), and who later became one of the founders of *Kadro Dergisi* (1932).[38]

According to İskit, Tör shut the magazine down after becoming the Director General of the Press (*Matbuat Umum Müdürü*); his colleagues had also been appointed to official positions.[39] The Directorate General of the Press was under the Ministry of Foreign Affairs in 1929–31, and subsequently subsumed by the Ministry of Interior.[40] After his position as director (1933–7) Tör became Chief of Ankara Radio (1938–43).[41] He remained a key figure in the politics of culture in Turkey, and was active for decades in Yapı Kredi and Akbank's culture and arts policy. Selim Rauf Sarper, a well-known foreign affairs diplomat, also became the Director General of the Press (1940–4).[42]

A March 1944 report signed by Sarper, translated by Mithat Akdora, and presented to the Prime Minister, cited *Halk Salnamesi*'s contention that Papadopulos, the editor-in-chief of the Greek newspaper *Metapolitefsis*, had been courageous enough to request a special appointment with the Prime Minister in order to discuss the circumstances of the people who were sentenced to service in labour camps as compensation for their Wealth Tax debts. The same article states that Ahmet Emin Yalman had also praised him for his courage in writing about the 'miserable conditions' (*elim durumları*) of the labourers. A third point in the article was that the same people who had insulted the labourers on their way to their work stations welcomed them on their way back. The report concerning this article ends on the contention that 'no other harmful element was found in the contents' – thereby implying that all of the above was considered harmful.[43]

The bans continued in the following years. In a list prepared in 1959, three Armenian books, dated 1958, 1954 and 1946, and listed among 'Arabic and Greek books, magazines and newspapers', were in fact the two editions of Vahe Haig's *Hatreni Tızıhan/Ana Vatandan tüten baca dumanı* (*sic*; published in Boston by Baikar in 1946 and by Gotchnag Publishing Houses in 1954),[44] and *Ermenistan Güneşi/The Sun of Armenia* (published by Hmayak Intoyan in 1958). All of these books were published in the USA.[45] The state ordered such lists until well into the 1970s.[46] Keeping track of the Armenian press as Director General of the Press apparently opened up a good career in the Ministry of Foreign Affairs; Nedim Veysel İlkin, the Director of the Press in 1946, became ambassador by 1957.[47]

Another very interesting document from 1944 that I found in the Prime Ministry Archives proves that the surveillance was multi-layered and indeed could reach far beyond professional matters. An accountant working in the army, Sabri Karayalçın, lost his job because he had been living with an Armenian woman, which shows that members of the army were prohibited from having relationships with Armenians.[48] Moreover, the fact that the decision was signed by President İsmet İnönü and Prime Minister Şükrü Saraçoğlu proves the standpoint of the state vis-à-vis Armenians in general. The highest representative of the state had to be informed of and confirm the expulsion of a regular accountant officer in the army, who in this case would have never been known to the president had he not had an Armenian partner.

There are various reports on the Armenian press in the Prime Ministry Archives in Istanbul, one of which was prepared on 1 February 1946,[49] after *Nor Lur*'s publication of Zaven Biberyan's article '*Badmagan Nshmarner*' (translated as: '*Tarihten İşaretler*'/'Signs from History').[50] Biberyan's articles must have been closely scrutinised after the notorious 'Enough is Enough' ('Al Gĕ Pavē') published on 5 January 1946, since İlkin prepared rather long reports on both *Nor Or* and *Nor Lur* (of which more later). '*Badmagan Nshmarner*' provides a rough summary of Armenian history and advocates immigration to Soviet Armenia, arguing, 'Just like there is a Jewish Question, there has been an Armenian Question, since half of the Armenian population lives away from their homeland.'[51] Biberyan thus draws a parallel between Jews and Armenians right after World War II. On the other hand, the report, along with the translation, emphasises Biberyan's endorsement of immigration to Soviet Armenia and assumes that the newspaper must be in the service of certain special interests and in solidarity with that country.[52] The report claims:

The editor-in-chief of *Nor Lur*, Vahan Toşikyan, is a person who has never been a friend of the Turks, and yet has never had an outburst throughout his 30 years in journalism. He is quite an unsympathetic character and rather weak. Nowadays he is very much in need, and his financial situation unfavourable. He has never been a member of a party or let his newspaper be the instrument of any movement. Because of his financial needs, he might attempt to take advantage of [his position or his newspaper] for profit.[53]

A second, 20-page-long report submitted on 2 April 1946 includes a translation of the *Nor Or* editorial (the third instalment of an editorial series) of 9 February 1946 in the first of its four sections. The first instalment of the original series assesses the fulfilment of Republican elites' promises to the Armenians.[54] The second and the third specifically discuss the principle of equality.[55] It is not by sheer coincidence that the Armenian translator picked up a specific article from this series: Whereas the first article mildly confirms fulfilment of the expectations and promises of equal citizenship, the second opines more comprehensively on the merits of the Republican constitution and the principle of equality, on the youth's lack of awareness of the tragic events of World War I, as well as its embrace of non-segregationist approaches to race or religion, in the name brotherhood with the Turkish people.[56] The third article in this series focuses intently on the discrimination against Armenians on the level of state policies that include the Wealth Tax and the unequal treatment of non-Muslims in the military. The editor problematizes the fact that Armenian men were not allowed to become high-ranking officers in the military even if they graduated from Turkish universities. The discussion of *Yirmi Kura Askerlik* points out that young non-Muslim men drafted into the military were not even provided with a proper uniform and were forced to carry stones as labourers in road construction. The Wealth Tax is also problematised as a special tax posing particular difficulties for non-Muslim citizens. Finally, the editorial refers to an article published in *Marmara* under the title 'Love Armenians!',[57] in order to argue, 'We love and we are loved ... This is a LIE. In order to love and to be loved, both sides should stand on equal footing.'[58] The article ends on a declaration:

As long as 'superiors' and 'inferiors' [...] exist in a society, they will always stand against each other. The superiors will look down on their inferiors; the inferiors will be suspicious of their superiors. In order to put an end to this, we need equality. Equality cannot be regarded as a favour: it is a 'right.'[59]

The third part of this article series is therefore the most straightforward and compelling: interestingly, the previous two articles on the theme of brotherhood and rapprochement did not appear to merit the same attention as the points of the last.

In the same file is a report prepared on 21 February 1946 on *Nor Lur* and *Nor Or*. Regarding the former, the translator mentions Zaven Biberyan and his pro-Soviet writings. About *Nor Or*, the translator points out that 'even the name of the newspaper was written in red'.[60] The Armenian translator informs the government about Aram Pehlivanyan – a communist and a Law School graduate with the pen-name Şavarş – to claim that the newspaper had mostly communists among its staff and contributors. In this report, the translator emphasises that *Marmara* also made Soviet propaganda. The third part of the report is the translation of a news item from the 2 February 1946 issue of *Nor Lur*, again concerning the immigration issue. The article instructs the reader on where to apply for the immigration process, providing an address in Yerevan (18 Nalbandyan St). The Armenian translator, again Mithat Akdora, assumes that the address provided in the newspaper is evidence that the latter had special information sources and thus various contacts and a mission to accomplish.[61] The fourth part of the report, signed by Nedim Veysel İlkin, is a letter that was sent to and published in *Nor Lur* of 19 March 1946, threatening the paper with a raid by university students and hostile Armenians to protest Zaven Biberyan's oppositional article.[62] A reference is made to the raid on Tan printing house in early December 1945. In its own editorial, *Nor Lur* informs its readers of this threatening letter, noting that the 'university students would destroy the *Nor Lur* Printing House just as they did *Tan*'.[63]

Again in the same file we find that the Armenian translator prepared an additional report on *Nor Lur* (15 March 1946) that closely scrutinises the editorial policy of the newspaper: it first points out that 'the newspaper is involved in direct propaganda of a foreign state [Soviet Union]' and second, that 'its aim is to promote and disseminate communist ideology and ideas'.[64] All of Zaven Biberyan's articles on 19 February and 9 March 1946 were labelled pro-Soviet. The report also provides a translation of Biberyan's 19 February 1946 article in *Nor Lur*. Furthermore, the 'tendency of the newspaper' is represented through information on the contents of the issues of 19 and 23 February 1946. The last paragraph of the report presents the internal turmoil of the Armenian newspapers published in Istanbul: *Marmara* complained about *Nor Lur*, which caused drops in readership, while *Jamanak*, known for its loyalty to Turkishness, continued to enjoy good circulation.[65]

The last part of this report cites another article, 'Struggle Between the Two Worlds', by Ares.[66] Here, again, the world political conjuncture is discussed in terms of Soviet and Anglo-Saxon tension. Parts of Biberyan's articles of 19 and 23 February 1946, 'Capitalism is a Catastrophe for Mankind', were translated as a second attachment. Submitted to the Prime Minister's office on 9 August 1946 was another 12-page-long report that provides a general picture of the Armenian press in Istanbul and that dwells upon the newspapers separately by way of commenting on *Jamanak*, *Marmara*, *Nor Lur* and *Nor Or*.[67] The first important criterion for the report seems to be the existence of comments or news from other Armenian communities: the absence of such reports was favourable. The reporter, again Mithat Akdora, found a remarkable difference between *Jamanak* and *Marmara*. According to the report, the former published very little news related to the Armenian communities and their activities abroad, while the latter regularly and visibly reported on Armenian life outside Turkey. Furthermore, *Marmara* was keen on disseminating Armenian culture and published articles on the importance of the day-to-day connection of Armenian youth to its culture.[68] According to Akdora, *Jamanak* was pro-CHP and *Marmara* pro-Soviet Armenia: *Jamanak* reported news items from pro-CHP newspapers, while informing its readers on Turkey's internal politics, while *Marmara*'s points of reference were more oppositional newspapers. Moreover, the report drew attention to the fact that *Marmara* had published an article on Ottoman Armenian parliamentarians Vartkes (Vartkes Serengülyan) and Zohrab (Krikor Zohrab) as well as Zohrab's ideas on the freedom of the press and his related conflicts with Hüseyin Cahit Yalçın, head of the Press Association.[69] In the reporter's opinion *Nor Lur* acted as the administrative body of the community, mostly publishing news related to Armenians, and appearing to be pro-Soviet

Armenia. Akdora repeats his previous comments on *Nor Lur*, namely that this newspaper must be acting on special orders from Soviet officers. *Nor Or*, as mentioned in the earlier report, was regarded as a communist propaganda tool predominantly for publishing news and articles against the government. Interestingly, the report underlines a sentence from a *Nor Or* editorial: 'Our newspaper [...] is a newspaper of intellectual [*fikir*] struggle.' This report also provides a translation of Zaven Biberyan's articles, which dwell on the misery and poverty of villagers and which assert that only 'socialism' (underscored) could achieve recovery from the CHP policy mistakes.[70]

The second report makes the priorities of the state very clear through its selection of newspapers, namely *Nor Lur* and *Nor Or*. Criticism of state policies (articles on unequal treatment of non-Muslims, the *Yirmi Kura Askerlik*, the Wealth Tax) and discussions on communism and immigration to Soviet Armenia were all considered threatening. Writing about state policies like the *Yirmi Kura Askerlik* or the Wealth Tax was not simply undesirable, but sure to invite state reports. The issue of disloyalty is raised in these reports too. Newspapers publishing such articles and news are thus regarded as propagandists for foreign states or executioners of specific missions.

The third report presents a wider range; it encompasses the entire Armenian press and informs its readers separately on each newspaper, with news items or articles translated into Turkish. Here we can see that the most important criterion for the state was whether or not an Armenian newspaper contextualised itself within the 'Armenian world' by reporting news items or publishing opinion pieces and articles on diaspora Armenians' lives and organisations. The second most important criterion was its position regarding denial, namely whether the newspaper reminded its readers of policies like the Wealth Tax and the *Yirmi Kura Askerlik*. Third, communism and pro-Soviet Armenianism were framed within the fifth column debate, which could vary according to political conjunctures. *Marmara* was not considered communist, but out of favour due to its persistence on publishing news on immigration to Armenia.[71] Zaven Biberyan and Aram Pehlivanyan were two names under close scrutiny and reported on after 1946 as well. State reports tend to give information on competitions and conflicts internal to the Armenian community, as well as the personal problems of the editors-in-chief.

Although the competition between *Jamanak* and *Marmara* and between *Marmara* and *Nor Lur* were mentioned in these reports, I could not find any documents on the conflict between *Nor Or* and *Marmara*. There are at least two open letters in *Nor Or* targeting *Marmara* and its editor-in-chief, Suren Şamlıyan: the first, an open letter published in early October in 1945,[72] announces that he visited the offices of *Nor Or* on his way to Ankara to meet the Prime Minister on 2 October 1945, and insistently asked for a volume of *Nor Or* issues. Afterwards, Şamlıyan published a series of news items and articles regarding his visit to Ankara, where, as it turned out, there were discussions on the problems of the Armenian community. *Nor Or* published a second open letter upon Şamlıyan's answer where he had stated that he wanted a volume of *Nor Or* in order to sue the newspaper. The second open letter asserts that, despite perpetual threats of lawsuits against *Nor Or*, in order to request a compilation of a newspaper from its publisher, one had to be either a member of the police force or a prosecutor. The open letter dares Şamlıyan to clarify whether he was one or the other.[73] The conflict between *Marmara* and *Nor Or* continued: In June 1946, *Nor Or* published a column by the title 'To Our Readers' (*'Mer Ěnterts'oghnerun'*) and responded to Şamlıyan's harassments to *Nor Or* and its contributors.[74] *Nor Or* accused Şamlıyan of being the 'representative of an international fascist organisation in Istanbul'.[75]

It appears, however, that it was not only *Nor Or* and *Marmara* that had problems. According to the editorials published in *Nor Lur*, Şamlıyan had attacked *Nor Or*, *Nor Lur* and *Jamanak* all at once.[76] In retaliation, Şamlıyan penned the article 'Invitation to Caution' (*'Zkushutean Hraver'*) in January 1946, publicly attacking and threatening Zaven Biberyan.[77] Therein Şamlıyan referred to a letter published in *Yeni Sabah*, presumably sent by an Armenian by the name of Boğos Çinili, who was from Adapazarı but lived in Rumelihisarı. Whereas *Yeni Sabah* presents Çinili's ideas as representative of Armenian leanings in Turkey, Şamlıyan refers to Çinili and Biberyan as 'equally harmful' to the community for attributing their personal ideas to the entire community.[78] In turn, Biberyan revealed that no one by the name of Boğos Çinili lived in Rumelihisarı; this letter was most probably a fabrication of *Yeni Sabah* or, at best, someone's nickname.[79] Biberyan also accuses Şamlıyan of being an opportunist and retorts that a person like him could not even pronounce the name of *Nor Or* – the purely intellectual Armenian newspaper he seeks to incriminate.[80]

The conflicts between editors, writers and newspapers become apparent in these series of articles. As personal as they might seem, the problems are perhaps instead political and tactical. Şamlıyan's target was not only *Nor Or*, but also individuals who more or less followed their line of politics. Zaven Biberyan, who wrote for *Nor Lur* at the time, did not hide his sympathy for *Nor Or*. What may have been Şamlıyan's tactical reasons, given that his newspaper was known for its reports on Armenian life in the world? Most probably, Şamlıyan knew that *Jamanak* was much more favoured by the state. In this political context, publishing complaints on a critical, leftist newspaper such as *Nor Or* or a newspaper like *Nor Lur* may have been considered a path to prestige and credit in the eyes of the officials. However, the main target remained *Jamanak*, since it was legitimate to discredit this paper for its contact with *Nor Or* and *Nor Lur*. The hostility between *Marmara* and other newspapers was known to Saraçoğlu too. Şamlıyan reported, after a monthly press meeting in Ankara, that Saraçoğlu had asked him to explain the hostility among Armenian newspapers, which he in reply dismissed as merely personal.[81] However, Şamlıyan's efforts proved futile, since the report submitted to the Prime Minister's special secretary on 11 February 1948 made it clear that he had not garnered any favour from the government. *Jamanak* was still the government's favourite Armenian newspaper, while *Marmara* still appeared to focus on the ties between the Armenians in Turkey and those in the 'colonies', meaning Armenians in the diaspora.[82]

In the meantime, Turkish public opinion was prepared for another turning point since mid-1945: the necessity of at least a second party in the political system in order to end the authoritarian appearance of the one-party regime. The Democratic Party announced its foundation in the same days as Biberyan published the article 'Enough is Enough', where he expressed a naïve faith in the talks of the day on democracy and liberalism. However, such aspirations turned out to be irrelevant to the fate of Armenian intellectuals. Biberyan was incarcerated after the publication of the article.[83]

In October 1946, two different human rights organisations were established in the country, as Martial Law was declared on 20 October 1946 in Istanbul, Edirne, Kırklareli, Tekirdağ, Çanakkale and Kocaeli, then extended for six months in December 1946, and then, in May 1947, for another six months.[84] Some of the parliamentary discussions on Martial Law were translated and published in *Marmara*. For instance, Fahri Ecevit from the CHP argued that Martial Law was necessary for Istanbul, since the city had a special, varied demographic constituency, which made it easy for the enemy to penetrate, and Anatolia would follow.[85] After the extension of the Martial Law Order for another six months, several organisations and newspapers were banned, some of them only temporarily, and some for good. *Nor Or* was among the latter:[86] it appears to be the only Armenian and in fact the only non-Turkish newspaper that was banned in this period. *Nor Or*'s systematic struggle for justice and rights, protestations against anti-Armenian campaigns, and demands for democratic representation mechanisms for the community must have played an important role in this outcome, as did its editor's political stance. The editors Avedis Aliksanyan and Aram Pehlivanyan were duly arrested. The day after the bans, editorials in the Turkish press rallied in their support, including by such writers as Ethem İzzet Benice (*Son Telgraf*), Ahmet Emin Yalman (*Vatan*) and Nadir Nadi (*Cumhuriyet*).[87] The people around *Nor Or* established another newspaper called *Aysor*, which started publication on 19 July 1947. In its first editorial, Avedis Aliksanyan, who was by then released, stated that they were not even allowed to make public the reasons for the prohibition of *Nor Or*.[88]

The reports reveal that the Press Office and officer had sound knowledge of newspapers and publishers, including details of their private lives. *Jamanak*, for instance, had a history of 40 years by 1948, and was thoroughly known to the state. The reports were almost always positive, and at their most brief, when it came to *Jamanak*. The publishers and authors of *Marmara*, *Nor Or*, *Nor Lur* and *Aysor* were also well known to the state. Their personal lives, their financial situation and the history of their political positions seem to have been even more important to the government than the actual content of what they published. For instance, among the press reports found in the Prime Ministry Archives, there were three special reports on *Nor Lur* just during the time of Zaven Biberyan's contributions.[89] The reporter knew personal details about its editor-in-chief, Vahan Toşikyan, such as his financial situation or his personal political stance. Therefore, the fact that there were no other special reports on *Nor Lur* – at least, not any that I could find – implies that these special reports were prepared mainly because *Nor Lur* had Zaven Biberyan among its contributors during that time.

Another report about the Armenian press was prepared by the head of the Press Department, Hasan Refik Ertuğ, in February 1948.[90] More than half of the 12-page report was devoted to *Carakayt*, another Armenian newspaper published in 1947–52 (not extensively covered in this book).[91] *Aysor* was scrutinised closely as a 'communist' newspaper and 'leading communist' Avedis Aliksanyan was its editor-in-chief. Zaven Biberyan's name was mentioned along with Aliksanyan. The editorials of *Aysor* from 6–20 December 1947 were partly translated. Both articles dealt with traitors in the community; their titles were in fact translated as 'Pen for Hire' ('*Satılmışlar*') and 'Press for Hire' ('*Satılmış Basın*') respectively. They argued that the community was in complete disarray, and that institutions and individuals made good use of this situation at the expense of the community. Interestingly, another article from *Aysor*, 'Tomorrow', was also regarded as dangerous by the Press Office: in discussing New Year's Eve, the writer expressed no expectation of good tidings from 'tomorrow', but only yet another day of tears, submission to slavery, and abandonment in intoxicating hope. The report argued that these kinds of articles aimed at inciting discomfort, pessimism and hatred against the social order.[92]

Marmara, for its part, put all its effort into remaining in line with state policies and published articles on the invaluable presence of its editor-in-chief in the monthly press meetings in Ankara,[93] but the Press Office reports differed. The main point of criticism about *Marmara* remained the fact that the newspaper published news on Armenians living in various diaspora communities. According to the reporter, *Marmara* consistently tried to foster Armenian culture by keeping alive the ties between the community in Istanbul and outside Turkey. This point had been underscored in previous reports too.[94] The extreme discomfort with the efforts to foster ties with the diaspora can be seen as an expression of the hatred against diaspora Armenians. Moreover, according to the report, *Marmara* remained pro-Soviet. Regarding community issues, *Marmara* did not insist on having a secular committee (*Cismani Meclis*) and yet criticised the Single Trustee System. However, we should keep in mind that at the time no Armenian newspaper was fond of the Single Trustee System and all newspapers expressed concern about community administration. Moreover, all Armenian newspapers that I have examined were reporting on Armenian cultural life in various communities or trying to keep up with communities around the world; this, in turn, was projected in the report as a matter of discomfort. As I have already shown, the state scrutinised not only local publications on ties with the diaspora but even Armenians and their activities in various diasporic communities, censoring them with ban orders.

The anti-Armenianness of Kemalism was all-inclusive. Throughout the years of the institutionalisation of Kemalism and the Single Party Period, not only were Armenians living in Turkey unwanted, but also Armenian survivors all over the world were regarded as enemies of Turkey. Since hatred of the diaspora has been constitutive to Kemalism, it is not surprising to find a positive attitude towards *Jamanak*, which was considered to be reporting very little about the diaspora communities. The first sentence of the 9 August 1946 report states that *Jamanak* included very few news items about the Armenian diaspora, and thereby earned the highly valued status of 'safe reporting': 'These news items [about the diaspora] are mostly comprised of brief news disseminated by A. A. with no commentary.'[95] I will not elaborate on the editorial choices of *Jamanak*, first because *Jamanak* is only partly included in this book, and second because similar editorial choices might have been made by other newspapers in different periods as well. Thus, such statements in the archives first and foremost demonstrate the state's priorities.

In this section I have demonstrated, through the Prime Ministry Archival documents and Armenian sources, state surveillance of the Armenian press both in Turkey and all over the world. In this context, the careers and biographies of Vedat Nedim Tör, Nedim Veysel İlkin and the Armenian translator Mithat Akdora are compelling. The Armenian press was under strict scrutiny and pressure. The editors-in-chief of Armenian newspapers were not at the same time parliamentarians as many of their Turkish counterparts were. Their reactions or silence become grounds for prohibitions on their newspaper or magazine. The post-genocide habitus of Republican Turkey required the isolation of Armenians living in Turkey from other Armenian communities around the world and the advocacy by Armenians remaining in Turkey of official state policies. Second, a primary reason for the bans seems to be the writers' investment, as demonstrated in their publications in Turkey and elsewhere, in historical contextualisations implicitly or explicitly concerning Armenians. Third, I have shown that surveillance did not confine itself to the professional life of the editors, but included their personal and private lives. The state thus manifested a holistic and consistent approach toward the Armenian press and Armenian individuals or communities in general. Armenian newspapers had to operate within this social and political habitus in one way or another, finding themselves in the position of political actors who had to respond to international politics on slippery grounds and with limited means, sometimes at the expense of their very existence.

Anti-Armenian Campaigns during and after World War II

Anti-Armenian campaigns during and after World War II took place in a wider international context, of which one layer was the politics of Armenian political life in Soviet Armenia and elsewhere. Another layer was the shifting power relations during the postwar period and the position of Turkey. A third layer was the results with which the Armenian community in Turkey had to cope. This last seems to be the most disregarded outcome of the first two, since the community was not in a position to put forth political actors, even though it had to bear the consequences of the postwar international shifts of power. Therefore, it fell to the Armenian press to deal with anti-Armenian campaigns in the absence of any other political representative body.

As Pınar Dost has recently shown, the United States began to regard Turkey as an ally, not after, but during Wold War II.[96] On the one hand, the interests of the United States and the Soviet Union overlapped at the time; on the other hand, Turkey signed the German–Turkish non-aggression pact in June 1941, four days before the German attack on the USSR. The Turkish army was stationed on the Turkish–Soviet border in the autumn of 1942.[97] This situation posed a serious threat for Soviet Armenia. At the end of the war, Turkey manoeuvred to position itself on the side of the winners. The issues of the Straits and the eastern border proved instrumental for both the Soviet Union and Turkey, according to their own interests within changing post-war conjunctures. The American–Soviet alliance had a positive impact on Armenian organisations in the United States: Vahé Tachjian's article on the history of the Armenian General Benevolent Union (AGBU) in the context of World War II and its aftermath sheds light on American–Soviet relations and their repercussions on Armenians.[98] After severing relations with Soviet Armenia in 1937, the AGBU restored them during the war. The reason, according to Tachjian, should be sought in the changing attitude of the Soviets vis-à-vis the Armenian diaspora as based on massive human and material losses of war.[99]

One of the milestones of history in the post-World War II period was the founding conference of the United Nations in San Francisco in April 1945. A group organised under the name of the Armenian National Council of the Armenian (ANCA) sent a memorandum allegedly supported by 'all the Armenian civic, social, cultural and religious organizations in the United States, except a small fascist faction known as the Tashnags'.[100] The footnote inserted next to *Tashnags* stated that the Armenian Revolutionary Federation (ARF) had presented itself to the conference as the 'Armenian National Committee'.[101]

> [T]his our homeland, the Armenian provinces of Turkey, are [*sic*] separated from the free and independent Republic of Soviet Armenia, where those of our brethren who are fortunate enough to be living have made a magnificent beginning in the revival and the reconstruction of Armenian national life. What would be more natural for Armenians outside that budding new land than to want to return to their homeland and join hands with their brethren. The time has come that the Armenia which is under Turkish rule be joined to the existing free and independent Armenia within the bounds of Soviet Union and opportunities be granted abroad to return their own homes and pastures, their cities and villages and live their own lives.[102]

Thus, the ANCA presented a territorial claim, using the terminology 'Armenian provinces of Turkey' even though the text did not offer any specific geographic designation. As a united front of all non-ARF organisations, ANCA was in strong competition with the Armenian National Committee of the ARF. In the meantime, relations between the USSR and Turkey took a sharp turn when Stalin abrogated the Soviet–Turkish Treaty of Neutrality and Friendship in May 1945, right after the San Francisco Conference. The USSR requested a revision of the Montreux Convention regarding the control of the straits in time of war, as well as the reappropriation of the regions of Kars and Ardahan.

According to Ronald Grigor Suny, the Soviet initiative against Turkey began in post-Yalta euphoria, when relations between the Big Three were still warm:[103]

> Rather than primarily an effort to satisfy aspirations of the Armenian (or Georgian) people, or to promote the fortunes of the international Left, Stalin's policy towards Turkey, like that in Eastern Europe, was based on a rather traditional notion of developing spheres of influence. Turkey's vulnerability combined with the enormous prestige of the Soviet Union should have been sufficient. [. . .] Soviet pressure worked only to unify the Turks and drive them into the Western alliance.[104]

The Executive Director of the ANCA, Charles A. [Aznakian] Vertanes, wrote a letter to the *New York Tribune* on 6 March 1946 as a response to an article written by Major George Fielding Eliot. Referring to the author's interpretation of an overlap between the ANCA and Soviet demands, Vertanes writes: 'It is possible that the claims of the Armenian people coincide with the interest of the Soviet Union, but why should over a million human beings suffer for that? Is it not time that the Armenian Question was handled apart from the interests of this or that major power?'[105] According to Vertanes, the demand for territories had started through the initiative of the ANCA and not of the USSR.[106]

This demand was to be debated heatedly in the Turkish media. In 'The Application Made on Behalf of Armenians from Turkey' (*'Trk'ahayeru Anunov Gadaruadz Timumĕ'* 10 May 1945), the editor-in-chief of *Marmara*, Suren Şamlıyan made references to the Armenian National Committee, which was affiliated with the ARF and not the ANCA, and which had presented yet another memorandum in San Francisco.[107] Doğan Nadi, who first reported on the presentations of Armenians in San Francisco, apparently mentioned that it was an initiative of 'Armenians from Turkey',[108] translated into Armenian as *Trkahay*. However, since most Armenians living in the United States were originally from Turkey, the definition does not necessarily indicate that Armenians still living in Turkey were involved in the initiative. Doğan Nadi then wrote in another article, 'Sometimes it is impossible not to regret that we have not committed the tortures the way Americans did with Blacks.'[109] This was the turning point for the Armenian press. Under the pen name Prof Nargizyan, Şamlıyan wrote two articles in *Marmara*, 'You Are Wrong, Doğan Nadi' (*'Gě Skhalis Doghan Nadi'*)[110] and 'We Are Not Blacks' (*'Menk Khap'shig Chenk'*).[111] On 4 and 5 August, Şamlıyan published notes from an interview with Doğan Nadi, where Cihad Baban from *Tasvir* was also present.[112] The next day, Şamlıyan visited *Son Posta* and tried to make it clear that Armenians of Turkey wanted to live peacefully in the country and had nothing to do with the claims presented in the Conference of San Francisco.[113] *Nor Lur* too published a riposte to an editorial by Selim Ragıp Emeç in *Son Posta*: Nusret Safa Coşkun here underscored that Armenians living in Turkey had no *political* (emphasis mine) connection to the Armenians living in the diaspora (*sp'iwrk*), despite the fact that they were all from the same race.[114] The editor-in-chief of *Nor Lur*, Vahan Toşikyan, emphasised that Armenians living in Turkey had nothing to do with politics. The Armenian press is full of cases where the spade is only implied to be a spade; this was one such instance, where Toşigyan implied a historical referent without spelling it out: 'We Armenians living in Turkey are never involved in politics, since we felt under our skin what that meant. Therefore, our Turkish countrymen should feel one hundred per cent safe.'[115]

On 5 August, *Jamanak* published and *Marmara* reprinted another article by Doğan Nadi,[116] where he clearly differentiates between Armenians living in the diaspora and Armenians living in Turkey. Doğan claims that he wished neither to hurt the Armenians of Turkey, nor to frown upon a people among whom he had such close friends; his anger was directed only at the Armenians living in the United States, who instigated trouble.[117] Nadi seems to have felt the need to compensate for his first articles from San Francisco from early June, which had implicated the Armenians of Turkey in territorial demands, and to which Şamlıyan had drawn attention by reminding him of fascist Germany and of Turkey's alliance with the United States.[118] During the San Francisco Conference, Doğan Nadi was not alone, but in the company of Hüseyin Cahit Yalçın (*Tanin*), Ahmet Emin Yalman (*Vatan*), Falih Rıfkı Atay (Head of Press Association, parliamentarian *cum* editor-in-chief of *Ulus*), Cemil Bilsel and Şükrü Esmer.[119] According to *Marmara*, the official delegation stayed in the United States for 76 days and did not return until the first week of September 1945.[120]

But Doğan Nadi returned earlier, in August. Aram Pehlivanyan wrote in an editorial in the fourth issue of *Nor Or* (11 August 1945) that when Nadi first reported on the issue, he attacked all Armenians.[121] According to Pehlivanyan, Nadi realised his mistake upon his return to Turkey:

> In his article Nadi wants to wear a friendly mask, saying that he had Armenian friends. He might have personally beloved Armenian friends; however, he has to know that, that mask is transparent enough to show the true features of his face. He also has to know that Armenian living in Turkey do not need the friendship of the likes of Doğan Nadi.[122]

Pehlivayan also makes a reference to Doğan Nadi's older brother, Nadir Nadi, who gave a special interview to *Jamanak* to declare that he did not share his brother's ideas, and that he differentiated Armenians in Turkey from those living in other parts of the world. Pertinently, Pehlivanyan then asks why Nadir Nadi talked specifically to *Jamanak* when he could have written in his own newspaper, *Cumhuriyet*, which, unlike Armenian newspapers, was read by tens of thousands of people.

Hüseyin Cahit Yalçın too gave an interview to *Marmara* upon his return from San Francisco to describe Armenians who had left Turkey 30 years ago (i.e. in 1915), and who were full of nostalgia for their hometown, Amasya or Agn (Eğin). These Armenians, who were very nice to him in San Francisco, did not, of course, share the ideas of the memorandum presented at the San Francisco Conference.[123] The next day, Yalçın published another article in his newspaper *Tanin*, where he argued that if the problem (the Armenian Question) were to be solved in Turkey, Armenian *komitaci*s outside Turkey would starve to death; it was therefore the mission of those Armenians to create discomfort and confusion in Turkey.[124] A few days later, Falih Rıfkı Atay, parliamentarian *cum* editor-in-chief of *Ulus*, wrote to *Akşam* on the same issue.[125] According to *Marmara*, all Turkish newspapers reprinted Atay's article, which was also aired by TRT Radio. The editor-in-chief of *Son Posta*, Selim Ragıp Emeç, called on Armenians living in Turkey to express themselves the way (good) Armenians living in the US had: by opposing the claims stated in the memorandum.[126]

Ben sana ne yaptım eşek merkebyan?	What have I done to you, ass-donke*yan*
Şikayet etmişsin halimden heman.	For you to run complaining about my ways.
Hiç sıkılmadın mı söylerken yalan.	Had you no shame in lying?
Türkler bizi kesiyor demişsin.	You said the Turks have been cutting us.
Sen ne sanıyorsun Keloğlan beni?	Who do you take me for Keloğlan?
Göster bana bir eşek, bir nankör deni.	Show me a donkey, a despicable ingrate—
O senin dediğin nankör Ermeni.	Ungrateful Armenian he turns out to be,
Yemek yediği kapları kirletir.	Biting the hand that feeds him
Hem yalan uydurur hem titrer tir tir.	Making up lies and shaking like a leaf.
Dibinde durmadan bülbüller ötse,	Were nightingales to sing forever at his feet,
Şarktaki dağları garba yürütse,	Were the eastern mountains to move west,
Ermeni bin sene dirsek çürütse,	Were the Armenian to put his nose to the grindstone,
İnsanlık yolunu bulamaz eşek.[127]	He is an ass lost in human ways.

The most inflammatory and racist piece of writing was yet to be published by a local newspaper in Adana, *Keloğlan*, in Armeno-Turkish. *Marmara* reprinted the piece:

The piece caused deep disappointment in the Armenian press. Suren Şamlıyan raised the issue when he visited Ankara in October and met the brother of the editor-in-chief of *Keloğlan*. In January 1946, Zaven Biberyan's article, '*Al Gě Pawē*', among many others, responded to this piece as well.

There was no end to anti-Armenian news items. In July 1945, *Marmara* translated articles published in *Tasvir* and *Tanin*, claiming that the number of Armenians in Urfa was decreasing because they were crossing the Syrian border to organise anti-Turkish riots and campaigns.[128] In August, *Marmara* published another translation from *Yeni Sabah* based on the news published in a local newspaper, *Yeni Adana*. According to this piece, Armenians living on the border with Syria were leaving all their properties, sending their wives to Beirut, and moving to Aleppo in order to register themselves as policemen for the French mandate. Armenians reportedly insisted that they had to leave because of the hostile attitude of their Turkish neighbours.[129] This trend was to continue for some time. In January 1946, *Marmara* translated an article published in *Cumhuriyet* by Ömer Rıza Doğrul,[130] where he reported on his visit to Aleppo and argued that because Armenians acted as a fifth column in the service of the Soviets, everyone hated them.[131] Around the same time, Hewlett Johnson, Archbishop of Canterbury, reportedly commented on the San Francisco memorandum and was supportive of the ANCA's claims. Johnson was an enthusiastic supporter of the Soviet policy on religion and of Stalin's policy towards Turkey.[132] Soon afterwards, *Marmara* made references to two articles from *Tasvir* which posited that Johnson was 'a red ecclesiastic' instrumentalised by the Soviet Union.[133] Meanwhile, *Marmara* reported that during the regular press meeting in Ankara, Prime Minister Saraçoğlu had praised the stance of Armenian newspapers and Armenians living in Turkey in general regarding the San Francisco memorandum.[134] In July 1945, Aka Gündüz, an enthusiastic ex-member of the CUP, like many other parliamentarian *cum* editors-in-chief of Turkish press, wrote an article in *Cumhuriyet* where he argued that 'the soul of the CUP starts to operate almost automatically when there is a threat from outside'.[135] The San Francisco memorandum was the most tangibly threatening matter at the time; Gündüz drew a continuous line in his article from the ideas of the Ottomans in the years following 1918 and those of Republican leaders. Furthermore, Gündüz claimed that the party to be founded should resurrect the principles of the CUP. The tension increased with the telegraph sent to the Potsdam Conference and the article published in *The New York Times* by (Souren) Saroyan, which repeated the claims for Kars and Ardahan.[136] On 24 July 1945, *Marmara*'s headline was 'The Big Victory of Lausanne'.[137] *Marmara* also translated *Vakıt*'s editorial piece 'The Armenian Question Has Already Been Sorted Out',[138] where editor *cum* parliamenterian Ahmed Us argued that the Treaty of Lausanne had brought to an end the problems of Armenians from Turkey. Ahmed Daver wrote a similar article in *Cumhuriyet*.[139]

Thus, the whole issue of territorial claims was first brought to the international arena by the Armenian National Council of America. Nonetheless, as Tachjian has pointed out, the Armenian General

Benevolent Union and the Soviet Union had already established good relations in 1940 with the first fundraising campaign for the benefit of 'Armenian war victims'.[140] The AGBU–USSR negotiations were around the *repatriation* campaign, which was to be launched at the end of 1945 by the Soviet government. Within the framework of friendly relations with the USSR, the AGBU was asked to do fundraising for the Red Army as well.[141] AGBU's financial aid to Soviet Armenia continued, while the New York committee of the AGBU was actively involved in the repatriation campaign.[142] In November 1945, the USSR's demand of Kars and Ardahan was already discussed in Armenian and Turkish newspapers. A letter by Kevork VI, Catholicos of All Armenians in Echmiadzin, confirms official support of territorial claims. On 22 October 1945, the Catholicos wrote a two-and-a-half-page-long letter to the Soviet government with a detailed historical account of the Armenians in the Ottoman Empire throughout the nineteenth century and afterwards, and expressed official support of territorial claims, asking to annex the Armenian *vilayet*s to Soviet Armenia.[143] Territorial demands, followed by the immigration call to Soviet Armenia, were serious challenges for Turkey. This situation in the aftermath of World War II must have motivated Turkey to consider a closer alliance with the United States; nonetheless, these challenges were then instrumentalised by Turkey. This about-face was possible due to reasons I analyse below.

Kevork VI was elected Catholicos of All Armenians in 1945, seven years after the suspicious death of Khoren I.[144] Catholicos Kevork VI expressed his full support for Soviet claims of territory and for the immigration call for Armenians, while attacking the Vatican for supporting the Nazis,[145] thus drawing the image of a leader actively involved in world politics. *Marmara* reprinted an article based on Syrian Armenian newspapers and statements of Cardinal Aghagianian,[146] where he persistently declared that Catholic Armenians were against socialism and against the call of immigration to Armenia. He had reportedly declared, 'Catholics are enemies of socialist administration. [...] The call of immigration did not solve the Armenian issue; on the contrary, it created various new problems and disappointments.'[147] Both for the Soviet government and for the Catholicosate, regaining the interest and loyalty of diaspora Armenians toward Echmiadzin was a strategic step. Stalin had promised the launching of the immigration call in April

1945 and issued the decree on 21 November 1945.[148] This wave of immigration to Armenia would have a completely different impact and context than the previous ones since Soviet Armenia had ceased all relations with the diaspora in 1937.[149] Therefore, the new call for immigration and the territorial claim generated considerable sympathy towards the Soviet Union among Armenian communities, which was relevant for the Catholicosate of All Armenians in Echmiadzin: By supporting the immigration, Echmiadzin went through a revival thanks to the support of diaspora communities. Immigration actually started in May 1946 and continued through 1948. Armenians moved to Soviet Armenia from Syria, Lebanon, Iran, Greece, Romania, Bulgaria, Egypt, Palestine, Iraq, France and the United States.[150] Although the immigration campaign was intended to attract hundreds of thousands of people, the number of immigrants throughout three years (1946–8) totalled 102,277 according to Soviet Armenian sources.[151]

A glance at the Armenian newspapers of the day reveals the repercussions of this issue within both Turkish public opinion and the Armenian community. After the Anglo–American–Soviet meeting of Moscow on 15 December 1945,[152] Turkish newspapers launched a campaign against Armenians. When the *Tan* printing house was raided on 4 December, yet another dimension had exacerbated Turkish public opinion, according to Ronald Suny:[153] On 27 November 1945, Kevork VI sent a note to all three Great Powers, calling them to support the return of Armenian lands as guaranteed by the Treaty of Sevres,[154] which amounted to much more than requesting Kars and Ardahan. General Kazım Karabekir proclaimed that the Turks would fight for every inch of their territory: 'The world must know that the Straits form the throat of the Turkish nation and the Kars Plateau, its backbone.'[155] This was the context in which the raid of the Tan printing house took place and the press once again fuelled public and state-sponsored anti-Armenianism. News items, editorials and commentaries on the Soviet calls of immigration followed one another. *Marmara* translated items from *Yeni Sabah*,[156] *Gece Postası*,[157] *Vatan*,[158] *Cumhuriyet*,[159] *Akşam*,[160] *Tasvir*,[161] the above-mentioned daily from Adana, *Keloğlan*,[162] *Son Telgraf*[163] and *Tanin*,[164] among other newspapers and magazines. The language used in these articles was always racist and hostile to Armenians, threatening them by implying that the hospitality and the patience of Turks might come to an end. Most of them 'waved good-bye'. Asım Us, for instance, asked Armenian intellectuals in his editorial for *Vakıt* 'to be conscientious and fulfil their duties'.[165]

However, such typical pressure was not restricted to that period alone. All through the year after the San Francisco Conference, numerous articles along the same lines were published. Peyami Safa, for instance, called the Armenians of Turkey to duty with his article, 'Armenians of Turkey, where are you?', which was published in *Tasvir* in September 1945.[166] Safa referred to the document submitted by the ANCA to the San Francisco Conference in April:

> [S]ome brethren of yours puke meaningless thoughts on your behalf. Whenever there is an international conference, these clowns appear on stage and submit letters, despite the fact that even they themselves do not know where they got their representative power. [...] We are sure you know very well that whatever catastrophe happened to the Armenian race in history was a result of these kinds of efforts. [...] Considering that time has not yet passed, our beloved Armenian citizens would not miss the golden historic opportunity to testify their solid bind to this land.[167]

The next day, *Marmara* published an article by the title 'We are here, Peyami Safa', where editor-in-chief Suren Şamlıyan argued that Armenians from Turkey had already written exactly what Safa wanted to hear, but that he was unaware of the voices already raised by Armenians.[168] In November 1945, *Marmara* reported that bombs were found in the Armenian cemetery in Pangaltı and the culprits already arrested. After this incident, Patriarch Mesrob Naroyan paid a visit to the governor of Istanbul, Lütfü Kırdar, to emphasise Armenians' loyalty.[169] *Marmara* published an editorial in Turkish, 'There Is No Armenian in Turkey to be Instrumentalised by Foreigners', in order to reach Turkish public opinion makers.[170] The Armenian press in Istanbul was overflowing with articles responding to these allegations.

The socio-political conditions and the field of power created and reproduced by Turkish newspapers cannot be considered separately from the state policies of the time, since many press editors were also parliamentarians. Cemil Koçak has shown that the Turkish press in fact published many of these articles upon direct orders from Prime Minister Saraçoğlu and the Ministry of Foreign Affairs.[171] In December 1945, US

Undersecretary of State Dean Acheson and Turkish Ambassador to Washington Hüseyin Ragıp Baydur held a meeting where Baydur argued that the Turkish people felt targeted and that it was therefore difficult to keep them in check.[172] The Armenian community in Turkey entered 1946 under these circumstances. During the first days, Prime Minister Saraçoğlu stated that Armenians should feel safe, that the government was convinced of their loyalty to the country, and that they enjoyed the protection of the law.[173] Şamlıyan claimed that Saraçoğlu's statement would bring to an end the Armenian community's psychological limbo.[174] A couple of days later, *Marmara* published an article signed by V. Bartevyan in lieu of the editorial, 'Love Armenians!'[175] In the very first sentence, Bartevyan revealed his target: the Turkish editors-in-chief.

> You, editors-in-chief, administrators of Turkish journalists, neighbouring newspapers, younger and older writers, we talk to you: love Armenians! [...] Armenians, Armenians, Armenians! Isn't it this word that you keep repeating, from your newspapers to the theatres, from markets to shops, from trains to ships [...] What about that huge prejudice '*gavur*' [infidel] [...] This word freezes Armenians' blood.[176]

Bartevyan's article may be read as an outcry provoked by the pressure on Armenian community both during that particular period and on a daily basis. While calling for 'love', Bartevyan actually points to the outright hatred against Armenians in Turkish society. In 1935, Bedros Zeki Garabetyan,[177] the founder of Turkish–Armenian Society for Advancement (*Türk–Ermeni Teali Cemiyeti*), wrote a similar piece, a poem devoted to Mustafa Kemal Atatürk and ending on the appeal: 'Love us'. A loaded gesture: If Atatürk would love 'us', then there might be a chance that the whole nation would love 'us' too.[178]

In his famous article 'Enough is Enough', Zaven Biberyan too confronts the entire anti-Armenian habitus of Turkey, which posits Armenians as internal enemies, spies, a fifth column, traitors, bomb-makers or '*komitacı*'-trainers.[179] Making references to the articles of famous journalists such as Asım Us[180] and Peyami Safa,[181] Biberyan argues that leaving any room for the charges that Armenians were a fifth column sufficed to fuel hatred against them. Biberyan sees the pro-German attitude in Turkey throughout the war and the ongoing debates in the Turkish public sphere as a manoeuvre to make Armenians foot the bill for Turkish wartime foreign policy. He also notes that there was not even a single Armenian among the alleged spies who were tried at court at that time. Biberyan's second point is related to immigration calls by the Soviet government. As previously noted, conscious efforts were made to point the finger at Armenians in Turkey and pressure them to respond positively to this call. Biberyan argues in his article that the Soviet calls for immigration provided yet another opportunity to express anti-Armenian sentiments in the Turkish public realm. He clarifies that he does not want to comment on the call itself, because neither he nor anyone else could talk on behalf of Armenians precisely because of the complete absence of a representative or administrative body or person. Ten days later, Biberyan wrote another article, 'Last Notice to the Provocateurs' ('*Verchin Aztararut'iwn Krkrich'nerun*'), where he criticises the editors of *Son Posta*, Selim Ragıp Emeç and Ekrem Uşaklıgil:[182] Although *Son Posta* attempted a balancing act by publishing Şükrü Saraçoğlu's view that Turkey had no complaints about Armenians, just a month before, the same *Son Posta* and Selim Ragıp had condemned all Armenians as suspect. Such abrupt changes in attitude led Biberyan to argue that the ideas and principles of Turkish public opinion makers and journalists could waver with every changing wind. To Ekrem Uşaklıgil's article claiming that Armenians wished solely to live like a Turk on Turkish soil, Biberyan responds:

> Uşaklıgil should not forget that Armenians in Turkey are Armenians before being Turks and human before being Armenian. [...] There is no doubt that if someone forced Ekrem Uşaklıgil to deny his Turkishness, he would have opposed and rejected that. [...] No one has the right to forbid us to live as humans and as Armenians, since we were born Armenian. Furthermore, no one can argue that it is a sin to be born Armenian.[183]

Not bothering to refer to or publicly ask his 'Armenian friends/ colleagues' how they want to live, Uşaklıgil had simply opined on their behalf, presuming that no Armenian would dare to raise such an objection as Biberyan's.

On 24 December 1945, *Tasvir* started to publish a series of articles presumably written by an Azerbaijani former minister.[184] The news item seems to be based on İbrahim Suphi Soysaloğlu's article in

Tasvir,[185] 'Armenians, Be Careful! There Is Freedom But No Betrayal in This Country',[186] where he cites some remarks by an unnamed 'former Azerbaijani minister'. *Marmara* translated the piece with the subtitle 'Thoughts of a Former Minister of Azerbaijan'. In response, Biberyan wonders whether the personage really was a former minister, and points out that he put all Armenians in the world, regardless of political stance, in the position of the usual suspects and enemies of Turks or Islam. The only aim of the series was to incite hatred, open up old accounts and create an inimical atmosphere for Armenians:

> If it is necessary to open up the old accounts, we can do that too. If it is necessary to count each and every corpse of the past, we too can count them. For, like any other people of the world, and even more than they, we have our corpses to count. We have no less to say to *Tasvir* and the Tasvircis. They and their likes are responsible for the millions of dead lying around.[187]

With this response to *Tasvir*, Biberyan confronted not only a newspaper, but also the whole state mechanism that produced denial and anti-Armenianism. Soysaloğlu's article and many others published in the same period in various newspapers were direct threats to Armenians, and Biberyan chose to confront them by saying that, unless they put an end to their harassment, he would harass them back, and without accountability.[188]

Interestingly enough, the international press had already blamed Armenians for being a fifth column since 1 June 1940, even before the meeting between the American ambassador to Turkey, John Van A. McMurray, and Turkish Prime Minister Refik Saydam.[189] *Marmara* gave a detailed account of anti-Armenian publications in Europe, the Middle East and elsewhere: According to Şamlıyan, the first accusation appeared in the British daily *News Chronicle* on 27 May 1940;[190] the correspondent claimed that German officers were trying to create a fifth column from the Armenians of Istanbul, which proved easy to do as they were ferociously anti-Turkish.[191] Şamlıyan's first contribution in this series also dealt with an article by Cedric Salter, who later published *Introducing Turkey*,[192] and who argued that the Armenians in Turkey were instrumentalised by German ambassador Franz von Pappen as a fifth column.[193]

Fervent debates, with detailed political contextualisations and rebuttals, were aired in the international public sphere from the 1940s to the 1950s. In *Summer of '42*, an informative book on German–Armenian relations during World War II, Levon Thomassian writes: 'Armenian representation in Germany had a strong *émigré* influence. This was mainly due to the massive exodus of Armenians out of Ottoman Turkey prior to and during the Armenian Genocide. Additional migrations ensued when Armenia became a Soviet republic in 1920.'[194] One reason may be that public opinion makers in Turkey relied on the fact that many Armenians in Germany were survivors and therefore should be considered Armenians from Turkey. However, a larger political context better explains the background of anti-Armenian campaigns, as exemplified by a letter penned by Jirair Missakian, the representative of the Bureau of the Armenian Revolutionary Federation in London. Missakian visited newspapers, trying to correct falsified information, before he wrote a letter to *The London Times*, where he refutes political allegations about Armenians:

> Sir – Fantastic reports have appeared lately in the British and American press suggesting that the Armenians in diaspora show pro-German leanings in the present War. Your paper inserted tentative hints to this effect in its issue of March 14, May 5 and June 24. An American periodical makes the absurd suggestion that the Nazis have picked out the Armenian Dashnak party to do fifth column work, promising the party an autonomous state for their cooperation.
>
> I vehemently protest against these malicious accusations, which are entirely devoid of foundation. They are instigated by certain anti-Armenian elements, and are indicative of a deliberate yet futile attempt designed to alienate the Armenian people from Great Britain and her Allies. The absurdity of the suggestion that Armenians can indulge in antidemocratic activities is manifest to the student of Germany's Drang Nach Osten policy of the last 60 to 70 years. Space does not permit to show in the light of documentary evidence how successive German governments behaved towards the Armenians. Suffice it to say that the utterances of German statesmen from Bismarck to Rethmann Hollweg, and the preachings of a galaxy of militant German

philosophers, cannot be described as manifestation of Tectonic [*sic*; read 'Teutonic'] affection for our people. There is no reason to believe that the present rulers of Germany will not follow their predecessors' steps where the Armenians are concerned.

The Armenian people fought by the side of Great Britain and France in the last war under the leadership of the Dashnak Party now accused of collusion with the Germans. They were neglected at the peace conferences. The civilised world forgot them and the unsurpassed tragedy which befell them. Nevertheless they cannot help persisting in the firm belief that the emancipation of oppressed nations and the principles of justice and freedom for all can be achieved only by an Allied victory.[195]

Reprinting this letter from 1941, James Mandalian points out in 1950 that, after this letter, the ARF's anti-Nazi position was obvious to the German government.[196] According to Mandalian, it was John Roy Carlson who was responsible for the allegations about Armenians:

But we are offered an even more authentic source than *Mirror-Spectator*, which made the Congressional Record. There is that imposing six-line item in *News Week* which claimed that the Dashnaks were doing fifth column work for the Nazis with headquarters in Berlin.

The joker in quoting these two awe-inspiring sources and what the reader does not know is that Carlson was the author of both. An analysis of internal evidence – the content, the diction, the style and the virulence – makes it plain that Carlson himself wrote that *Mirror-Spectator* article, it was he who furnished the *News Week* with that scurillous [*sic*] six-line item against the Dashnaks. And that was not all that Carlson wrote in American newspapers against the Dashnaks. He was the one who placed articles, furnished the material, or inspired the innuendoes in *Newsletter*, *The Hour*, *The Nation* and many others in 1940 and 1941, in a desperate effort to knock out the Dashnaks. He was the author of a mimeographed memorandum entitled 'The Case For and Against the Armenian Revolutionary Federation, Also Known as Dashnaks,' published by a fictitious organization called 'American Friends of the Armenians,' which was nothing but an abominable

rehash of what he once splashed on the pages of Propaganda
Battlefront, and which he has spewed anew in the debut edition of
the Communist periodical 'Armenian Affairs.'

Carlson's technique is not difficult at all if you know how to go
about it. Carlson plants a smear in seven different newspapers,
then turns around and quotes them as seven different sources.[197]

John Roy Carlson was the pen name of Avedis Boghos Derounian, who
was born in Alexandroupoli, Greece in 1909, and who passed away in the
US in 1991. He is the author of the book *Under Cover* (1943),[198] which
became the target for various lawsuits.[199] In July 1933, the primate of
the Armenian Diocese of America, Archbishop Ghewont Tourian, who
had started a campaign against the ARF's influence on the church,
refused to speak at the Armenian Day's celebrations held in Chicago
World's Fair until the tricolour flag of the independent republic was
removed. A month later, he was beaten up by a group of Armenians and,
on 24 December 1933, killed in Surp Khach' Church in New York.[200]
The ARF officially denied having anything to do with the affair;
however, nine members of the party were arrested.[201] This incident left a
deep and lasting mark on the socio-political and religious sphere of
Armenian communities, and caused a rift in the Armenian-American
community that has remained to this day.

In Turkey, too, Armenian newspapers followed the case closely. The
suspicious death of the Catholicos of All Armenians, Khoren I, in his
residence in Holy Echmiadzin (1938) and John Roy Carlson's book
accusing the ARF of collaborating with the Nazis in the 1940s affected
Armenian politics, particularly in the diaspora.[202] Thus, anti-Armenian
publications in the Turkish media accusing the Armenian community in
Turkey of doing fifth-column work can be seen as a result of the debates
taking place in the US and in Europe. They fall squarely within the
context of the post-genocide habitus of Turkey and once again put it to
work. Non-Muslims remaining in Turkey faced the charges of fifth
column work after the Armistice period as well. Thus, these two
historically unrelated contexts intersected and reproduced the same
anti-Armenianism.

The correspondent of *The Observer* in Beirut wrote a similar article
that also included Kurds in the scenario by referring to the statements of
'a renowned [but unnamed] Kurdish leader' who claimed that the issue

of the Straits would lead to the establishment of Kurdistan and Armenia.[203] Claims about a pro-Soviet 'fifth column' appeared in the Syrian press too, according to the series in *Marmara*; the Syrian newspaper *El Kefah* assumed that Armenians were standard-bearers of communism.[204] *Marmara* translated the editorial, which stated that the Armenian youth in Kamishli were very active in Bolshevik propaganda and, in the area of Djezira, were organised along with the Kurds who hoped to obtain their independence with Russian help.[205] Right next to this article, *Marmara* published 'special correspondence' on Armenians living in Aleppo, according to which the Syrian state was glad to have hardworking Armenian people, and lamented that some of them would immigrate to Armenia.[206] This was a tactical choice, evidently, to reassure the reader that, contrary to what *El Kefah* claimed, Armenians in Aleppo were well-received by Syrians and lived in harmony with Syrian society. Those accusing Armenians in Syria and Lebanon of fifth column work saw them as communist satellites.[207] *Marmara* reported that another newspaper from Cairo, *Al Musawwar*, also published anti-Armenian news items in the context of communist movements and Armenian involvement.[208] *Marmara* continued its reports on anti-Armenian articles published in the Arab world. In February 1947, again in Cairo, *Dünya El-Cedid* drew parallels between the *destruction caused* (emphasis mine) by Jews in Germany and Armenians in the Ottoman Empire. Moreover, the newspaper issued a bid to drive Armenians out of Lebanon, Syria and Egypt.[209] A few days later, *Keloğlan* published a cartoon where 'Artin', an Armenian character with an enormous nose and a monstrous face, introduced himself to the five powers (China, Great Britain, United States, Soviet Union and France), saying that he was from Van but lived in the United States.[210] *Nor Lur* also covered the incident on the front page on 15 February, explaining that, as the territorial claim had been introduced by an Armenian from Van, Karagöz was making an offensive pun with the words '*hay*' ('Armenian' in Armenian) and 'Van' as his ancestral homeland, combining the two in the Turkish word '*hayvan*' (animal).[211]

Nor Or was very active in its responses to the anti-Armenian campaign in the Turkish press, which routinely engaged in discrimination and harassment, targeted the community or its members, and pushed incessantly for responses from the Istanbul community on world politics. Soviet immigration calls to Armenians around the world were

one of the most optimal occasions to reproduce anti-Armenian hatred in
society, when we take into consideration the international conjuncture of
the period and Turkey's harsh policy against communism and its
sympathisers. Aram Pehlivanyan's article in *Nor Or* describes the anti-
Armenian campaigns in the Turkish press:

> Some Turkish journalists taunt Istanbul Armenians incessantly by
> saying 'why does the Armenian community not respond,' 'why do
> our dear Armenians not raise their voices.' One may come across
> some such cant every other day. Recently, Peyami Safa also lined
> himself up with those who have asked these questions. [. . .] What
> is the reason for these questions? We think that it is literally and
> solely to provoke Turkish public opinion against the Armenian
> minority. People like Mr Safa do not attack as directly as Doğan
> Nadi does. They have more subtle, nice-looking ways of reaching
> their goals.[212]

On 26 January 1946, after Biberyan's article, Pehlivanyan wrote another
piece – this time in Turkish – entitled 'Hakikat!',[213] where he mentions a
piece published by a certain Ahmed Halil in *Cumhuriyet* on 25 December
1945. Halil had argued that Armenians in Turkey and all over the world
had collaborated with Germans. Pehlivanyan replied that *Cumhuriyet*,
whose pro-German bias was very well known, tried to pin the blame on
Armenians.[214] He placed Ahmed Halil's article within the context of anti-
Armenianism, as there was no evidence to prove Halil's arguments. In the
same article, Pehlivyan responded to the allegations that combined anti-
Armenianism with immigration calls from Soviet Armenia:

> Recently, Armenian immigration has been raised as an issue, and
> turned out to be a new opportunity for abuse, harassment and
> general outrage [. . .]. Yet, there is a forgotten matter in this debate.
> [. . .] Every democratic country enables its citizens to go and live
> wherever they would like to live. [. . .] In some of the newspapers
> there is a distinct wish to engender anti-Armenian opinions.[215]

Ares (Arshag Ezikyan) wrote another article along these lines on
9 February 1946, 'What Do We Expect from the Turkish Press?', where
he argued that the aim of the articles in the Turkish press was to

humiliate Armenians before Turkish public opinion and turn them into an undesired element of society.[216] The issue was debated throughout the year.[217]

The volume of the records on Biberyan and Pehlivanyan that I found in the Prime Ministry Archives also shows that they provided quite an intelligent analysis of the situation as a whole. Both were leftist Armenian authors and supported the immigration call. Zaven Biberyan wrote various articles expressing his enthusiasm, including 'Armenian Miracle' in March 1946:[218] 'Soviet Armenia stood unexpectedly on its feet throughout centuries of darkness. [. . .] People are progressing in the secure borders of a socialist state, wilful, healthy, lively, happy, away from all prejudice and horror.' In the postwar context, the Soviet Union was still regarded as a heroic power. Yet, Biberyan's enthusiasm had historical grounds. In the 1920s, a handful of Armenian intellectuals who had survived the Genocide, such as Zabel Yesayan, had placed all their efforts and hopes in Soviet Armenia, which was regarded as the only viable option, compared to living in constant existential struggle as a diaspora community anywhere else in the world. The full details of Stalinist purges and the murder of Armenian intellectuals were not yet known to the communities in the diaspora. Given the obscurity of the Stalinist regime, Soviet Armenia still instilled hope in the Armenian survivor generation. The same was true for Armenians remaining in Turkey as well; especially considering the habitus explained in this book, it was not unexpected that Armenians wished to immigrate. Immigration was ongoing – the only real question was the direction, east or west. The trajectory from Asia Minor to Istanbul and from there to Europe remained typical for decades. However, immigration to the east, i.e. Soviet Armenia, was not typical until the repatriation calls.

A news item published on 11 July 1946 in *Akşam* triggered a new discussion on whether the Wealth Tax should be reintroduced.[219] Vala Nured argued that the millionaires of Istanbul lived extravagantly at the expense of peasants and *mehmetçik*s.[220] Therefore, although the Wealth Tax had caused some injustices, it should still not be too negatively presented to the new generations.[221] This discussion was to come back on the agenda again in mid-December.

In August 1946, Aram Pehlivanyan pointed out in his editorial 'The Press and the Government' ('*Mamul Ew Garawarut'iwn*') that the anti-Armenian mentality reproduced by the press was already embraced by the government:[222]

If this anti-Armenian attitude were just the specialty of a newspaper, it would not be worth talking about. However, there is a mentality in the country, racist and especially anti-Armenian, which denies the existence of the other. [...] The press and the government are hooked on the same mentality, complementing each other. If the state changed its mentality, the press would not have the same courage. Shall we be hopeful or not? History cautions us not to be. Yet, there is still a way back to a healthy way of thinking.

The anti-Armenian campaigns fuelled by the Soviet calls for immigration and the territorial claims regarding the eastern provinces continued throughout 1946.[223] The ambiguity around the immigration of Armenians from Turkey became a cause for agitation and provocation. In July 1946, the Anadolu agency reported from Paris that an independent Kurdistan was going to be established comprising Kars, Ardahan and the region of Cilicia.[224] The Turkish press reacted to this news in unison; *Son Telgraf* ran a piece by the title 'Armenian Hallucinations Resurrected: Huge Case of Stupidity'.[225]

According to Avedis Aliksanyan's article of 27 August 1946, the newspapers *Tasvir* and *Son Saat* continued their insults against Armenians. The latter argued that the Armenians who chose to immigrate to the Soviet Union were the homeless living under bridges, vagabonds, *apatrides* and 'xenophiles' who do not sufficiently love their own country or compatriots. Indeed, Aliksanyan pointed out that *Tasvir* was aimed at declaring traitors not only those Armenians who wanted to immigrate, but also those who stayed.[226] *Son Saat* claimed that 700 Armenians from Turkey had prepared their papers for departure.[227]

Tasvir continued its publications against Armenians. An editorial by Aram Pehlivanyan noted that the paper published news about a map disseminated among Armenians where the eastern provinces of Turkey were shown as part of Soviet Armenia. This time, he drew attention to *Tasvir*'s attitude by linking fascism and anti-Armenianism:

Tasvir and others like *Tasvir* have traded their fascist masks of yesterday for liberal ones. However, their attitude towards Armenians reveals from time to time how deeply engrained their fascist principles are. [...] They look forward to hearing an

Armenian name mixed in some international affair and to present the Armenians of Turkey as guilty and suspect in [Turkish] public opinion. As long as [...] they remain unpunished, the responsibility of their deeds falls on the government, because it is the government's duty to protect the honour of the citizens.[228]

Pehlivanyan pointed out a very important characteristic of both the media and the state. As previously noted, Cihad Baban, parliamentarian *cum* editor-in-chief (he was Istanbul representative of the DP in 1946), had worked for various newspapers as columnist or editor-in-chief throughout the 1930s and 1940s, including *Cumhuriyet*, *Tasvir-i Efkar*, *Yeni Sabah* and *Son Posta*.[229] He was a member of the Ottoman elite and a prominent opinion maker during the post-1923 period. Along with other Turkish editors, he was a member of the San Francisco delegation. Furthermore, as a pro-Nazi wartime writer, he authored *Hitler ve Nasyonal Sosyalizm* in 1933, the year of Hitler's ascension to power,[230] which was not forgotten when he became a parliamentarian from the Democratic Party in 1946.[231] Hence, when Aram Pehlivanyan wrote 'Tasvir and its likes,' he implied the existence of deep-rooted racism and anti-Armenianism among opinion makers. News pieces and editorials define public opinion making in the post-genocide habitus of the country. *Tasvir* continued its anti-Armenian publications: this time, another news item claimed that Syrian Armenians were very upset that the Armenians of Istanbul did not show enthusiasm for the calls to immigrate to Armenia.[232] The same news item claimed that a certain Hrant from Hatay, who lived in Syria, was harassing the Turkish villages near Latakieh.[233]

It is quite interesting that in mid-December, rumours about restoring the Wealth Tax resurfaced in *Yarın*,[234] but this time around, an official statement refuted the news.[235] DP members, who were previously CHP parliamentarians, had defended the Wealth Tax when it was first introduced. Moreover, it does not seem likely that these rumours casually materialised right after the meeting in Paris, where, it was claimed, eastern provinces would be established as Kurdistan. Maps showing the eastern provinces in Soviet Armenia had been published from time to time since October 1946. The weekly *Millet* reprinted one such map on the cover, showing Kars, Ardahan, Erzurum and Bitlis as part of Soviet Armenia.[236] It was said that the map had reached *Millet* from the United

States. In the top part of the map, a statement by Senator Charles W. Tobey suggests that Armenians should place their case before the UN and demand to have their homeland back.[237] On the right is the figure of a woman, who *Millet* names 'Vartuhi' and supplies with the caption 'She/ This must be a symbol of Armenians' ('*Bu Ermeni sembolü imiş*'); the title of this part is 'The Human Side of the Armenian Question'. On the same page is a map of 'The Political Side of the Armenian Question'.[238] In November 1946, the local newspaper of Adana, *Keloğlan*, ran another article on the Soviet Armenian immigration campaign and wrote: 'We would be more than happy, in fact gleefully jump up and down [*hoplaya zıplaya*] to help them leave, if only they took action. *Efendim* … They have to leave anyway – Yerevan is their heaven.'[239] The article in *Keloğlan* claimed that the *Daily Telegraph* also reported on the Armenian immigration to the Soviet Union.[240] By not rejecting these claims until mid-December, the government perpetuated the atmosphere of unease and insecurity for non-Muslims on the eve of the declaration of Martial Law in December 1946. The situation did not improve after Martial Law interfered in the public realm by banning a number of organisations and newspapers.

The issue of the eastern provinces became a pretext to reproduce the anti-Armenian and denialist habitus of Turkey on the level of both public opinion makers and legislation. A document signed by President İsmet İnönü shows that the state undertook other security measures as well. The order issued on 18 September 1946 forbade the settlement of foreigners in Kars, Erzurum, Ağrı and Muş.[241] I could not trace how this order was applied or how it affected people's lives in those regions. However, Agop Arslanyan wrote about the social impact of the Soviet Armenian immigration calls in Tokat. According to Arslanyan, Armenians were both surprised and eager to immigrate to Armenia at that time. However, their willingness was a source of discomfort among their Turkish neighbours. Ohanik and Hamazasp, both ready to immigrate, sold everything they had and prepared to go to Armenia, and yet they could only move to Istanbul, since the Soviet Union did not accept any Armenians from Turkey.[242] Ohanik and Hamazasp lived in poverty in Istanbul. Whether the Soviet Union did not accept Armenians from Turkey or whether there was another obstacle before their immigration is not clear to me. However, various accounts and news items show that no Armenian from Turkey immigrated in 1946–8, despite the fact that, according to the sources, hundreds of people, if not thousands, had registered. Abidin Daver stated in *Cumhuriyet* that, although many people were in the queue in front of the Soviet embassy, no Armenian from Turkey immigrated.[243]

Armen Melqumyan published a short list of people who registered themselves at the Soviet Embassy in Istanbul on 1–29 July. According to this list, more than 1,000 people had applied, but the number of accepted applications was around 200.[244] In the end, no Armenian from Turkey could immigrate. The list consulted by Daniela De Maglio Slavich cites the number of Armenian immigrants from Turkey to Soviet Armenia as zero.[245] I could not find any official declaration addressing the reason.

A Russian document – not a final decree but a draft – stated that there would be no mass immigration from Turkey, the United States, France, Iraq or Egypt in 1946. However, according to this document, committees should be established and preparations made for future immigration campaigns.[246] Immigration from the US and other places did actually take place. Based on American consular archives, Dilek Güven wrote that in the summer of 1946, Soviet ships carrying Armenians from the eastern Mediterranean region passed through the Bosphorus, and yet there were no ships for Armenians applying for immigration from Turkey until the end of 1946. US consular reports indicate that the registration of Armenians was an even greater cause for suspicion.[247]

By 1947, the first wave of immigration had already arrived in the Soviet Union. Meanwhile, according to Ronald Suny, both the US and the USSR distanced themselves from the territorial claims by August 1946 and stepped back on the issue of Kars and Ardahan.[248] For Truman, it was more important to have bases in Turkey, while the American military concluded that Turkey should be equipped accordingly.[249] Upon the announcement of the Truman doctrine on 12 March 1947, the Armenian National Council of America submitted a memorandum on the proposed aid to Greece and Turkey.[250] According to the memorandum, Greece deserved the aid, but Turkey did not:

> The proposal of financial and military assistance to Turkey however, falls under a different category altogether, and can never be justified. It will not further our own national interest and security, and cannot promote justice and peace in the Near East.[251]

The memorandum listed seven arguments against providing military and financial assistance: Turkey was not a democracy; it was an aggressor nation; it had plans of expansion via pan-Turanism and pan-Islamism; it was an ally of the United States's enemies in World War I and of the Axis Powers in World War II; it did not fulfil its obligations under the Treaty of Mutual Aid signed in 1939; it received the Sancak of Alexandretta as a courtesy; it robbed and economically crushed all its minorities with the Wealth Tax. Economic and military aid would strengthen Turkey in the Middle East and revive the danger of pan-Islamism and pan-Turanism.[252] Through *Vatan*'s correspondent Feridun Demokan, *Marmara* reported on the World Armenian Congress (organised by the Armenian National Council of America), which took place in New York on 30 April–4 May.[253] The illustration on the cover of the conference programme features President Woodrow Wilson standing in front of a map at the Allied Supreme Council and requesting that Trabzon, Erzurum, Erzincan, Bitlis, Muş and Van, in addition to Kars and Ardahan, become part of Armenia.[254] This five-day congress included speeches on 'Repatriation and Rehabilitation' and 'Armenian Territorial Claims'.[255] After the Congress, a letter was submitted to the UN demanding a solution to the Armenian Question on the principles of the Treaty of Sevres, and also stating that Armenians had already participated in the May 1947 meeting of Ministers of Foreign Affairs in Moscow.[256] Armenian support for Soviet claims of Kars and Ardahan as well as the reaction to territorial claims in Turkey paved the way for the United States to support Turkey against the Soviet threat, and legitimise military and financial aid to Turkey. Although Armenian organisations' role in the international arena could not accurately be called decisive, it became evident that their demands were instrumental in making anti-Armenian and later anti-Soviet campaigns, as well as instigating a political shift in the fragile conjuncture of the post-World War II period.

Following the news in the Turkish press on the World Armenian Congress, the newspaper *Şark Yolu* posed the perennial question, 'Why do Turkish Armenians keep silent?' and argued that the silence of 'Turkish Armenians' signified agreement with American Armenians.[257] The same day, *Marmara* published an editorial specifically in Turkish to announce that Armenians living in Turkey made no contribution to and had no connection whatsoever with the World Armenian Congress.[258] This editorial found a response the next day in *Cumhuriyet*, which mentioned the unease expressed by Armenians living in Turkey; *Marmara* had thus become their representative.[259] According to *Cumhuriyet*, the Armenians in Turkey were powerful enough to reach out to the government and obtain results. *Cumhuriyet* drew on the case of the Armenian properties of the church of Kayseri, whose auction had been prevented at the last minute by state intervention, in order to show how powerful Armenians were.[260] Two days later, *Son Saat* published a report by Cehdi Şahingiray from New York on the World Armenian Congress.[261] Shortly afterwards, the weekly magazine *Bekri Mustafa* announced that, in case of a new war with Russia, 'we would be obliged to take new measures in order to maintain internal security'.[262] The article claimed that Armenians were 'armed to the teeth with the soul of *komitacı*s', and that they were ready to cause any kind of harm to Turkey as children and grandchildren of the assassins of Said Halims, Bahaeddin Şakirs and Talats – their hands were drenched in blood.[263] *Bekri Mustafa* thus mentions some of the names of the perpetrators of the Armenian Genocide: honouring the memory of genocide executioners is a result of the denialist habitus of the Republic of Turkey; it was the same habitus that made possible the relocation of Talat's remains from Germany and their reinterment in Turkey in 1943. In fact, when the Turkish Hearths (*Türk Ocakları*) were reopened in 1949, there was discussion of erecting a mausoleum for Talat.[264] *Marmara* translated the entire article by *Bekri Mustafa* with the new headline, 'Threatening Armenians', and requested that the authorities take action against the threats.

The border issue was cause for heated debates once again in December 1948. The headlines in *Marmara* were brimming with news and commentaries on territorial claims and the reaction of Armenians living in Turkey. On 13 December 1948, *Cumhuriyet* published a news item on the 'Russian provocation of Kurds and Armenians' according to which the Russian radio had reported the presentation of another Armenian memorandum of territorial claims to the United Nations.[265] The next day, Şamlıyan stated again in his editorial that the Armenians of Turkey were not part of this initiative. He recalled that in 1946, with the first debates around the San Francisco Conference, Armenians in Turkey had been put under heavy pressure and represented as suspect people; two years later, the same phenomenon was recurring. In both cases, Şamlıyan wrote, Armenians were required to make statements and distance themselves from those who took such initiatives.[266] One of the points that Şamlıyan repeated in this editorial was that the Armenian community living in Turkey no longer had anything to do with politics. Şamlıyan requested that the government issue a public statement in order to dispel suspicions about Armenians living in Turkey. On 15 December, Berç Türker, acting as though he were a designated representative of Armenians in Turkey, wrote a letter to *Cumhuriyet*, which *Marmara* also published in translation. Here Türker claimed that the Armenians living in Turkey were happy to have nothing to do with the Armenians in the diaspora, and that Russian intrigues were known to Armenians anyway:[267] 'Oh you, the great Turkish nation, never suspect your brethren Armenians who have been so loyal to you and who refuse to listen to the demonising propaganda of the outside world. Armenians of Turkey despise these things.'[268]

The next day, Nureddin Artam, from Radio Ankara, reported on the memorandum and insisted that the Armenians of Turkey had nothing to do with it. This was presented as the government's official attempt to dispel suspicions about Armenians in the public realm.[269] The news on the radio was embraced as the confirmation of the 'official recognition of Armenian right-mindedness'.[270] However, it seems that official recognition did not suffice, since the representatives of Surp P'rgich' Armenian Hospital issued a statement in *Son Telgraf* the very next day: 'As a Turkish citizen, I love my country and feel deeply connected to it. [...] These initiatives have nothing to do with Armenians living in Turkey.'[271] On 15 December, *Son Posta* reported from Adana a fatal fight in Aleppo among Armenians and pro-Turkish Arabs following the stoning of a Turkish train by local Armenians. The news item on this incident, which had taken place four days before (and one day before news of the Armenian memorandum of territorial claims), was translated into Armenian and published in *Marmara*. *Son Posta* brought the news item to the fore, once again fuelling anti-Armenian sentiments by revealing activities beyond the borders of Turkey. The next day, however, the news item was declared a complete fabrication by *Cumhuriyet*, which interviewed travellers on the train and found that they had been welcomed in Aleppo with chants ('Viva Turkey') and even a Turkish flag on the fortress of Aleppo. As for the stoning of the train, it turned out to be a case from Baghdad and unrelated to Armenians.[272] This example shows how easily anti-Armenian public opinion could be manipulated, if need be. In March 1949, Nureddin Artam responded to the territorial claims of Armenians by publishing a letter by Dr Mustafa Selçuk Ar, who claimed that Armenians had never been natives of Anatolia, since Hittites, who could be proven to be Turks, were in Anatolia long before Armenians.[273] Ar quoted a certain German scientist, von Brandenstein, to prove that Armenians were incomers and not indigenous.

Although Soviet territorial claims faded away by the end of 1946, anti-Armenian campaigns recurred on cue.[274] The reporting of anti-Armenian campaigns based on the Soviet immigration call decreased with the patriarchal election crisis. In 1949–50 Armenian newspapers were mostly concerned with patriarchal elections and other adminis-trative issues such as the local elections of pious foundations. The Democratic Party came to power in Turkey with the parliamentary elections of 14 May, which ended three decades of CHP rule. However, as previously noted, Armenian opinion makers were not enthusiastic about this change. *Tebi Luys* stated: 'We have to admit that the Democratic Party owes its success [...] to the failures of the CHP. [...] We cannot help saying this, since there is no difference between the programmes of the two parties. [...] The only thing that differentiates them might be [...] personal sympathies or antipathies. [...] The Democratic Party was born out of the CHP.'[275] Therefore, the victory of the DP was not a source for hope in the Armenian community. The pogrom of 6–7 September 1955 proved the accuracy of such sentiments.

In fact, anti-Armenian campaigns have remained a constitutive part of the denialist habitus in Turkey: they have served to perpetuate anti-Armenianism, to silence the voices of the victims and their descendants who remained in Turkey, to reproduce official historiography, to isolate the Armenian community in Turkey from their relatives in other parts of the world, and to obligate them to profess views in line with the Turkish official position – all of which amount to actively propagating denialism. The calls on Armenians to represent themselves in an anti-Armenian public sphere also aimed to dissimulate not only the annihilation of their grandparents, but also the fact that they themselves were the children of survivors. Thus, Armenians in Turkey were expected to make their own contribution to the denialist habitus.

CHAPTER 4

THE PATRIARCHAL ELECTION CRISIS: 1944–50

Background of the Crisis

The years 1944–50 were a period of crisis in the Patriarchate of Istanbul. Despite the fact that the patriarchal election crisis has great significance in the history of the Armenian Patriarchate in Istanbul, I have come across the issue neither in English nor in Turkish-language sources. In this chapter I analyse the few accounts of this crisis in Armenian. A history without this crisis and its repercussions on the social life and the institutions of the Armenian community in Turkey would exclude one of the major conflicts of the community.

In a remarkable historical coincidence, both the Patriarchate of Jerusalem and the Catholicosate in Echmiadzin were headed by deputies, Archbishop Giwregh Israelyan (1944) and Archbishop Kevork Chorekchyan (1938–45), respectively. Karekin I Hovsēp'yan (1943– 52) was the Catholicos of the historical Catholicosate of Sis (Kozan), which was re-established in Antelias, Lebanon. A summary of the political situation of Echmiadzin is pertinent: According to Felix Corley, who has written extensively on the history of the Armenian Apostolic Church, Soviet authorities decided to dissolve the structure of the Armenian Church in the country in the 1930s.[1] After the death of Catholicos Khoren I in August 1938, the Armenian Communist Party decided to shut down the monastery of Echmiadzin, though Moscow does not seem to have approved.[2] The election process did not prove to be easy for the Armenian Church in Echmiadzin either, if for different reasons. Corley points out that the Russian Orthodox Church had long been prohibited from electing a new Patriarch, as had the Armenian Church after the death of Khoren I:[3]

> The Church had effectively ceased to exist in the Soviet Union as an entity – Echmiadzin functioned only minimally, isolated from the outside world, while a handful of individual parishes and priests struggled on in Armenia, Georgia and southern Russia. The Armenian population in the Soviet Union had largely lost any organic connection to the Church.[4]

In the early 1940s, things started to change. Archbishop Kevork Chorekchyan was designated *locum tenens* after the suspicious death of Khoren I, which was followed by permission to hold new elections.[5] The electoral process for the Catholicos of All Armenians started on 16 June 1945. Eight days later, Kevork VI was consecrated Catholicos. During his time, the Armenian Church went through a considerable revival.

In Istanbul, after the sudden death of Patriarch Mesrob Naroyan on 31 May 1944, Archbishop Kevork Arslanyan was appointed *locum tenens* by the Religious Assembly on 2 June. I have drawn on three sources for biographical information on Archbishop Arslanyan: Karnik Step'anyan's *Gensakragan Pararan*,[6] Kevork Pamukciyan's contribution in *Biyografileriyle Ermeniler*[7] and Toros Azadyan's biographical work, *Kevork Arch. Arslanyan (1867–1951)*.[8] According to this last, Arslanyan was born with the baptismal name Karekin in 1867 in the village of Pingean of Agn/ Eğin. After attending the local Mesrobyan School, he worked in the pharmacy belonging to his uncle, Dr Kevork Bekyan, in 1882–5.[9] He was then appointed principal of the Mesrobyan School, married Nazeni, and had five children. In 1890 he relocated to Istanbul and, along with his brother, opened a factory of underwear and socks. The following year, he was entitled '*Fanilacıbaşı*' (Chief Lingerie Producer) by the Court.[10] According to Kevork Pamukciyan, because of some calamity in his family on which no further details are given, he decided to embrace religion.[11] The catastrophe hinted at by Pamukciyan is the Hamidian massacres. Arslanyan lost his wife, father and children during these massacres. Only one of his daughters, Hripsime, survived.[12] In 1898 he was appointed director of orphanages in Divrighi and served in

Tokat and then in Sivas.[13] After receiving his religious degree (*apegha*, or celibate monk), he became deputy director of the monastery of Surp Nshan. He was then appointed as the religious leader of Tokat.[14] In 1904–14 he served in Malatya, Kharpert (Harput), Tekirdagh and Adana as a religious leader.[15] After the Adana massacres of 1909, he went to the region and brought some of the orphaned girls to the *arhesdanots'* (workshops) of Istanbul, where they could learn handicrafts to earn a living.[16] Step'anyan's account notes that he was in exile at wartime,[17] while Pamukciyan's account shows a gap between his religious leadership in 1914 and his arrival to Istanbul in 1921. Azadyan provides a detailed account of those years. According to this source, Arslanyan was exiled to Idlib (Syria), where he contracted typhoid. US Ambassador Morgenthau intervened to send him to Aleppo.[18] After a stay in Beirut for medical treatment, he returned to Adana by the end of 1919.[19] In late 1920, he had a confrontation with members of the ARF at church and was wounded. He left Adana for Istanbul in March 1921.[20] In 1922, he was consecrated archbishop in Echmiadzin, and became *locum tenens* of the Patriarchate of Istanbul (1922–7). He was sent to Ethiopia in 1928 to consecrate the Armenian church of Surp Kēōrk in Addis Ababa.[21] Upon his return, he wrote a travelogue, *Ugheworut'iwn Et'ovhia*, in addition to an unpublished study on Armenians in Pingyan. He had been writing articles in Armenian newspapers and magazines both in Istanbul and abroad since 1890.[22] Arslanyan was again *locum tenens* from 1944 to 1950, the period marked by the patriarchal election crisis.

The disputes began in June 1944 and made problematic the mechanism of Arslanyan's appointment as *locum tenens* to the Patriarchate of Istanbul for the second time. In *Lipananean Husher*, Toros Azadyan refers to the minutes of the process that led to Arslanyan's re-appointment – although incomplete, the minutes remain the only accessible record. According to Azadyan, since the Civil/ Political Assembly was inactive, the approval of prominent members of the community was required, along with the eight votes of the 14-member Religious Assembly.[23] This means that some non-elected members of the community played an important role in the appointment of the *locum tenens*. After Archbishop Arslanyan's appointment, only a few meetings were held with the Religious Assembly before he dissolved it on 21 August 1944.[24] Some members submitted a letter to Arslanyan in July 1944, requesting the appointment of an administrative body that would counterbalance the heavy duties of the Religious Assembly. According to the report presented to the GNA on the day of the patriarchal election, 2 December 1950, Archbishop Arslanyan refused to convene the Religious Assembly and argued that it had lost the majority of its members.[25] Consequently, the abovementioned members of the Religious Assembly issued a press release opposing his decision on the grounds that he had been appointed by the same Religious Assembly; Archbishop Arslanyan should have called the Assembly for a meeting in order to clarify his points, as the Assembly was the only body elected by the community and recognised by the state in the administration of the community's religious affairs.[26] Hence, with a public statement, the Religious Assembly invited Archbishop Arslanyan to return to the legal tradition of the church.[27] This incident was reported in *Lipananean Husher*:

> Six members of the Religious Assembly have requested that the legal authority of the Civil Assembly be transferred to the Religious Assembly, which was against the [Armenian National] Constitution. Thus, upon the rejection of their request, the members resigned on their own volition, while the *locum tenens* formed a Temporary Religious Assembly with the participation of two out of the eight former members, who remained loyal to the Constitution.[28]

The Administrative Committees' situation was no better than the Religious Assembly's. Many of their members had passed away, some had resigned, and many others remained on duty long past their term.[29]

However, beside serious issues of administration, there were other, less important problems that caused unease in the community, one of them being the issue of the seat. Archbishop Arslanyan wanted to use the handmade seat that was prepared in 1904 for Catholicos Sahak of Cilicia (Sis/Kozan) on the occasion of his visit to Istanbul.[30] According to the official report of the Investigation Committee, his request was denied, and another seat offered. The seat became an important enough issue for Arslanyan to express his discontent to the governor of Istanbul.[31] I only came across this incident in the Investigation Committee's explicitly anti-Arslanyan report.

There were other incidents involving Arslanyan that adversely affected his popularity: Patriarch Mesrob Naroyan was planning to will his property to the Surp P'rgich' Hospital, and discussed the issue with the chief physician of the hospital, Bağdasar Manuelyan, and with the head of the hospital administration, Hrant Peştimalcıyan.[32] However, he suddenly passed away, before the formalities were completed. *Locum tenens* Archbishop Kevork Arslanyan interfered with the process by confiscating the Patriarch's belongings in his office,[33] which included 50 Egyptian shares, 182 pieces of Ottoman gold money, an emerald ring, and his memoirs, among other items.[34] The conflict turned into a legal process by the end of 1944. The court confirmed the legal validity of late Patriarch Naroyan's will and ordered that the belongings be returned to their new rightful owner, the hospital. Arslanyan did not accept the court's decision, arguing that it was the Patriarchate, and not the late Patriarch, who had previously owned these items.[35] Besides, a sum of 15,560 Turkish lira had been found on the late Patriarch after his death and trusted to Khachig (Haçik) Batmayan;[36] however, Arslanyan argued that this money was also national property. Although it was stated that Batmayan had returned the money to the hospital upon the court decision,[37] we understand from the news items of 1947 that another court case was still in progress. After long discussions and conflicts, an agreement was reached through arbitrage, but could not be put into effect due to Archbishop Arslanyan's withdrawal. The court battle lasted three years, until April 1947, when Arslanyan lost and was forced to deliver the aforementioned goods and money to the owners.[38] However, the freezing of the Patriarch's personal account in the Dutch Bank and the account of the Patriarchate by the Armenian Hospital administration was only lifted in October 1947.[39] The two officially recognised community institutions, the Patriarchate and the Surp P'rgich' Armenian Hospital thus came into longstanding conflict because of this incident. Though not the only serious issue that occupied the community's agenda right after the death of Patriarch Naroyan, the case escalated the patriarchal election crisis on which there are very few sources. However, it is interesting to note that the two major sources do not mention this background.[40]

After the death of Patriarch Naroyan, the inheritance issue and the entire legal procedure, along with the existing legal, administrative and social problems, divided the Armenian community into two main camps. The positions of these camps became even more pronounced throughout the drawn-out process of the patriarch's non-election, which lasted until the end of 1950. *Marmara* was in the anti-Arslanyan camp, while *Nor Lur* and *Jamanak* sided with Arslanyan. According to the oral historical account of Varujan Köseyan, the supporters of each group would buy all the opponent newspapers from vendors to prevent circulation.[41] The crisis was not limited to the community in Istanbul. The process of non-election soon became an issue for Armenians all over the world, including the Catholicosates of Cilicia and of Echmiadzin, and various other centres.

In June 1945, Kevork VI became Catolicos of all Armenians in Echmiadzin. The *locum tenens* of the Patriarchate of Istanbul was expected to have attended the election. However, according to the news published in *Nor Lur*, Archbishop Kevork Arslanyan and his delegation could not receive their Soviet visas in time to attend the election process.[42] The Patriarchal delegation of Istanbul consisted of clergymen and a group of prominent members of the community, but the latter created another debate, since the prominent members in question were not elected and, therefore, their capacity for representation was questionable. Dr Peştimalcıyan, who was both the administrator of the hospital and a member of the General National Assembly, sent a telegram to Echmiadzin in this latter capacity, stating that the lay members of the delegation were not authorised to represent the community.[43] The official report of the GNA Investigation Committee referred to this point and stated that paragraphs 60 and 61 of the *Nizamname/* Constitution required a special meeting of the Civil–Political Assembly to choose members of the committee for the election of Catholicos.[44] According to the report of the Committee, Arslanyan intended to go to Echmiadzin with arbitrarily chosen persons, and had even auctioned the Echmiadzin journey to the most compliant, highest bidders.[45] In August 1945, an Armenian newspaper from Egypt, *Araks*, criticised the telegram sent to Echmiadzin by the representatives of the Armenian community in Istanbul, condemning their initiative as inconvenient.[46] In September 1945, according to the news item published in *Nor Lur*, Prime Minister Şükrü Saraçoğlu expressed his appreciation of the Armenian community: 'The Armenians of Turkey consulted us when they were invited to participate in the catholicosate elections in Echmiadzin. We told them that they were free to go, undoubtedly without forgetting their Turkish citizenship throughout their trip.'[47] An editorial note attached to the news item confirmed that the Armenian delegation of

Turkey had never forgotten its deeply cherished Turkish citizenship during this trip and would never allow it to be maligned.[48] Saraçoğlu's statement should be read in the context of the post-San Francisco Conference process, when debates about a fifth column were in full force and the shock of territorial claims was a scathing issue. The religious leader of the Armenian community in Bulgaria, Archbishop Krikor Garabetyan, issued a statement when he visited his family members in Istanbul, to clarify that although the telegram from Istanbul to Echmiadzin caused pain, the delegation accomplished its work satisfactorily.[49] The delegation reached Yerevan after the election and could not participate in the election process.

An Institutional Crisis Turns Social

Among the disputes that arose in the churches in 1947, two took place in Feriköy and Balat during services. The latter subsided only after police intervention.[50] Incidents continued. *Nor Lur* reported again in June 1947 about a fight during the liturgy between the priest and his assistant on the altar, reportedly because the latter did not obey ceremonial etiquette.[51]

In December 1948, B. Hovnan Palakashyan (Palakaşyan) published an open letter to the priest of Gedikpaşa, Hosrof Misakyan, asking him not to mention the name of the *locum tenens* during the liturgy, repeating the news in *Marmara* that the Armenian community in Paris had undertaken such a protest.[52] If his request were to go disregarded, Palakashyan threatened to shout in the church, 'Do not mention his name!'[53] A couple of days later, columnist Dr K. Shahnazaryan (Şahnazaryan) cited examples from the history of the Armenian Church to show that the community had effectively revolted against the Patriarch in the churches by shouting 'Do not mention his name!'[54] There were other such incidents in the community administration as well. *Marmara* reported that, in one of the biggest communities in Feriköy, a self-appointed group administered the community affairs, although their names were not even mentioned in the circulars.[55] According to *Marmara*, as a rule, local communities used to elect their own administrators, but in this case there was a self-appointed local administrator on duty.

While Armenian socio-political life was defined by the conflict over the patriarchal election crisis, in January 1949, Archbishop Athenagoras was elected Patriarch of the Ecumenical Orthodox Church in Istanbul. Athenagoras I arrived from the United States on Air Force One.[56] He first paid a visit to the statue of Mustafa Kemal in Taksim Square and then to the Patriarchate in Fener.[57] Athenagoras I gave his first speech in Turkish, whereas the Metropolitan Bishop of Bursa, who welcomed Athenagoras at the airport, made his in Greek.[58] Athenagoras stated in an interview that he had travelled from the United States to Turkey with a group of Turkish journalists whose presence was useful to him,[59] and that he intended to rescue millions of Orthodox people from the Soviet regime.[60] He carried a personal letter from President Truman, which he delivered to President İnönü during his visit to Ankara on 5 February. The relations between other non-Muslim groups and the state affected each community. Therefore Archbishop Athenagoras' policy vis-à-vis the state had implications for the Armenian Patriarchate as well.

In the meantime, the crisis within the Armenian community continued to grow. On 7 March 1949, Archbishop Kevork Arslanyan received two petitions requesting a meeting with him. The signatories were 38 ecclesiastics (out of 47), of which nine withdrew their signatures in the next couple of days because they chose to wait in the patriarchate for the *locum tenens* to arrive and ask for a meeting.[61] Arslanyan reportedly told them that he was going to discuss the request with the Religious Assembly after Easter.[62] However, the opposing clergy did not agree. On 10 March, Arslanyan responded to these petitions by suspending five clergymen as organisers. The official response of the Patriarchate was sent to both daily newspapers, *Marmara* and *Jamanak*. *Marmara* published the Patriarchate's text next to the ecclesiastics' response to the *locum tenens*.[63] *Nor Lur* did not publish the original petition of the clerics, but printed a lengthy editorial whose arguments closely resembled the response by the *locum tenens* a few days later. However, *Nor Lur* made a rather interesting point about the religious leader of the Armenians in Bulgaria, Archbishop Kusan, who was still in town. According to *Nor Lur*, he was the most probable candidate for Patriarch of Istanbul, given the age and the health problems of the *locum tenens*.[64]

Another long editorial published in *Nor Lur* on 12 March quoted *Jamanak*, making it clear that *Jamanak* too found the initiative of the clergy inappropriate.[65] Thus, *Nor Lur* and *Jamanak* were in the same camp, while *Marmara* had chosen the other side. According to *Nor Lur*, the whole crisis was a part or result of the decades-long administrative crisis and, therefore, Archbishop Arslanyan could not be held responsible for the current situation. Moreover, based on the legal tradition of the Patriarchate, *Nor Lur* argued that the action of the clerics was unacceptable.[66] On the other hand, the clerics did not comply with their suspension and continued their duties in the churches, still refusing to mention the name of the *locum tenens* during liturgy.[67] The mention of his name became an issue in most churches throughout the period of crisis. On 16 March the suspended clerics appointed Archimandrite Superior Hmayag Bahtiyaryan as *locum tenens*.[68] *Nor Lur* always referred to Bahtiyaryan mockingly as '*bantogĕndir*', ie. 'elected in a hotel', for being appointed *locum tenens* by his supporters in a hotel. A patriarch or a catholicos would be *azkĕndir*, elected by the *azk* ('nation'). On 18 March, Bahtiyaryan went to Ankara in order to ratify his mandate and received a register number.[69] In the meantime, the Turkish press took an interest in the conflict. Priest Tovma Shigaher (Şigaher) gave an interview to *Yeni Sabah* and Hmayag Bahtiyaryan gave one to *Son Telgraf*.[70] While *Marmara* translated and published these news items and commentaries, *Nor Lur* just responded to the situation and refused to have its columns taken up by the oppositional clerics. *Yeni Sabah* reported the incident as the 'Bifurcation in the Armenian Patriarchate' and *Son Telgraf*, as the 'Incident at the Armenian Patriarchate'. The former also published Archbishop Arslanyan's statement. The next day, another street quarrel took place between Toros Azadyan, who was pro-Arslanyan, and Dikran Karakızyan. The incident came to an end only through police intervention.[71] The following day, *Marmara* reported that the Armenian communities in Belgium and France did not mention the name of the *locum tenens*, but continued to mention the name of the late Patriarch Naroyan.[72] A four-and-a-half-page letter from Arslanyan to Kevork VI on 16 March 1949 starts with a reminder of the historical background that Arslanyan had provided for the Catholicos in 1945, when he was in Echmiadzin on the occasion of the election of Kevork VI:

> The national and religious life of the Armenians in Turkey has continued under dire [...] circumstances for decades. [...] The General National Assembly, the administration and the committees had already ceased their activities; only the religious assembly still maintained its majority of members and yet, because

of resignations and the death of one or two of its members, it had
to cease activities as well. We established a temporary religious
assembly based on the authority accorded to us in accordance with
our regulations.[73]

Archbishop Arslanyan's statements confirm the fact that there was no
administration per se, and that he had allowed himself to constitute a
Religious Assembly. He writes about the opposing clerics' petition and
statement concerning the election of a new Religious Assembly, which,
he argues, would normally be the duty of the currently inoperative
General National Assembly but was now undertaken by a temporary
religious committee. Another argument Arslanyan makes is that the
Patriarchate should have waited for the new law on minorities to be put
into effect by the government. He also provided a long report on three of
the suspended clerics and the coverage in the Turkish press.[74]

While Armenian churches as institutions were having various political
problems in the countries where they operated, in Turkey the church was
the only institution to regulate the entire community. However, as shown
in Chapter 2, because post-1923 policies undermined the administrative
mechanisms of the community, situations like the sudden death of the
Patriarch could easily turn into a crisis with immediate social and
international repercussions in all Armenian institutions and communities.
From the perspective of power relations, these were the most opportune
occasions to create arbitrary solutions and practices as power dictated, with
neither legal basis nor community approval. On the other hand, the social
impact of the patriarchal crisis is worthy of scrutiny in demonstrating the
general involvement of the people and their will to participate in
administration and decision-making processes.

Clashes of Power

By 1949 the political conflict had already reached international
dimensions. The power claims of Echmiadzin and the Patriarchate,
and as well as the reactions of the state and society, all clashed with
one another. It is interesting to note who tried to obtain legitimacy
from whom.

According to the news published in the Turkish press, Arslanyan sent
two letters to the Ministry of Interior, the Prime Minister and the

governor.[75] Despite the fact that this piece of news was published on 13 March and his letter to Echmiadzin was dated 16 March, the *locum tenens* did not mention his letters to the Turkish government in the latter. On 18 March the issue took another dimension with the intervention of the GDPF, reportedly upon the Patriarchal order to suspend priests' salaries in Beyoğlu, Kadıköy and Yeniköy. The article stated that the foundations of these churches were directly administered by the GDPF,[76] and that the priests of these churches belonged to the opposing group. The next day, *Marmara* reported that both Arslanyan and the opposing priests had visited the governor, and that the issue had been covered in the Turkish newspapers *Tasvir*, *Hürriyet*, *Yeni Sabah* and *Son Telgraf*.[77] On 21 March, *Marmara* ran an article on the visit of the opposing clerics in Ankara.[78] In the same issue, it enthusiastically reported that the oppositional group had appointed Bahtiyaryan as *locum tenens*. Upon their arrival to Ankara, the priests first visited Atatürk's temporary mausoleum and then the Prime Minister and the Minister of Interior.[79] Turkish newspapers also closely followed the situation. On 23 March, Archbishop Arslanyan issued a press release stating that he was still *locum tenens* and that any information to the contrary was unfounded.[80]

By the end of March, another protest took place during the funeral of Hosrof Misakyan, who was one of the members of the Religious Assembly. Meanwhile, the priest of Kayseri, Fr Haygazun, condemned the acts of the oppositional group, which constituted the only news item from the provinces regarding the situation in Istanbul.[81]

Around the same time, Nusret Safa wrote in *Son Posta* that, if Echmiadzin intervened in the affairs of the Armenian Church in Turkey, the whole issue might turn political.[82] Another crisis was simultaneously brewing in Egypt within the local Armenian community, with a similar dimension of state–community conflict. According to the story published in *Marmara*, the Catholicos of All Armenians had requested that certain rules be followed for an election process in Egypt, but the government refused this intervention by the Catholicos and renounced any authority other than its own.[83] Soon afterwards, a similar incident took place in Bulgaria: Archbishop Kusan, who was the religious leader of the Armenian Church in Bulgaria and had Turkish citizenship, was removed from his post because the Bulgarian government required clerics to have Bulgarian citizenship.[84] Archbishop Kusan himself might have wanted to keep his citizenship in order to be able to pose his candidacy for the patriarchal elections in Turkey. The Armenian Church thus had to struggle with changing political and legal structures in three countries at once: Turkey, Egypt and Bulgaria. There were thus clashes due to the international conjuncture, especially to the fact that the centre of the Armenian Church was in the Soviet Union, and that legal mechanisms had to be in place to protect the authority of the nation state. Nusret Safa's statement, 'If Echmiadzin interferes, our stomach might get upset',[85] thus points to a conflict that was a matter of postwar international politics, and no longer a communal conflict of Armenians in Istanbul. First, communities became a space for the power struggle of nation states and, second, they remained squeezed between the national authorities of the host countries and the Church headquarters in Echmiadzin, which in turn had its own power struggle with the Soviet government. In terms of the hierarchy within the Armenian Church, the special position of the Patriarchate in Istanbul is noticeable, along with the Patriarchate in Jerusalem and the Catholicosate in Antelias, which enjoyed a wide range of autonomy in the Armenian ecclesiastical system.

By mid-April, the issue had already turned into an information war, with interventions, statements and news widely published in the Turkish press, especially after Bahtiyaryan's 14 April letter to Arslanyan regarding his removal from office.[86] In order to become a point of reference for the Turkish press, *Marmara* started to publish a Turkish section (which hardly lasted a week) by the title 'Factions in the Armenian Patriarchate' ('*Ermeni Patrikahnesi İhtilafı*') 'to inform the Turkish press of the inner layers of the conflict'.[87] The Turkish press again started to call on Armenian individuals to express their thoughts and, in one way or another, to become representatives of their community. *Marmara* reported that *Tasvir* had published a long article with statements from Archbishop Arslanyan and a certain Hagop Chnaryan (Çınaryan), who was said to be a member of the (then non-existent) General National Assembly. Chnaryan claimed that Arslanyan was loyal to the Turkish state, although he had been threatened in Adana and in Beirut because of his pro-Turkish stance.[88] Another Armenian from Hatay, Misak Bey, confirmed his claims by saying that Arslanyan had been threatened by the Armenian Revolutionary Federation and that all Armenians in Europe were against him.[89] Misak Bey referred to the ARF, the Armenians in Beirut, or the Armenians in Europe (which were not objective categories, as they were all embedded in the discourse of anti-Armenian campaigns) in order to whitewash Arslanyan's image, implying the 'good Armenian / bad Armenian' divide. In this context, as an Armenian from Hatay, Misak Bey was the 'good' Armenian, as was Hagop Chnaryan, while the ARF and others were the 'bad' Armenians. The attempt to secure the position of a *locum tenens* by asserting his pro-Turkishness in the overly anti-Armenian newspaper *Tasvir*, and by using a language that marginalised the Armenian Catholicosate of Cilicia in Beirut, positioned the crisis squarely within anti-Armenian discourse.

In April 1949 *Marmara* reported the mention of Archimandrite Superior Bahtiyaryan as *locum tenens* during the Sunday mass in the Armenian church of Gedikpaşa. The article explained that deputies had never been mentioned in the Armenian church tradition, but the name of the late Patriarch had been always mentioned until the election of its successor.[90] *Nor Lur*, which was not very much in favour of publishing the incidents taking place in the churches, wrote of awkward situations in various churches such as Beşiktaş, Feriköy and Kadıköy, among others.[91] The incident of the Easter mass in the church of the Patriarchate explains the gravity of the situation. According to *Nor Lur*, the Single Trustee of the church in Kumkapı had invited the self-appointed *locum tenens* Bahtiyaryan to conduct the religious ceremony of Easter.[92] According to Azadyan, on 17 April, when Arslanyan wanted to attend Easter mass, he confronted Archmadrite Superior Bahtiyaryan and his group of followers who had entered the church at night to conduct the mass.[93] *Marmara* reported that Bahtiyaryan presided over the ceremony, while Archbishop Arslanyan could not enter from the door of the central church.[94] *Marmara* estimated the number of attendants of the Easter mass to be 3,000.[95] This figure may have been exaggerated, but still gives an idea about the public response to, or support for, the oppositional clerics. *Marmara* reported various cases from different churches on Easter day; for instance, a quarrel between pro-Arslanyan and pro-Bahtiyaryan priests in the Armenian cemetery of Bakırköy was only brought to an end through police intervention.[96] On 21 April, Bahtiyaryan announced that the seat in the main church in Kumkapı belonged to him:[97] Both deputies, one recognised by the state, and the other the alternative deputy, were across from each another on the same street, thus positioned literally against each other. According to an article in *Marmara*, Arslanyan asked the police to take Bahtiyaryan out of the church, but the police did not comply, arguing that the Turkish state was secular.[98] Although the truth of these dialogues cannot be confirmed, it is obvious that there was a confrontation on Easter Sunday. Toros Azadyan also confirmed that Archbishop Arslanyan could not enter the central church across the patriarchate.[99]

In early May, *Baikar*, an Armenian newspaper from Boston affiliated with the Ramgavar Party, ran a commentary on the situation in Istanbul and condemned *Marmara*'s position.[100] Five trustees from five local communities asked Arslanyan to resign in front of his house.[101] Lütfü Kırdar, Governor of Istanbul, held meetings with the *locum tenens* and the opposition groups, and announced that the patriarchal election would take place soon.[102] After the meeting with Arslanyan, on 7 May 1949, *Jamanak* reported that the governor requested the preparation of 'a legal code responding to the current needs' in order to proceed with the patriarchal election process.[103] It is not clear what kind of legal code was being negotiated. On 11 May, *Marmara* issued a peculiar report on the meeting between the governor and Bahtiyaryan's group: the article was written in the passive tense and presented the whole crisis as resolved by the rightful intervention of the governor or the state.[104] On 16 May, *Marmara* reported about a two-hour-long meeting at the governor's office, together with the editor-in-chief of *Jamanak*. The governor was well aware of the nature of the conflict and the two camps. A telegram from the Catholicosate of Echmiadzin, dated 18 May, followed suit in a facsimile published in *Marmara* and *Nor Lur* on 20 May, albeit with a remarkable difference in presentation. *Nor Lur* published the photograph of Catholicos Kevork VI with a full front-page coverage. Kevork VI approved the suspension and did not recognise Bahtiyaryan as *locum tenens*.[105] The letter had a certain impact; for instance, *Marmara*'s language about the crisis became remarkably more cautious. However, the crisis had already become widespread, and a letter from Echmiadzin was not enough to bridge the gap that had grown over the past five years. Churches had turned into fields of struggle between the two camps. Easter, funerals, or regular Sunday mass were all occasions for outbursts of tension in the community. The social aspect of the conflict could also be seen in the press release of the Koghtan Choir, of the central Armenian church of Istanbul, which stated their discontent 'on behalf of the majority of Armenians in Kumkapı' concerning the unresolved problem of suspensions, as well as their refusal to sing in the case where arbitrary decisions by Archbishop Arslanyan continued.[106] There was a similar situation in Gedikpaşa, where six choirs united to hold mass for the late priest Hosrov. Although Arslanyan refused the united choir's participation in the mass because Hosrov's funeral had turned into a battle, the ceremony did take place with the participation of the six choirs.[107]

The position of the administration becomes a point of curiosity in the discussions of the affairs of the church. It is mystifying to read these newspapers and to occasionally see mentions of 'the administration' without any actual quote or statement. During the first weeks of July, the newspapers were preparing the reader/ community for the upcoming patriarchal elections, although it was still not clear how and when they would take place.[108] The preparations for elections was a result of the appeals to the governor's office by the opposing clergy, who requested permission to start the electoral process. The governor of Istanbul responded that his office would not interfere in the conflict,[109] which was interpreted as permissiveness by the opposing clergy. On the other hand, citing *Jamanak*, *Marmara* reported that some people had visited the shops of Armenian jewellers in the Covered Bazaar to ask for money for the churches, which were deprived of their budget because of the conflict with the Patriarchate. There had even been a quarrel with a certain Davud Şükrü, in which the Armenian jewellers and police had to intervene.[110] *Nor Lur* alluded to similar fights in the church and elsewhere, as well as reporting on Davud Şükrü and the money-collection, without reference to the quarrel and the police intervention.[111]

Yet, the core of the problem lay in the fact that the legal structure of the community had been bypassed in 1934. For the sake of state-enforced secularism, the patriarch had lost the social and secular role of the leader of the Armenian *millet*, and become an exclusively religious leader.[112] To legitimise its new way of existence, the administration of the day issued a new official letterhead and stamp.[113] A *de facto* administration was formed and remained in power until the introduction of the Single Trustee System. While all this was taking place, the General National Assembly had more than 50 members, some of whom had compiled a regulation in reference to the *Nizamname*/Constitution and presented it to the governor with the support of the extant administration.[114] According to an article published in *Nor Lur*, this amounted to 'giving up'.[115] As far as I understand, the author, Datevatsi, wanted to point out an issue that has remained crucial to this day: Two parallel processes were taking place, the first being the limitation of the patriarch's authority to the religious realm, which undermined the influence and the cooperation of elected bodies (comprised of laymen) in decision-making processes regarding religious issues. Yet, secondly, as I understand from various articles, there was a state intervention or in fact hindrance, in the call for a meeting of the General National Assembly.

Thus, although a General National Assembly existed, it was not functional; its existence and functioning depended on governmental permission.[116] After the resignation of Zaven Patriarch in 1922, Archbishop Kevork Arslanyan was *locum tenens* until the election in 1927. Varujan Köseyan states in his book on the Armenian Hospital that Arslanyan foresaw the danger of not having any Civil–Political Assembly and called the members of the GNA who were still in Istanbul; they then voted for the formation of a Civil Assembly headed by Artur Maghakyan.[117] Maghakyan had put all his effort into making the administrative system of the community functional; a new Civil–Political Assembly was elected in 1927 and the patriarchal election proceeded.[118] Both the accounts of Köseyan and *Nor Lur* make it clear that the major challenge was to obtain permission to meet for the GNA; without that mechanism, the other steps could not follow. The same problem recurred in 1949, namely, the need for governmental permission to proceed with the election. Oppositional ecclesiastics asked for permission from the governor in early June.[119] Although I could not find the original permission document, *Marmara* assumed that the government had allowed the committee to organise the patriarchal elections.[120] On the other hand, on 15 June Arslanyan sent a letter to Prime Minister Şemseddin Günaltay, requesting permission to reconstitute the GNA.[121] Upon these developments in Istanbul, the Catholicosate of Echmiadzin asked the Catholicosate of Cilicia in Antelias to take care of the crisis.[122] In the meantime, *Marmara* was enthusiastically preparing its readers for the patriarchal election, which was apparently a process run by the opposition. The government and the Patriarchate were both trying to intervene.

The report of the Investigative Committee of the GNA includes minutes of the meeting held on 26 July 1949[123] by Archbishop Arslanyan, in his house.[124] According to these minutes, Arslanyan, along with Toros

Azadyan, Mardiros Koç (editor-in-chief of *Jamanak*), and two more people, met the Prime Minister Şemseddin Günaltay in his house in Erenköy.[125] Günaltay was briefed about the conflict, after which he declared his willingness to intervene in the illegal process and send a response to the Patriarchate.[126] Following the meeting with Günaltay, the permission to organise the GNA was cancelled and, instead, a document was presented to the National Assembly of Turkey regarding the administration of Armenians in Turkey. This document stated that the patriarch was a mere ecclesiastic and had no right to represent the community. Second, only the clergy could elect the patriarch, and laymen had no right to interfere with the election process,[127] which, again, was tantamount to the repeal of the *Nizamname*/Constitution. Minutes stated that a delegation visited President İnönü to explain the secular nature of the Armenian Constitution. The proposal was withdrawn before ratification.[128] On the other hand, Bahtiyaryan's group organised the meeting on July 18 despite its absolute prohibition by Arslanyan. As a result, a list was compiled, comprising six candidates for patriarch.[129] *Marmara* published the list of possible GNA members: 22, including the editor-in-chief of *Nor Lur*, Vahan Toşikyan,[130] were members of the former GNA, while 71 people asked to become members in order to organise the election.

The Intervention of the Catholicos

On July 29 Catholicos Kevork VI of Holy Echmiadzin sent an investigation request to the Armenian Patriarchate of Istanbul, asking to send delegates to Antelias to solve the problem,[131] while Karekin I, the Catholicos of Cilicia, called both sides of the conflict to Antelias, as ordered by Kevork VI.[132] On 1 and 6 August, *Marmara* published both letters in facsimile.[133] On 6 August, *Nor Lur*[134] published a message from Kevork VI, in which he declared all assemblies, civil and religious, defunct.[135] However, none of these developments brought the churches any peace; the newspapers were filled with incidents, quarrels, and police interventions throughout.

On 8 August, Hayganuş Mark, who was a regular contributor to *Nor Lur* and the wife of Vahan Toşikyan, its editor-in-chief, wrote a letter to her colleague Avedik Isahakyan, a celebrated writer in Armenia. She asked him to talk to the Catholicos, to explain the severity of the situation, and to help re-establish peace in the churches.[136]

Unfortunately, some suspicious laymen, with the definite support of a newspaper, and all those who had deep-seated ill will, united to form an opposition with no regard for the decision of suspension of His Holiness. [. . .] These days, the church has turned into a cinema [or] a battlefield: they refuse all [. . .] orders and measures. Brothers are armed against each other, as if the blood in their veins were not the same Armenian blood.[137]

On 15 August, four representatives of the opposition group had already arrived in Antelias, but the *locum tenens* refused to send representatives. Instead, he submitted a 31-page report on the crisis.[138] Upon the insistence of the Catholicos, just one person, Toros Azadyan, arrived in Antelias on 9 September as the representative of Archbishop Arslanyan.[139] Both Puzant Yeghiayan and Toros Azadyan described the situation as a trial. The minutes of the trial where both sides came together on 22 September, after separate meetings with Catholicos Karekin I, can be found in Azadyan's book, *Lipananean Husher*.[140] The decision was sent to Echmiadzin on 24 September 1949.[141] Catholicos Karekin wrote a letter to Echmiadzin, asking Kevork VI to allow the suspended clerics to return to their duties, prohibiting their participation in the upcoming patriarchal elections, and asking *locum tenens* Kevork Arslanyan not to pose his candidacy in the patriarchal elections.[142] On the same day, *Marmara* published an unusual official letter by the GDPF Head of Beyoğlu, which wrote that the priest Husig had been dismissed on 22 August 1949 upon the request of the Patriarchate.[143] Turkish newspapers followed the issue closely. The echoes of the meeting in Beirut also reached them: *Son Telgraf* reported about the cancellation of the suspensions and *Cumhuriyet* was rather suspicious about the possible results of the meetings held in Beirut.[144] Nonetheless, the decision of the Catholicos of Cilicia remained undisclosed for quite some time and had still not reached Istanbul in August 1950 – a situation harshly criticised by *Marmara*.[145]

Upon the cancellation of the Single Trustee System, toward the end of October 1949, local communities started to prepare for the election of the administration of foundations. These elections were also part of the patriarchal election crisis, since all communities on the local level were split into pro- and anti-Arslanyan factions. On the one hand, the reintroduction of the election system was heartily welcomed; on the other, it opened up a new space of conflict in the context of the patriarchal election crisis. When a call for local elections was made by the Central Administration and signed by Vartan Akgül and Levon Papazyan, yet another discussion arose as to whether the Central Administration had the authority to call for such an election.[146] According to the pro-Arslanyan camp, the Central Administration was no longer in power and therefore had no right to call for elections;[147] but on the other side, the argument was that the Central Administration had never resigned and therefore still maintained authority. The former's argument was based on the abolishment of the Central Administration during the term of Patriarch Naroyan. As there had been no General National Assembly since then, there was no Central Administration either. Thus, there could be no legitimate mechanism of community administration for the pro-Arslanyan camp. On the other hand, many local communities responded to the call positively. On the administrative level, the non-existence of the GNA was a real problem that affected the community as a whole; for instance, the administration of the Surp P'rgich' Hospital could not be appointed. The hospital administration should have been changed every two years after the elections, but by 1950, for the first time in the history of the Hospital, an administration had remained on duty for 16 years due to the absence of the GNA. As a result, the administration invited new candidates to its organisation in order to produce a solution to the *de facto* situation.[148]

By the end of 1949, local communities started to organise elections for the administration of their respective foundations. The election process was complete chaos. In Beyoğlu, Feriköy and Gedikpaşa the problems were multi-layered: In the case of Beyoğlu more than one administration had the right to organise the election: One was authorised by the government through the STS, while the other had been the administration before the STS, working on the assumption that it retained the right to organise the elections because it had never resigned. The conflicts could not be resolved and the police intervened to stop several quarrels. Through the election process, the whole tension of the past six years of non-election (a result of the STS) and the abolition of communal administrative systems exploded in a way that was unique in the preceding century. The candidates of the opposition won the local elections, which in turn accelerated the patriarchal election process.

Under these socio-political conditions, a new newspaper, *Paros*, started publication as a daily on 23 November 1949 and then turned into a weekly. In its first issue, editor-in-chief Takvor Acun (1894–1976) stated that the rationale of publication was the bifurcation created and fuelled by the two daily newspapers, *Marmara* and *Jamanak*. By contrast, *Paros* wanted to provide unbiased information on the entire crisis.[149] While the birth of a newspaper from such social and political chaos shows the depth of the community's upheaval, it also reflects the lasting dynamism in the society. In its first issue, *Paros* writes, 'We must sincerely admit that we do not and cannot like Arslanyan, and we hate Bahtiyaryan and Şigaher, among others, because we know them very well.'[150] As I have already argued in this book, *Paros* diagnosed that the existing crisis was a result of the process that started in 1923, with the loss of sovereignty over communal affairs.

Varujan Köseyan's account about the years of crisis confirms that even the church across from the Patriarchate and the Patriarchate itself had turned into a space of struggle. Köseyan told me that Archbishop Arslanyan's opponents prevented him from even entering the church. The official report of the Investigation Committee also stated that the Patriarchate was mostly empty since the *locum tenens* did not regularly come to his office, and that the Patriarchate was even closed and under special protection for a period of time in 1949 against possible attempts at occupation.[151]

On 28 January 1950, the Administration, along with 18 members of the GNA, invited the *locum tenens* to leave his position. This letter was also sent to the Prime Minister.[152] Archbishop Arslanyan and his Advisory Committee decided to go to Ankara to declare the illegitimacy of the Administration.[153]

In February, Kevork VI issued an order suspending three opposing clergymen[154] and barring another three[155] from Armenian church service.[156] The most acrimonious part of the three-page-long document concerns Bahtiyaryan's declarations to *Yeni Sabah*, which quotes the following excerpt *verbatim*:

All our actions are within the limits of legality. The government knows every step we take. We inform the government of our actions. It is not accurate to say that we were punished by Yerevan, and even if that were the case, we would not have listened. It is a lie that we appealed to Yerevan and received no answer. An appeal to Yerevan means ignoring the Turkish government. We would not do such a terrible thing.[157]

It is obvious that this statement especially incited anger in Echmiadzin. In a letter written in February 1950, Kevork VI stated that he had received Karekin's conclusion, but not the grounds for it, and therefore could not make a final decision.[158]

In June 1950 Kevork VI corresponded with Hrach'ya Grigoryan, the chairman of the Committee of Affairs of the Armenian Church adjunct to the Council of Ministers of Soviet Armenia (1948–57), requesting permission 'to send his decision regarding the punishments for the clerics of the opposition in order to bring peace and put an end to the Janus-faced policy of the Turkish state'.[159] This letter shows that not only was there strict control over correspondence, but correspondence itself was a matter of permission.

Interestingly, neither the decision of the Catholicos of Cilicia nor the telegram of Catholicos Kevork VI to President Celal Bayar, dated 2 August 1950, were published by the Armenian press of Istanbul. The full text of the telegram, however, appeared in the press in the diaspora. For instance, the newspaper *Zartonk* of Beirut published it on 12 November 1950, and was the source for the reprint in *Hasg*, the monthly of the Catholicosate of Cilicia:

The Historical Telegram of His Holiness, Patriarch Kevork VI, Catholicos of All Armenians, to the President of the Republic of Turkey, Celal Bayar, Concerning the Election of the Armenian Patriarch of Turkey

To the President of the Republic of Turkey, Ankara
Mr President:
The order issued by the Governor of Istanbul concerning the election of the Patriarch of Istanbul violates not only the canonical laws and the historically consecrated rights of the Armenian Church, but also the National Constitution of 1862, which was approved by the Turkish government and has historically remained in effect by custom. At the same time, this order constitutes an unacceptable violation of the internal affairs of the Armenian Church. For this reason, we, as the head of the unified Armenian

Apostolic Church, firmly protest against the abovementioned measure of the Governor of Istanbul *and hope that you will kindly cancel the Governor's electoral order, thereby instructing that the elections be held according to the regulations of the National Constitution of the Armenian Church, which, with the permission of the government, formed the basis of the election of Patriarch Mesrob Naroyan in 1927*, and which your government had ordered Patriarchal *locum tenens* Archbishop Arslanyan to observe during the following elections. Otherwise, as head of the unified Armenian Church, we will be constrained to deem the patriarchal elections illegal, and deny consecration to the patriarch-elect. [my emphasis][160]

Yeghiayan, who quotes only the italicised section, concludes that the conflict was resolved and that the election date was set for December upon this telegram.[161] Whether the telegram of the Catholicos of Echmiadzin to President Bayar played any role in the resolution of the conflict remains unclear, although *Hasg* printed a short article noting, 'With deepest joy we report that, on the demand made by the telegram of His Holiness Patriarch Kevork VI, Catholicos of All Armenians, the Turkish government has allowed the election of the Armenian Patriarch of Turkey according to the dispositions of the National Constitution.'[162]

Armenian newspapers were still discussing the decisions of the Governor of Istanbul in October 1950, which shows by omission that Bayar did not hinder his initiative. At the end of October 1950, *Tebi Luys* asked in the headline (even changing the layout of the newspaper), 'What Is the Nature of the Governor's Order?',[163] arguing that the governor's order was against the Constitution of Turkey, the Armenian Constitution, and the Treaty of Lausanne all at once. According to the editorial, the order of the governor, Prof Fahrettin Kerim Gökay, dated 19 September 1950 (decision no. 11824), suppressed both the General Assembly and the administration, thus leaving no way to reconcile the presumed permission and the preconditions of the Armenian *Nizamname* for the patriarchal election process.[164]

In mid-November, *Paros* published the official announcement of the Patriarchate signed by *locum tenens* Arslanyan, which described the whole process of the patriarchal election, and maintained that an election of the General National Assembly should have taken place with its Religious and Administrative Councils, each of them consisting of 14 people.[165]

The Election Process

The election procedures started on 2 December 1950. The government evidently allowed the community to convene the General National Assembly for one time only, to elect the patriarch. On 25 November, 14,000 people voted in local communities to elect representatives, of which 69 were anti-Arslanyan and 15 pro-Arslanyan.[166] The official report of the Investigation Committee of the GNA included an interesting, unsigned letter that seems to have been sent by the Armenian Patriarchate, as it carries its address. The letter was addressed to Fr Haygazun Garabetyan, the priest of Kayseri, who was asked to organise everything in such a way as to bypass the election and to sort things out by appointment. He was requested to await subsequent orders in this regard.[167] There is no other source to verify the authenticity of this letter.

The minutes of the GNA meeting are a very valuable historical source in revealing the main administrative conflicts and the socio-political situation of the community at the time. According to the permitted election process, 'Armenians would congregate in every church in Istanbul and elect two representatives from the provinces.'[168] Thus, the representatives were elected from Istanbul and from Kayseri, Kırıkhan, Everek, İskenderun, Antakya-Vakıfköy, Diyarbakır (S. Sarkis and S. Giragos, two ballot boxes) and Ordu. Some of the names from the provinces show that the representatives were not from the local communities, but were people living in Istanbul who had been elected in the provinces. I understand from the minutes of the GNA that there were ballot boxes in Gümüşhacıköy and Talas also, and that representatives were elected by the votes of the locals. However, there was a debate in the GNA meeting about these two places (which had ballot boxes, but no churches) as to whether there could be an election process if there was no church, but a community. Some members requested the annulment of these votes, which would also mean rejecting the representatives. The discussion ended with a vote, and these two ballot boxes were declared null and void by 42 to 38.[169] A total of 99 representatives were elected for the GNA. The conversations in the GNA meeting are informative: The representative of Beykoz, H. Hayrabedyan, requested to run the GNA according to the Armenian Constitution, which had the precondition that Administrative (Civil) and Religious Assemblies appoint a patriarchal candidate to the GNA. Hayrabedyan asked to form these bodies in order to proceed with the patriarchal elections.[170] Some of the representatives appear to have agreed upon an agenda with the governor before the GNA meeting; the day of election and the topics of this agenda were distributed in the meeting and included in Turkish at the back of the minutes booklet. Other members opposed the prepared agenda topics and wanted to set their own; the head of the GNA, Kegham Kavafyan, argued that the Assembly had met under extraordinary conditions and that this was a good chance to revive the communal mechanisms to put an end to the ongoing crisis. The bid to directly elect the patriarch, without following the Constitution, was not accepted by Dr Manuelyan, who argued that the GNA could not be convened for such a long time, and that the administrative mechanism of the community had remained inoperative for so long that this was a good chance to start over and follow the guidelines of the Constitution.[171] Another representative from Antakya–Vakıfköy, Garbis Ersan, stuck to the point that the GNA should proceed as instructed by the governor's office and elect the patriarch without establishing the assemblies.[172] Thus, the GNA meeting started with a discussion on whether the principles of Armenian Constitution or the principles of the governor of Istanbul should be followed. It was decided that first the Religious Assembly (14 people) and then the Administrative Assembly (20 people) should be elected.

The GNA met for the patriarchal election at 21:30 with two candidates, which later became five: Archbishop Kevork Arslanyan, Archbishop Karekin Khachaduryan, Bishop Khoren Paroyian, Archbishop Mampre Kalfayan and Bishop Krikor Garabetyan.[173] After another round of discussions, the number of candidates was brought down to two: if one of them refused the post, the other would be the new patriarch. Another round of discussions addressed whether this was allowed by the Constitution. The urgency of electing a patriarch and avoiding any extension to the crisis by failing to elect prevailed. Two names were selected for the voting tickets: Archbishop Karekin Khachaduryan, who had been the Catholicosal Legate to South America (with headquarters in Argentina since 1938) was elected with 67 votes; Bishop Khoren Paroyian, who was Sacristan and Bishop of the Door of Antelias, received 63 votes and came in second.[174] Former *locum tenens* Arslanyan received only two votes, which drastically revealed the community's reaction.[175]

The Investigation Committee of the GNA issued a 95-page report demonstrating, in a nine-point indictment in the first three pages, the breaches of the Armenian Constitution committed by Archbishop Arslanyan during his tenure as *locum tenens*.[176] According to this indictment, Arslanyan had trampled upon the Armenian National Constitution and the centuries-long tradition of the Armenian Apostolic Church, thus going against its democratic and religious principles, among other violations:

(1) Paragraph 11 of the Constitution: Arslanyan infringed it by abolishing the Religious Assembly that had appointed him as well as the Administrative Committee.
(2) Paragraph 8: Arslanyan violated it by monopolising all community affairs, without consulting with its administrative bodies as based on the Constitution.
(3) Paragraph 10, which clearly states that the Patriarch could only suggest suspending clergymen from the GNA in cases where they breached the principles of the Constitution.
(4) Paragraph 25: Arslanyan violated it by appointing new members to the Religious Assembly.
(5) Paragraph 29: Arslanyan suspended the clergymen who asked to discuss the problems of the community, and manipulated the Catholicos of All Armenians in Echmiadzin.
(6) Paragraph 30: All official reports had to be signed by the majority of the Religious Assembly.
(7) Paragraph 31: Arslanyan breached it by arbitrarily granting ecclesiastical rank.
(8) Paragraph 8: Arslanyan negotiated the principles of the Constitution with the state.[177] The Investigation Committee advises the refusal of Archbishop Arslanyan's patriarchal candidacy as per paragraph 1 of the Constitution, according to which the patriarch-to-be must have gained the respect and the trust of 'the nation' (*'azk'*).

The election was a turning point in the community crisis, which had started in 1923 and deepened during the Single Party years, especially during the seven years of tenure of the *locum tenens*. After the elections, the Joint Assembly (Religious and Civil) requested Archbishop Arslanyan to lead the community until Patriarch Khachaduryan's arrival from Argentina. The Assembly also requested him to concentrate all administrative and financial issues in the patriarchate. However, the *locum tenens* did not comply with the requests and, in return, the Assembly decided to dismiss him from his position. Arslanyan rejected the decision of the Assembly and replied to their request with a notarised letter. The conflict continued on a legal level through various reciprocal notarised letters.[178] As the Investigation Committee wryly noted at the end of its official report, 'This is not a history of a period, since it does not include all the incidents with their causes and consequences. Nor is this someone's biographical account. This is only one page of the overall crisis that our community has been going through for the last 30 years.'[179]

The Crisis between Istanbul and Echmiadzin Continues

Archbishop Karekin Khachaduryan sent two letters to Echmiadzin to receive the approval of Kevork VI in his capacity as Patriarch of the Armenians in Turkey. In the second letter, Khachaduryan also asked Kevork VI for authorisation to solve the current problem of suspensions and removals from office in the clergy. These letters were followed by a third written by the GNA of Istanbul, asking Kevork VI to grant the new patriarch the authority to solve the crisis.[180] Kevork VI sent his congratulatory letter on 20 March, almost four months after the election, which bore no direct reference to the suspensions and prohibitions. Instead, in the final paragraphs, Kevork VI also sent his blessings to Archbishop Kevork Arslanyan, who 'remained loyal to the traditional laws of the Armenian Church and the Constitution',[181] which can be taken an expression of support for Arslanyan after the seven-year crisis in the Istanbul Patriarchate. The next day, on 21 March, two of the suspended clerics appealed to the newly elected Patriarch for amnesty.[182] On 22 March, the other three who were prohibited from Armenian religious service appealed to Khachaduryan with a letter.[183] These letters were sent to Echmiadzin on 4 April 1951, with a cover letter by Patriarch Khachaduryan.

The letters sent and received by Kevork VI are published in a book that unfortunately does not include them all. The dates of the letters are not always mentioned either, as they might not have existed in the originals. According to the introduction of the book, the letters were chronologically ordered. I assume that the letter sent on 4 April was written on 21–2 March by the suspended and prohibited clergy, since there are no other letters published in between. The response of Kevork VI is undated. From the date of the following letter, I understand that Kevork VI did not answer the letter written by the Patriarch in April until October. As a matter of fact, I found references to two other letters written on 9 July and 10 September to Kevork VI,[184] which support my claim that he did not respond to any of these letters and telegrams until October. From this letter, I deduce that, although the suspensions were abolished, the issue of suspended clerics remained unresolved.[185] Kevork VI replied, 'We received your letter dated 4 April. We read it and were puzzled, because the style and the tone of your letter were different from those of the religious leader of [the Armenians of] South America.'[186] Following these initial lines, a scolding tone makes clear that, as a 'lower ranking' cleric, Khachaduryan had no right to re-examine an issue that had already been examined by two Catholicoi and a *locum tenens*.[187] The letter ends: '[W]ith this letter we wish that your reputation will remain intact. You decide what is in your interest.'[188] Patriarch Khachaduryan, in his turn, wrote another letter to Echmiadzin where he states that he had lost some of his respect for His Holiness because of his resoluteness to issue a one-sided decision on the basis of mostly fabricated and distorted information: 'If this is and will be your decision, the respectful and deep relation that we have maintained must change.'[189] He then rationalises his will to grant amnesty to those who were suspended and removed from service: 'We do not have the clergy to reach and serve the broken segments of our people in the provinces. [...] You have to know that we cannot hire colleagues from elsewhere; we must do our work with who we have.'[190] The tone of the letters from both sides grew increasingly tense, as can be seen in Khachaduryan's statement: 'We did everything to maintain the authority of Your Holiness at the highest level, which you did not perceive. [...] I am writing to the Armenian Catholicos and not to the Pope in Rome; therefore, I have the right to request that you listen to me.'[191] Patriarch Karekin Khachaduryan indicated at the end of his letter that it was not official, as also implied by his statement '*srdkrutiwn antsnagan*' at the top, or 'writing what privately passes through one's heart.' It is unclear whether or not Kevork VI responded to this letter. However, this correspondence clearly shows the degree of the crisis. It also demonstrates that the conflict continued after the election.

Although Kevork VI did not respond to the letter sent on 4 April 1951, the all-Soviet Council of Ministers in Moscow was working on the issue of the patriarchal crisis in Istanbul. According to their letter from 10 April 1951, marked 'secret' and signed by I. V. Poliansky, Patriarch Khachaduryan had already contacted the opposition clerics upon his arrival to Istanbul, but refused to meet with Archbishop Arslanyan. The report claimed that Khachaduryan had called Suren Şamlıyan, editor-in-chief of *Marmara*, who advocated the break of relations with Echmiadzin. Arslanyan, on the other hand, needed Echmiadzin's support in resolving his problems. The Council asked whether the letter to Khachaduryan should include anything about Archbishop Arslanyan or confine itself to confirming his election as patriarch, which supports my abovementioned contention about the paragraph on Arslanyan in the letter of congratulations.[192] Moreover, after reading that paragraph in the light of the letter sent by the Council of Ministers, it can be argued that Kevork VI wrote those words of support to ease the situation for Archbishop Arslanyan in Istanbul and offer him protection. On the same day, 10 April, the Council of Ministers wrote another letter, informing the Catholicos about a meeting in Milan between Patriarch Khachaduryan and Hrant Samuelyan, the Secretary General of the Armenian Revolutionary Federation.[193] This information had been provided by Arslanyan's cousin. The letter also stated that Turkish newspapers had written about Khachaduryan's visit to Milan, as he was suspected of supporting the ARF back in Argentina.[194] There are several reports in Pehputyan's book going back to the early 1940s that similarly accuse him.[195] The particular letter has an accusatory tone, as having relations with the ARF during Stalin's time was tantamount to spying and thus reason enough for incarceration or exile.

Archbishop Kevork Arslanyan passed away in June 1951. In a letter written after 28 August to Kevork VI,[196] Patriarch Khachaduryan writes: 'We have respected the authority of Your Honour, putting aside our own legal jurisdiction. We still wish to solve the problem within your authority, according to the proposal we made in our letter dated 9 July. However, we would like to ask you to urgently issue Papazyan's amnesty by telegram.'[197] I would like to draw attention to the wording here: *heghinagut'iwn* and *irawasut'iwn*, the former meaning 'authority,' and the latter, 'jurisdiction'. Thus, the Patriarch of Istanbul was trying to remain on good terms with the Catholicos of Echmiadzin on the one hand, while, on the other, the last sentence still conveyed the tone of an order.

The exchange of letters between the highest-ranking clerics of the Armenian Church intensified in October 1951. The primate of Egypt, Archbishop Mampre Sirunyan, visited Istanbul, where he stayed for two months, and penned a letter to Kevork VI, asking to grant amnesty to the punished clerics.[198] The *locum tenens* of the Catholicosate of Cilicia, Yeghishe Derderyan, also wrote a letter to Echmiadzin in October, addressing, among other things, the unresolved issue of the punishments. Interestingly, Derderyan complained in this letter about Sirunyan for unrelated (financial) reasons, which proves that they did not collude to send the letters.[199] Patriarch Khachaduryan wrote yet another letter on 31 October and asked Kevork VI to forgive the punished clergymen, and to save the honour and the authority of Echmiadzin by granting amnesty.[200] The expected amnesty arrived from Echmiadzin at the beginning of December.[201] However, the issue had left its mark on the relations between the parties. For instance, Catholicos Kevork VI wrote a letter in June 1952 to Archbishop Sirunyan on a different issue, and devoted three pages out of six to the latter's role in the crisis of the punished clergy. The Catholicos did not discredit Archbishop Sirunyan's approach. Moreover, he stated that he regarded Patriarch Karekin Khachaduryan's attitude as completely misguided and dishonourable.[202] We can thus see that, despite the fact that the crisis in Istanbul had somehow been resolved, it proved difficult to restore relations.[203]

The period 1915–23 and its aftermath also weakened the Patriarchate as an institution and the Patriarch as a symbol of power and representation. As Armenian institutions gradually became diasporic in the context of the Cold War, the election crisis carried double significance, with Echmiadzin trying to gain power under the auspices of the Soviet government and the Catholicosate of Cilicia establishing itself in Antelias. In this context, the Patriarchate of Istanbul was suffering a crisis of legitimacy and authority, which further fuelled anti-Armenianism in Turkey, and strained the relations between other Armenian communities around the world.

CONCLUSION

This book aimed at writing a socio-political history of Armenians in Turkey up until the 1950s. It is one of the first such attempts. I remember the words of Kevork Hintlian, who for me represents the living memory of Armenians making their way to Jerusalem after 1915: 'You should go and talk to people in the Armenian nursing home in Istanbul.' Although at the time I had not yet realised just how important his advice was, this book is the result of my work both in the nursing home of the Armenian Hospital and the archives stored therein. In general, oral historical accounts have been the most enriching experiences in the writing of this book, which made me understand the importance of explaining *what constitutes the ordinary*.

Whenever Armenians stand in the middle of crisis situations in Turkey, we start reading articles about what it means to be an Armenian in Turkey. This is a question that transcends personal experience, and can never be answered in full, because words would fail and the responses can hardly be understood by the wider public.[1] In my view, the deeper reason is the absence of context for this question itself. The question must thus be formulated differently: Why do Armenians so easily become targets for and victims of various physical or verbal attacks? The answer lies in the historical context that has constituted the 'social' environment for the majority in Turkey, the post-genocide habitus of denial.

Therefore I put at the core of my book the concept of post-genocide habitus of denialism stemming from the state and reproduced by the larger layers of society. The process of becoming diaspora for Armenians remaining in Turkey also is a central theme. I have thus far demonstrated the coherence of official practices, official denial, and its social repercussions, as well as their significance for Armenians in particular. Silencing through 'Citizen, Speak Turkish' campaigns, lawsuits based on 'denigrating Turkishness', intimidation on a daily basis, confiscation of properties, normalised kidnapping of Armenian women survivors, all day-to-day occurrences of discrimination and social pressure put the habitus to work to such an extent that it defines social reality. In tandem, on the level of official policies, a series of juridical measures facilitated and legitimised systematic exclusion. The destruction of the cultural heritage, the legitimisation of the confiscation of abandoned properties, settlement policies, bans on travel and the prohibition of certain professions, the *Yirmi Kura Askerlik* compulsory military service, and the Wealth Tax were among the policies that the state applied to non-Muslims. All these constitute the post-genocide habitus, the concept that I suggest as a tool to understand the state and society formation, in the constitution of which the genocide and its denial have been an important generator. Furthermore, I demonstrated the institutionalisa-tion of denial during the Single Party years, which I find central to the understanding of the socio-political conditions of the period.

Among the aims of state policies after 1923 was the systematic undermining of the legal basis for the merest existence of the Armenian community in Turkey, namely of the *Nizamname* and its attendant institutional structures. The process, ongoing since 1915, was systematised during the first three decades of the post-1923 era. These policies, as well as their indirect consequences, forced the community to abolish institutional representative bodies like the Civil Assembly, to disallow the GNA meetings, and instead to introduce the Single Trustee System. Thus, the Armenian Patriarchate and the structures stemming from the *Nizamname* largely lost their agency (in relation to the state) along with the social influence they had gained over the two preceding centuries. The patriarchal election crisis was a result of the decades-long policies of structural eradication. The state intervention in the crisis, the legitimation sought by the actors, in addition to the social and legal context I describe in the last chapter of this book, demonstrate that state policies systematically aimed at the abolition of the existing structures. At the same time, state policies found their echo within the community as well. Thus, the post-genocide habitus was partly internalised by prominent figures of the community who wanted their share in arbitrating power.

The claim to equality was denied by both public opinion-makers and the state. If a group loses its agency and institutional representation in part or in whole, this results in the loss of the legitimacy of claiming rights and equality. Representation and agency become diffuse when it is the state that determines whom to address, to marginalise, or even to erase completely. Armenian intellectuals who struggled for equality and coexistence were not only marginalised, but also imprisoned; their newspapers were banned and eventually many were forced to leave the country. Thus, the first generation of Armenian intellectuals after the genocide by and large lost contact with the community to which they belonged. By working on this period, I gained valuable insight into what it means to be a conscious pariah, or, in Arendt's terms, to '[accept] the challenge and responsibility of being an outsider even among one's own people'.[2] For the Armenians in Turkey, there is a historicity to being conscious pariahs, which came at a high price. The experience of the generation of *Nor Or* should be taken into consideration when approaching Armenian intellectual life in the post-1923 period in future studies.

Moreover, the post-genocide habitus of the Republic of Turkey set and legitimised a series of practices. With the establishment and institutionalisation of denial on both the state and the society levels, a series of social and legal practices were normalised and reproduced after 1923: kidnapping Armenian women, pushing the remaining Armenians out from Asia Minor and Northern Mesopotamia throughout the Republican years, prohibiting guaranteed rights such as opening schools in the provinces, confiscating properties, discriminating against Armenian children in school, daily harassment and physical attacks on the street, and lawsuits based on 'denigrating Turkishness', among others. Official and social Republican policies were the leading reason for the extinction of Armenian cultural and social life in the provinces, which was noticeable from the 1920s until the 1950s, when there was still a significant Armenian population living in the provinces.

A second set of practices includes the state's coercion of Armenians living in Turkey to endorse official policies, and their consequent isolation from other Armenian communities around the world, which were strictly dehumanised and demonised. The Armenian press was expected to support the Turkish official position and advocate Turkish international policy. The publication of historical accounts of the existence of Armenians in the pre-Ottoman period and histories of the early twentieth century was cause for bans or censorship. Not only was the press closely scrutinised, but also the private lives of editors too were kept under close surveillance. It would therefore not be wrong to say that there was a consistent, holistic perspective on the part of the state in its approach to Armenians all over the world as well as in Turkey. Thus, the separation of 'our good Armenians' and 'bad diaspora Armenians' was nothing more than a Kemalist construct, a discursive separation aimed at severing connections between the community in Turkey and elsewhere, that has in fact succeeded for decades. Armenians remaining in Turkey were politically and socially marginalised since they were not allowed to unite their voices with those of their relatives living in other countries. On the contrary, they were expected to take the side of the Turkish state for the sake of their own security.[3] Anti-Armenian campaigns – a constitutive part of the denialist habitus of Turkey – have served to reproduce anti-Armenianism in the country and silence the victims. Calling Armenians to represent themselves within anti-Armenian structures meant requiring them to assimilate themselves within anti-Armenianism. Thus, Armenians in Turkey were expected to participate in the denialist habitus by operating within its own framework.

As is the case with Ottoman history writing, the post-1923 history of Turkey should be reconsidered and rewritten in the light of the sources of 'the other', and with a methodological consciousness of the fact that those sources are themselves interpellated by the post-genocide habitus: they are called into being, determined and constrained by that habitus itself. The histories of the Armenian communities in the Middle East or elsewhere are part of Ottoman and Republican history. In other words, the histories of Armenians from Diyarbekir living in Los Angeles or Armenians from Van living in Armenia or in Beirut are part of Ottoman history, and history (writing) of/in Turkey, as are the histories of Rums, Jews, Assyrians, Alewis, or Kurds who were exiled or driven out of their hometowns in one way or another. We have to keep in mind that not only the late Ottoman Empire, but also the Republic of Turkey has created a series of diasporas whose histories belong to the histories of both the Ottoman Empire and modern Turkey.

The court cases relating to the properties that belonged to the communities, especially those remaining outside Istanbul, the confiscation processes and the properties subjected to the Law of Abandoned Properties should be further researched. Armenian newspapers constitute a very rich source for the legal bases of Republican Turkey, as well as the prevailing notion of justice both for the state and for society. Likewise, extensive research on the existence of Armenians – whether Islamicised or not – in the provinces during the first decades of the post-1923 era would fill a central gap in the field of social history.

To this day, the post-genocide denialist habitus has defined the existence of Armenians in every way and the lives of other groups whose conflicts with the state remain unresolved. More importantly, the mechanisms of the same habitus operate in all social segments. Thus, throughout the decades, not only Armenians but also the majority population have been affected by the mechanisms of denial, which the minority–majority dichotomy does not suffice to explain. Not only the legal context, but also the entire denialist habitus plays a decisive role in the generation of apparatuses of exclusion, in the construction of a model of citizenship, and, consequently, in the affective attachment to all dimensions of the denialist habitus itself.

NOTES

Prelims

1. http://www.loc.gov/catdir/cpso/romanization/armenian.pdf.

Introduction

1. I better understood this difficulty, or rather impossibility, after reading Marc Nichanian, *Writers of Disaster: Armenian Literature in the Twentieth Century* (Princeton: Gomidas Institute, 2002) and idem, *The Historiographic Perversion* (New York: Columbia University Press, 2009), and listening to his lectures both in Armenia in 2007 and in Turkey.
2. UNESCO has included Western Armenian in the list of 'definitely endangered languages' since 2010. For more see www.guardian.co.uk/news/datablog/2011/apr/15/language-extinct-endangered (accessed 23 February 2013). Western Armenian is one of the standardised forms of the Armenian language.
3. Heidrun Friese, 'The Silence-voice-representation', in Robert Fine and Charles Turner (eds), *Social Theory After the Holocaust* (Oxford: Liverpool University Press, 2000), p. 175.
4. Ibid. The author refers to Jean-Luc Nancy, *The Birth to Presence* (Stanford: Stanford University Press, 1993).
5. On Catholic and Protestant Armenians, see Raymond Kevorkian, *1915 Öncesinde Osmanlı İmparatorluğu'nda Ermeniler* (Istanbul: Aras Yay., 2012), pp. 87–8.
6. A. Giragosyan (ed.), *Hay Barperagan Mamuli Madenakidut'yun (1794–1967)* (Yerevan: Haygagan SSH Guldurayi Minisdrut'yun, 1970), pp. 499–513. I thank Kevork Kirkoryan for making this source available to me.
7. Ibid., pp. 551–2.
8. One example is *Keheni Jampun Vra* by Adrine Dadryan, published in *Marmara* for seven months and later released as a book in 1966, in Istanbul. Adrine

Dadryan was one of the most prominent Armenian woman novelists of the Republican era. She started to publish the children's magazine *Bardez* with Dr Armenuhi Özer in 1947. According to Pakarat Tevyan, the content of *Bardez* was similar to European children's magazines. Yet, because of financial problems, the publication was irregular. On Dadryan, see Pakarat Tevyan *Erchanig Darekirkʻ 1950* (Istanbul: Doğu Basımevi, 1949), pp. 5–6. Adrine Dadryan was the sister of Vahakn Dadrian, the sociologist and historian. According to Pakarat Tevyan, she was the most audacious and outspoken authors among women writers. Other women writers mentioned in the same article are: Lilit Koç, Sirvart Gülbenkyan, Araksi Babikyan, Roz Vartanyan, Manişak Giragosyan, Verjin Hacınlıyan, Armenuhi Özer, Malvine Valideyan, and Diana and Sona Der Markaryan. See Pakarat Tevyan, *Erchanig Darekirkʻ 1946* (Istanbul: Ak-Ün Basımevi, 1945), pp. 12–17. The following year, in the *Erchanig Darekirkʻ 1947*, Tevyan wrote briefly on Dadrian's series, which was being published in *Jamanak* under the title *Martgayin Tsʻutsʻahantēsē*, noting that her work had definitely reached literary maturity. See Pakarat Tevyan, *Erchanig Darekirkʻ 1947* (Istanbul: Doğu Basımevi, Bardez Gazetesi Neşriyatı, 1946), pp. 11–12. In the *Erchanig Darekirkʻ 1949*, I found a satirical piece on Adrine Dadryan by Varujan Acemyan, who also wrote a similar piece on Zaven Biberyan. See Tevyan, *Erchanig Darekirkʻ 1949*, p. 104.

9. Giragosyan (ed.), *Hay Barperagan*, p. 144.

10. Toros Azadyan, *Jamanak: Kʻaṟasnamea Hishadagaran 1908–1948* (Istanbul: Becid Basımevi, 1948), p. 188.

11. Kaṟnik Stepʻanyan, 'Tʻoshigyan Vahan', in *Gensakragan Paṟaran*, Vol. 1 (Yerevan: Hayasdan Hradaragchʻutʻiwn, 1973), p. 367. In Stepʻanyan's book, the first publishing date of *Nor Lur* was given as 1923.

12. Stepʻanyan, 'Vahan Toshigyan', in *Gensakragan Paṟaran*, p. 367.

13. Ibid.

14. Ibid. He passed away in Kars, on the way to the funeral of the Catholicos of All Armenians Kevork VI, in 1954.

15. Sarkis Boghossian, *Iconographie Arménienne*, Vol. 2: *Catalogue de reproductions en noir et en couleurs de 756 pièces originales du XVe au XXe siècle suite de la collection: nos. 704–1365* (Paris: 1988), p. 439. I thank Vahé Tachjian for bringing this source to my attention.

16. Giragosyan (ed.), *Hay Barperagan*, p. 133.

17. Kevork Kirkoryan is an Armenian novelist and researcher who has been working on Armenian biographies for some years. I am thankful to him for graciously sharing his unpublished data.

18. I thank Vartan Matiossian for bringing this source to my attention.

19. Kevork Kirkoryan's unpublished research (data provided in 2009).

20. Stepʻanyan, 'Suren Shamlyan', in *Gensakragan Paṟaran*, Vol. 3 (Yerevan: Khorhrtayin Krogh, 1990), pp. 170–1.

21. See Giragosyan (ed.), *Hay Barperagan*, p. 82. Also see, Toros Azadyan, *Mshaguytʻ Azkakragan Darekirkʻ 1948* (Istanbul: Mshaguyt Kradun, Becid Basımevi, 1947), p. 113.

22. There is no statistical data on the regular circulation of Armenian newspapers in the provinces, and I could not find any references to regular circulation in the sources that I consulted. However, Kēōrk Halajian mentions in his memoirs the prohibition on the circulation of Armenian newsapapers in the eastern provinces. See T'ap'aragan (Kēōrk Halajian), *Tebi Gakhaghan* (Boston: Hairenik Publ., 1932), p. 144.

23. Giragosyan (ed.), *Hay Barperagan*, p. 150.

24. Avedis Aliksanyan was born in Üsküdar and attended the Berberyan and Getronagan Armenian schools. He was imprisoned after the banning of *Nor Or* in 1946. After his release, he published *Aysor* until his emigration to France in 1948. He continued his editorial activities in Paris. For more information, see *Ashkharh* (Aşğharh), 29 December 1979, No. 1119, Paris, in Aram Pehlivanyan, *Özgürlük İki Adım Ötede Değil* (Istanbul: Aras Yay., 1999), p. 99. He was the editor-in-chief of *Ashkharh* from 1960 onwards, had previously published *Luys Parizi* in 1957 and *Lusaghpiwr* in 1958, and was a member of the Communist Party of France. For more information, see *Haygagan Sovedagan Hanrakidaran*, Vol. 1 (Yerevan: 1974), s.v. 'Alik'sanyan'. I thank Ararat Şekeryan for scanning and sending me these two sources.

25. See Introduction, footnote 23.

26. For Keçyan's detailed biography, see www.arasyayincilik.com/tr/yazarlar/s-k-zanku/58 (accessed 25 November 2012).

27. For Pehlivanyan's detailed biography, see www.arasyayincilik.com/tr/yazarlar/aram-pehlivanyan/10 (accessed 25 November 2012).

28. For Koçunyan's detailed biography, see www.arasyayincilik.com/tr/yazarlar/ara-kocunyan/8 (accessed 25 November 2012).

29. Pakarat Tevyan, *Erchanig Darekirk' 1948* (Istanbul: Doğu Basımevi, 1947), p. 5.

30. See also www.arasyayincilik.com/tr/yazarlar/rupen-masoyan/57 (accessed 4 November 2012).

31. Transliteration offered by Aras Publishing.

32. See Introduction, footnote 26.

33. For Gobelyan's detailed biography see www.arasyayincilik.com/tr/yazarlar/yervant-gobelyan/79 (accessed 25 November 2012).

34. Ibid.

35. Giragosyan (ed.), *Hay Barperagan*, p. 72.

36. *Tebi Luys*, 29 April 1950, No. 9.

37. Pakarat Tevyan, *Erchanig Darekirk' 1953* (Istanbul: Varol Matbaası, 1952), p. 9.

38. Pakarat Tevyan, *Erchanig Darekirk' 1954* (Istanbul: Varol Matbaası, 1953), p. 10.

39. Teodoros Lapçinciyan (Teotig) (Istanbul 1873 – Paris 1929) worked for the newspapers *Piwzantion*, *Manzume-i Efkar*, *Ceride-i Şarkiye* and *Dzaghik*. He published *Amēnun Darēts'oyts'ě* with his wife Arşaguhi Teotig (Cezveciyan) starting in 1907, and continued alone after her death in 1921. In 1912 he published his first book, *Dib u Dar*, on the occasion of the 400th anniversary of Armenian printing. He was imprisoned in 1915 and exiled the following year first to Izmit and then on to the Eskişehir–Konya–Pozantı route, where he

was rescued by members of the Armenian community. He made his way back to Istanbul and, like many others, left in 1923, first for Corfu, then for Cyprus and finally for Paris. For his detailed biography, see Teotig, *11 Nisan Anıtı*, ed. Dora Sakayan (Istanbul: Belge Yay., 2010).

40. Pakarat Tevyan (1893–1967) started *Erchanig Darēkirk'* in 1928 and continued publication for 40 years. See Arsen Yarman, 'Sunum', in *Surp Pırgiç Ermeni Hastanesi 1900–1910 Salnameleri*, Vol. 13 (Istanbul: Surp Pırgiç Ermeni Hastanesi Vakfı Kültür Yay., 2012), p. 312.

41. Server R. İskit, *Türkiyede Neşriyat Hareketleri Tarihine Bakış* (Ankara: Milli Eğitim Basımevi, 2000), pp. 232–9.

42. Toros Azadyan (1893–1955). One of the most productive writers of the Republican era. Author and publisher. Some of his books are *Hushamadean Karagēözyan Orpanots'i 1913–1948, Lipananean Husher* and *Kevork Ark. Arslanyan (1867–1951)*. He was also the publisher of *Mshaguyt' Azkakragan Darekirk' 1948*. Azadyan was sent to the Catholicosate of Cilicia as the representative of *locum tenens* Kevork Arslanyan in 1949.

43. Mardiros Koç was then the editor-in-chief of *Jamanak*.

44. Kevork A. Sarafian, *Armenian History of Aintab/Badmut'iwn Antebi Hayots* (Los Angeles, CA: Union of Armenians of Aintab in America, 1953).

45. Aram Sahagian, *Tiwtsaznagan Urfan Ew Ir Hayortinerě* (Beirut: Dbaran Atlas, 1955).

46. Garo Sasuni, *Badmut'iwn Darōni Ashkharhi* (Beirut: Dbaran Sevan, 1956).

47. Vahe Haig (ed.), *Kharpert Ew Anor Osgeghēn Tashdě* (New York: Kharpert Armenian Patriotic Union, 1959).

48. Howag Hagopian, *Badmut'iwn Baghnadan* (Boston: Hayrenik Publ., 1966).

49. Antranig L. P'oladian, *Badmut'iwn Hayots' Arapgiri* (New York: Hradaragut'iwn Amerigayi Arapgiri Miut'ean, 1969).

50. Haygazn Ghazarian, *Badmakirk' Chmshgadzaki* (Beirut: Hamazkayin Publ., 1971).

51. Misak' Siseṛian, *Badmut'iwn Zeyt'uni (1409–1921)* (Lebanon: No Publisher, 1996).

52. Badrig Aṛak'el, *Hushamadean Sepasdio Ew Kavaṛi Hayut'ean*, Vols 1 and 2 (Beirut: Mshag Dbaran, 1979 and New Jersey, 1983).

53. It is different in nature from the aforementioned books. The author of the four-volume *Bolis Ew Ir Terě* was H. J. Siruni, one of the most renowned Turcologists who lived in Romania after 1915.

54. Toros Azadyan, *Lipananean Husher* (Istanbul: Doğu Basımevi, 1949).

55. Santro Pehputyan (ed.), *Vaverakrer Hay Yegeghetsu Badmut'ean: Kevork VI. Gat'oghigos Amenayn Hayots' (1938–1955)*, Kirk'Z. (Yerevan: Osgan Yerevants'i Publ., 1999).

56. Seda Altuğ, paper presented at LMU, 'Viewing state and society relations in Ottoman–Kurdistan from post-Ottoman Syria', Calouste Gulbenkian Foundation, Gomidas Institute and LMU Turkish Studies Lecture Series: The Ottoman Empire and Its Eastern Provinces, 9 January 2013.

57. Hans-Lukas Kieser, *Iskalanmış Barış: Doğu Vilayetleri'nde Misyonerlik, Etnik Kimlik ve Devlet 1839–1938* (Istanbul: İletişim Yay., 2005), pp. 27–8.
58. See Biray Kolluoğlu Kırlı, 'Forgetting the Smyrna fire', *History Workshop Journal* lx/1 (2005), pp. 25–44; Dora Sakayan (ed.), *Smyrna 1922: Das Tagebuch Des Garabed Hatscherian* (Klagenfurt: Kitab-Veri Yay., 2006).
59. For more see Şükrü Aslan (ed.), *Herkesin Bildiği Sır: Dersim* (Istanbul: İletişim Yay., 2010), İzzettin Çalışlar (ed.), *Dersim Raporu* (Istanbul: İletişim Yay., 2011), Yalçın Doğan, *Savrulanlar Dersim 1937–1938 Hatta 1939* (Istanbul: Kırmızıkedi Yay., 2012), Özgür Fındık, *Kara Vagon: Dersim–Kırım ve Sürgün* (Istanbul: Fam Yay., 2012), Cihangir Gündoğdu and Vural Genç, *Dersim'de Osmanlı Siyaseti: İzâle-i Vahşet, Tahsis-i İtikât, Tasfiye-i Ezhân 1880–1913* (Istanbul: Kitapyayınevi, 2013).
60. Karnig Step'anyan, 'Naroyan Mesrob', in *Gensakragan Pararan*, Vol. 3 (Yerevan: Khorkhrtayin Krogh, 1990), p. 128. He was born in Hartert, a village of Daron, and attended the St Garabed Monastery of Mush. In 1895 he attended the Armash Monastery (Akmeşe, near Bahçecik today) and graduated in 1899. In 1904–9 he taught at Armash and was elected patriarch of Istanbul in 1927. Starting in 1900 he published literary and philological articles and critiques in Armenian newspapers and year books. These articles were compiled in the posthumous volume *Nshkharner*; another book, *Nshanavor Tebk'er Haygagan Ants'yalēn*, was published in Jerusalem (biographical information compiled from Step'anyan).
61. Arslanyan twice held the position of *locum tenens* of the Istanbul Patriarchate – first, after Zaven Patriarch left his post in 1922 until 1927, and then upon Naroyan Patriarch's death in 1944 until 1950. Toros Azadyan wrote a biographical work, *Kevork Ark. Arslanyan (1867–1951)* (Istanbul: Mshagoyt Hradaragch'adun, 1952).
62. Telegram 280 from the US Secretary of State (Hull) to US Ambassador to Turkey (Steinhardt) in Ankara, 30 March 1944, *FRUS, 1944* Vol. 5, p. 822, in Levon Thomassian, *Summer of '42: A Study of German–Armenian Relations During the Second World War* (Atglen, PA: Schiffer Publ., 2012), p. 93.
63. Cordell Hull, *The Memoirs of Cordell Hull*, Vol. 2 (New York: Macmillan Company, 1948), p. 1372, in Thomassian, *Summer of '42*, p. 93.
64. Telegram 689 from the US Ambassador to Turkey (Steinhardt) in Ankara to the US Secretary of State (Hull) 15 April 1944, *FRUS, 1944*, Vol 5, pp. 827–8, in Thomassian, *Summer of '42*, p. 93.
65. Telegram 717 from the US Ambassador to Turkey (Steinhardt) in Ankara to the US Secretary of State (Hull) 15 April 1944, *FRUS, 1944*, Vol 5, p. 831 in Thomassian, *Summer of '42*, p. 93.
66. Maarif Vekaleti, *Irkçılık Turancılık* (Ankara: Türk Inkılap Tarihi Enstitüsü Yay., no. 4, 1944).
67. Cemil Koçak, *Türkiye'de İki Partili Siyasi Sistemin Kuruluş Yılları: İkinci Parti* (Istanbul: İletişim Yay., 2010), pp. 80–1.

68. Among inspiring works that use Pierre Bourdieu's theory are: George Steinmetz, *The Devil's Handwriting: Precoloniality and the German Colonial State in Qingdao, Samoa and Southwest Africa* (Chicago and London: University of Chicago Press, 2007) and Timothy Mitchell, *Colonizing Egypt* (Berkeley and Los Angeles: University of California Press, 1991).

69. Martin A. Conway and David C. Rubin, 'The structure of autobiographical memory', in Alan F. Collins et al. (eds), *Theories of Memory* (Hillsdale, NJ: Lawrence Erlbaum Associates, 1993), pp. 103–37. Also see Martin A. Conway, 'Memory and the self', *Journal of Memory and Language* 53 (2005), pp. 594–628 and Darryl Bruce et al., 'Memory fragments as autobiographical knowledge', *Applied Cognitive Psychology* xxi/3 (2007), pp. 307–24.

70. See, for instance, Niklas Radenbach and Gabriele Rosenthal, 'Das Vergangene ist auch Gegenwart, das Gesellschaftliche ist auch individuell. Zur Notwendigkeit der Analyse biographischer und historischer Rahmendaten', *Sozialer Sinn: Zeitschrift für hermeneutische Sozialforschung* xiii/1 (2012), pp. 3–37. Family research has been institutionalised in German-speaking academia. Among the academic journals in the field is *Zeitschrift für Familienforschung*, and there are various institutions such as the *Institute for Family Research & Counseling at University of Fribourg (Switzerland)* or *Institute für angewandte Biografie und Familienforschung Kassel*. There are also regional and social institutions such as *Die Westfälische Gesellschaft für Genealogie und Familienforschung (WGGF)*.

71. Loïc Wacquant, 'Habitus', in Jens Beckert and Milan Zafirovski (eds), *International Encyclopaedia of Economic Sociology* (London: Routledge, 2004), pp. 315–19.

72. Pierre Bourdieu and Loïc Wacquant, *An Invitation to Reflexive Sociology* (Chicago: The University of Chicago Press, 1992), pp. 120–1.

73. Ibid.

74. Loïc Wacquant, 'Habitus', in Jens Beckert and Milan Zafirovski (eds), *International Encyclopaedia of Economic Sociology* (London: Routledge, 2004), pp. 315–19.

75. Ibid.

76. Bourdieu and Wacquant, *An Invitation*, p. 124. For more on the agency–structure debate, see William H. Sewell Jr, 'A theory of structure: Duality, agency, and transformation', *American Journal of Sociology* xcviii/1 (1992), p. 1. For an interesting debate between Judith Butler and Pierre Bourdieu, see Judith Butler, *Excitable Speech: A Politics of the Performative* (London: Routledge, 1997) and Pierre Bourdieu, *Pascalian Meditations* (Cambridge: Polity Press, 2000). Also see Lois McNay, 'Agency and experience: Gender as a lived relation', *Sociological Review* 52 (2004), pp. 173–90 and Terry Lovell, 'Resisting with authority: Historical specificity, agency and the performative self', *Theory, Culture & Society* xx/1 (2003), pp. 1–17.

77. Bourdieu and Wacquant, *An Invitation*, p. 135.

78. Bourdieu, *The State Nobility: Elite Schools in the Field of Power*, transl. Loretta C. Clough (Cambridge–Oxford: Polity Press, 1996). p. 3.

79. Bourdieu and Wacquant, *An Invitation*, p. 126.

80. George Steinmetz, 'Bourdieu, history and historical sociology', *Cultural Sociology* v/1 (2011), p. 51. For more see James Bohman, 'Practical reason and cultural constraint: Agency in Bourdieu's theory of practice', in Richard Shusterman (ed.), *Bourdieu: A Critical Reader* (Oxford: Blackwell, 1999), pp. 129–52 and Ciaran Cronin, 'Bourdieu and Foucault on power and modernity', *Philosophy and Social Criticism* xxii/6 (1996): pp. 55–85.

81. Pierre Bourdieu, *The Political Ontology of Martin Heidegger* (Oxford: Polity, 1991), p. 252, quoted in Steinmetz, 'Bourdieu, history', p. 51.

82. Pierre Bourdieu, *Outline of a Theory of Practice* (Cambridge: Cambridge University Press, 1977), p. 80.

83. Uğur Ümit Üngör and Mehmet Polatel, *Confiscation and Destruction: The Young Turk Seizure of Armenian Property* (London: Continuum International Publ., 2011), p. 12.

84. Bourdieu, *Outline of a Theory of Practice*, pp. 78–9.

85. Ayşe Zarakol, *Yenilgiden Sonra Doğu Batı ile Yaşamayı Nasıl Öğrendi* (Istanbul: Koç Üniversitesi Yay. 2012), p. 27.

86. From the very beginning of her book, Zarakol refers to 'Turks' with no further elaboration in terms of the socio-political layers of identity politics. Ibid., pp. 25–6. For an analysis of identity construction and habitus in Turkey, see Barış Ünlü, 'Türklüğün halleri: Barış Ünlü'yle Türklük sözleşmesi ve Türkiye entelektüelliği üzerine', interview with Eren Barış, *Express* 133 (2013), pp. 24–7 and Ünlü, 'Türklüğün Kısa Tarihi', *Birikim* 274 (2012), pp. 23–34.

87. Nick Crossley, 'The phenomenological habitus and its construction', *Theory and Society* xxx/1 (2001), p. 83, in Zarakol, *Yenilgiden Sonra*, p. 33.

88. Zarakol, p. 136.

89. Ibid., p. 138.

90. Ibid.

91. Ibid., p. 179. The first sentence regarding the numerical data is footnoted as 'Osmanlı Arşivleri'. I could not make sense of this information, as I could not find the reference in the bibliography and in the previous footnotes. This, too, should be considered as part of the manipulation of sources, as there cannot be a source entitled 'Ottoman Archives'.

92. In his interview with the Swiss *Tages Anzeiger*, Pamuk said, 'a million Armenians and 30,000 Kurds were killed in this country'. (Available at www.tagesanzeiger.ch/ausland/europa/LiteraturNobelpreistraeger-Orhan-Pamuk-m uss-vor-Gericht/story/30060283 and www.theguardian.com/world/2005/oct/ 23/books.turkey, accessed 1 February 2015). Zarakol rather reports: '[Pamuk] said [in the interview] that he was willing to the discuss massacres of Armenians and the issues related to Kurdish minorities in Turkey.' Her use of the concept 'minority' for Kurds and the choice of 'discussing the issues' along with the avoidance of using the numbers participates in denialist discourse.

Nonetheless, even the use of numbers (on the part of Pamuk) would not necessarily carry much significance until it is conceptually defined.

93. C. Charle and D. Roche, 'Pierre Bourdieu et l'histoire', *Le Monde* (6 February 2002), in Steinmetz, 'Bourdieu, history', p. 46. Steinmetz also shows the interconnectedness of history and sociology in Bourdieu's work, especially on the subject of the French academic system.
94. Bourdieu, *Outline of a Theory of Practice*, p. 82.
95. Bourdieu and Wacquant, *An Invitation*, p. 131.
96. Ivan Ermakoff, 'Rational choice may take over', in Philip S. Gorski (ed.), *Bourdieu and Historical Analysis* (Durham: Duke Univ. Press, 2013), p. 93.
97. Bourdieu and Wacquant, *An Invitation*, p. 133.
98. This should be read not as an idealised depiction, but an open-ended process that started after World War II and that continues with its own difficulties and achievements.
99. For a detailed analysis of Treaty of Lausanne see Taner Akçam and Ümit Kurt, *Kanunların Ruhu* (Istanbul: İletişim Yay., 2012), pp. 107–213.
100. Ibid., p. 212.
101. Akçam and Kurt, *Kanunların Ruhu*, p. 12.
102. Khatchig Tölölyan, 'Elites and institutions in the Armenian transnation', in *Diaspora* 9 (2000), pp. 118–9; 120.
103. Mihran Dabag, 'Diaspora als gelebtes Wissen', in Mihran Dabag, Martin Sökefeld and Matthias Morgenstern, *Diaspora und Kulturwissenschaften* (Leipzig: Gustav-Adolf-Werk Verlag, 2011), p. 14. For the discussions on the concept diaspora see Sökefeld, 'Das Diaspora Konzept in der neueren sozial-und kulturwissenschaftlichen Debatten', in *Diaspora und Kulturwissenschaften*, pp. 18–33.
104. Ibid., p. 17.
105. Raymond Kevorkian, *Ermeniler*, p. 11.
106. Ibid.
107. Ulf Björklund, 'Armenians of Athens and Istanbul: The Armenian diaspora and the "transnational" nation', *Global Networks* 3 (2003), p. 349.
108. Some examples are: Khatchig Tölölyan, 'Elites and institutions in the Armenian transnation', *Diaspora* 9 (2000), pp. 107–36; Kim Butler, 'Defining diaspora, refining a discourse', in *Diaspora* x/2 (2001), pp. 189–219; Andre Levy, 'Diasporas through anthropological lenses: Contexts of postmodernity', in *Diaspora* ix/1 (2000), pp. 137–57.
109. Melissa Bilal, 'Longing for home at home: the Armenians of Istanbul', in Marie-Aude Baronian, Stephan Besser and Yolande Jansen (eds), *Diaspora and Memory: Figures of Displacement in Contemporary Literature, Arts and Politics* (Amsterdam–New York: Rodopi B.V., 2007), p. 62.
110. Björklund, 'Armenians of Athens and Istanbul', p. 345.
111. Hrant Dink, 'Ermeni kimliği üzerine (I): Kuşaklara dair', *Agos*, 7 November 2003, No. 397. This article series occasioned a lawsuit in which Dink was prosecuted under article 301 of the Penal Code for 'denigrating Turkishness'.

112. Hrant Dink, 'Zorunlu bir saptama', *Agos*, 27 February 2004, No. 413. This was two weeks after publishing a news item on the Armenian roots of Sabiha Gökçen, the adopted child of Mustafa Kemal and the first woman military pilot of Turkey. Both this news and the series had already turned him and his newspaper into a target of racist attacks.
113. 'Türkiye bizimle güzel', *Agos*, 5 March 2004, No. 414.
114. Bilal, 'Longing for home at home', p. 55.
115. Ibid., p. 62.
116. Akçam and Kurt, *Kanunların Ruhu*, pp. 179–204.
117. For more on the discussion of Armenian community as diaspora see hetq.am/eng/articles/953/, Kurken Berksanlar, hyetert.blogspot.de/2011/05/turkiye-ermenileri-diaspora-m.html, Vartan Matossian, azadalik.wordpress.com/2011/07/05/istanbul-diyaspora-midir-degil-midir/, Talin Suciyan, www.taraf.com.tr/haber/diaspora-kim.htm. For the dehumanisation and demonisation of the diaspora, see Ayda Erbal and Talin Suciyan, 'One hundred years of abandonment', *The Armenian Weekly Special Issue 2011*, pp. 41–5, avaiable at www.armenianweekly.com/2011/04/29/erbal-and-suciyan-one-hundred-years-of-abandonment/ (accessed 13 March 2013).
118. Hagop Mıntzuri, *Istanbul Anıları*, transl. Silva Kuyumciyan (Istanbul: Tarih Vakfı Yurt Yay., 1993), p. 143 (the English translation is mine).

Chapter 1   Social Conditions of Armenians Remaining in Istanbul and in the Provinces

1. See Taner Akçam and Ümit Kurt, *Kanunların Ruhu* (Istanbul: İletişim Yay., 2012) and Uğur Ümit Üngör and Mehmet Polatel, *Confiscation and Destruction: The Young Turk Seizure of Armenian Property* (London: Continuum International Publ., 2011).
2. Erik Jan Zürcher, *Turkey: A Modern History* (London: I.B.Tauris, 2004), pp. 381–407.
3. Taner Akçam, *From Empire to Republic: Turkish Nationalism and The Armenian Genocide* (London: Zed Books, 2004), p. 11.
4. Akçam, *From Empire to Republic*, p. 12.
5. See Donald Quataert, *The Ottoman Empire 1700–1922* (New York: Cambridge University Press, 2005), pp. 54–90.
6. Şerif Mardin, 'Center–periphery relations: A key to Turkish politics?', in Engin Akarlı and Gabriel Ben-Dior (eds), *Political Participation in Turkey: Historical Background and Present Problems* (Istanbul: Bogazici University Press, 1975), pp. 7–32. For more on the Menemen incident and Sheikh Said, see Zürcher, *Turkey*, pp. 169–74; 179.
7. Ibid., p. 23.
8. Ibid.

9. Cihangir Gündoğdu and Vural Genç, *Dersim'de Osmanlı Siyaseti: İzâle-i Vahşet, Tashih-i İtikâd, Tasfiye-i Ezhân 1880–1913* (Istanbul: Kitap Yay., 2013), pp. 15–17. For policies specific to nineteenth-century Ottoman Empire, see Reşat Kasaba, *Bir Konargöçer İmparatorluk, Osmanlıda Göçebeler, Göçmenler ve Sığınmacılar*, transl. Ayla Ortaç (Istanbul: Kitap Yay., 2012).

10. Gündoğdu and Genç, *Dersim*, pp. 13–14.

11. *Layiha*s are state reports prepared on the regions that are considered to have political, economic, military or administrative problems and contain suggestions for solutions. For more see Mübahat Kütüoğlu, '*Layiha*' DIA (Ankara, 2003), pp. 116–17 in Gündoğdu and Genç, *Dersim*, p. 11.

12. Martin van Bruinessen, *Agha, Shaikh and State: The Social and Political Structures of Kurdistan* (London–New Jersey: Zed Books, 1992), p. 175.

13. For *Vilayet Reformu* and administrative/demographic changes undertaken by the state, see Roderic H. Davidson, *Reform in the Ottoman Empire* (New York: Gordian Press, 1973), and Raymond H. Kevorkian, 'The administrative divisions', in idem, *The Armenian Genocide: A Complete History* (London: I.B. Tauris, 2011), pp. 266–7.

14. Hans-Lukas Kieser, *Iskalanmış Barış: Doğu Vilayetleri'nde Misyonerlik, Etnik Kimlik ve Devlet 1839–1938* (Istanbul: İletişim Yay., 2005), p. 66. Kieser uses the word '*Binneneroberung*' in his original work, the English translation of which is 'internal conquest'. However, the Turkish translation has favored '*iç sömürgeleştirme*' – literally 'internal colonisation'. I translated the concept from the German original into English as internal conquest, which Kieser prefers (e-mail, 23 February 2015).

15. Gündoğdu and Genç, *Dersim*, p. 16. For more on Land Code see Martin van Bruinessen, *Agha, Shaikh and State*, pp. 182–5.

16. Ussama Makdisi, 'Ottoman Orientalism', *American Historical Review* cvii/3 (2002), pp. 768–96.

17. Gündoğdu and Genç, *Dersim*, p. 52.

18. Ibid., p. 53.

19. Ibid.

20. See the works of Selim Deringil, *The Well-Protected Domains: Ideology and the Legitimation of Power in the Ottoman Empire 1876–1909* (London, 1998) and '"They live in a state of nomadism and savagery": The late Ottoman Empire and the post-colonial debate', *Comparative Studies in Society and History* xlv/2 (2003), pp. 311–42; Thomas Kühn, *Empire, Islam and Politics of Difference: Ottoman Rule in Yemen, 1849–1919* (Leiden: Brill Publ., 2011); Isa Blumi, *Rethinking the Late Ottoman Empire: A Comparative Social and Political History of Albania and Yemen, 1878–1918* (Istanbul: Isis Press, 2003), Marc Aymes, 'Many standards at a time', *Contributions to the History of Concepts* viii/1 (2013), pp. 26–43; and *A Provincial History of the Ottoman Empire: Cyprus and the Eastern Mediterranean in the Nineteenth Century* (London: Routledge, 2014).

21. Krikor Zohrab, 'Pnagch'ut'iwn', in Alperd Sharuryan (ed.), *Krikor Zohrab Yergeri Zhoghovadzu*, Vol. 3, pp. 519–23.

22. Ibid., p. 520. Zohrab uses the extra amount added on *bedel-i askeri* upon the request of the Patriarchate of Constantinople for the purposes of paying off the debt of the Patriarchate of Jerusalem. He compares the amount collected with the amount foreseen by the council of ministers and calculates the Armenian population as over three million as of 1884; he then compares this with the statistics of the Patriarchate.

23. Masayuki Ueno, 'For the fatherland and the state: Armenians negotiate the Tanzimat reforms', *International Journal of Middle East Studies* 45 (2013), pp. 93–109.

24. Ibid., p. 96.

25. Ibid.

26. Ibid., p. 99.

27. Ibid.

28. Şerif Mardin, 'Center–periphery', p. 25.

29. Ibid., p. 25. This article was first published in *Daedalus* cii/1 (1973), pp. 169–90. However in the version printed in the *Political Participation in Turkey* there are slight differences and additional sentences. For instance, this sentence was not included in the first version.

30. Here I am translating the passage from the German original, as the Turkish translation seems modified: Hans-Lukas Kieser, *Der Verpasste Friede* (Zürich: Chronos, 2000), p. 500. Kieser also discusses Yehuda Bauer, who argued that the mass destruction of the Armenian people was the rehearsal of the Holocaust. For more see Yehuda Bauer, *A History of the Holocaust* (New York: F. Watts, 1987), p. 57 in Kieser, *Iskalanmış Barış*, p. 712.

31. Further analysis of the state and the government in Turkey would exceed the limits of this book, especially considering the fact that the state as a concept in Turkey has been in the process of reconceptualization, with lines of continuity drawn from the Special Organisation of 1915 to such structures as the 'deep state', or even the 'diffuse state' (groups organised within the society but working for the state). For this terminology see *Agos*, 1 February 2013, available at http://www.agos.com.tr/yazdir.php?detay=4218 (accessed 15 February 2013).

32. Zaven Der Yeghiayan, *My Patriarchal Memoirs*, transl. Ared Misirliyan, ed. Vatche Ghazarian (Barrington: Mayreni Publishing, 2002), p. 202. In the original text, the wording is *kaghakatsi gam hbadag*, which can be translated as 'citizens or subjects'. See Zaven Der Yeghiayan, *Badriarkagan Hushers: Vgayakirner Ew Vgayut'iwnner* (Cairo: Nor Asdgh Publishing, 1947), p. 326.

33. Der Yeghiayan, *My Patriarchal Memoirs*, pp. 242–3. Soon after this meeting, Patriarch Zaven was put in the position of a *persona non grata* by Mustafa Kemal and had to leave Istanbul. Der Yeghiayan writes that Mustafa Kemal stated, 'Another unforgettable disastrous hero for us was the Armenian Patriarch Zaven. Forgetting their old quarrels with the Greek Patriarchate, this Patriarch too, committed all kinds of accursed acts for the purpose of ruining the Turkish Fatherland' (*Aztarar*, 21 July 1928, quoted in Der Yeghiayan, *My Patriarchal Memoirs*, p. 248).

34. In his capacity as legal inspector of the *vilayet* of Manastir, Harutyun Mosdichian was also a member of the delegation sent to investigate the massacres of Adana in 1909. See the report by Hagop Babigyan, *Adanayi Yeghernĕ* (Aleppo: Ayk Madenashar-6, Hradaradgut'iwn Beiruti Hayots' Temi, 2009), p. 23. I have preserved the orthography of the names in Der Yeghiayan, *My Patriarchal Memoirs*.
35. Der Yeghiayan, *My Patriarchal Memoirs*, p. 243.
36. TBMM–Gizli Celse Zabıtları, 1934: Vol. 4, 2 March 1339 (1923), p. 5.
37. Ibid., pp. 7–8.
38. Ibid., p. 8.
39. Ibid., p. 9.
40. In the same section, Riza Nur provides details about the duties of the Patrirachate: '[A]s you know, the Patriarchate had political, administrative, juridical, and religious responsibilities. They have had their own courts and stuff (*bilmem neleri vardır*) for centuries [...] The Patriarch would come and our soldier at the office of the *vezir* would greet him.'
41. Ibid., p. 7.
42. Ibid.
43. Ibid., p. 8.
44. Patriarch Maghak'ia Ōrmanyan wrote in his posthumously published memoirs, *Khōsk' Ew Khohk'*, that Armenians from provinces increasingly tried to go to Istanbul for work after the Hamidian massacres. However, they were sent back to their villages because of the prohibition against Armenians' migration to Istanbul. Those who fled to foreign countries were not allowed to return to Ottoman territories. According to Ōrmanyan, 300,000 Armenians were killed during the Hamidian massacres of 1894–7. See Maghak'ia Ōrmanyan, *Khōsk' Ew Khohk'* (Jerusalem: Dbaran Srpots Hagopeants, 1929), pp. 177–8; 187.
45. See Elif Babul, 'Home or away: On the connotations of homeland imaginations of *imvros*', in Baronian, Besser, Jansen (eds), *Diaspora and Memory*, pp. 43–54.
46. Rıfat N. Bali, *Cumhuriyet Yılarında Türkiye Yahudileri: Bir Türkleştirme Serüveni (1923–1945)* (Istanbul: İletişim Yay., 2003), p. 45.
47. I translated *Üsküdar Valiliği* as 'governorate of Üsküdar'. Üsküdar was a *vilayet* in 1924–6. I also checked with the authors: Taner Akçam confirmed that the newspapers in 1925 used this terminology. Personal correspondence with Akçam on 24 July 2013.
48. *Tevhid-i Efkar*, 26 December 1340 (1924) and *Son Telgraf*, 3 February 1341 (1925), in Akçam and Kurt, *Kanunların Ruhu*, p. 210.
49. BCA/TİGMA, 030-0-18-01-01-10-36-6-00, decree dated 27 July 1340 (1924), in Akçam and Kurt, *Kanunların Ruhu*, p. 211.
50. Elçin Macar, *Cumhuriyet Döneminde İstanbul Rum Patrikhanesi* (Istanbul: İletişim Yay., 2003), p. 171.
51. For panopticism see Michel Foucault, *Discipline and Punish: The Birth of the Prison*, transl. Alan Sheridan (New York: Vintage Books, 1995), pp. 195–228.
52. BCA, 030-0-18-01-02-3-29-003, decree dated 8 May 1929, in Akçam and Kurt, *Kanunların Ruhu*, p. 213.

53. N. D., oral historical account, 16 September 2012.
54. Ibid.
55. Arshag Alboyadjian, *Badmut'iwn Malatio Hayots'* (Beirut: Sevan Press, 1961), pp. 966–7. See also Vahé Tachjian, *La France en Cilicie et en Haute-Mesopotamie: Aux Confins de la Turquie, de la Syrie et de l'Irak (1919–1933)* (Paris: Edition Karthala, 2004), pp. 259–60.
56. Ibid.
57. Ibid.
58. Ibid.
59. Kevorkian, *Armenian Genocide*, p. 748. For more see also pp. 745–50.
60. See Chapter 1, footnote 67.
61. Der Yeghiayan, *My Patriarchal Memoirs*, p. 180.
62. Ibid., p. 176.
63. Kevorkian, *Armenian Genocide*, p. 759, uses the English translation 'National Relief Mission'.
64. Der Yeghiayan, *My Patriarchal Memoirs*, p. 177.
65. Köseyan, *Hushamadean Surp P'rgich' Hiwanatanots'i- Surp Pırgiç Hastanesi Tarihçesi* (Istanbul: Murat Ofset, 1994), p. 146. The orphanages mentioned in Köseyan's book are: Karagözyan, Esayan, Ortaköy Orphanage of Girls, Kalfayan, Kadıköy, Bakırköy, Narlıkapı, Arnavutköy, Boyacıköy, Beyoğlu St. Anna Orphanage, Samatya Orphanage, Kadıköy St Penedigoros.
66. See Chapter 1, footnote 52.
67. APC/APJ, The Patriarchate's Constantinople Information Bureau, Ě 181–6, no. 193, letter from the Patriarchate to the Ministry of Justice, January 3, 1920, in Kevorkian, *Armenian Genocide*, p. 759.
68. The Beylerbeyi orphanage used to be the Turkish military school. The British gave the building to the Armenians.
69. Der Yeghiayan, *My Patriarchal Memoirs*, pp. 178–9.
70. Ibid., p. 178.
71. Köseyan, *Hushamadean*, p. 149.
72. *Ěntartsag Darets'oyts' Surp P'rgich' Hiwantanots'i 1924*, p. 139, cited in Armaveni Miroğlu, 'G. Bolsoy Azkayin Khnamadarut'iwně', *Handes Amsorya* 124 (2010), p. 428. See also *Vat'sunameag (1866–1926) Kalfayan Aghchgants' Orpanots' Khaskiwghi* (G. Bolis: Dbakrut'iwn H.M. Setyan, 1926), p. 30.
73. According to Fr Zaven Arzumanian, there were four orphanages in Kayseri (two in Talas, one in Efkere and one in Zincirderesi) in 1922. See Fr Zaven Arzumanian, *Azkabadum*, Vol. 4, Book I (1910–30) (New York: St Vartan's Press, 1995), p. 224.
74. Ibid., p. 223.
75. Ibid., p. 222.
76. Oral historical account of Varujan Köseyan, 13 September 2010, in Armenian.
77. Armaveni Miroğlu, 'G. Bolsoy', pp. 428; 430. *Kaght'agan* and *Kaght'agayan* were two terms that could be found in all Armenian texts of the period and that refer to the people who have left their houses in the provinces 1915

onwards. During the Republican years, Armenians who could make their way back to their cities or villages or to any city or village in Asia Minor and Northern Mesopotamia were perpetually exiled because living in the provinces as Armenians was extremely difficult. Thus, Armenians in provinces have been uprooted for at least the second or even the third time. In those days *kaght'agan* had such a connotation, of 'perpetual exodus', and the bleak living conditions in the *kaght'agayan* (*kaght'agan* centres). I prefer not to translate the concept into English because the probable translations such as 'exile, deportee, migrant, refugee, internally displaced, forcefully displaced' fall short of explaining the situation in its entirety, or the experience of being a *kaght'agan*.

78. Toros Azadyan, *Hushamadean Karagēōzyan Orpanots'i 1913–1948 (Şişli)* (Istanbul: Becid Basımevi: 1949), p. 90.

79. *Panper*, 22 April 1933, No. 3.

80. Ibid.

81. Toros Azadyan, (ed.), *Ĕntartsag Darets'oyts' Surp P'rgich' Hiwantanots'i 1932* (Istanbul: H.M. Basımevi), p. 305.

82. About Azkayin Khnamadarut'iwn, see also Madt'os Ēblighatyan, *Azkayin Khnamadarut'iwn: Ĕnt'hanur Deghegakir Arachin Vetsamea (1 Mayis 1919–1 Hokdemper 1919)* (Beirut: Dbaran Kat'oghigosutean Hayots' Medzi Dann Giligio, 1990).

83. Miroğlu, 'G. Bolsoy', p. 434.

84. *Nor Lur*, 30 December 1947, No. 301; *Nor Lur*, 20 January 1948, No. 307. This number was 107 in 1933 according to a news item in *Panper*, 22 April 1933, No. 3. Karagözyan received around 100 orphans in 1913 when the orphanage of Surp Hagop next to the Surp P'rgich' Armenian Hospital was closed. Karagözyan was newly opened at that time. Surp Hagop Orphanage was famous for its rebellious orphans. According to Pakarat Tevyan, who was one of the orphans of Surp Hagop, orphans took over the administration from 6–7 November 1908. They rebelled against the hospital administration, as well as the whole hierarchy mechanisms of the community. The children went as far as taking the teachers as hostages and take over their own education. The situation turned into a crisis. Orphans were called for a meeting in the hospital with the participation of the Patriarch. See Pakarat Tevyan, *Erchanig Darekirk': Bardez Kutlu Yıllar Dergisi 1958* (Istanbul: Varol Matbaası, 1958), pp. 28–47. In fact, in Toros Azadyan's history of the Karagözyan Orphanage (*Hushamadean Karagēōzyan Orpanots'i 1913–48*), one can trace the destiny of the rebellious orphans of Surp Hagop: there were 101 orphans, yet 16 of them were not transferred to Karagözyan, probably due to the rebellion. Thus, 85 orphans were transferred in September 1913. See Azadyan, *Hushamadean*, p. 27.

85. *Paros*, 17 January 1950, No. 21.

86. A nun, *mayrabed* in Armenian, can also mean a woman who chose not to marry. See *Vat'sunameag (1866–1926) Kalfayan Aghchgants' Orpanots' Khaskiwghi*, p. 3.

87. The Kalfayan boarding school had 90 girl students in 1933, according an article by Baruyr Püzant Keçyan in *Panper*, 11 May 1933, No. 6.
88. Azadyan, *Hushamadean*, p. 107.
89. Ibid., p. 111.
90. Dilek Güven, *Nationalismus und Minderheiten: Die Ausschreitungen gegen die Christen und Juden der Türkei vom September 1955* (Munich: Oldenbourg Verlag, 2012), p. 107.
91. Soner Cagaptay, *Islam, Secularism, and Nationalism in Modern Turkey: Who is a Turk?* (London–New York: Routledge Publ., 2006), p. 33.
92. FO371/13818/E6101 in ibid., p. 35.
93. Ibid.
94. Murat Bebiroğlu, http://www.hyetert.com/prnyazi3.asp?s=&Id = 442& Sayfa = 0&DilId = 1&AltYazi (accessed 25 February 2012).
95. NARA 867.4016 Jews/13 US Embassy, to State Department from Ankara 24 July 1934, in Dilek Güven, *Cumhuriyet Dönemi Azınlık Politikaları ve Stratejileri Bağlamında 6–7 Eylül Olayları* (Istanbul: Tarih Vakfı Yurt Yay., 2005), p. 103.
96. Ibid., p. 105.
97. Ibid., p. 104.
98. Ibid. Güven points out that this number was provided by the Armenian Patriarch. The American Embassy in Beirut gave the number of emigrants as 4,000. NARA 867.404/208. No. 946, the US Consulate, from Istanbul to the State Department, 24 February 1930.
99. SD 867.4016, From Crew (Istanbul) to Washington, 12 February 1930 in Cagaptay, *Islam, Secularisms*, p. 35.
100. FO 371/14587/E729 and FO 371/14567/EE886 in ibid., p. 36.
101. *Ngar* was a weekly newspaper published in 1933–4 by Krikor Mhitaryan.
102. *Ngar*, 25 March 1934, No. 25.
103. *Panper Weekly* was launched on 8 April 1933 by Aram Dağlaryan and Yetvart Simkeşyan.
104. Suren Şamlıyan, 'Panperi bduydnerĕ: Inch'bēs gabrin Samat'ioo gayanin kaght'agannerĕ', in *Panper*, 27 April 1933.
105. Miroğlu, 'G. Bolsoy', p. 432.
106. *Ĕntartsag Darets'oyts' Surp P'rgich' Hiwantanots'i 1932*, p. 306.
107. *Panper*, 27 April 1933.
108. Ibid.
109. *Ngar*, 25 March 1934, No. 25. The same news item stated that there were *kaght'agan*s from Bebek (a village of Yozgat), a total of 200 people.
110. *Nor Lur*, 9 January 1935, No. 5001; *Nor Lur*, 7 January 1935, No. 5150; *Nor Lur*, 26 July 1935, No. 5199; *Nor Lur*, 28 July 1935, No. 5201.
111. *Nor Lur*, 27 April 1935, No. 5108.
112. *Nor Lur*, 3 August 1935, No. 5207.
113. The former monastery of the Armenian Catholic congregation of the Andoneants' Monastery in Ortaköy was used as *kaght'agan* centre.

114. *Nor Lur*, 16 November 1935, No. 5312.
115. *Nor Lur*, 14 December 1935.
116. *Nor Lur*, 12 June 1935, No. 5155.
117. *Nor Lur*, 16 November 1935, No. 5312.
118. *Nor Lur*, 30 May 1935, No. 5141.
119. *Ēntartsag Darekirkʻ Hiwantanotsʻi, 1939* (Istanbul: O. Aktaryan Basımevi, 1938), p. 100.
120. Ibid.
121. *Ēntartsag Darekirkʻ Hiwantanotsʻi, 1938* (Istanbul: O. Aktaryan Basımevi, 1937), p. 87.
122. A. B., oral historical account, 13 March 2013, Munich.
123. Ibid.
124. See Toros Azadyan and Mardiros Koçunyan, *Armağan: Türkiye Cumhuriyeti 15. Yıldönümü 1923-38* (Istanbul: Gutemberg Matb., G.N. Makasciyan, 1938), p. 80. The editors explained the rationale of the title *Armağan*, which is also an Armenian noun for 'gift', the same as in Turkish. They consult various dictionaries to prove their argument.
125. BCA 030.10.85.558.7.
126. For a summary of the Sancak's annexation see Zürcher, *Turkey*, pp. 202-3.
127. Azadyan and Koçunyan, *Armağan*, pp. 2-12.
128. His name was most probably written as Civan Aşıkyan.
129. For more see, Vakıflar Kanunu (Law of Pious Foundations) www.hukuki.net/kanun/2762.13.text.asp (accessed 25 January 2015).
130. In the case of Diyarbekir, data varies according to the sources. According to Kēōrk Halajian's memoirs (1925), Müftüzade Abdurrahman Şeref Bey, who was the representative of Diyarbekir at the time, related the following about the Armenian population of the city. 'After the armistice the number of Armenians in Diyarbekir increased to 13,000-14,000. This was a real concern for us. [...] But in 1920-2 emigration started and the numbers decreased. Today there are almost 2,500-3,000 Armenians in the city and perhaps a little bit more on the mountains', T'apʻaragan (Kēōrk Halajian), *Tebi Gakhaghan* (Boston: Hairenik Publ., 1932), p. 143. We learn from the travel account of Bedros Zobyan and William Saroyan in 1964 that there were 1,500 Armenians living in the area; see Bedros Zobyan, *Tebi Bitlis William Saroyani Hed* (Istanbul: Aras Yay., 2007), p. 247. In 1935 *Nor Lur* reported the existence of a total of 200 Armenian families in Diyarbekir (*Nor Lur*, 20 November 1935, No. 5316). In an oral historical account, I came across a number much higher than these, from the 1960s: 'We arrived in Diyarbakır and lived in the church house in Hançepek. There were approximately 10,000 Armenians living in Hançepek in those days', K. B., Oral historical account, 21 January 2009, Berlin.
131. Azadyan and Koçunyan, *Armağan*, pp. 41-2.
132. Ibid.
133. Ibid.

134. *Ēntartsag Daretsuyts Surp P'rgich' Azkayin Hiwantanots'i 1932*, p. 303. These data were utilised in the books on historical Armenian cities published in various communities of the diaspora. For instance, the information of the Yearbook of 1932 of the Armenian Hospital is found in Armēn Tarian and Antranig Erganian (eds), *Badmut'iwn Yozgadi Ew Shrchagayits' (Kamirk') Hayots'* (Beirut: Hradaragut'iwn Yozgadi Ew Shrchagayits' (Kamirk') Hayrenagts'agan Miut'ean, 1988), p. 913.
135. Ibid., p. 304.
136. Hrant Güzelyan, in Yervant H. Kasuni (ed.), *Bolso Badanegan Dunĕ: Mnats'ortats'i Duntartsi Badmut'iwn Mĕ* (Beirut: 2007), p. 4.
137. Ibid., p. 22.
138. Antranig L. P'oladian, *Badmut'iwn Hayots' Arapgiri* (New York: Hradaragut'iwn Amerigayi Miut'ean, 1969), p. 741.
139. Ibid., p. 742.
140. BCA 030.18.01.03.84.79.8.
141. For Efkere's local history and Armenians, see www.efkere.com (accessed 12 March 2013).
142. *Ēntarts'ag Darekirk' Hiwantanots'i 1944* (Istanbul: W. Der Nersēsyan Ew Ortik'/ Güzeliş Basımevi), p. 233.
143. A document in the Prime Ministry Archives shows the close control of activities of priests in Asia Minor were controlled. The sermon of 10 April 1938 by priest Haygazun Garabetyan in the church of Kayseri was reported to Prime Minister, Chief of Staff and Minister of Foreign Affairs. It was noted that he had called the community to pray for Atatürk's health, as he had 'rescued the country from the hands of foreign powers'. See BCA 030.10.109.721.21.
144. *Marmara*, 7 July 1945, No. 713.
145. Tavra is a village couple of kilometres away from Sivas. Before 1915 it had an Armenian population of 1,500 people. The village had two monasteries, Surp Hagop and Surp Anabad, and one church, Surp Asduadzadzin. There were two Armenian schools, Aramyan and Tavityan. See bianet.org/bianet/biamag/115648-sivas-ermenileri-bin-varmis-bir-yokmus (accessed 8 July 2012) and Arsen Yarman, *Sivas 1877: Boğos Natanyan* (Istanbul: Birzamanlar Yayıncılık, 2008).
146. *Nor Lur*, 26 April 1947, No. 230.
147. *Marmara*, 25 May 1947, No. 1647.
148. *Marmara*, 25 August 1950, No. 2317.
149. Ibid.
150. Ibid.
151. *Marmara*, 5 July 1946, No. 1325.
152. *Nor Lur*, 5 November 1949, No. 494.
153. Köseyan, *Hushamadean*, p. 180.
154. Şavarş Balımyan, *U Yes Gertam* (Istanbul: Aras Yay., 2005), p. 263. This is the transliteration suggested by Aras Publishing.

155. *Ĕntartsag Darekirk' Surp P'rgich' Hiwantanots'i 1948, Türk Ermeni Hastanesi Salnamesi* (Istanbul: Akın Basımevi, 1947), p. 376. *Ĕntartsag Darekirk' Surp P'rgich' Hiwantanots'i 1949* (Istanbul: Becid Basımevi, 1948), p. 413. The same information is included also in *Ĕntartsag Darekirk' Surp P'rgich' Hiwantanots'i 1944*.

156. Civan Çakır, Oral historical account, 8 April 2012, Montreal, in Armenian.

157. *Marmara*, 6 May 1947, No. 1628.

158. *Marmara*, 1 May 1947, No. 1623. On 9 and 16 May 1947, *Marmara* published the memoirs of Father Serope Burmayan, who wrote that there were three churches in Kayseri: Surp Lusaworich' (with the Giwmiwshyan School nearby), Surp Asduadzadzin and Surp Sarkis (with the Hagopyan School nearby). After 1919, Burmayan served in Kayseri for 13 years. Burmayan's memoirs state that two of the three churches were confiscated with all their properties during the Republican period. Surp Sarkis Church was going to be turned into a cinema, but Burmayan argued that this did not happen since it would have dishonoured the religious feelings of Armenians; even turning the church into a mosque would have been better. He also wrote about the Talas Armenian Church and social life during the early Republican period.

159. *Marmara*, 1 May 1947, No. 1623.

160. *Marmara*, 6 May 1947, No. 1628.

161. *Ülke*, 7 March 1950, quoted in *Marmara*, 16 March 1950, No. 2156.

162. Ibid.

163. Ibid.

164. Ibid.

165. *Marmara*, 20 March 1950, No. 2160.

166. Ibid.

167. *Marmara*, 26 March 1950, No. 2166.

168. K. A., oral historical account, 13 March 2013, Munich.

169. Funda Tosun, 'Bir canavarmışım gibi subaylar beni görmeye geliyordu', interview with Garabet Demircioğlu, *Agos*, 20 May 2011, No. 789. See also www.bianet.org/biamag/azinliklar/130311-bir-canavarmisim-gibi-subaylar-beni-gormeye-geliyordu (accessed 30 November 2012).

170. Yaşar Kemal and Alain Bosquet, *Yaşar Kemal Kendini Anlatıyor* (Istanbul: Toros Yay., 1993), pp. 67–9.

171. Üngör and Polatel, *Confiscation and Destruction*, p. 166.

172. Vahé Tachjian, 'Gender, nationalism, exclusion: The reintegration process of female survivors of the Armenian Genocide', *Nations and Nationalisms* xv/1 (2009), pp. 60–80.

173. Ara Sarafian, 'The absorption of Armenian women and children into Muslim households as a structural component of the Armenian Genocide', in Omer Bartov and Phyllis Mack (eds), *In God's Name: Genocide and Religion in the Twentieth Century* (USA: Berghahn Books, 2001), pp. 209–21.

174. Katharine Derderian, 'Common fate, different experience: Gender-specific aspects of the Armenian Genocide, 1915–1917', *Holocaust and Genocide Studies* xix/1 (2005), pp. 1–25.
175. Vahé Tachjian & Raymond H. Kévorkian, 'Reconstructing the nation with women and children kidnapped during the genocide', transl. Marjorie R. Appel, *Ararat* xlv/185 (2006), pp. 5–14, and Kévorkian, *Armenian Genocide*, pp. 757–62.
176. Taner Akçam, *Ermenilerin Zorla Müslümanlaştırılması: Sessizlik, İnkâr ve Asimilasyon* (Istanbul: İletişim Yay., 2014).
177. Talin Suciyan, 'Tachjian: Her üç aileden birinde böyle bir olay yaşanmış olmalı', interview with Vahé Tachjian, *Agos*, 4 June 2010, No. 740, pp. 10–11.
178. Civan Çakır, oral historical account, 8 April 2012.
179. See Chapter 1, footnote 124.
180. Agop Arslanyan, *Adım Agop Memleketim Tokat* (Istanbul, Aras Yay., 2008), p. 119; for male converts, p. 143.
181. See Yorgos Andreadis, *Tamama: Pontus'un Yitik Kızı* (Istanbul: Belge Yay., 2012); Gülçiçek Günel Tekin, *Kara Kefen: Müslümanlaştırılan Ermeni Kadınların Dramı* (Istanbul: Belge Yay., 2011); Fethiye Çetin, *Anneannem* (Istanbul: Metis Yay., 2004); Fethiye Çetin and Ayşegül Altınay, *Torunlar* (Istanbul: Metis Yay., 2009).
182. FO, 371/13827/E6397 in Cagaptay, *Islam*, p. 33.
183. W. Y., email, 12 May 2007.
184. K. B., Oral historical account, 21 January 2009, Berlin.
185. T'ap'aragan (Kēōrk Halajian), *Tebi Gakhaghan*, p. 157.
186. Ibid.
187. Ibid., p. 73.
188. Ibid., p. 75–9.
189. Ibid., p. 88.
190. Mıgırdiç Margosyan attended the same school in Diyarbakır. See *Tespih Taneleri* (Istanbul: Aras Yayıncılık, 2008), p. 83.
191. Tosun, 'Bir canavarmışım gibi'.
192. Güzelyan, *Bolso Badanegan Duně*, p. 35.
193. Sending children to Istanbul was not always regarded as something positive, since Tbrevank was first designed to be a clerical school. In Margosyan's book, there is a passage explaining the discomfort expressed by an Armenian about sending children to Istanbul to become clerics. 'A *vertabed* [celibate priest in Armenian] has come here from Istanbul, collecting kids ... He takes the kids to Istanbul, to make them *vertabed* [*Istanbol'dan bir tene* vertebed *gelmiş, çocığ topli ... Çocığlari İstanbol'a götıri,* vertebed *yapmağ isti...*] He says he comes to make a home, but where was he till now? Our spawn is all in Kafle [Kafle, another word used for exile] barely surviving extinction, now he's taking our kids to Istanbul to make them *vertabed*, so now we'll never get to see the progeny of the kids that we do have. Do they not have Armenians in Istanbul, such that he comes all the way here to get them? For forty years we haven't

heard peep from Istanbul, and now they come for our kids? No sir, no good will come to us from those Istanbulites ... *[Baş göz üzerine gelmiş; hama şimdiye kadar ecep ali nerdeymiş? Zatani züryetımız Kafle'de kökınden kurıtmağtan zor kurtılmış, şimdi çocığlarımız İstanbol'a götıre, vertebed yapa ki, oliğ çocığımızın da züryetini heç görmiyağh! Niye İstanbol'da Ermeni yoğh mi ki, kağhmiş buralara gelmiş? Kırğh senedır Istanbol'dan bıze bi ğheber yoğhken, şimdi bızım çoliğ çocığımıza mi göz tikmişler? Yoğh babam yoğh, İstanbollilardan bıze heç bi zaman ne gher gelır ne de bereket ...]'*, Margosyan, *Tepsih Taneleri*, p. 85.

194. This figure must be Müftüzade Abdurrahman Şeref Uluğ, who was the representative of Diyarbekir at that time. He was well known for his involvement in genocidal acts. See Uğur Ümit Üngör, *The Making of the Modern Turkey: Nation and State in Eastern Anatolia 1913–1950* (Oxford University Press, 2012), p. 237 and Kevorkian, *Armenian Genocide*, pp. 359–65.

195. T'ap'aragan (K.H.), *Tebi Gakhaghan*, p. 144.

196. Ibid.

197. Ibid.

198. Hayguhi Çakır, Oral historical account, 8 April 2012, Montreal.

199. Macar, *Cumhuriyet Döneminde*, p. 168.

200. Cemil Koçak, 'Ayın karanlık yüzü', *Tarih ve Toplum Yeni Yaklaşımlar* 1 (2005), p. 149.

201. Ibid., p. 153.

202. Ibid.

203. Ibid., www.duzceyerelhaber.com/Cemil-KOCAK/3055-Gayri-Muslimler-ve-Turkluge-Hakaret-Davalari-Ayin-karanlik-yuzu (accessed 10 December 2014).

204. Baghdik Hagopyan, oral historical account, 6 April 2012, Montreal.

205. Ara Garmiryan, oral historical account, 3 April 2012, Montreal.

206. Civan Çakır, oral historical account, 2012.

207. Koçak, 'Ayın karanlık yüzü', pp. 174–200.

208. *Marmara*, 8 October 1949, No. 1999.

209. Evdoksi Suciyan Parsehyan, oral historical account.

210. *Nor Or*, 1 September 1946, No. 23.

211. Ibid.

212. Rifat N. Bali, www.birgun.net/forum_index.php?news_code=1150985306& year = 2006&month = 06&day = 22 (accessed 8 December 2012).

213. Cihad Baban, *Ulus*, 4 September 1960, in Rifat N. Bali, 'Vatandaş Türkçe konuş!', www.rifatbali.com/images/stories/dokumanlar/turkce_konusma_bi rgun.pdf (accessed 8 December 2012).

214. *Vakit*, 27 April 1925, quoted in Füsun Üstel, *İmparatorluktan Ulus-devlete Türk milliyetçiliği: Türk Ocakları (1912–1931)* (Istanbul: İletişim Yay., 1997), p. 173.

215. Necmeddin Sadak, 'Türkleştirme', *Akşam*, 30 April 1925, quoted in NARA 9 May 1925, 867.9111/95, quoted in Rifat N. Bali, *Cumhuriyet Yıllarında Türkiye Yahudileri: Bir Türkleştirme Serüveni (1923–1945)* (Istanbul: İletişim Yay., 2005), p. 107.

216. 'L'intransigeance municipale a Brousse', *La République*, 30 July 1925; 'Le Turc obligatoire entre Turcs', *Stamboul*, 12 January 1926, quoted in Bali, *Cumhuriyet Yıllarında*, p. 108.

217. Günver Güneş, 'Türk devrimi ve İzmir Türk Ocağı', *Çağdaş Türkiye Tarihi Araştırmaları Dergisi* iii/8 (1988), pp. 115–35, quoted in Bali, *Cumhuriyet Yıllarında*, p. 109.

218. For *Vilayet Gazetesi*, see Horst Unbehaun www.tubar.com.tr/TUBAR% 20DOSYA/pdf/2001GUZ/1.1svas%20vlayetnde%20basinin%20douu.pdf and Nesimi Yazıcı, dergiler.ankara.edu.tr/dergiler/37/781/10025.pdf (accessed 7 July 2012).

219. *Marmara*, 6 March 1947, No. 1568. According to *Marmara*, MUTLU was the nickname of the *mektubci* of Isparta, i.e. Agah Yüce.

220. *Isparta*, 5 February 1947, No. 1214, See BCA 030.10.88.577.4. Pari Siragan must have been Paresiragan, which means 'benevolent'. Charity organisations existed in many communities in order to help the community members in need. They did not necessarily belong to political organisations.

221. Ibid.

222. Ibid.

223. Güven, *Cumhuriyet Dönemi*, p. 106.

224. Ayşe Hür, derinsular.com/cumhuriyetin-amele-taburlari-yirmi-kura-ihtiya-tlar-ayse-hur/ (accessed 20 October 2012).

225. Rıfat N. Bali, *II. Dünya Savaşında Gayrimüslimlerin Askerlik Serüveni: Yirmi Kur'a Nafıa Askerleri* (Istanbul: Kitabevi Yay. 2008), p. 1.

226. See Leyla Neyzi, *Amele Taburu: The Military Journal of a Jewish Soldier During the War of Independence* (Istanbul: Isis Yay., 2005).

227. TBMM–Gizli Celse Zabıtları, p. 6.

228. See Bali, *Yirmi Kur'a Nafıa Askerleri*; Idem, 'İkinci Dünya Savaşı yıllarında Türkiye'de azınlıklar:Yirmi Kur'a ihtiyatlar olayı', *Tarih ve Toplum* 179 (1998), pp. 4–18; Ayşe Hür, derinsular.com/cumhuriyetin-amele-taburlari-yirmi-kura-ihtiyatlar-ayse-hur/ (accessed 20 October 2012); Güven, *Cumhuriyet Dönemi*, pp. 106–8; Vartan İhmalyan, *Bir Yaşam Öyküsü* (Istanbul: Cem Yayınevi, 1989), pp. 67–74.

229. Publisher Yervant Gobelyan (1923–2010) met Haygazun Kalustyan during the Yirmi Kura Askerlik and served four years. See www.arasayıncilik.com/tr/yazarlar/yervant-gobelyan/79 (accessed 4 November 2012).

230. Haygazun Kalustyan (1920–85), poet. He also worked as a teacher at Tbrevank Boarding School (see Margosyan, *Tespih Taneleri*, p. 82), as well as in Aram Pehlivanyan's *Ashkhadank*, and later in 1938, along with Garbis Cancikyan and Avedis Aliksanyan, in the monthly *Amsvan Kirk'*, where he published a poem with a female pen name, Alis Erēts'yan. See Haygazun Kalustyan, 'Istanbulahay nor panasdeghdzner: Haykazun Kalustyan (Inknatadut'iwn)', *Tebi Luys*, 8 July 1950, No. 19. He later immigrated to Armenia, where he became a researcher on Turkey at the Academy of Sciences, and died there.

231. Talin Suciyan, 'Baron Varujan İstanbul Ermenilerinin tarihini kurtardı', *Agos*, 29 April 2011, No. 786, pp. 10–11.
232. Güzelyan, *Bolso Badanegan Dunĕ*, p. 5.
233. Civan Çakır, oral historical account.
234. Ibid.
235. Arslanyan, *Adım Agop*, p. 41.
236. Ara Koçunyan, *Voğçuyn Amenkin* (Istanbul: Aras Yay. 2008), p. 36.
237. See www.sabah.com.tr/fotohaber/kultur_sanat/istanbulun-100-spor-kulubu/39415 (accessed 11 July 2012). For Armenian sport clubs in the Republican era, see *Aysor*, 26 July 1947, No. 2.
238. Talin Suciyan, 'Baron Varujan İstanbul' and azadalik.wordpress.com/2011/05/07/ermeniler-varujan-koseyana-tarihlerini-borcludur/.
239. Evdoksi Suciyan Parsehyan, oral historical account 1–8 April 2012.
240. During World War I, the Armenian orphanage in Şişli was occupied by the military authorities in 1916 and the orphanage was evacuated, with its many of its beds, utensils, and various household goods reappropriated by the military. The orphanage could be only used again in 1919. See *Hushamadean Karēōgzyan Orpanots'i*, pp. 52 and 57.
241. S. {Stepan} Gülbenkyan and H. {Hrant} Peştimalcıyan, 'Deghegakir Surp P'rgich' Azkayin Hiwantanots'i Hokapartsutean 1944–45i shrchani (113.rt Dari)', in *Ēntartsag Darekirk' Surp P'rgich' Azkayin Hiwantanots'i 1946* (Istanbul: Dbakrut'iwn H. Aprahamyan, 1946), p. 418.
242. Köseyan, *Hushamadean*, p. 181.
243. *Han* can be an inn or a building for small businesses. Ibid., p. 174.
244. *Nor Lur*, 21 July 1947, No. 246.
245. Evdoksi Suciyan Parsehyan, oral historical account.
246. Ibid.
247. Arslanyan, *Adım Agop*, p. 32.
248. Ibid.
249. Ara Garmiryan, oral historical account, 3 April 2012, Montreal.
250. Azadyan and Koçunyan, *Armağan*, pp. 76–9. The authors obviously felt the need to explain the rationale for devoting a special section to Hatay. After explaining how Armenians had come to be instrumentalised in the hands of foreign powers, the authors celebrate the very existence of Atatürk, who they argue protected both Armenians and Turks in Hatay. Atatürk 'rescued' Armenians from becoming victims again in the hands of 'new adventurers'. The special section on Hatay consists of three parts: I. Hatay and the New Sunrise of People of Hatay, II. Armenians in Hatay, III. Armenian Press in the World and Turkey.
251. Information on the election results was also provided in the same pages: 'According to the legislation, they elected the following five members of parliament: Mihran Keshishyan (a teacher at Nubaryan school), Hovhannēs Kazanjyan (trade expert), Khachadur Karabajakyan (tradesmen and AGBU Beylan representative), H. Tavityan (geometry teacher and one of the teachers of Melkonyan), Marsel Balit (Armenian Catholic).'

252. Movses Der Kalustian was one of the main leaders of the Musa Dagh resistance in 1915.
253. *Kulis* was published by Hagop Ayvaz in 1946–96. It was the longest-lasting theatre magazine of Turkey.
254. A. K., oral historical account, Berlin, 20 January 2009.
255. BCA 030.10.225.515.26.
256. A. K., oral historical account, Berlin, 20 January 2009.
257. Ibid.
258. Ibid.
259. *Nor Lur*, 5 January 1946.
260. *Marmara*, 26 July 1947. This means that Armenians did not just live in Vakıf, but also in the surrounding villages at the time. According to the travel account of Bedros Zobyan and William Saroyan in 1964, the number of Armenian families was 20–5 in İskenderun, 15–20 in Kırıkhan and 40–50 in Vakıf. See Zobyan, *Tebi Bitlis*, p. 291.
261. The original phrase is *gayri Türk* in the report, BCA 030.10.24.136.3 – not an uncommon usage. In the daily *Cumhuriyet*, an article on the settlement of Karapapaks referred to them as non-Turkish Muslims (*gayri Türk Müslümanlar*). This definition makes it clear that Turkishness was specifically regarded as a racial category, especially because the *İskan Talimatnamesi* not only aimed at demographic engineering of Turkish-speaking people, but more importantly, it was a demographic engineering project. See 'Karapapaklar ve iskan talimatnamesi', *Cumhuriyet*, 13 July 1934.
262. Ibid.
263. Mentioned as *ırki milliyetler.*
264. Unlike Bulgarians and Slavic groups, Molokans are a religious group, a sect derived from the Russian Orthodox Church.
265. *Cumhuriyet*, 10 July 1934. According to the news, special police units were stationed in Galata and Sirkeci in order to secure that the new immigrants would not be raped/abused/attacked/harrased (*iğfal edilmelerine meydan vermemek üzere* in the original) in Istanbul.
266. Ibid.
267. The last digit is hardly visible, but I identify it as per the date of the law mentioned in the text, 15 July 1949. BCA 030.18.01.02.120.65.17.
268. The first penalisation of hate speech against Armenians was applied to the racist slogans used during the Khojalu demonstration in Istanbul of February 2012. See marksist.org/haberler/9274-azinliklara-yonelik-nefret-soylemine-ilk-ceza (accessed 2 February 2013).
269. For his speech see Talât Paşa, *Hatıralarım ve Müdafam* (Istanbul: Kaynak Yay. 2006).
270. I thank Taner Akçam for bringing these sources to my attention: *Aspiration et Agissenments Revolutionnaires des Comitas Armenies avant et après la Proclamation de la Constition Ottomane* (Istanbul: 1917); *Ermeni Komitelerinin Âmâl ve Harekât-ı İhtilâliyesi (İlân-ı Meşrutiyetten Evvel ve Sonra, 1916)* (Istanbul: Matbaa-i

Amire, 1916). The original book in Ottoman is available at https://ia802604. us.archive.org/14/items/ermenikomiteleri00istauoft/ermenikomiteleri00is- tauoft.pdf and in print, Talât Paşa, *Ermeni Vahşeti ve Ermeni Komitelerinin Âmâl ve Harekât-ı İhtilâliyesi (İlân-ı Meşrutiyetten Evvel ve Sonra) 1916*, ed. Ö. Andaç Uğurlu (Istanbul: Örgün Yay. 2006).

271. Taner Akçam, *A Shameful Act: The Armenian Genocide and the Question of Turkish Responsibility* (New York: Metropolitan Books, 2006), pp. 243–302.

272. Ibid., pp. 349–67.

273. Ibid. p. 374.

274. 'TBMM'nin Ermeni Komiteleri Tarafından Şehit Edilenlerin Ailelerine Yaptıkları Yardımlar.' Available at www.atam.gov.tr/dergi/sayi-55/turkiye- buyuk-millet-meclisinin-ermeni-komiteleri-tarafından-sehit-edilenlerin-ai lelerine-yaptiklari-yardimlar.

275. Donald Bloxham, 'The roots of American Genocide denial: Near Eastern geopolitics and the interwar Armenian question', *Journal of Genocide Research* viii/1 (2006), pp. 27–49.

276. Ibid., p. 37.

277. Ibid., p. 38.

278. 867.00/1578, *Bristol Diary*, 4 November 1922, meeting with Wirt; 867.00/1583, *Bristol Diary*, 27 November 1922, meeting with Barton, both quoted in Bloxham, 'The roots of American Genocide denial', p. 39.

279. 867.00/1884, *Bristol Diary*, 13 July 1925, meeting with King, quoted in Bloxham, 'The roots of American Genocide denial', p. 39.

280. Charles H. Sherrill, *A Year's Embassy to Mustafa Kemal* (New York: Charles Scribner's and Son, 1934), pp. 171 and 208, quoted in Bloxham, 'The roots of American Genocide denial', p. 39.

281. Bloxham, 'The roots of American Genocide denial', p. 39.

282. Ibid., p. 41.

283. Ibid., p. 44.

284. Akçam and Kurt, *Kanunların Ruhu*, p. 182.

285. United States Department of State, *Papers Related to the Foreign Relations of the United States*, Vol. 2 (1923), p. 1195, in Akçam and Kurt, *Kanunların Ruhu*, p. 184.

286. MAE, Levant 1918–40, Turquie, Vol. 260, lettre de Charles de Chambrun, ambassadeur de France en Turquie à Locquin, député, vice-président de la Commission des Finances, Chambres des députés, 10 juillet 1929, Constantinople, f° 27, in Vahe Tachjian, 'An attempt to recover Armenian properties in Turkey through the French authorities in Syria and Lebanon in the 1920s', unpublished article. See also Akçam and Kurt, *Kanunların Ruhu*, p. 154.

287. Hilmar Kaiser, 'From Empire to Republic: The continuities of Turkish denial', *Armenian Review* 48 (2003), p. 3.

288. Alexander Aaronsohn, *With the Turks in Palestine* (London: Constable &. Co. Ltd., 1917), pp. 47–56, quoted in Kaiser, 'From Empire to Republic', p. 3.

289. Ahmed Cemal Bey, *Hatıralar*, ed. Behçet Cemal (Istanbul: Selek Yay., 1959) in Hilmar Kaiser, 'From Empire to Republic', p. 6.
290. Kaiser, 'From Empire to Republic', p. 8.
291. Kaiser, 'From Empire to Republic', p. 10.
292. I have counted 44 articles in *Marmara* on Esat Uras's book, including an interview with him. The articles appeared on 29 August–10 October 1950.
293. Ibid., p. 14.
294. Ibid.
295. *Marmara*, 31 October 1946, No. 1443.
296. On the Turkish Hearths, Erik J. Zürcher writes in *Turkey: A Modern History*: 'It had been reactivated under the leadership of the minister of education, Hamdullah Suphi (Tanrıöver), and it tried to spread nationalist, positivist and secularist ideas in the country through lectures, courses and exhibitions. [...] From 1932 it was replaced by the so-called *Halk Evleri* (People's Homes) in towns and by *Halk Odaları* (People's Rooms) in large villages; they served essentially the same function but were tightly controlled by the provincial branches of the party. By the end of World War II there were nearly 500 of these People's Homes in all parts of the country.' (p. 180).
297. Büşra Ersanlı, *İktidar ve Tarih: Türkiye'de 'Resmi Tarih' Tezinin Oluşumu (1929–1937)* (Istanbul: İletişim Yay., 2011), pp. 110–2. See also the Turkish Historical Association website, www.ttk.gov.tr/index.php?Page=Sayfa&No = 1 (accessed 24 July 2013):
For this reason, on the date of 28 April 1930, in the final sitting of the sixth Convention of the Turkish Hearths (*Türk Ocakları*) attended and led by Atatürk, Âfet İnan and 40 signatories presented a motion which read, 'We propose the formation of a permanent committee for scientific inquiry into Turkish history and civilisation and the Central committee's authorisation for the election of the members of the said scientific committee.' On the same day, following the discussions, (the relevant clause) was added to the Turkish Hearths Statute as clause 84. As per this ruling, a 'Committee for the Inquiry of Turkish History' of 16 members was founded, and the first meeting held on 14 June 1930 for the election of the board of management and other members. Board: President Tevfik Bıyıklıoğlu, Vice-Presidents Yusuf Akçura and Samih Rıfat, Secretary-General Dr Reşit Galip; Members: Âfet İnan, İsmail Hakkı Uzunçarşılı, Hâmid Zübeyir Koşay, Halil Edhem, Ragıb Hulûsi, Reşid Safvet Atabinen, Zâkir Kadîrî, Sadri Maksudi Arsal, Mesaroş (expert, Ankara Ethnography Museum), Mükrimin Halil Yinanç, Vâsıf Çınar and Yusuf Ziya Özer. This committee then published its first work, 'An Outline for Turkish History'. The Turkish Historical Society, which had thus been formed, was reorganised after the decision for closing in the seventh convention of the Turkish Hearths on 29 March 1931, and resumed activities on 12 April 1931 as the 'Turkish Society for Historical Inquiry' as per the principles established in 1930. In 1935, the institution was renamed as 'Turkish Historical Research Association', and then as 'Turkish Historical Association'.

298. See Nazan Maksudyan, *Türklüğü Ölçmek: Bilimkurgusal Antropoloji ve Türk Milliyetçiliğinin Irkçı Çehresi* (Istanbul: Metis Yay., 2005).

299. Ibid., p. 153.

300. See Falih Rıfkı Atay, *Çankaya: Atatürk Devri Hatıraları 1918–1938*, Vol. I (Dünya Yay., Ekicigil Matbaası, 1953), p. 205 in İsmail Beşikçi, *Cumhuriyet Halk Fırkası'nın Tüzüğü (1927) ve Kürt Sorunu* (Ankara: Yurt Kitap Yay., 1991), p. 100. I thank Nevra Ünver Lischewski for bringing this source to my attention. For more, see Falih Rıfkı Atay, 'Hitlerin Doğumgünü', *Ulus* (20 April 1939); Hüseyin Cahit Yalçın, 'Hitlerin 50. Senesi', *Yeni Sabah* (26 April 1939); Nadir Nadi, *Perde Aralığından* (Istanbul: Cumhuriyet Yay., 1965), p. 22.

301. For more on *aşiret mektebi* see Eugene L. Rogan, '*Aşiret mektebi*: Abdülhamid II's school for tribes (1892–1907)', *International Journal of Middle East Studies*, xxviii/1 (1996), pp. 83–107.

302. The relation – if there is one – between the *aşiret mektebi* practice and the boarding schools in the provinces would be an interesting topic for future research.

303. Ayşe Hür, 'Avar, ne olur kızımı götürme...', *Taraf*, 4 October 2009, available at http://arsiv.taraf.com.tr/yazilar/ayse-hur/avar-ne-olur-kizimi-goturme/7767/ (accessed 24 February 2015). Also see the memoirs of Sıdıka Avar, *Dağ Çiçeklerim*, ed. Suat Akgönül (Ankara: Berikan Yay., 2011).

304. Ibid.

305. For the 'race code' see, 'Cumhuriyetin gilzli soy kodu', www.agos.com.tr/tr/yazi/5390/turkiye-soy-kodunu-tartisiyor (accessed 15 March 2015).

306. *Tedvir* means administration. See http://tdk.gov.tr/index.php?option=com _gts&arama = gts&guid = TDK.GTS.54f48860ac56b6.91276290 (accessed 2 March 2015).

307. Emre Ertani, 'Dikkat "Türk müdür" konuşuyor', *Agos*, 20 July 2012, No. 849. See also Emin Keşmer, *Bir Poşet İstanbul Toprağı* (Istanbul: Siyah Beyaz, 2012). The implementation of the Turkish deputy principal system in non-Muslim and foreign schools may be seen within the same framework of social engineering as that inherited from the 'School for Tribes' (*aşiret mekteps*). Very different in nature, 'School for Tribes' was part of a social engineering project during the Abdul Hamid II period that aimed at controlling the empire's tribes to gain their loyalty to the Ottoman state and to create intermediaries between the state and its tribes. For more, see Rogan, 'Aşiret mektebi', p. 83.

308. See Sezen Kılıç, http://atam.gov.tr/cumhuriyet-doneminde-yabanci-okullar-1923-1938/ (accessed 2 February 2013).

309. For more, see Fuat Dündar, *İttihat ve Terakki'nin Etnisite Mühendisliği 1913– 1918* (Istanbul: İletişim Yay., 2008). Talin Suciyan, 'Dündar: İttihat ve Terakki Anadolu'da sistematik etnisite mühendisliği yaptı', interview with Fuat Dündar, *Agos*, 6 April 2007, No. 575.

310. Cemil Koçak, *Umumi Müfettişlikler (1927–1952)* (Istanbul: İletişim Yay., 2003), p. 293.

311. Ibid.

312. The quotation marks are Koçak's.

313. Ibid., p. 294.

314. Ibid., pp. 252–3.

315. Janet Klein, *The Margins of Empire: Kurdish Militias in the Ottoman Tribal Zone* (Stanford: Stanford University Press, 2011), p. 6.

316. Zürcher, *Turkey*, p. 181.

317. Pierre Bourdieu and Loïc Wacquant, *An Invitation to Reflexive Sociology* (Chicago: The University of Chicago Press, 1992), p. 121.

Chapter 2 The Legal Context

1. For the full text of the Treaty of Lausanne, see www.lib.byu.edu/index.php/ Treaty_of_Lausanne (accessed 2 December 2012).

2. For more see Zaven Der Yeghiayan, *My Patriarchal Memoirs*, transl. Ared Misirliyan, ed. Vatche Ghazarian (Barrington: Mayreni Publishing, 2002).

3. Kezban Hatemi and Dilek Kurban, *Bir Yabancılaştırma Hikayesi: Türkiye'deki Gayrimüslim Azınlığın Vakıf ve Mülkiyet Sorunları* (Istanbul: TESEV, 2009), p. 7.

4. Murat Bebiroğlu, www.hyetert.com/prnyazi3.asp?s=&Id = 442&Sayfa = 0& DilId = 1&AltYazi, 2009 and Dimitri Kamouzis, 'İstanbul Rum Ortodoks azınlığının tabi olduğu hukuki rejim ve işleyişi, 1923–1939', in Foti Benlisoy, Annamaria Aslanoğlu and Haris Rigas (eds), *İstanbul Rumları:Bugün ve Yarın* (Istanbul: Istos, 2012), p. 45.

5. Step'an Gülbenkyan, 'Hayots' Badriark'arani Ganonakirě i zōru ě', in *Ěntartsag Darets'oyts' Surp P'rgich' Hiwantanots'i 1946* (Istanbul: Aprahamyan Matbaası, 1946), p. 29.

6. Varujan Köseyan, *Hushamadean Surp P'rgich' Hiwanatanots'i- Surp Pırgiç Hastanesi Tarihçesi* (Istanbul: Murat Ofset, 1994), p. 41, where Patriarch Maghak'ia Ōrmanyan, *Azgapatum*, 3 vols (Constantinople and Jerusalem: 1913–1927) and Piwzant K'ech'yan, *Badmut'iwn Surp P'rgich' Hiwantanots'i Hayots'* (Constantinople: 1887) are also referenced.

7. Hagop Barsoumian, *The Armenian Amira Class of Istanbul* (Yerevan: American University of Armenia, 2007), pp. 118–19. See also *Nor Luys*, 20 September 1933, No. 62.

8. Arus Yumul, 'Osmanlı'nın ilk anayasası', in Vartan Artinian (ed.), *Osmanlı Devleti'nde Ermeni Anayasası'nın Doğuşu* (Istanbul: Aras Yay. 2004), p. 178.

9. Arşag Alboyacıyan, 'Azkayin Sahmanatrut'iwně, ir dzakumě ew girarut'iwne', in *Ěntartsag Orats'oyts' Surp P'rgich' Hiwantanots'i* (Istanbul: Madt'ēosyan Matbaası., 1910), pp. 76–528.

10. Avedis Berberyan, *Badmut'iwn Hayots'* (Istanbul: B. Kirişçiyan Matbaası, 1871).

11. Yumul, 'Osmanlı'nın ilk anayasası', p. 169.

12. Artinian, 'Appendix IX: Nizamname-i millet-i Ermeniyan', in *Osmanlı Devleti'nde Ermeni Anayasası'nın Doğuşu*, p. 243.

230   NOTES TO PAGES 93–4

13. There are differences between the Armenian and the Armeno-Turkish originals of the *Nizamname*, on which Vartan Artinian, Arşag Alboyacıyan and Arus Yumul have written in more detail. See Artinian, *Osmanlı Devleti'nde Ermeni Anayasası'nın Doğuşu*, pp. 117, 176). See also 'Appendix V' and Arşag Alboyacıyan, '1860 Anayasası ile 1863 Anayasası arasındaki farklılıklar', pp. 151–62 in the same source.

14. This concept of the Integrated/ Mixed Assembly was not used in the Ottoman version of the text. Arus Yumul refers to this assembly, in Turkish translation, as *Muhtelit Meclis* (Artinian, *Osmanlı Devleti'nde Ermeni Anayasası'nın Doğuşu*, p. 172).

15. Ibid., p. 245. See Armenian text of Nizamname in Artinian, 'Appendix IX', in *Osmanlı Devleti'nde Ermeni Anayasası'nın Doğuşu*, p. 39.

16. *Deghegakir Ēnthanur Zhoghovo K'nnich' Hantsnazhoghovi* (Istanbul: Foti Basımevi, 1951), p. 15.

17. Toros Azadyan, *Lipananean Husher* (Istanbul: Doğu Basımevi, 1949), p. 132.

18. *Nor Lur*, 9 July 1949, No. 460.

19. Ibid.

20. Murat Bebiroğlu, www.hyetert.com/prnyazi3.asp?s=&Id = 442&Sayfa = 0& DilId = 1&AltYazi (accessed 30 August 2012).

21. I have come across a footnote in *Paros* (3 October 1950, No. 58) about the person of Vahan Surēnyan and his period: 'Surēnyan's administration (1927–37) was the most harmful during the last constitutional period (more accurately, it acted against the constitution); it was an administration that wasted the funds of the community.' The author (most probably editor-in-chief Takvor Acun, since the text was written on behalf of *Paros*) argued that three Surēnyan relatives with different positions enabled this administration: Vahan was head of the administration, Arşag was administrator of properties, and Levon was a member of the local administration in Beyoğlu. Their family relationship is not mentioned; they may have been brothers or first paternal cousins. Apparently, Vahan Surēnyan had previously worked as a teacher at the Halkalı Ziraat Mektebi. About the school, see Özgür Yıldız, 'The history of Halkalı School of Agriculture', *International Journal of Social Science* v/4, pp. 293–306, or see the Turkish version, www.jasstudies.com/Makaleler/11260937_yıldız_özgür_mTT. pdf (accessed 2 December 2012). *Paros* continued to write about the Surēnyan administration; according to Takvor Acun, Vahan Surēnyan had previously worked in the Ministry of Agriculture as an executive director. See *Paros*, 17 October 1950, No. 60.

22. *Nor Lur*, 9 July 1949, No. 46.

23. *Nor Lur*, 13 September 1934.

24. Different sources referred to the name of the newly established body in different ways. However, Toros Azadyan's book on the history of Karagözyan includes a copy of an official letter where its name appears as Azkayin Varch'agan Zhoghov. See Toros Azadyan, *Hushamadean Karagēōzyan Orpanots'i 1913–1948 (Şişli)* (Istanbul: Becid Basımevi: 1949), p. 108.

25. *Nor Lur*, 14 September 1934.

26. Ibid.

27. On the other hand, the meetings of GNA have been a constant issue after 1915 because of deaths, exile and pressures. See Patriarch Zaven Der Yeghiayan's memoirs.

28. *Bashdonagan Hradaragut'iwn Azkayin Badriark'arani: Adenakrut'iwn Azkayin Ĕnthanur Zhoghovo* (Istanbul: Ak-Ün Matbaası, 2 December 1950), p. 3.

29. Azadyan, *Lipananean Husher*, p. 134.

30. *Cumhuriyet* quoted in *Nor Lur*, 14 September 1934.

31. Ibid.

32. *Nor Lur*, 15 September 1934.

33. Murat Bebiroğlu, http://www.hyetert.com/prnyazi3.asp?s=&Id = 442& Sayfa = 0&DilId = 1&AltYazi, 2009 (accessed 10 August 2012).

34. *Milliyet* quoted in *Nor Lur*, 15 September 1934.

35. Ardaşes Kalpakcıyan, 'Azkayin Sahmanatrut'iwne ew mer hamaynk'in paghtsankĕ', *Nor Luys*, 20 September 1934, No. 62.

36. *Nor Lur*, 16 September 1934.

37. *Marmara*, 1 July 1949, No. 1900.

38. Ibid.

39. Artinian, 'Appendix', p. 24.

40. *Nor Lur*, 14 October 1947, No. 279, also *Nor Lur* 22 November 1947, No. 290.

41. The signature, A.P.K., belonged to Vahan Toşikyan himself. See Toros Azadyan, *Jamanak: K'aṛasnamea Hishadagaran 1908–1948* (Istanbul: Becid Basımevi, 1948), p. 209.

42. *Marmara*, 5 August 1947, No. 1718 and 6 August 1947, No. 1719.

43. *Marmara*, 27 June 1949, No. 1896.

44. Ibid.

45. Ibid.

46. Ibid.

47. Ibid.

48. Ibid.

49. *Marmara*, 1 July 1949, No. 1900.

50. *Paros*, 23 November 1949, No. 1.

51. A report of 8 June 1937 in the Prime Minister's Archive on the Republican period shows that the civil assembly still existed as a concept. The reporter who translated a news item from *Nor Lur* wrote that a special report was to be prepared on the Civil Assembly and its legal procedence (See BCA 030.10.109.720.13). However, I could not locate this report and do not know whether it was indeed prepared. The Civil Assembly legally ceased to exist in 1961, after the *coup d'état* of 1960. It ceased to function *de facto* after September 1934. With the election of Patriarch Karekin Khachaduryan (Haçaduryan) in 1950, a GNA meeting was held and the Civil Assembly was formed, but it hardly lasted a decade; such entities were prohibited after the *coup d'état* of 1960.

52. See the full text of the *3512 Cemiyetler Kanunu* of 26 June 1938 in *Resmi Gazete*, 14 July 1938.
53. *Tebi Luys*, 17 June 1950, No. 16.
54. See the full text of the changes in Law of Pious Foundations published in *Resmi Gazete*, 14 July 1938, No. 3959 http://www.resmigazete.gov.tr/arsiv/3959.pdf (accessed 2 December 2012).
55. Toros Azadyan and Zarmayr Dz. V. Geziwryan, *Hay Hosnak Salnamesi / Hay Khosnag Darekirk' I. Dari, 1941* (Istanbul: Dbakrutiwun Hagop Aprahamyan, 1941), p. 198.
56. *Marmara*, 19 June 1947, No. 1671.
57. *Nor Lur*, 27 June 1947, No. 248.
58. For more see BCA 030.10.000.000.191.308.11.
59. *Marmara*, 27 October 1948, No. 1655.
60. *Marmara*, 18 December 1948, No. 1707.
61. *Deghegakir Ĕnthanur Zhoghovo K'nnich' Hantsnazhoghovi*, p. 24.
62. Ibid., p. 35.
63. Ibid., pp. 36–7.
64. Köseyan, *Hushamadean*, pp. 168–9.
65. Ibid.
66. *Marmara*, 14 September 1949, No. 1975.
67. Ibid.
68. *Marmara*, 26 September 1949, No. 1987.
69. *Marmara*, 10 October 1949, No. 2001.
70. Ibid.
71. Elçin Macar, 'Başbakanlık Cumhuriyet Arşivi belgelerine göre tek parti döneminde cemaat vakıflarının sorunları', www.bolsohays.com/yazarmakale-73/anonim-tek-parti-doneminde-cemaat-vakiflarinin-sorunlari.html, 2011 (accessed 15 August 2012) and *Cumhuriyet Döneminde İstanbul Rum Patrikhanesi* (Istanbul: İletişim Yay., 2003), pp. 176–9.
72. Ibid.
73. BCA 030.10.109.723.1.
74. BCA 030.10.191.307.9.
75. Editorial, 'Hamaynkayin hartser: Anhrajeshd baymannerēn min', *Nor Or*, 10 November 1945.
76. Ahmet Emin Yalman (Thessaloniki 1888–Istanbul 1972), prominent author, opinion maker, journalist. He pursued an academic career as well. His memoirs were published in four volumes: *Yakın Tarihimizde Gördüklerim ve Geçirdiklerim* (Istanbul: Rey Yay., 1970).
77. *Marmara*, 2 March 1947, No. 1561.
78. Ibid.
79. *Marmara*, 22 March 1947, No. 1584; 23 March 1947, No. 1585; 28 March 1947, No. 1590; 2 April 1947, No. 1595; 3 April 1947, No. 1596; 4 April 1947, No. 1597; 8 April 1947, No. 1600; 18 April 1947, No. 1610.
80. *Marmara*, 22 March 1947, No. 1584.

81. *Nor Lur*, 29 March 1947, No. 222; *Jamanak*, quoted in *Marmara*, 3 May 1947, No. 1625.
82. *Nor Lur*, 12 April 1947, No. 226.
83. Ibid.
84. *Marmara*, 8 April 1947, No. 1600.
85. *Marmara*, 14 July 1947, No. 1697.
86. Prof A. Nargizyan (Suren Şamlıyan)'s series of articles were published on 14–20 July 1947 in the column 'Badmutean hamar' and under the section 'Ēvkafi dnorēnĕ inch'bēs chure tskets' Vakĕfneru Orēnk'in parep'okhumĕ'.
87. *Marmara*, 16 July 1947, No. 1699.
88. *Marmara*, 18 July 1947, No. 1701.
89. Ibid.
90. Ibid.
91. Ibid.
92. *Marmara*, 18–20 July 1947, No. 1701–3.
93. *Marmara*, 18 July 1947, No. 1701.
94. Ibid.
95. Ibid.
96. For the confiscation of Sanasaryan Han see Hüseyin Şengül, www.bianet.org/biamag/azinliklar/135782-sanasaryan-han-gaspin-ve-zulmun-dikilitasi (accessed 30 November 2012). See also http://www.istanbulermenivakiflari.org (accessed 1 December 2012).
97. For the confiscation of the Armenian cemetery of Pangaltı, see Armaveni Miroğlu, www.hyetert.com/yazi3.asp?Id=323&DilId = 1 (accessed 30 November 2012).
98. As Çobangil explains, paragraph 9 of the Law of Foundations states clearly that a property could not be sold if the beneficiaries of that property continued to exist.
99. *Mülhak Vakıflar* were established prior to the enactment of the Civil Code and are mostly registered on the names of saints, like Jesus, Holy Saviour, St Maria, etcetera.
100. *Marmara*, 18 July 1947, No. 1702. Çobangil gives the date of the law as 1328 AH, which corresponds to 1912.
101. *Marmara*, 19 July 1947, No. 1703.
102. Ibid.
103. *Marmara*, 20 July 1947, No. 1703.
104. Ibid.
105. For more see 'Surenyan varch'ut'iwnĕ ew ir kordzunēut'iwnĕ', *Paros*, 24 October 1950, No. 61. The article draws attention to the relations between CHP and Vahan Surēnyan.
106. Lütfik Kuyumcuyan, 'Ĕngeragts'utyants' Ōrēnk'č', in *Ermeni Hastanesi Salnamesi/ Ĕntarts'ag Darekirk' Hiwantanots'i 1938* (Istanbul: O. Aktaryan Matbaası, 1938), pp. 37–44.
107. *Marmara*, 20 July 1947, No. 1703.

108. Ibid. *Takvim-i Vekayi*, 28 'Temmuz' 1332 AH Solar / 11 Şevval 1334 AH Lunar (11 August 1916), No. 2611. Available at http://gazeteler.ankara.edu.tr/dergiler/milli_kutup/865/865_37//0470.pdf (accessed 1 February 2015).

109. Ibid. *Takvim-i Vekayi*, 20 Teşrin-i Sani 1334 AH Solar /13 Safer 1337 AH Lunar (18 November 1918), No. 3399. Available at http://gazeteler.ankara.edu.tr/dergiler/milli_kutup/865/865_42//0495.pdf (accesed 1 February 2015). See also Dr Ali Güler, 'Ermenilerle ilgili 1916 ve 1918 yıllarında yapılan hukuki düzenlemeler', in http://dergiler.ankara.edu.tr/dergiler/19/1152/13543.pdf (accessed 1 February 2015).

110. Ibid. These bylaws are about the attribution of the Patriarchate. The legal status and the authority of Patriachate were changed in 1916 and the bylaws were restored in 1918 (*Takvim-i Vekayi*, No. 3399, in *Marmara*, 22 November 1947, No. 1818, and Gülbenkyan, 'Hayots'', pp. 26–8).

111. In 1916–18 new bylaws were enacted. There is a footnote on these bylaws in Puzant Yeghiayan's book, *Jamanagagits' Badmut'iwn Gatoghigosut'ean Hayots' Giligyo 1914–1972* (Antilias: Dbaran Gat'oghigosut'ean Hayots' Medzi Dann Giligio, 1975), p. 61. The bylaws were published as a separate booklet by the publishing house of the Patriarchate of Jerusalem in 1917. They are also included in their entirety in Papkēn Giwlēsēryan, *Badmut'iwn Gat'oghigosats' Giligio* (Antelias: Dbaran Gatoghigosut'ean Hayots' Medzi Dann Giligio, 1990), pp. 933–48.

112. *Marmara*, 20 July 1947, No. 1703.

113. *Marmara*, 25 July 1947, No. 1708.

114. Ibid.

115. *Arevelk* quoted in *Marmara*, 13 February 1948, No. 1900. The editor-in-chief of *Arevelk* was Minas Tololyan, a former Armenian from Istanbul.

116. Foundation Law 5404 was modified on 31 May 1949. For the text, see www.hukuki.net/kanun/2762.13.text.asp (accessed 30 July 2012), and also *Resmî Gazete*, No. 7224, 4 June 1949, in Macar, 'Başbakanlık Cumhuriyet Arşivi Belgelerine', p. 8.

117. *Marmara*, 14 May 1949, No. 1852.

118. *Marmara*, 15 February 1950, No. 2127; 18 February 1950, No. 2130; 20 February 1950, No. 2132; 25 February 1950, No. 2137.

119. *Marmara*, 5 March 1950, No. 2145.

120. *Marmara*, 18 March 1950, No. 2158.

121. *Bēyoghlui Egeghets'eats' Ew Anonts' Ent'aga Hasdadut'eants Madagararut'ean K'aramea Deghegakir 1950–1953* (Istanbul: Dbakrut'iwn Narin, 1954), p. 7.

122. Ibid., p. 8.

123. Ibid.

124. H. Peştimalciyan (Dr), *Hrabaragayin Niwtagan Ew Paroyagan Hamaraduut'iwn 1933–1949* (Istanbul: Varol Matbaası, 1961), p. 8.

125. Zygmunt Baumann, *Modernity and Ambivalence* (Great Britain: Polity Press, 1991), p. 104.

126. Ibid., p. 106.
127. Emphasis in the original.
128. Ibid., p. 111.
129. Biberyan was drafted during the *Yirmi Kura Askerlik*, where he met the editor-in-chief of *Jamanak* newspaper, Ara Koçunyan. After his return, Biberyan started writing a series of articles in *Jamanak* under the title 'The Death of Christianity'. These articles were harshly criticised. He lost his job shortly thereafter. See www.arasyayincilik.com/tr/yazarlar/zaven-biberyan/83 (accessed 4 November 2012).
130. Zaven Biberyan, 'Al gĕ pawē', *Nor Lur*, 5 January 1946.
131. *Marmara*, 4 October 1945, No. 1058.
132. *Marmara*, 5 October 1945, No. 1059.
133. Şamlıyan refers to Prime Minister Şükrü Saraçoğlu as 'his excellency'.
134. *Marmara*, 7 October 1945, No. 1061.
135. *Marmara*, 10 October 1945, No. 1064.
136. *Marmara*, 7 September 1945, No. 1031.
137. *Marmara*, 21 June 1946, No. 1313.
138. Ibid.
139. *Darekirk' Surp P'rgich' Hiwantanots'i 1947*, p. 376.
140. *Marmara*, 21 June 1946, No. 1313.
141. Ibid.
142. According to Ali İhsan Ökten, Mustafa Kemal used the name of Asım Us when he wrote his famous articles in *Vakıt* (22–5 January 1937) on the annexation of Hatay. If this is true, Asım Us was the embodiment of the establishment itself. See www.hekimedya.org/index.php/yazarlar/dr-ali-ihsan-okten/465-savan-goelgesinde-hatayda-hekimlik-ve-sorunlar.html (accessed 31 January 2015).
143. Hayk Açıkgöz, *Bir Anadolulu Ermeni Komünistin Anıları* (Istanbul: Belge Yay., 2006), p. 102.
144. www.arasyayincilik.com/index.php?dispatch=pages.view&page_id = 520 (accessed 6 August 2012). According to his birth register (*nüfus tezkeresi*), he was born on 9.7.1333 AH, that is 1 August 1917. In his two-page, hand-written autobiography, Pehlivanyan states that he was born in 1919. This autobiographical text was written on 22 April 1955 and made available to me by his daughter Meline Pehlivanyan.
145. Krikor Sarafyan, chemist, and one of the former principals (1933–6) of Getronagan High School, was born in Kadıköy in 1909. I thank Silva Kuyumcuyan, the principal of Getronagan High School, for providing this biographical data.
146. Pehlivanyan, autobiographical notes written on 22 April 1955. Pehlivanyan wrote that they were arrested in 1943. However, this is most probably incorrect, since the arrests took place in 1944.
147. Ibid.

148. Vartan İhmalyan was a graduate of the American boys college, i.e. Robert College, now Bogazici University. For his biography see Vartan İhmalyan, *Bir Yaşam Öyküsü* (Istanbul: Cem Yayınevi, 1989).
149. For Sarkis Keçyan's biography, see Introduction, footnote 26.
150. www.arasyayincilik.com/tr/yazarlar/s-k-zanku/58 (accessed 8 March 2013).
151. Pehlivanyan, autobiographical notes on 22 April 1955.
152. *Nor Or*, 21 July 1945, No. 1.
153. *Nor Or*, 26 November 1946, No. 109.
154. *Nor Or*, 13 October 1945, No. 13.
155. *Nor Or*, 21 October 1946, No. 73.
156. *Nor Or*, 29 June 1946, No. 50.
157. *Nor Or*, 6 July 1946, No. 51.
158. Ibid.
159. *Nor Or*, 20 July 1946, No. 1.
160. Ibid.
161. Ibid.
162. Berç Keresteciyan received his Turkish family name Türker from Mustafa Kemal after the Surname Law of 1934. Berç Türker posed his candidacy from Istanbul with Hüseyin Cahit Yalçın, Kazım Karabekir, Refet Bele, Yahya Kemal Beyatlı, Ahmet Şükrü Esmer and Hamdullah Suphi Tanrıöver, among others.
163. *Nor Lur*, 20 July 1946, No. 150.
164. Ibid.
165. Ibid.
166. Cemil Koçak, *Türkiye'de İki Partili Siyasi Sistemin Kuruluş Yılları: İkinci Parti* (Istanbul: İletişim Yay., 2010), p. 525. See also Metin Toker, *Tek Partiden Çok Partiye* (Istanbul: Milliyet Yay., 1970), pp. 171–2.
167. According to official detailed results, Türker received 135,913 votes, as opposed to Dr Kirkor Keşişyan, who received 158,793 votes. See *Marmara*, 27 July 1946, No. 1345.
168. *Nor Or*, 28 July 1946, No. 2.
169. *Nor Or*, 3 August 1946, No. 3.
170. *Nor Or*, 11 August 1946.
171. Ibid.
172. *Nor Or*, 13 August 1946, No. 4.
173. Aram Pehlivanyan, 'Mer tsaverě', *Nor Or*, 21 August 1946, No. 12.
174. *Nor Or*, 14 August 1946, No. 5.
175. Ibid.
176. *Nor Or*, 14 October 1946, No. 66. In the second and third parts, Aliksanyan discusses the issue from the perspective of the working classes and the attitude of Köprülü and Menderes regarding class issues.
177. *Nor Or*, 19 September 1946, No. 41.
178. Aram Pehlivanyan, 'Anhrajeshd lusapanut'iwn mě', *Nor Or*, 15 November 1946, No. 98.

179. *Marmara*, 26 March 1947, No. 1588.
180. *Marmara*, 28 March 1947, No. 1590.
181. *Marmara*, 29 March 1947, No. 1591.
182. Ibid.
183. Zaven Biberyan, 'Och' ok'', *Aysor*, 8 August 1947, No. 4.
184. Ibid.
185. *Nor Lur*, 9 August 1947, No. 260.
186. *Aysor*, 16 August 1947, No. 5.
187. Irazeg is a very common pseudonym in the Armenian press. Irazeg, 'Getronagan madagarar marmin', *Aysor*, 6 September 1947, No. 8.
188. Zaven Biberyan, 'Kordzik' chllank'', *Aysor*, 13 September 1947, No. 9.
189. *Nor Lur*, 16 September 1947, No. 271.
190. *Aysor*, 4 October 1947, No. 12.
191. *Nor Lur*, 13 November 1947, No. 289.
192. Ibid.
193. *Marmara*, 17 November 1947, No. 1813.
194. Ibid.
195. *Nor Lur*, 22 November 1947, No. 290.
196. Ibid.
197. *Aysor*, 27 December 1947, No. 24.
198. *Marmara*, 1 January 1948, No. 1858; 5 January 1948, No. 1862.
199. *Nor Lur*, 3 January, 10 January, 13 January, 17 January, 20 January, 23 January, 27 January, 10 February, 17 February, 21 February, 6 March, 13 March, 20 March, 3 April 1948.
200. *Aysor*, 3 January 1948, No. 25.
201. Hamdullah Suphi Tanrıöver (Istanbul 1885–1966), Minister of Education and head of the Turkish Hearths (*Türk Ocakları*) organisation, both until its banning in 1931 and after its reestablishment in 1949. He was elected to the parliament in 1950.
202. *Tebi Luys*, 3 June 1950, No. 14.
203. Ibid.
204. *Tebi Luys*, 17 June 1950, No. 16.
205. Ibid.

Chapter 3   State Surveillance and Anti-Armenian Campaigns

1. The high number of Armenian owners of publishing houses exclusively in Istanbul, according to the list compiled in 1934, confirms this argument. See Server İskit, *Türkiye'de Neşriyat Hareketleri Tarihine Bir Bakış* (Ankara: Milli Eğitim Basımevi, 2000), pp. 193–6.
2. *Mayr hayrenik* is the translation of the French *mère patrie*.
3. Ara Koçunyan, *Voğçuyn Amenkin* (Istanbul: Aras Yay., 2008), pp. 78–9. Koçunyan did not mention the exact date of this incident, which must have

taken place in 1936 or 1937. Aslanyan left the country after the closure of his newspaper. He first went to Syria and then to Lebanon. In 1942 he reissued *Aztarar* in Beirut, which continued publication until 1955. See Amalia Giragosyan (ed.), *Hay Barperagan Mamuli Madenakrut'yun (1794– 1967)* (Yerevan: 1970), p. 36. Manuk Aslanyan passed away in 1944 in Beirut.

4. For the full text of the law, see www.resmigazete.gov.tr/arsiv/87.pdf (accessed 7 January 2015).
5. Mustafa Yılmaz and Yasemin Doğaner, 'Demokrat Parti döneminde Bakanlar Kurulu ile yasaklanan yayınlar', *Kebikeç* 22 (2006), pp. 151–204. See also Mustafa Yılmaz, 'Cumhuriyet döneminde Bakanlar Kurulu kararı ile yasaklanan yayınlar 1923–45', *Kebikeç* 6 (1998), pp. 53–80, and with Yasemin Doğaner, '1961–63 yılları arasında Bakanlar Kurulu kararı ile yasaklanan yayınlar', *Atatürk Yolu* (2006), pp. 247–99.
6. Server İskit, *Türkiyede Matbuat İdareleri ve Politikaları* (Istanbul: Başvekalet Basın ve Yayın Umum Müdürlüğü Yayınlarından, 1943), p. 205.
7. Ibid., p. 249.
8. For the full text of the law, see www.tbmm.gov.tr/tutanaklar/KANUNLAR_ KARARLAR/kanuntbmmc013/kanuntbmmc013/kanuntbmmc01302444. pdf (accessed 8 December 2012).
9. See Melissa Bilal and Lerna Ekmekçioğlu, *Bir Adalet Feryadı: Osmanlı'dan Türkiye'ye Beş Ermeni Feminist Yazar 1862–1933* (Istanbul: Aras Yay., 2006).
10. *Nor Or, Yığın, Gün, Ses, Sendika* and *Dost* were all banned on 16 December 1946. www.tarihtebugun.org/tarihte_bu_sene/1946-senesi-yasananlar.html, see also www.pirvakfi.8m.com/sansur.html, www.nesinvakfi.org/aziz_nesi n_ayrintili_yasamoykusu.html (accessed 18 June 2012).
11. See Elçin Macar, *Cumhuriyet Döneminde İstanbul Rum Patrikhanesi* (Istanbul: İletişim Yay., 2003), p. 168.
12. Mustafa Yılmaz, www.ait.hacettepe.edu.tr/akademik/arsiv/ysk.htm#_ftn211 (accessed 20 April 2012).
13. BCA, 030.18.01.02.118.100.18.
14. Vartan Matiossian drew my attention to the fact that the title must have been *Ermeni Tarihi*, which was published until 1934. Therefore it is not clear to me which publication exactly was banned.
15. BCA, 030.18.02.105.47.6.
16. Mihran Dabağ, oral historical account, 27 January 2015, Konstanz. In Talin Suciyan, 'Dört nesil: Kurtarılamayan son', *Toplum ve Bilim* 132 (2015), pp. 132–49.
17. A. K. Berlin 2009, ibid.
18. Press Code of 1931, Law no. 1881, paragraph 51: 'The entry and dissemination in Turkey of a newspaper or a magazine published in a foreign country can be prohibited by Cabinet Council Decision' ('*Yabancı bir memlekette çıkan bir gazete veya mecmuanın Türkiyeye sokulması ve dağıtılması İcra Vekilleri Heyeti Kararı ile menolunabilir*').

19. BCA, 030.18.01.02.1.1.14. In fact, *Harach* was published by Shavarsh Misakian himself; though always a private publication, it simply followed the line of the ARF.
20. BCA, 030.18.01.02.45.35.4.
21. BCA, 030.18.01.02.44.25.15. In fact, *Troshag* ceased publication in 1933.
22. BCA, 030.18.05.84.73.12.
23. BCA, 030.18.01.02.25.2.19.
24. BCA, 030.18.01.02.35.30.3.
25. BCA, 030.18.01.02.36.33.6.
26. BCA, 030.18.01.02.50.89.17.
27. BCA, 030.18.01.02.49.77.15.
28. BCA, 030.18.01.01.61.10.15.
29. BCA, 030.10.108.712.17.
30. BCA, 030.18.01.02.71.69.
31. BCA, 030.18.01.02.51.32.
32. BCA, 030.10.111.745.11.
33. Marie Sarrafian Banker's book, *My Beloved Armenia: A Thrilling Testimony* was first published in 1936 and reprinted several times.
34. BCA, 030.18.01.02.79.82.14.
35. BCA, 030.18.01.02.86.40.18. Bishop Mushegh Seropian was prelate of Adana in 1909.
36. BCA, 30.10.109.720.12. I could not find any information on this person. The document was submitted to the office of the Prime Minister and the Minister of Foreign Affairs.
37. 'Ankarayi mēch Hay lezui pdzakhntir bashdonadar mě' *Marmara*, 12 October 1945, No. 1066 and 13 October 1945, No. 1067.
38. Abdullah Muradoğlu, yarin1ist.tripod.com/mayis/34.htm (accessed 24 April 2012).
39. Server İskit, *Türkiyede Matbuat*, p. 271.
40. Ibid.
41. Vedat Nedim Tör (Istanbul 1897–1985) was the son of Nedim Bey, the General Secretary of the Ministry of War (*Harbiye Nezareti Müsteşarlık Başkatibi*). See İskit, *Türkiyede Matbuat*, pp. 271–2, and also his memoirs: Vedat Nedim Tör, *Yıllar Böyle Geçti* (Istanbul: Milliyet Yay., 1976).
42. www.mfa.gov.tr/sayin_-selim-r_-sarper_in-ozgecmisi.tr.mfa (accessed 24 April 2012).
43. BCA, 30.10. 86.570.5; *Halk Salnamesi* was printed by A. Abrahamyan Printing House.
44. The title of Vahe Haig's book may be translated as *The Chimney of the Fatherland*. The Turkish translation given in the document is far-fetched. This was a collection of short stories in five volumes, authored by Vahe Haig (1900–83), an Armenian-American writer and survivor from Kharpert. He is also the editor of *Kharpert Ew Anor Osgeghēn Tashdĕ*. See Introduction, footnote 47.

45. BCA, 030.18.01.151.69.19.
46. BCA, File No. 52–117 1730, 1973. The document mentions a book published in Iran, *Katliam-ı Ermeniyan*, along with two other books published in West Germany.
47. Available at rabat.be.mfa.gov.tr/MissionChiefHistory.aspx (accessed 24 April 2012).
48. BCA, 030.11.165.2.15.
49. BCA, 030.01.101.623.4.
50. *Nor Lur*, 22 January 1946, No. 100.
51. Ibid.
52. BCA, 030.01.101.623.4.
53. Ibid.
54. *Nor Or*, 19 January 1946, No. 27.
55. *Nor Or*, 2 February 1946, No. 29 and *Nor Or*, 9 February 1946, No. 30.
56. Ibid.
57. V. Bartevyan, 'Siretsek Hayerě', *Marmara*, 7 January 1946, No. 1153.
58. See Chapter 3, footnote 38.
59. Ibid.
60. BCA, 030.01.101.623.6.
61. BCA, 030.01.101.623.6.
62. Ibid.
63. Ibid.
64. Ibid.
65. Ibid.
66. Pen name of Arshag Ezikyan. See Toros Azadyan, *Jamanak: K'aṛasnamea Hishadagaran 1908–1948* (Istanbul: Becid Basımevi, 1948), p. 209.
67. BCA, 030.10.87.573.6.
68. Ibid.
69. Prof A. Nargizyan, 'Aṛachin demokratnerě ew Hay yerespokhanneru terě Osm. khorhrtaranin měch', *Marmara*, 2–5 July 1946, No. 1322, 1323, 1324, 1325. Prof A. Nargizyan was one of the pen names of Suren Şamlıyan. The article series presents a broad picture of the press and the freedom of the press in the nineteenth century and the late Ottoman period, providing detailed information on the Armenian contribution to Ottoman state and society.
70. BCA, 030.10.87.573.6.
71. There is a variety of news in *Marmara* on immigration; for instance, two lengthy articles on the immigration of Armenians from Bulgaria and Lebanon (28 August 1946, No. 1379).
72. *Nor Or*, 6 October 1945, No 12.
73. *Nor Or*, 20 October 1945, No. 14.
74. *Nor Or*, 29 June 1946, No. 50.
75. Ibid.
76. *Nor Lur*, 20, 24 and 27 November 1945.
77. Suren Şamlıyan, 'Zkushutyan hraver', *Marmara*, 24 January 1946, No. 1170.

78. Ibid.
79. Ibid.
80. *Nor Lur*, 29 January 1946, No. 102.
81. *Marmara*, 7 January 1946, No. 1153.
82. BCA, 030.01.101.626.6.
83. Available at www.arasyayincilik.com/tr/yazarlar/zaven-biberyan/83 (accessed 16 November 2012). See also the biography of Biberyan in Zaven Biberyan, *Mrchiwnneru Verchaloysĕ* (Istanbul: Aras Yayıncılık, 2007), p. 7.
84. See Cemil Koçak, *Türkiye'de İki Partili Siyasi Sistemin Kuruluş Yılları: İkinci Parti* (Istanbul: İletişim Yay., 2010), pp. 311–3 and *Marmara*, 21 May 1947, No. 1642.
85. *Marmara*, 5 December 1946, No. 1478.
86. *Marmara*, 17 December 1946, No. 1490. The Turkish Socialist Labour Party, the Turkish Socialist Party, their trade unions, and the newspapers *Sendika, Ses, Gün, Yığın* and *Dost* were all banned. *Yarın* and *Büyük Doğu*, regarded as reactionary, were temporarily closed down.
87. *Son Telgraf, Vatan* and *Cumhuriyet* quoted in *Marmara*, 18 December 1946, No. 1491.
88. *Aysor*, 19 July 1947, No. 1. There was an article on the communists who were released in *Marmara*, 16 March 1948, No. 1932, which for the first time mentioned the names of Armenians who got arrested: Aram Pehlivanyan, Jak İhmalyan, tailor Levon, Barkev and Dr Hayk. *Marmara* published another piece of news about the court decision on 15 July 1948, No. 1551. Aram Pehlivanyan and Dr Hayk Açıkgöz were sentenced to three years of imprisonment, while Barkev Şamigyan was sentenced to two. Nubar Acemyan and Hraç Akmanoğlu were released. This information was confirmed in the memoirs of Dr Hayk Açıkgöz, according to whom Nubar Acemyan was an architect and Hraç Akmanoğlu, a labourer. There was another person arrested by the name of Mıgırdiç. See Hayk Açıkgöz, *Bir Anadolulu Ermeni Komünistin Anıları* (Istanbul: Belge Yay., 2006), pp. 236–7. Upon his release, Aram Pehlivanyan was conscripted, knowing that, as an Armenian communist, and given experiences of imprisonment and torture, this was a one-way ticket. He wrote that he left the country in agreement with the Turkish Communist Party's central committee decisions. He lived in Aleppo and Beirut, where he established a business in biscuit production. He then moved to Germany. Jak İhmalyan and Dr Hayk Açıkgöz were to face the same outcome and left the country. With the help of Armenians in Syria and Lebanon, they made their way to Beirut. Zaven Biberyan joined them in Beirut (ibid., pp. 267–77 and 310–11). Thus, Beirut became an important centre for the leftist Armenians of Turkey at the end of the 1940s and the beginning of the 1950s. The existence of a large Armenian community in Beirut was decisive, rather than the relative strength of leftist movements in Lebanon. Indeed, Dr Açıkgöz wrote about Turkish leftists coming to Beirut and getting false identity cards through the connections of

local Armenians and Armenian members of the Turkish Communist Party, i.e. Aram Pehlivanyan and Hayk Açıkgöz, among others (see ibid., pp. 397–8).

89. BCA, 030.01.101.623.6.

90. BCA, 030.01.101.626.6.

91. *Carakayt* was published by Haçik Amiryan in 1947–52. Amiryan later moved to Soviet Armenia and taught at the Yerevan State University.

92. Ibid.

93. See the chapter on legal issues.

94. BCA, 030.01.101.623.6.

95. BCA, 030.10.87.573.6.

96. See Pınar Dost, 'Amerika'nın Türkiye politikasının oluşumu üzerine yeni bir okuma', *Tarih ve Toplum Yeni Yaklaşımlar* 13 (2011), pp. 177–98.

97. Edward Melkonyan, 'Stalini ashkharhakragan ngrdumnerĕ ew Hayeru hayrenatarts 'utiwunē 1946–48', in *1946–1948 Hayrenatarts'utiwunē Ew tra Taserē: Hayrenatarts'utyan Himnakhntirn Aysōr. Hamahaygagan Kidazhōghōvi Zegutsumneri Zhōghōvadzu*, 2008, available at hayrenadardz.org/eduard-melkonyan.html (accessed 15 July 2012).

98. Vahé Tachjian, '"Repatriation": A new chapter, studded with new obstacles, in the history of AGBU's cooperation in Soviet Armenia', in Raymond H. Kevorkian and Vahé Tachjian (eds), *The Armenian General Benevolent Union: A Hundred Years of History (1906–2006)*, Vol. 2 (1941–2006), pp. 291–309.

99. Ibid., p. 291.

100. The Delegation of the Armenian National Council of America, *The Case of the Armenian People: Memorandum to the United Nations Conference On International Organization in San Francisco* (New York: 1945).

101. Ibid.

102. Ibid.

103. Ronald Grigor Suny, *Looking Toward Ararat: Armenia in Modern History* (Bloomington: Indiana University Press, 1993), p. 166.

104. Ibid.

105. Charles A. Vertanes, Executive Director of ANCA, Letter sent to *New York Tribune*, Inc., New York, on 6 March 1946. I thank Marc Mamigonian, Academic Director of NAASR, for making these sources available to me.

106. Ibid.

107. Prof A. Nargizyan [Suren Şamlıyan], 'Trk'ahayeru anunov gadaruadz timumĕ', *Marmara*, 10 May 1945, No. 655.

108. *Marmara*, 20 June 1945, No. 696 – special interview with Hüseyin Cahit Yalçın, the editor-in- chief of *Tanin*, on Doğan Nadi's reports and on the issue in general.

109. *Jamanak*, quoted in *Marmara*, 31 July 1945, No. 737.

110. *Marmara*, 1 August 1945, No. 738.

111. *Marmara*, 3 August 1945, No. 740.

112. *Marmara*, 4 August 1945, No. 741 and 5 August 1945, No. 742.

113. *Marmara*, 6 August 1945, No. 743.

114. *Nor Lur*, 11 August 1945, No. 53.
115. Ibid.
116. *Jamanak*, quoted in *Marmara*, 10 August 1945, No. 747.
117. Ibid.
118. Suren Şamlıyan, 'Gě skhalis Doghan Nadi', *Marmara*, 3 August 1945, No. 740 and 'Menk khap'shig chenk', *Marmara*, 1 August 1945, No. 738. In the first article Şamlıyan provides some interesting historical details. Şamlıyan claims that two Armenians, Harutiwn Kuyumjiyan and Vartan Tovmasyan, saved the lives of the Nadi family, and that therefore the latter received a grant until the end of his life. Based on this incident, Yunus Nadi always wrote and talked very positively about Armenians, unlike Doğan Nadi. However, Şamlıyan does not refer to the incident itself. Furthermore, Şamlıyan argues that Madt'ēosyan Printing House was founded by *Cumhuriyet*.
119. Other members of the group, according to the news item, were Abdühlak Şinasi Hisar, Hasan Nureddin, Tahsin Gönden, Şinasi Devrim, Abdullah Zeki Polat, Hazım Atıf Kuyucak, Süreyya Anderiman (*Marmara*, 9 September 1945, No. 1033). See www.unmultimedia.org/s/photo/detail/613/0061360.html (accessed 10 January 2015).
120. *Marmara*, 8 September 1945, No. 1032. *Marmara* reprinted the news from *Cumhuriyet*: 'Finally our representatives were able to come back to the country.'
121. Aram Pehlivanyan, 'Mer badaskhanē Doghan Nadiin', *Nor Or*, 11 August 1945, No. 4.
122. Ibid.
123. *Marmara*, 20 June 1945, No. 696.
124. *Marmara*, 21 June 1945, No. 697.
125. *Akşam*, quoted in *Marmara*, 23 June 1945, No. 698.
126. *Son Posta*, quoted in *Marmara*, 23 June 1945, No. 698.
127. *Keloğlan*, quoted in *Marmara*, 24 June 1945, No. 700. I thank Burcu Gürsel for the translation of this piece.
128. *Tanin*, quoted in *Marmara*, 6 July 1945, No. 712.
129. *Cumhuriyet*, quoted in *Marmara*, 8 July 1945, No. 713.
130. Ömer Rıza Doğrul (Cairo 1893–Istanbul 1952) was a well-known journalist specialised in religious issues.
131. *Cumhuriyet*, quoted in *Marmara*, 12 January 1946, No. 1158.
132. Felix Corley, 'The Armenian Church under the Soviet Regime, part 1: Leadership of Kevork', *Religion, State and Society* xxiv/1 (1996), p. 19. Johnson writes, 'I completely and wholeheartedly agree that the regions seized by Turkey must be returned to Armenia as quickly as possible – with unbelievable cruelty Turkey exterminated the Armenian population. The victorious powers declared after the First World War that justice demanded the return of these territories to their rightful owners' (*Pravda*, 29 June 1945). According to Corley, Archbishop Johnson was decorated with the highest honour of the Armenian Church, the Order of St Gregory the Illuminator. Corley refers to a letter in the State Archives of the Russian Federation (GARF) written by Nersesovich Ovanesyan,

a major in the Armenian NKVD (Peoples' Commissariat for Internal Affairs), to Ivan Polyansky, head of CARC (Council for Affairs of the Armenian Church). The letter was dated 25 April 1947; it noted the award and approved of Johnson's support for the annexation of eastern Turkey (GARF, f. 6991, op. 3. d. 234, pp. 152–3).

133. *Tasvir*, quoted in *Marmara*, 5 July 1945, No. 711 and 7 July 1945, No. 713.
134. *Marmara*, 9 July 1945, No. 715.
135. *Cumhuriyet*, quoted in *Marmara*, 22 July 1945, No. 728.
136. Ibid.
137. *Marmara*, 24 July 1945, No. 730.
138. *Vakıt*, quoted in *Marmara* 24 July 1945, No. 730.
139. *Cumhuriyet*, quoted in *Marmara*, 24 July 1945, No. 730.
140. Tachjian, '"Repatriation": A new chapter', p. 291.
141. Ibid., p. 292.
142. The AGBU was active in the repatriation campaigns during the 1920s and 1930s too. See www.AGBU.org/publications/article.asp?A_ID=643 (accessed 7 May 2012).
143. Santro Pehputyan (ed.), *Vaverakrer Hay Yegeghetsu Badmut'ean: Kevork VI. Gat'oghigos Amenayn Hayots' (1938–1955)*, Kirk' Z. (Yerevan: Osgan Yerevants'i Publ., 1999), p. 299.
144. Corley, 'The Armenian Church', p. 9. See also idem, 'The Armenian Apostolic Church', in Lucian N. Leustean (ed.), *Eastern Christianity and the Cold War, 1945–91* (Abingdon, Oxon: Routledge, 2010), p. 196. According to Corley, Catholicos of All Armenians Khoren I (Muradbekyan) was found dead at the church headquarters at the Holy Echmiadzin monastery, probably murdered by the NKVD (Peoples' Commissariat for Internal Affairs).
145. Corley, 'The Armenian Church', p. 19.
146. Cardinal Krikor Bedros Aghagianian (Akhaltskhe 1895–Rome 1971) was Catholic Patriarch of Cilicia in 1937–62 and was elevated to cardinalate in 1946 by Pope Pius XVII. For more see encyclopedia.thefreedictionary.com/Krikor + Bedros + Cardinal + Aghajanian (accessed 15 July 2012).
147. *Marmara*, 12 February 1948, No. 1899. Cardinal Aghagianian made his ideas public by his two encyclicals, entitled 'T'ught' hovuagan', on 6 July 1946 (criticised by *Nor Or*, 14 August 1946, No. 5; 6 September 1946, No. 28; and 6 December 1946). They were referenced in Zaven Biberyan's article in *Aysor*, 28 February 1948, No. 33.
148. *Soviet News*, 30 June 1945, quoted in Corley, 'The Armenian Church', p. 18.
149. Ētuart Melk'onyan, 'Stalini ashkharhakragan ngrdumnerě ew Hayeri hayrenatartsutiwně 1946–1948', in hayrenadardz.org/eduard-melkonyan.html (accessed 15 July 2012). See Chapter 3, footnote 97.
150. Tachjian, '"Repatriation": A new chapter', pp. 300–3.
151. Daniela De Maglio Slavich, *Il rimpatrio degli Armenia nell'immediato dopoguerra* (Milan: ICOM, 1980), p. 25.
152. Koçak, *Türkiye'de İki Partili*, p. 824.

153. Suny, *Looking Toward Ararat*, p. 168.

154. Ibid. See also the letter written by the Soviet Ministry of Foreign Affairs on 11 April 1946 and sent to the embassies of US, France and Turkey, as well as Soviet missions in Egypt and Iraq about the organisation of repatriation of Armenians, in the National Archives of Armenia, F. 326, 'Ministry of Foreign Affairs of Soviet Union', catalogue 1, file 117, folder 1, quoted in Armen Melqumyan, 'Turkagan ishkhanut'yunneri k'aghak 'aganut 'yuně ew Bolsahay hamaynkě 1945–1947 t't'', in *Mertsavor Arevelk (VII): Badmut'yun, K'aghak'aganutyun, Mshaguyt': Hotvadzneri Joghovadzu*, S. Krikoryan et al. (ed.), RA National Academy of Sciences, Institute of Orientalism (Yerevan:Lusagn Publ., 2011), p. 198; available at serials.flib.sci.am/openreader/merc_arev_7/book/index.html#page/198/mode/2up (accessed 25 March 2013).

155. Ibid. For Karabekir's quote in Turkish, 'Boğazlar boğazımız, Kars–Ardahan bel kemiğimizdir', see the official website of the Ministry of Culture and Tourism on Ardahan, www.ardahankulturturizm.gov.tr/belge/1-45876/tarihcesi.html (accessed 15 March 2013).

156. *Yeni Sabah*, quoted in *Marmara*, 18 December 1945, No. 1133.

157. *Gece Postası*, quoted in *Marmara*, 17 December 1945, No. 1132. The editor-in-chief of *Gece Postası*, Ethem İzzet Benice, former representative of Kars, wrote an article on the issue, 'Armenians of Turkey and the Invitation of Soviets' where he suggested that those who want to leave, should leave, and 'good-bye!'

158. *Vatan*, quoted in *Marmara*, 18 December 1945, No. 1133. The editor-in-chief of *Vatan*, Ahmet Emin Yalman, wrote that any decision that went against the honour and the interests of Turkey should take people's opposition into consideration. His statement referred to the issue of the eastern borders.

159. *Cumhuriyet*, quoted in *Marmara*, 18 December 1945, No. 1133. According to the translation in *Marmara*, *Cumhuriyet* described the crowd in front of the Soviet Embassy in Istanbul, trying to provide a social analysis of the applicants in terms of their ages, employment status, sense of purpose, etc. In *Marmara* (26 December 1945, No. 1141), Suren Şamlıyan mentioned an article written by Ahmed Halil in *Cumhuriyet* the day before, 'The Armenian Question during the Second World War' ('İkinci Dünya Harbinde Ermeni Meselesi'). Aram Pehlivanyan responded to this same article with a Turkish editorial in *Nor Or* on 26 January 1946.

160. *Akşam*, quoted in *Marmara*, 18 December 1945, No. 1133. The editor-in-chief of *Akşam*, Necmeddin Sadak, who was at the same time representative of Sivas, wrote: 'Whoever wants to leave should leave, and whoever wants to stay should stay.' He wrote his column under the pen-name 'Democrat'. Sada stated that Armenians preferred to remain minorities, speak their own language, and attend their own schools; thus, they chose to be foreigners.

161. *Tasvir*, quoted in *Marmara*, 24 December 1945, No. 1139, where the translation was: 'We have a right to be suspicious of the entire Armenian community. [...] Armenians stabbed the Turkish Army in the back, which met with the most legitimate response.'

162. *Keloğlan*, quoted in *Marmara*, 24 June 1945, No. 700 (written in Armeno-Turkish). According to *Marmara*, *Keloğlan* published this piece on 20 December 1945: 'Some disconnected Armenians applied to the Moscow Embassy in Istanbul and reported to the Moscow Embassy General that they wish to leave. This news gladdened us. May they leave, whether willingly or merrily, so long as they just leave' (*'Bazı kopuk Ermeniler İstanbul'daki Moskof elçiliğine başvurup, Moskof büyükelçiliğine gitmek istediklerini bildirmişler. Bu haber bizleri mutlu etti. İster oynayarak, ister gülerek gitsinler, yeter ki gitsinler'*). (*Keloğlan*, quoted in *Marmara*, 24 December 1945, No. 1139.)

163. *Son Telgraf*, quoted in *Marmara*, 25 December 1945, No. 1140. *Son Telgraf* interviewed some Armenians who reportedly said: 'We are Turks. What business do we have in Russia? It is stupid to go there.'

164. *Tanin*, quoted in *Marmara*, 25 December 1945, No. 1140.

165. *Vakıt*, quoted in *Marmara*, 25 December 1945, No. 1140.

166. *Tasvir*, quoted in *Marmara*, 22 September 1945, No. 1046.

167. Ibid.

168. Suren Şamlıyan, 'Hos enk' P'ēyami Safa', *Marmara*, 23 September 1945, No. 1450.

169. Suren Şamlıyan, 'Türkiye'de yabancılara alet olacak Ermeni yoktur', *Marmara*, 26 December 1945, No. 1141. I could not trace when the bombs were planted in the Pangaltı Cemetery or exactly when Patriarch Naroyan visited the governor of Istanbul. In any case, this must have been before the sudden death of Patriarch Naroyan in 1944.

170. Ibid.

171. Koçak, *Türkiye'de İki Partili*, p. 835.

172. Ibid., p. 840.

173. *Marmara*, 7 January 1946, No. 1153.

174. Ibid.

175. *Marmara*, 11 January 1946, No. 1157.

176. Ibid.

177. In 1926, Bedros Garabetyan and his friends established the choir 'Hilal,' which participated in the celebrations of Republican Day. See Bedros Garabetyan, *Hnktarean Hishadagaran Samatio Surp Kēōrk Yegeghetso 1461–1935* (Istanbul: Terzyan Kardeşler Matbaası–Yeni Türkiye Basımevi, 1935), p. 336.

178. Garabetyan, *Hnktarean Hishadagaran*, p. 5.

179. *Nor Lur*, 5 January 1946, No. 95.

180. A translation of Asım Us's article appeared in *Marmara*, 16 December 1945, No. 1131. Us combines the issues of Kars, Ardahan and Artvin with the Soviet calls for immigration and asks the government how the Soviet Embassy was able to register the names and addresses of Armenians of Turkey without having made an agreement with Turkey. Another article by Us, 'Let's speak frankly with our Armenian citizens' ('Ermeni vatandaşlarımızla açık konuşalım'), was published on 26 December 1945 in *Vakıt*.

181. Peyami Safa, 'Turkish Armenians, where are you?' ('Türkiye Ermenileri neredesiniz?'), in *Tasvir*, 22 September 1945. See also, 'A whole new Armenian nonsense' ('Yeni bir Ermeni saçması') in *Tasvir*, 19 September 1945 and 'The Armenian Congress refreshes the story' ('Ermeni Kongresi hikayeyi tazeledi'), in *Tasvir*, 28 September 1945.

182. Zaven Biberyan, 'Verchin aztararut'iwn krkrich'nerun', *Nor Lur*, 15 January 1946, No. 98.

183. Ibid.

184. *Tasvir*, quoted in *Marmara*, 24 December 1945, No. 1139.

185. Representative of Burdur in the parliament of 1920.

186. See Chapter 3, footnotes 97 and 149.

187. Biberyan, 'Verchin aztararut'iwn krkrich'nerun'.

188. Biberyan, 'Verchin aztararut'iwn'.

189. *Dost*, 'Amerika'nın Türkiye politikasının oluşumu üzerine', p. 187.

190. *News Chronicle*, 27 May 1940, quoted in Suren Şamlıyan, 'Hagahay krut'iwnner Londoni mamulin mech', *Marmara*, 5 November 1946, No. 1448.

191. Ibid.

192. Cedric Salter, *Introducing Turkey* (London: Methuen, 1961, reprinted in 1996).

193. Şamlıyan, 'Hagahay krut'iwunner'.

194. Levon Thomassian, *Summer of '42: A Study of German–Armenian Relations During the Second World War* (Atglen, PA: Schiffer Publ., 2012), p. 28.

195. Jirair Missakian, 'Armenians and the War', *The London Times*, 19 July 1941, quoted in James G. Mandalian, 'The smearer: A reply to Roy John Carlson', *Armenian Review* 3 (1950), p. 8. A partial Armenian translation of the letter could be found in *Marmara*, 6 November 1946, No. 1449. I thank Vartan Matiossian for bringing Mandalian's article to my attention and also Marc Mamigonian from NAASR, who scanned and sent the material.

196. Mandalian, 'The smearer', p. 9.

197. Ibid.

198. John Roy Carlson, *Under Cover: My 4 Years in the Nazi Underworld of America. The Amazing Revelation of How Axis Agents and Our Enemies Within Are Now Plotting to Destroy the United States* (Philadelphia: Blakiston, 1943).

199. For more, see Mandalian, 'The smearer', p. 19.

200. Suny, *Looking Toward Ararat*, p. 223.

201. Liana Sayadyan, 'New book sheds light on 1933 murder of Archbishop Tourian and Church split' in old.hetq.am/en/culture/terry-phillips-2/ (accessed 18 March 2013).

202. For more see Suny, *Looking Toward Ararat*, p. 224.

203. *Marmara*, 6 November 1946, No. 1449.

204. *El Kefah*, quoted in *Marmara*, 7 November 1946, No. 1450.

205. Ibid.

206. Ibid.

207. *Marmara*, 8 November 1946, No. 1451.

208. *Al Musawwar*, quoted in *Marmara*, 8 November 1946, No. 1451.

209. *Dünya El Cedid*, quoted in *Marmara*, 7 February 1947, No. 1541.
210. *Keloğlan*, quoted in *Marmara*, 13 February 1947, No. 1547. The conversation was included in Armeno-Turkish: 'Enough with these atrocities sir. Only Mega Asdvadz [God] and Hampartsun Papaz knows what we have suffered from the hands of the Turks. Even if I live in America, my origins are Hay/Armenian, and my land of birth Van.' (*'Bu vahşetlikler yeter olsun efendim. Türk milletinden çektiğimizi bir Meg{h}a Asdvadz {Ya Rab} bir de Hampartsum Papaz bilior. Bendeniz Amelikada ikamet edorsam da, aslım Hay, topraga indiğim yer ise Van.'*). Karagöz then tells the United Nations, *'Çelebi*s, [Gentlemen], what can I say – Artin Domuzyan has confessed that he is a Hayvanoğlu Hayvan ['animal–son of animal']' (*'Çelebiler, sözüm yok, Artin Domuzyan itiraf etti ki Hayvanoğlu Hayvandır'*). See also Talin Suciyan, 'Bir Cumhuriyet açmazı: Ermeni karşıtlığı ortamında Ermeni temsiliyeti', *Toplumsal Tarih* 224 (2012), pp. 76–9.
211. *Nor Lur*, 15 February 1947, No. 210.
212. *Nor Or*, 13 October 1945, No. 13.
213. *Nor Or*, 26 January 1946, No. 28.
214. Suciyan, 'Bir Cumhuriyet açmazı'.
215. Aram Pehlivanyan, 'Hakikat', *Nor Or*, 26 January 1946, No. 28.
216. *Nor Or*, 9 February 1946, No. 30.
217. *Nor Or*, 27 August 1946, 28 August 1946, 29 August 1946, 30 August 1946, 13 September 1946, 22 October 1946, 28 October 1946.
218. Zaven Biberyan, 'Haygagan hrashkě', *Nor Lur*, 12 March 1946, No. 114.
219. *Akşam*, quoted in *Marmara*, 11 July 1946, No. 1331.
220. Vala Nureddin (1901–67), journalist and author who studied in Vienna and Moscow. He was the author of the biographical work *Bu Dünyadan Nazım Geçti*. See www.iisg.nl/archives/en/files/n/ARCH02057full.php (accessed 23 June 2012).
221. *Akşam*, quoted in *Marmara*, 11 July 1946, No. 1331.
222. Aram Pehlivanyan, 'Mamul ew garavarut'iwn', *Nor Or*, 30 August 1946, No. 21.
223. For instance, see *Yeni Türkiye*, quoted in *Nor Or*, 13 September 1946, No. 35; *Vatan*, quoted in *Nor Or*, 15 September 1946, No. 37; *Cumhuriyet*, quoted in *Nor Or*, 17 October 1946, No. 69; *Tasvir*, quoted in *Nor Or*, 28 October 1946, No. 80.
224. *Anadolu Ajansı*, quoted in *Marmara*, 6 July 1946, No. 1326.
225. *Son Telgraf*, quoted in *Marmara*, 6 July 1946, No. 1326.
226. *Nor Or*, 27 August 1946, No. 18.
227. *Son Saat*, quoted in *Nor Or*, 27 August 1946, No. 18.
228. See Chapter 3, footnote 211.
229. Cihad Baban (Istanbul 1911–84), author of various books, journalist, editor-in-chief, parliamentarian, Minister of Press and Tourism (1960–1), Minister of Culture (1980). For more, see www.timas.com.tr/yazarlar/cihad-baban.as px?hA.R.F.=&list = 1 (accessed 12 March 2013).
230. Cihat Hikmet (Cihad Baban), *Hitler ve Nasyonal Sosyalizm* (Istanbul: Şafak Kütüphanesi, 1933).

231. *Marmara*, 14 August 1946, No. 1365.
232. *Tasvir* quoted in *Nor Or*, 28 October 1946, No. 80.
233. Ibid.
234. *Yarın*, quoted in *Nor Or*, 14 December 1946, No. 127.
235. *Yarın*, quoted in *Nor Or*, 15 December 1946, No. 128.
236. *Millet*, reprinted in *Marmara*, 17 October 1946, No. 1429. *Millet* was a weekly published by Cemal Kutay. It started publication on 31 January 1946. Available at e-dergi.atauni.edu.tr/index.php/taed/article/viewFile/2248/2249 (accessed 24 June 2012).
237. Ibid.
238. Ibid.
239. Keloğlan, quoted in *Marmara*, 4 November 1946, No. 1447.
240. Ibid.
241. BCA, 030.18.01.02.111.59.17.
242. Agop Arslanyan, *Adım Agop Memleketim Tokat* (Istanbul: Aras Yay., 2008), pp. 66–8.
243. *Cumhuriyet*, quoted in *Marmara*, 24 January 1948, No. 1880.
244. Minutes of talks at the Soviet Embassy in Istanbul, 29 July 1946, National Archive of Armenia, F. 326. 'Fund of Ministry of Foreign Affairs of Soviet Union', Catalogue 1, File 134, Folder10, in Melqumyan, 'Turkagan ishkanut'yunneri k 'agahak 'aganutyuně ew Bolsahay hamaynkě 1945–1947 T'T'', p. 199.
245. Slavich, *Il rimpatrio degli Armenia nell'immediato*, p. 25.
246. hayrenadardz.org/wp-content/uploads/2012/06/1946-04-11.pdf (accessed 17 July 2012), I thank Hrach Bayadyan for the translation of the document.
247. NARA, 867.4016/5-1449, Ankara, 3 December 1946, in Dilek Güven, *Nationalismus und Minderheiten: Die Ausschreitungen gegen die Christen und Juden der Türkei vom September 1955* (Munich: Oldenbourg Verlag, 2012), p. 125.
248. Suny, *Looking Towards Ararat*, p. 175.
249. Ibid. For more see *Foreign Relations*, Vol. 7 (1946), pp. 857–8 quoted in the same source.
250. Armenian National Council of America, *Memorandum on the Proposed Aid to Greece and Turkey, Presented to the Government of the United States*, March 1947. I thank Marc Mamigonian and NAASR for bringing this source to my attention and making it available to me.
251. Ibid.
252. Ibid.
253. *Marmara*, 3 May 1947, No. 1625. According to Demokan, 1,200 Armenians from all over the world participated in the Congress. This figure is exaggerated. According to an article by Aris Gazinyan and Suren Musaelyan, the actual figure is 715 delegates from 22 countries and 31 church eparchies. See www.AGBU.org/publications/article.asp?A_ID=643 (accessed 6 July 2012).

254. Programme of World Armenian Congress, 30 April–4 May 1947, Waldorf Astoria Hotel, New York, and also Vahe Haig (ed.), *Kharpert Ew Anor Osgeghēn Tashdē* (New York: Kharpert Armenian Patriotic Union, 1959), p. 1475.
255. Programme of World Armenian Congress, 30 April–4 May 1947, Waldorf Astoria Hotel, New York.
256. *Marmara*, 16 June 1947, No. 1668.
257. *Şark Yolu*, 7 May 1947, quoted in *Marmara*, 9 May 1947, No. 1631.
258. *Marmara*, 7 May 1947, No. 1629.
259. *Cumhuriyet*, quoted in *Marmara*, 8 May 1947, No. 1630.
260. Ibid.
261. *Son Saat*, quoted in *Marmara*, 10 May 1947, No. 1632.
262. Bekri Mustafa, 17 May 1947, No. 8, quoted in *Marmara*, 17 May 1947, No. 1639.
263. Ibid.
264. *Marmara*, 21 September 1949, No. 1982.
265. *Marmara*, 13 December 1948, No. 1702.
266. *Marmara*, 14 December 1948, No. 1703.
267. Ibid.
268. Ibid.
269. Radio programme of Nureddin Artam quoted in *Marmara*, 15 February 1948, No. 1704.
270. Ibid.
271. *Marmara*, 16 February 1948, No. 1705.
272. *Cumhuriyet*, quoted in *Marmara*, 17 December 1948, No. 1706.
273. *Marmara*, 1 April 1949, No. 1811.
274. See Talin Suciyan, 'Armenian representation in Turkey', in *The Armenian Weekly*, Special Issue, April 2012, available at www.armenianweekly.com/2012/06/12/suciyan-armenian-representation-in-turkey/ (accessed 17 November 2012), and idem, 'Bir Cumhuriyet açmazı'.
275. *Tebi Luys*, 20 May 1950.

Chapter 4   The Patriarchal Election Crisis: 1944–50

1. Felix Corley, 'The Armenian Apostolic Church', in Lucian N. Leustean (ed.), *Eastern Christianity and the Cold War, 1945–91* (Abingdon, Oxon: Routledge, 2010), p. 190.
2. Ibid.
3. Ibid.
4. Ibid.
5. Ibid.
6. Karnik Step'anyan, *Gensakragan Pararan*, Vol. 1 (Yerevan: Hayastan, 1973), p. 116.
7. Kevork Pamukciyan, in Osman Köker (ed.), *Ermeni Kaynaklarından Tarihe Katkılar IV: Biyografileriyle Ermeniler* (Istanbul: Aras Yay., 2003), pp. 46–7.

8. Toros Azadyan (ed.), *Kevork Arch. Arslanyan (1867–1951)* (Istanbul: Mshaguyt Hradaragchagan, 1952), p. 7.
9. Pamukciyan, *Ermeni Kaynaklarından*, pp. 46–7.
10. Ibid.
11. Ibid.
12. Azadyan (ed.), *Kevork Arch. Arslanyan*, p. 8.
13. Ibid., p. 9.
14. Pamukciyan, *Ermeni Kaynaklarından*, p. 47.
15. Step'anyan, *Gensakragan Pararan*, p. 116.
16. Azadyan (ed.), *Kevork Arch. Arslanyan*, p. 11.
17. Step'anyan, *Gensakragan Pararan*, p. 116.
18. Azadyan (ed.), *Kevork Arch. Arslanyan*, p. 13.
19. Ibid.
20. Ibid., p. 14.
21. Step'anyan, *Gensakragan Pararan*, p. 116.
22. Pamukciyan, *Ermeni Kaynaklarından*, p. 47.
23. Toros Azadyan, *Lipananean Husher* (Istanbul: Doğu Basımevi, 1949), p. 134.
24. *Deghegakir Ĕnthanur Zhoghovo K'nnich' Hantsnazhoghovi* (Istanbul: Foti Basımevi, 1951), p. 10.
25. Ibid., p. 11.
26. *Marmara*, 8 July 1949, No. 1907; *Jamanak*, 30 September 1944; *Bashdonagan Hradaragut'iwn Azkayin Badriark'arani: Adenakrut'iwn Azkayin Ĕnthanur Zhoghovo* (Istanbul: Ak-Ün Matbaası, 2 December 1950), p. 3; and *Deghegakir Ĕnthanur Zhoghovo K'nnich'*, p. 12.
27. Ibid. and *Jamanak*, 1 September 1944.
28. Azadyan, *Lipananean Husher*, p. 135.
29. *Bashdonagan Hradaragut'iwn Azkayin Badriark'arani*, p. 3.
30. *Deghegakir Ĕnthanur Zhoghovo K'nnich'*, p. 30.
31. Ibid.
32. Gülbenkyan and Peştimalcıyan, 'Deghegakir Surp P'rgich' Azkayin Hiwantanots'i hokapartsutean 1944–45i shrchani (113.rt Dari)', in *Ĕntartsag Darekirk' Surp P'rgich' Azkayin Hiwantanots'i 1946 (General Yearbook of Surp P'rgich' National Hospital 1946)* (Istanbul: Dbakrut'iwn H. Aprahamyan, 1946), p. 421.
33. Varujan Köseyan, *Hushamadean Surp P'rgich' Hiwanatanots'i- Surp Pırgiç Hastanesi Tarihçesi* (Istanbul: Murat Ofset, 1994), p. 176.
34. The amount inheritance varies according to the source. For instance, according to *Marmara*, the amount of gold money was 186 (*Marmara*, 14 January 1947, No. 1517).
35. Gülbenkyan and Peştimalcıyan, 'Deghegakir Surp P'rgch'i Azkayin Hiwantanots'i hokapartsutean', in *Ĕntartsag Darekirk' {...} 1946*, p. 422.
36. This amount was given as 15,650 and 16,650 in *Nor Lur*, 2 June 1945, No. 33 and *Nor Lur*, 7 July 1945, No. 43. However, it might be a typographical mistake.

37. See Chapter 4, footnote 16.

38. *Marmara*, 19 April 1947, No. 1611.

39. *Nor Lur*, 10 November 1947, No. 278.

40. Zaven Arzumanyan, *Azkabadum*, Vol. 4.ii (1930−55) (New York: St Vartan Matenashar, 1997), pp. 263−9 and Puzant Yeghiayan, *Jamanagagits' Badmut'iwn Gatoghigosut'ean Hayots' Giligyo 1914−1972* (Antilias: Dbaran Gat'oghigosut'ean Hayots' Medzi Dann Giligio, 1975), pp. 617−23.

41. Talin Suciyan, 'Baron Varujan İstanbul', *Agos*, 29 April 2011, No. 786 or see azadalik.wordpress.com/2011/05/07/ermeniler-varujan-koseyana-tarihlerini-borcludur/ (accessed 1 September 2012). Armenian newspapers are sold by newspaper vendors, in certain districts where Armenians live, such as Beyoğlu, Kurtuluş, Yeşilköy, Bakırköy etc.

42. *Nor Lur*, 16 July 1945, No. 37.

43. *Marmara*, 21 June 1945, No. 697, *Nor Lur*, 10 July 1945, No. 44.

44. *Deghegakir Ënthanur Zhoghovo K'nnich'*, p. 25.

45. Ibid., p. 26.

46. *Araks*, quoted in *Nor Lur*, 7 August 1945, No. 5.

47. *Nor Lur*, 11 September 1945, No. 62.

48. Ibid.

49. *Nor Lur*, 14 December 1946, No. 192.

50. *Nor Lur*, 8 April 1947, No. 225.

51. *Nor Lur*, 7 June 1947, No. 242.

52. *Marmara*, 22 December 1948, No. 1711.

53. Ibid.

54. *Marmara*, 25 December 1948, No. 1714.The author mentions the names of Patriarchs Sarkis Kuyumcuyan and Boghos Taktakyan, who were forced to resign because of these protests.

55. *Marmara*, 11 January 1949, No. 1730.

56. *Marmara*, 27 January 1949, No. 1746, and 29 January 1949, No. 1748.

57. Ibid.

58. Ibid.

59. *Vatan*, quoted in *Marmara*, 29 January 1949, No. 1748.

60. *Marmara*, 29 January 1949, No. 1748.

61. Santro Pehputian (ed.), *Vaverakrer Hay Yegeghets'u Badmut'ean: Kevork VI. Gat'oghigos Amenayn Hayots' (1938−1955)*, Kirk' Z. (Yerevan: Osgan Yerevants'i Publ., 1999), p. 497.

62. Varujan Köseyan also told me about the appointment, referring to the *locum tenens'* promise to discuss the issue after Easter, although no such development took place. See *Agos*, 29 April 2011, No. 786.

63. *Marmara*, 11 March 1949, No. 1789.

64. *Nor Lur*, 8 March 1949, No. 425.

65. *Nor Lur*, 12 March 1949, No. 426.

66. Ibid.

67. *Deghegakir Ĕnthanur Zhoghovo K'nnich'*, p. 29 and Azadyan, *Lipananean Husher*, p. 162.
68. *Nor Lur*, 18 March 1949, No. 428.
69. Azadyan, *Lipananean Husher*, p. 163.
70. *Marmara*, 13 March 1949, No. 1791; *Yeni Sabah*, 13 March 1949, No. 3579 and *Son Telgraf*, 13 March 1949, No. 4405, quoted in Pehputyan, *Vaverakrer Hay Yegeghetsu*, p. 499.
71. *Marmara*, 14 March 1949, No. 1792.
72. Marmara, 15 March 1949, No. 1793.
73. Pehputyan, *Vaverakrer Hay Yegeghets'u*, Letter No. 348, p. 496.
74. Ibid., pp. 499–500.
75. *Yeni Sabah*, quoted in *Marmara*, 13 March 1949, No. 1791.
76. *Marmara*, 18 March 1949, No. 1796.
77. *Tasvir*, *Hürriyet*, *Yeni Sabah* and *Son Telgraf* quoted in *Marmara*, 19 March 1949, No. 1797.
78. *Marmara*, 21 March 1949, No. 1799.
79. Ibid.
80. *Marmara*, 23 March 1949, No. 1801.
81. *Nor Lur*, 2 April 1949, No. 432.
82. *Son Posta* quoted in *Marmara*, 31 March 1949, No. 1809.
83. *Marmara*, 1 April 1949, No. 1810.
84. *Marmara*, 8 April 1949, No. 1816 and *Nor Lur*, 9 April 1949, No. 434.
85. *Son Posta* quoted in *Marmara*, 31 March 1949, No. 1809.
86. Azadyan, *Lipananean Husher*, p. 164.
87. *Marmara*, 14 April 1949, No. 1823.
88. Ibid.
89. Ibid.
90. *Marmara*, 5 April 1949, No. 1814.
91. *Nor Lur*, 12 April 1949, No. 435.
92. *Nor Lur*, 7 May 1949, No. 442.
93. Azadyan, *Lipananean Husher*, p. 165.
94. *Marmara*, 19 April 1949, No. 1827.
95. Ibid.
96. Ibid.
97. *Marmara*, 21 April 1949, No. 1829.
98. Ibid.
99. Azadyan, *Lipananean Husher*, p. 165.
100. *Nor Lur*, 7 May 1949, No. 442.
101. *Nor Lur*, 10 May 1949, No. 443.
102. *Marmara*, 7 May 1949, No. 1845; 8 May 1949, No. 1846; 9 May 1949, No. 1847.
103. *Deghegakir Ĕnthanur Zhoghovo K'nnich'*, p. 56.
104. *Marmara*, 11 May 1949, No. 1849.

105. *Marmara*, 20 May 1949, No. 1858, and *Nor Lur* (20 May 1949). The issue of *Nor Lur* had neither date nor number. I dated it according to its publishing frequency.
106. *Marmara*, 18 June 1949, No. 1887.
107. *Marmara*, 19 June 1949, No. 1888.
108. *Nor Lur*, 12 July 1949, No. 461.
109. *Deghegakir Ĕnthanur Zhoghovo K'nnich'*, p. 59.
110. *Marmara*, 9 July 1949, No. 1908.
111. *Nor Lur*, 16 July 1949, No. 462.
112. Azadyan, *Lipananean Hushers*, p. 133.
113. *Nor Lur*, 30 July 1949, No. 466.
114. Ibid.
115. Ibid.
116. Ibid. and Köseyan, *Hushamadean*, p. 189.
117. Köseyan, *Hushamadean*, p. 156.
118. Ibid.
119. *Marmara*, 15 July 1949, No. 1914.
120. Ibid.
121. Ibid. See also Azadyan, *Lipananean Husher*, p. 171.
122. *Nor Lur*, 6 August 1949, No. 468, *Marmara*, 17 July 1949, No. 1916 and Yeghiayan, *Jamanagagits'*, p. 620.
123. Azadyan, *Lipananean Husher*, p. 182. In this book this date was given as 25 July 1949.
124. *Deghegakir Ĕnthanur Zhoghovo K'nnich'*, p. 61.
125. Ibid.
126. Ibid.
127. Ibid.
128. Ibid., p. 62.
129. Ibid., p. 177.
130. *Marmara*, 24 July 1949, No. 1924.
131. Azadyan, *Lipananean Husher*, p. 184.
132. Ibid., p. 184.
133. *Marmara*, 1 August 1949, No. 1931 and 6 August 1949, No. 1936.
134. *Nor Lur*, 6 August 1949, No. 468.
135. Azadyan, *Lipananean Husher*, p. 185.
136. Pehputyan, *Vaverakrer Hay Yegeghets'u*, p. 518.
137. Ibid.
138. *Nor Lur*, 3 September 1949, No. 476; see also Yeghiayan, *Jamanagagits'*, p. 621.
139. Ibid.
140. Azadyan, *Lipananean Husher*, pp. 189–99.
141. Yeghiayan, *Jamanagagits'*, p. 622.
142. File 54/3, Catholicos Karekin I, copies of sent letters, No. 41, in ibid., p. 622.
143. *Marmara*, 24 September 1949, No. 1985.
144. *Marmara*, 29 September 1949, No. 1990.

145. *Marmara*, 3 August 1950, No. 2295.

146. *Marmara*, 17 October 1949, No. 2008.

147. *Nor Lur*, 5 November 1949, No. 494.

148. Köseyan, *Hushamadean*, p. 180. The head of the Armenian Hospital of Surp P'rgichʻ, Dr Peştimalcıyan, stayed in his position even after 1950. His official attempt at resignation in 1951 was not accepted by the Patriarch, and he was still on duty in 1961. See H. Peştimalcıyan, *Hrabaragayin Niwt'agan Ew Paroyagan Hamaraduutiwn, 1933–1949* (Istanbul: 1961).

149. *Paros*, 23 November 1949, No. 1.

150. Ibid.

151. *Deghegakir Ĕnthanur Zhoghovo K'nnichʻ*, p. 39 and Suciyan, 'Ermeniler Varujan Köseyan'aʻ', or see azadalik.wordpress.com/2011/05/07/ermeniler-varujan-koseyana-tarihlerini-borcludur/.

152. *Deghegakir Ĕnthanur Zhoghovo K'nnichʻ*, p. 65.

153. Ibid.

154. Zarmayr Geziwryan, Apraham Ebeyan, Serope Burmayantsʻ.

155. Hmayag Bahtiyaryan, Tovma Shigaher, Sahak Papazyan.

156. Pehputyan, *Vaverakrer Hay Yegeghets'u*, p. 567.

157. Ibid., p. 566, and Azadyan, *Lipananean Husher*, p. 140.

158. Pehputyan, *Vaverakrer Hay Yegeghets'u*, p. 560.

159. Ibid., pp. 591–2.

160. *Zartonk*, 12 November 1950. I thank Vartan Matiossian for bringing this source to my attention and making it available for me.

161. *Hasg*, November 1950 (Beirut: Hradaragut'iwn Giligio Gat'oghigosutean), p. 356, in Yeghiayan, *Jamanagagitsʻ Badmut'iwn Gatoghigosut'ean Hayotsʻ*, p. 622.

162. *Hasg*, November 1950, p. 356.

163. *Tebi Luys*, 28 October 1950, No. 34.

164. Ibid.

165. *Paros*, 14 November 1950, No. 64.

166. *Deghegakir Ĕnthanur Zhoghovo K'nnichʻ*, pp. 85–6.

167. Ibid.

168. *Bashdonagan Hradaragut'iwn Azkayin Badriark'arani: Adenakrut'iwn Azkayin Ĕnthanur*, p. 3.

169. Ibid., p. 12.

170. Ibid., p. 8.

171. Ibid., p. 9.

172. Ibid., p. 10.

173. Ibid., p. 14.

174. Yeghiayan, *Jamanagagitsʻ*, p. 622.

175. Ibid., p. 16.

176. *Deghegakir Ĕnthanur Zhoghovo K'nnichʻ*, pp. 3–6.

177. Ibid.

178. Ibid., p. 90.

179. Ibid., p. 94.

180. Pehputyan, *Vaverakrer Hay Yegeghets'u*, pp. 607–8.
181. Ibid., p. 623.
182. Ibid., p. 626.
183. Ibid., p. 627.
184. Ibid., p. 634.
185. Ibid., p. 745. In his letter of 15 May 1951, Kevork VI wrote: 'Upon the letter of the suspended clerics, we granted them amnesty, although we considered their regret as mere formality and their letters did not convey any credibility' (Ibid., p. 653).
186. Ibid., p. 628.
187. Ibid., p. 629.
188. Ibid., p. 630.
189. Ibid., p. 631.
190. Ibid., p. 632.
191. Ibid.
192. Ibid., p. 642.
193. Ibid., p. 643.
194. Ibid.
195. See the report of Arsen Arch. Ghldchyan in 1942 to the Supreme Spiritual Council of Holy Echmiadzin, in Pehputyan, *Vaverakrer Hay Yegeghets'u*, p. 146.
196. The letter is undated, but it starts with a quote from Archbishop Eghishē, the *locum tenens* of Jerusalem, written on 28 August. Ibid., p. 634.
197. Ibid., p. 635.
198. Ibid., p. 678.
199. Ibid., pp. 679–81.
200. Ibid., p. 683.
201. Ibid., p. 685.
202. Ibid., pp. 768–73.
203. At the time of writing, I came across a footnote in Yeghiayan's book, *Jamanagagits' Badmut'iwn Gat'oghigosut'ean Hayots' Giligio 1914–1972*, where he states that there was a 200-page special file on the patriarchal crisis of Istanbul. I contacted the Catholicosate in Antelias. Unfortunately, due to some changes in the classification, the file could not be located. However, I was invited to conduct research on the topic, and I would not rule out the possiblity of finding the file during my research. I believe that the archives of both Patriarchates, Istanbul and Jerusalem, as well as both Catholicosates, Echmiadzin and Cilicia, would provide more information on the issue.

Conclusion

1. See Ayda Erbal, 'We are all oxymorons', *The Armenian Weekly*, 24 April 2007, Special Insert, pp. 14 and 27. See azadalik.wordpress.com/2013/01/21/we-are-all-oxymorons/ (accessed 15 March 2013).

2. Richard Bernstein, *Hannah Arendt and the Jewish Question* (Cambridge, MA: MIT Press, 1996), p. 18.
3. For instance, they had to stage a book burning ceremony in Istanbul, as depicted in Franz Werfel's *The Forty Days of Musa Dagh* (1933). See Rifat N. Bali, *Musa'nın Evlatları, Cumhuriyet'in Yurttaşları* (Istanbul: İletişim Yay., 2001), p. 133. Or they had to lay a wreath on the Republican Statue in 1965 as a response to the 50th anniversary of the genocide commemoration taking place in other parts of the world. See Kersam Aharonian, *Khoher Hisnameagi Avardin* (Beirut: Dbaran Atlas, 1966), p. 149 and footnote 113.

BIBLIOGRAPHY

I. Primary Sources

a. Prime Ministry Archives (Başbakanlık Cumhuriyet Arşivi)
BCA, 030.10.85.558.7.
BCA, 030.18.01.03.84.79.8.
BCA, 030.10.109.721.21.
BCA, 030.10.88.577.4.
BCA, 030.10.88.577.4.
BCA, 030.10.225.515.26.
BCA, 030.18.01.02.120.65.17.
BCA, 030.10.24.136.3.
BCA, 030.10.109.720.13.
BCA, 030.10.191.308.11.
BCA, 030.10.109.723.1.
BCA, 030.10.191.307.9.
BCA, 030.18.01.02.118.100.18.
BCA, 030.18.02.105.47.6.
BCA, 030.18.01.02.1.1.14.
BCA, 030.18.01.02.45.35.4.
BCA, 030.18.01.02.44.25.15.
BCA, 030.18.05.84.73.12.
BCA, 030.18.01.02.25.2.19.
BCA, 030.18.01.02.35.30.3.
BCA, 030.18.01.02.36.33.6.
BCA, 030.18.01.02.50.89.17.
BCA, 030.18.01.02.49.77.15.
BCA, 030.18.01.01.61.10.15.
BCA, 030.10.108.712.17.
BCA, 030.18.01.02.71.69.
BCA, 030.18.01.02.51.32.
BCA, 030.10.111.745.11.

BCA, 030.18.01.02.79.82.14.
BCA, 030.18.01.02.86.40.18.
BCA, 030.10.109.720.12.
BCA, 030.10.86.570.5.
BCA, 030.18.01.151.69.19.
BCA, 030.11.165.2.15.
BCA, 030.01.101.623.4.
BCA, 030.01.101.623.6.
BCA, 030.10.87.573.6.
BCA, 030.01.101.626.6.
BCA, 030.18.01.02.111.59.17.
BCA, File No. 52–117 1730, 1973.

b. Yearbooks

Azadyan, Toros, *Mshaguyt' Azkakragan Darekirk' 1948* (*Culture Ethnographical Yearbook*) (Istanbul: Becid Basımevi, 1947).
Azadyan, Toros and Zarmayr Dz. V. Geziwryan (eds), *Hay Hosnak Salnamesi / Hay Khosnak Darekirk' I. Dari, 1941* (Istanbul: No publisher, 1941).
Azadyan, Toros and Mardiros Koçunyan, *Armağan: Türkiye Cumhuriyeti 15. Yıldönümü 1923–38* (Istanbul: Dbakrut 'iwn Giwt 'ēmberg, G.N.Makascıyan, 1938).
Ĕntartsag Darekirk' Azkayin Hiwantanots'i 1937 (*General Yearbook of National Hospital 1937*) (Istanbul: Dilberyan Basımevi, no date).
Ĕntartsag Darekirk' Azkayin Hiwantanots'i 1938 (*General Yearbook of National Hospital 1938*) (Istanbul: O. Aktaryan Matbaası, 1938).
Ĕntartsag Darekirk' Azkayin Hiwantanots'i 1939 (*General Yearbook of National Hospital 1939*) (Istanbul: O. Aktaryan Matbaası, 1938).
Ĕntartsag Darekirk' Surp P'rgich' Azkayin Hiwantanots'i 1944 (*General Yearbook of Surp P'rgich' National Hospital 1944*) (Istanbul: V. Der Nersēsyan Ew Ortik' / Güzeliş Basımevi, 1943).
Ĕntartsag Darets'oyts' Surp P'rgich' Hiwantanots'i 1932 (*General Almanac of Surp P'rgich' Hospital 1932*) (Istanbul: Dbakrut'iwn H.M. Sētyan, no date).
Ĕntartsag Darets'oyts' Surp P'rgich' Azkayin Hiwantanots'i 1945 (*General Almanac of Surp P'rgich' National Hospital 1945*) (Istanbul: Ak-Ün Basımevi, Dbakrut'iwn M. Der Sahakyan, 1944).
Ĕntartsag Darekirk' Surp P'rgich' Azkayin Hiwantanots'i 1946 (*General Yearbook of Surp P'rgich' National Hospital 1946*) (Istanbul: Dbakrut'iwn H. Aprahamyan, 1946).
Ĕntartsag Darekirk' Surp P'rgich' Azkayin Hiwantanots'i 1947 (*General Yearbook of Surp P'rgich' National Hospital 1947*) (Istanbul: O. Aktaryan Basımevi, 1946).
Ĕntartsag Darekirk' Surp P'rgich' Azkayin Hiwantanots'i 1948 (*General Yearbook of Surp P'rgich' National Hospital 1948*) (Istanbul: Akın Basımevi, 1947).
Ĕntartsag Darekirk' Surp P'rgich' Hiwantanots'i 1949 (*General Yearbook of Surp P'rgich' Hospital 1949*) (Istanbul: Becid Basımevi, 1948).
Malkhasyan, Sirvart and Arsen Yarman (eds), *Surp Pırgiç Ermeni Hastanesi 1900–1910 Salnameleri* (Istanbul: 2012).
Tevyan, Pakarat, *Erchanig Darekirk' 1946* (*Happy Yearbook 1946*) (Istanbul: Ak-Ün Basımevi, 1945).

—— *Erchanig Darekirkʿ 1947* (*Happy Yearbook 1947*) (Istanbul: Doğu Basımevi, Bardez Gazetesi Neşriyatı, 1946).

—— *Erchanig Darekirkʿ 1948* (*Happy Yearbook 1948*) (Istanbul: Doğu Basımevi, 1947).

—— *Erchanig Darekirkʿ 1949* (*Happy Yearbook 1949*) (Istanbul: Doğu Basımevi, Hermon Dizgievi, no date).

—— *Erchanig Darekirkʿ 1950* (*Happy Yearbook*) (Istanbul: Doğu Basımevi, 1949).

—— *Erchanig Darekirkʿ 1953* (*Happy Yearbook 1953*) (Istanbul: Varol Matbaası, 1952).

—— *Erchanig Darekirkʿ 1954* (*Happy Yearbook 1954*) (Istanbul: Varol Matbaası, 1953).

—— *Erchanig Darekirkʿ: Bardez Kutlu Yıllar Dergisi 1958* (Istanbul: Varol Matbaası, 1958).

c. Newspapers

Agos, 2003–13 (according to topic).

Aysor, 1947–8.

Cumhuriyet, 1934.

Hasg, November 1950.

Jamanak, 1941–4 (according to topic).

Marmara, 1945, 1946, 1947, 1948, 1949, 1950.

Ngar, 1933–4.

Nor Lur, 1934, 1935, 1945, 1946, 1947, 1948, 1949.

Nor Luys, 1933.

Nor Or, 1945–6.

Panper, 1933.

Paros, 1949, 1950.

Takvim-i Vekayi, No. 2611, available at http://gazeteler.ankara.edu.tr/dergiler/milli_kutup/865/865_37//0470.pdf; and No. 3399, available at http://gazeteler.ankara.edu.tr/dergiler/milli_kutup/865/865_42//0495.pdf (accessed 1 February 2015).

Tasvir, September–October 1945.

Tebi Luys, 1950.

Zartonk, November 1950.

d. Unpublished Sources

Aram Pehlivanyan's autobiographical note written on 22 April 1955 and provided by his daughter Meline Pehlivanyan, Berlin.

The Delegation of the Armenian National Council of America, 'The case of the Armenian People: Memorandum to the United Nations Conference on International Organisation in San Francisco' (New York, 1945).

Kevork Kirkoryan's unpublished research, data provided in 2009.

Programme of World Armenian Congress, 30 April–4 May 1947, Waldorf Astoria Hotel, New York.

Russian archival document on repatriation. Available at hayrenadardz.org/wp-content/uploads/2012/06/1946–04–11.pdf (accessed 17 July 2012).

W. Y.'s email/letter written on 12 May 2007.

e. Published Primary Sources

Açıkgöz, Hayk (Dr), *Bir Anadolulu Ermeni Komünistin Anıları* (Istanbul: Belge Yay., 2006).

Arslanyan, Agop, *Adım Agop Memleketim Tokat* (Istanbul: Aras Yay., 2008).

Azadyan, Toros, *Jamanak: K'aṙasnamea Hishadagaran 1908–1948* (Istanbul: Becid Basımevi, 1948).

——— *Lipananean Husher* (Istanbul: Doğu Basımevi, 1949).

Babigyan, Hagop, *Adanayi Yegheṙně* (Aleppo: Ayk Madenashar–6. Hradaragut'iwn Perio Hayots' Temi, 2009).

Balımyan, Şavarş, *U Yes Gertam* (Istanbul: Aras Yay., 2005).

Bashdonagan Hradaragut'iwn Azkayin Badriark'arani: Adenakrut'iwn Azkayin Ěnthanur Zhoghovo (Istanbul: Ak-Ün Matbaası, 2 December 1950).

Běyoghlui Egeghets'eats' Ew Anonts' Ent'aga Hasdadut'eants Madagararut'ean K'aṙamea Deghegakir 1950–1953 (Istanbul: Dbakrut'iwn Narin, 1954).

Boghossian, Sarkis, *Iconographie Arménienne/2: Catalogue de Reproductions en Noir et en Couleurs de 756 Pièces Originales du XVe au XXe Siècle Suite de la Collection: nos. 704–1365* (Paris: 1998).

Deghegakir Ěnthanur Zhoghovo K'nnich' Hantsnazhoghovi (Istanbul: Foti Basımevi, 1951).

Der Yeghiayan, Zaven, *Badriarkagan Hushers: Vgayakirner Ew Vgayut'iwnner* (Cairo: Nor Asdgh Press, 1947).

Halajian, Kēōrk (T'ap'aragan), *Tebi Gakhaghan* (Boston: Hairenik Publ., 1932).

İhmalyan, Vartan, *Bir Yaşam Öyküsü* (Istanbul: Cem Yayınevi, 1989).

Koçunyan, Ara, *Voğçuyn Amenkin* (Istanbul: Aras Yay., 2008).

Maarif Vekaleti, *Irkçılık Turancılık* (Ankara: Türk Inkılap Tarihi Enstitüsü Yay., Vol. 4, 1944).

Ōrmanyan, Arch, Maghak'ia, *Khōsk 'Ew Khohk': Ir Geank 'in Verchin Shrchanin Měch* (Jerusalem: Dbaran Srpots' Hagopeants' 1929).

Pehlivanyan, Aram, *Özgürlük İki Adım Ötede Değil* (Istanbul: Aras Yay., 1999).

Pehputyan, Santro (ed.), *Vaverakrer Hay Yegeghetsu Badmut'ean: Kevork VI. Gat'oghigos Amenayn Hayots' (1938–1955)*, Kirk' Z. (Yerevan: Osgan Yerevants'i Publ., 1999).

Peştimalcıyan, Hrant (Dr), *Hrabaragayin Niwt'agan Ew Paroyagan Hamaraduut'iwn, 1933–1949* (Istanbul: No publisher, 1961).

TBMM–Gizli Celse Zabıtları 1934, Vol. 4–5, Ankara.

Yeghiayan, Zaven Der, *My Patriarchal Memoirs*, transl. Ared Misirliyan, copyedited and annotated by Vatche Ghazarian (Barrington, 2002).

Zobyan, Bedros, *Tebi Bitlis William Saroyani Hed* (Istanbul: Aras Yay., 2003).

f. Oral History

A. B., 13 March 2013, Munich, in Turkish.
A. K., 20 January 2009, Berlin, in Turkish.
Ara Garmiryan, 3 April 2012, Montreal, in Armenian.
Baghdik Hagopyan, 6 April 2012, Montreal, in Armenian.
Civan Çakır, 8 April 2012, Montreal, in Armenian.
Evdoksi Suciyan Parsehyan, 1–8 April 2012, Montreal, in Armenian.
Hayguhi Çakır, 8 April 2012, Montreal, in Armenian.
K. A., 13 March 2013, Munich, in Turkish.

K. B., 21 January 2009, Berlin, in Turkish.
N. D., 16 September 2012, Istanbul, in Turkish.
Varujan Köseyan, 13 September 2010, Istanbul, in Armenian.

II. Reference Books and Online References

a. Biographies

Aghajanian, Krikor Bedros (Cardinal). Available at encyclopedia.thefreedictionary.com/Krikor + Bedros + Cardinal + Aghajanian (accessed 15 July 2012).
Baban, Cihad. Available at www.timas.com.tr/yazarlar/cihad-baban.aspx?hARF=&list=1 (accessed 12 March 2013).
Biberyan, Zaven. Available at www.arasyayincilik.com/tr/yazarlar/zaven-biberyan/83 (accessed 16 November 2012).
Gobelyan, Yervant. Available at www.arasyayincilik.com/tr/yazarlar/yervant-gobelyan/79 (accessed 25 November 2012).
Koçunyan, Ara. Available at www.arasyayincilik.com/tr/yazarlar/ara-kocunyan/8 (accessed 25 November 2012).
Maşoyan, Rupen. Available at www.arasyayincilik.com/tr/yazarlar/rupen-masoyan/57 (accessed 4 November 2012).
Nureddin, Vala. Available at www.iisg.nl/archives/en/files/n/ARCH02057full.php (accessed 23 June 2012).
Pehlivanyan, Aram. Available at www.arasyayincilik.com/tr/yazarlar/aram-pehlivanyan/10 (accessed 25 November 2012).
Sarper, Selim. Available at www.mfa.gov.tr/sayin_-selim-r_-sarper_in-ozgecmisi.tr.mfa (accessed 24 April 2012).
Zanku, Sarkis Keçyan. Available at www.arasyayincilik.com/tr/yazarlar/s-k-zanku/58 (accessed 25 November 2012).

b. Other Reference Books and Online References

Armenian Pious Foundations. Available at www.istanbulermenivakiflari.org/ (accessed 1 December 2012).
Cemiyetler Kanunu of 26 August 1938. *Resmi Gazete*, 14 July 1938.
Giragosyan, Amalia (ed.), *Hay Barperagan Mamuli Madenakrut'yun (1794–1967)* (Yerevan: 1970), pp. 499–513.
Güzelyan, Hrant, *Bolso Badanegan Dunĕ: Mnats'ortats'i Duntartsi Badmut'iwn Mĕ*, ed. Yervant H. Kasuni. Available at http://tert.nla.am/archive/HAY%20GIRQ/Ardy/2001–2011/patanekan_2007.pdf (accessed 12 February 2015).
Haygagan Sovetagan Hanrakidaran (Armyanskaya sovetskaya entsiklopediya), Vol. 1, 1974, s.v. 'Alik'sanyan'.
International Encyclopedia of Economic Sociology, ed. Jens Beckert and Milan Zafirovski (London, 2004).
Marksist.org. Available at marksist.org/haberler/9274-azinliklara-yonelik-nefret-soylemine-ilk-ceza (accessed 2 February 2013).
Matbuat Umum Müdürlüğü Teşkilâtına ve Vazifelerine Dair Kanun (Publication Law). Available at tbmm.gov.tr/tutanaklar/KANUNLAR_KARARLAR/kanuntbmmc013/kanuntbmmc013/kanuntbmmc01302444.pdf (accessed 8 December 2012).

Nesin Vakfı. Available at www.nesinvakfi.org/aziz_nesin_ayrintili_yasamoykusu. html (accessed 18 June 2012).

Nor Şişli Spor Klübü. Available at www.sabah.com.tr/fotohaber/kultur_sanat/ istanbulun-100-spor-kulubu/39415 (accessed 11 July 2012).

Pir Vakfı. Available at www.pirvakfi.8m.com/sansur.html (accessed 18 June 2012).

Step'anyan, Karnik, *Gensakragan Pararan*, Vol. 1 (Yerevan: Hayasdan Hradaragch'ut'iwn, 1973).

T.C. Dışişleri Bakanlığı (Ministry of Foreign Affairs). Available at rabat.be.mfa.gov. tr/MissionChiefHistory.aspx (accessed 24 April 2012).

Takrir-i Sükun Kanunu. Available at www.resmigazete.gov.tr/arsiv/87.pdf (accessed 15 March 2013).

Tarihtebugün.org. Available at www.tarihtebugun.org/tarihte_bu_sene/1946-senesiyasananlar.html (accessed 18 June 2012).

Treaty of Lausanne. Available at wwi.lib.byu.edu/index.php/Treaty_of_Lausanne (accessed 2 December 2012).

Türk Tarih Kurumu (Turkish Historical Association). Available at www.ttk.gov.tr/ index.php?Page=Sayfa&No=1 (accessed 24 July 2013).

Vakıflar Kanunu of 5 June 1935 (Law of Pious Foundations). Available at www. hukuki.net/kanun/2762.13.text.asp (accessed 25 January 2015).

Vakıflar Kanunu of 14 November 1938 (Law of Pious Foundations). Available at www.resmigazete.gov.tr/arsiv/3959.pdf (accessed 2 December 2012).

Vakıflar Kanunu of 31 May 1949 (Law of Pious Foundations). Available at www. hukuki.net/kanun/2762.13.text.asp (accessed 30 July 2012).

III. Secondary Sources

Akçam, Taner, *From Empire to Republic: Turkish Nationalism and The Armenian Genocide* (London: Zed Books, 2004).

———— *A Shameful Act: The Armenian Genocide and the Question of Turkish Responsibility* (New York: Metropolitan Books, 2006).

Akçam, Taner and Ümit Kurt, *Kanunların Ruhu* (Istanbul: İletişim Yay., 2012).

Alboyadjian, Arshag, *Badmut'iwn Malatio Hayots / History of Armenians in Malatia* (Beirut: Sevan Press, 1961).

Altuğ, Seda, 'Viewing state and society relations in Ottoman-Kurdistan from postOttoman Syria', Calouste Gulbenkian Foundation, Gomdias Institute, and LMU Turkish Studies Lecture Series: The Ottoman Empire and its Eastern Provinces, 9 January 2013.

Andreadis, Yorgos, *Tamama: Pontus'un Yitik Kızı* (Istanbul: Belge Yay., 2012).

Aŕak'el, Badrig, *Hushamadean Sepasdio Ew Kavaŗi Hayutean*, Vol. 1 (Beirut: 1979) and Vol. 2 (New Jersey: Mshag Dbaran, Hradaragut'iwn Sepastahay Verashinadz Miut'ean, 1983).

Arendt, Hannah, *The Origins of Totalitarianism* (New York: Harcourt Brace, 1951).

Artinian, Vartan, *Osmanlı Devleti'nde Ermeni Anayasası'nın Doğuşu* (Istanbul: Aras Yay., 2004).

Arzumanian, Zaven, *Azkabadum*, Vol. 4.i, 1910–30 (New York: St. Vartan's Press, 1995).

Aslan, Şükrü (ed.), *Herkesin Bildiği Sır: Dersim* (Istanbul: İletişim Yay., 2010).

Azadyan, Toros, *Hushamadean Karageōzyan Orpanots'i 1913–1948 (Şişli)* (Istanbul: Becid Basımevi, 1949).

———— *Kevork Ark. Arslanyan (1867–1951)* (Istanbul: Mshaguyt' Hradaragch'agan: Madenashar T'iw 20, 1952).

Bali, Rifat N., 'İkinci Dünya Savaşı yıllarında Türkiye'de azınlıklar: Yirmi Kur'a ihtiyatlar olayı', *Tarih ve Toplum* 179 (1998), pp. 4–18.

———— *Cumhuriyet Yıllarında Türkiye Yahudileri: Bir Türkleştirme Serüveni (1923–1945)* (Istanbul: İletişim Yay., 2005).

———— *Yirmi Kur'a Nafıa Askerleri II. Dünya Savaşında Gayrimüslimlerin* (Istanbul: Kitabevi Yay., 2008).

———— 'Vatandaş Türkçe konuş!' Available at www.rifatbali.com/images/stories/dokumanlar/turkce_konusma_birgun.pdf (accessed 8 December 2012).

Baronian, Marie-Aude, Stephan Besser, and Yolande Jansen (eds), *Diaspora and Memory: Figures of Displacement in Contemporary Literature, Arts and Politicsed* (Amsterdam: Edition Rodopi B.V., 2006).

Barsoumian, Hagop, *The Armenian Amira Class of Istanbul* (Yerevan: American University of Armenia, 2007).

Baumann, Zygmunt, *Modernity and Ambivalence* (Great Britain: Polity Press, 1991).

Berberyan, Avedis, *Badmut'iwn Hayots'* (Istanbul: B. Kirişçiyan Matbaası, 1871).

Bebiroğlu, Murat, 'Cumhuriyet döneminde patrikler ve önemli olaylar'. Available at www.hyetert.com/prnyazi3.asp?s=&Id=442&Sayfa=0&DilId=1&AltYazi (accessed 25 February 2012).

Benlisoy, Foti, Annamaria Aslanoğlu, and Rigas Haris (eds), *İstanbul Rumları: Bugün ve Yarın* (Istanbul: Istos, 2012).

Berksanlar, Kurken, 'Türkiye Ermenileri diaspora mı?' Available at hyetert.blogspot.de/2011/05/turkiye-ermenileri-diaspora-m.html (accessed 15 February 2013).

Beşikçi, İsmail, *Cumhuriyet Halk Fırkası'nın Tüzüğü (1927) ve Kürt Sorunu* (Ankara: Yurt Kitap Yay., 1991).

Bilal, Melissa, and Lerna Ekmekçioğlu, *Bir Adalet Feryadı: Osmanlı'dan Türkiye'ye Beş Ermeni Feminist Yazar 1862–1933* (Istanbul: Aras Yay., 2006).

Björklund, Ulf, 'Armenians of Athens and Istanbul: The Armenian diaspora and the "transnational" nation', *Global Networks* 3 (2003), pp. 337–54.

Bloxham, Donald, 'The roots of American genocide denial: Near Eastern geopolitics and the interwar Armenian question', *Journal of Genocide Research* viii/1 (2006), pp. 27–49.

Boghossian, Sarkis, *Iconographie Arménienne/2: Catalogue de Reproductions en Noir et en Couleurs de 756 Pièces Originales du XVe au XXe Siècle Suite de la Collection: nos. 704–1365* (Paris: 1998).

Bourdieu, Pierre, *Outline of a Theory of Practice* (Cambridge: Cambridge University Press, 1977).

———— *The State Nobility: Elite Schools in the Field of Power*, Transl. Loretta C. Clough (Cambridge–Oxford: Polity Press, 1996).

———— *Practical Reason: On The Theory of Action* (Stanford: Stanford University Press, 1998).

Bourdieu, Pierre and Loïc Wacquant, *An Invitation to Reflexive Sociology* (Chicago: University of Chicago Press, 1992).

Cagaptay, Soner, *Islam, Nationalism and Secularism in Modern Turkey: Who is a Turk?* (London: Routledge, 2006).

Çalışlar, İzettin (ed.), *Dersim Raporu* (Istanbul: İletişim Yay., 2011).

Çetin, Fethiye, *Anneannem* (Istanbul: Metis Yay., 2004).

Çetin, Fethiye, and Ayşegül Altınay, *Torunlar* (Istanbul: Metis Yay., 2009).

266 THE ARMENIANS IN MODERN TURKEY

Corley, Felix, 'The Armenian Church under the Soviet regime, part 1: Leadership of Kevork', *Religion, State and Society* xxiv/1 (1996), pp. 9–53.

—— 'The Armenian Apostolic Church', in Lucian N. Leustean (ed.), *Eastern Christianity and the Cold War, 1945–91* (Abingdon, Oxon: Routledge, 2010), pp. 189–203.

Dabag, Mihran, Martin Sökefeld and Matthias Morgenstern, *Diaspora und Kulturwissenschaften* (Leipzig: Gustav-Aldolf-Werk Verlag, 2011).

Derderian, Katharine, 'Common fate, different experience: Gender-specific aspects of the Armenian Genocide, 1915–1917', *Holocaust and Genocide Studies* xix/1 (2005), pp. 1–25.

Doğan, Yalçın, *Savrulanlar Dersim 1937–1938 Hatta 1939* (Istanbul: Kırmızıkedi Yay., 2012).

Dost, Pınar, 'Amerika'nın Türkiye politikasının oluşumu üzerine yeni bir okuma', *Tarih ve Toplum Yeni Yaklaşımlar* 13 (2011), pp. 177–98.

Dündar, Fuat, *İttihat ve Terakki'nin Etnisite Mühendisliği 1913–1918* (Istanbul: İletişim Yay., 2008).

Ermakoff, Ivan, 'Rational choice may take over', in Philip S. Gorski (ed.), *Bourdieu and Historical Analysis* (Durham: Duke University Press, 2013).

Ersanlı, Büşra, *İktidar ve Tarih: Türkiye'de 'Resmi Tarih' Tezinin Oluşumu (1929–1937)* (Istanbul: İletişim Yay., 2011).

Ertani, Emre, 'Dikkat "Türk Müdür" konuşuyor', *Agos*, 20 July 2012, No. 849.

Eski, Beril, 'Mit raporu Dink, Zirve ve Santoro Cinayetleri Çözülebilir', *Agos*, 1 February 2013. Available at www.agos.com.tr/yazdir.php?detay=4218 (accessed 15 February 2013).

Fındık, Özgür, *Kara Vagon: Dersim–Kırım ve Sürgün* (Istanbul: Fam Yay., 2012).

Foucault, Michel, *Discipline and Punish: The Birth of the Prison*, transl. Alan Sheridan (New York: Vintage Books, 1995).

Friese, Heidrun, 'The Silence-voice-representation', in Robert Fine and Charles Turner (eds), *Social Theory After the Holocaust* (Oxford: Liverpool University Press, 2000), pp. 159–78.

Garabetyan, Bedros, *Hnktarean Hishadagaran Samat'io Surp Kēōrk Yegeghets'o 1461–1935* (Istanbul: Terzyan Kardeşler Matbaası / Yeni Türkiye Basımevi, 1935).

Ghazarian, Haygazn, *Badmakirk' Chmshgadzak'i* (Beirut: Hamazkayin Publ., 1971).

Gök, Salhadin, 'Tek Parti iktidarında basın muhalefeti: Millet Dergisi örneği', *A.Ü. Türkiyat Araş tırmaları Enstitüsü Dergisi* 41 (2009). Available at e-dergi.atauni. edu.tr/index.php/taed/article/viewFile/2248/2249 (accessed 24 June 2012).

Gündoğdu, Cihangir and Vural Genç, *Dersim'de Osmanlı Siyaseti: İzâle-i Vahşet, Tahsis-i İtikât, Tasfiye-i Ezhân 1880–1913* (Istanbul: Kitap Yay., 2013).

Güven, Dilek, *Cumhuriyet Dönemi Azınlık Politikaları ve Stratejileri Bağlamında 6–7 Eylül Olayları* (Istanbul: Tarih Vakfı Yurt Yay., 2005).

—— *Nationalismus und Minderheiten: Die Ausschreitungen gegen di Christen und Juden der Türkei vom September 1955* (Munich: Oldenbourg Verlag, 2012).

Hagan, John and Wenona Raymond-Richmond, 'The collective synamics of racial dehumanization and genocidal victimization in Darfur', *American Sociological Review* 73 (2008), pp. 875–902. Available at http://faculty.washington.edu/matsueda/courses/587/readings/Hagan%20Rymond-Richmond.pdf (accessed 16 February 2015).

Hagopian, Hovag, *Badmut'iwn Baghnadan* (Boston: Hayrenik Publ., 1966).

Haig, Vahe, *Kharpert Ew Anor Osgeghen Tashdĕ* (New York: Kharpert Armenian Patriotic Union, 1959).

Hatemi, Kezban and Dilek Kurban, *Bir Yabancılaştırma Hikayesi: Türkiye'deki Gayrimüslim Azınlığın Vakıf ve Mülkiyet Sorunları* (Istanbul: TESEV, 2009).

Hür, Ayşe, 'Cumhuriyetin amele taburları: Yirmi Kura ihtiyatlar'. Available at derinsular.com/cumhuriyetin-amele-taburlari-yirmi-kura-ihtiyatlar-ayse-hur/ (accessed 20 October 2012).

———— 'Avar, ne olur kızımı götürme...' Available at http://arsiv.taraf.com.tr/ yazilar/ayse-hur/avar-ne-olur-kizimi-goturme/7767/ (accessed 24 February 2015).

———— 'Nihal Atsız, Reha Oğuz Türkkan ve Turancılar Davası'. Available at www.radikal.com.tr/Radikal.aspx?aType=RadikalYazar&ArticleID=1120725&Yazar=AYSE-HUR&CategoryID=97 (accessed 15 February 2013).

İnsel, Ahmet (et al.), *Modern Türkiye'de Siyasi Düşünce: Kemalizm*, Vol. 2. (Istanbul: İletişim Yay. 2001).

İskit, Server R., *Türkiyede Matbuat İdareleri ve Politikaları* (Başvekalet Basın ve Yayın Umum Müdürlüğü Yayınlarından, 1943).

———— *Türkiyede Neşriyat Hareketleri Tarihine Bakış* (Ankara: Milli Eğitim Basımevi, 2000).

Kaiser, Hilmar, 'From Empire to Republic: The continuities of Turkish denial', *Armenian Review* 48 (2003), pp. 1–24.

Kemal, Yaşar and Alain Bosquet, *Yaşar Kemal Kendini Anlatıyor* (Istanbul: Toros Yay., 1993).

Keşmer, Emin, *Bir Poşet İstanbul Toprağı* (Istanbul: Siyah Beyaz, 2012).

Kevorkian, Raymond H., *The Armenian Genocide: A Complete History* (London: I.B. Tauris, 2011).

———— *1915 Öncesinde Osmanlı İmparatorluğu'nda Ermeniler* (Istanbul: Aras Yay., 2012).

Kieser, Hans-Lukas, *Der Verpasste Friede: Mission, Ethnie und Staat in den Ostprovinzen der Türkei 1839–1938* (Zürich: Chronos Verlag, 2000); Turkish transl. Atilla Dirim, *Iskalanmış Barış: Doğu Vilayetleri'nde Misyonerlik, Etnik Kimlik ve Devlet 1839–1938* (Istanbul: İletişim Yay., 2005).

Kılıç, Sezen, 'Cumhuriyet döneminde yabancı okullar'. Available at atam.gov.tr/ cumhuriyet-doneminde-yabanci-okullar-1923–1938/ (accessed 2 February 2013).

Kırlı, Biray Kolluoğlu, 'Forgetting the Smyrna fire', *History Workshop Journal* lx/1 (2005), pp. 25–44.

Klein, Janet, *The Margins of Empire: Kurdish Militias in the Ottoman Tribal Zone?* (Stanford: Stanford University Press, 2011).

Koçak, Cemil, *Umumi Müfettişlikler (1927–1952)* (Istanbul: İletişim Yay., 2003).

———— *Türkiye'de İki Partili Siyasi Sistemin Kuruluş Yılları: İkinci Parti* (Istanbul: İletişim Yay., 2010).

———— 'Ayın karanlık yüzü', *Star*, 20 August 2011. Available at www.stargazete.com/yazar/cemil-kocak/ayin-karanlik-yuzu-haber-375966.htm (accessed 20 August 2012) and *Tarih ve Toplum Yeni Yaklaşımlar* 1 (2005), pp. 147–208.

Köker, Osman, 'Sivas Ermenileri bin varmış bir yokmuş', 4 July 2009. Available at bianet.org/bianet/biamag/115648-sivas-ermenileri-bin-varmis-bir-yokmus (accessed 5 October 2011).

Köseyan, Varujan, *Hushamadean Surp P'rgich 'Hiwanatanots 'i- Surp Pırgiç Hastanesi Tarihçesi* (Istanbul: 1994).

Macar, Elçin, *Cumhuriyet Döneminde İstanbul Rum Patrikhanesi* (Istanbul: İletişim Yay., 2003).

—— 'Başbakanlık cumhuriyet arşivi belgelerine göre Tek Parti döneminde cemaat vakıflarının sorunları'. Available at www.bolsohays.com/yazarmakale-73/anonim-tek-parti-doneminde-cemaat-vakiflarinin-sorunlari.html (accessed 15 August 2012).

Maksudyan, Nazan, *Türklüğü Ölçmek: Bilimkurgusal Antropoloji ve Türk Milliyetçiliğinin Irkçı Çehresi* (Istanbul: Metis Yay., 2005).

Mardin, Şerif, 'Center-periphery relations: A key to Turkish politics?', in Engin Akarlı and Gabriel Ben-Dior (eds), *Political Participation in Turkey: Historical Background and Present Problems* (Istanbul: Bogazici University Press, 1975), pp. 7–32 and *Daedalus* cii/1 (1973), pp. 169–90.

—— *Religion and the Social Change in the Modern Turkey: The Case of Bediüzzaman Said Nursi* (Albany: State University of New York Press, 1989).

Margosyan, Mıgırdiç, *Tespih Taneleri* (Istanbul: Aras Yayıncılık, 2008).

Matiossian, Vartan, 'İstanbul diyaspora mıdır değil midir'. Available at azadalik.wordpress.com/2011/07/05/istanbul-diyaspora-midir-degil-midir/ (accessed 8 May 2011).

Melkonyan, Edward, 'Stalini ashkharakragan ngrdumnerĕ ew Hayeru hayrenatarts 'utiwunē 1946–48', in *1946–1948 Hayrenatarts 'utiwunē ew tra taserē: Hayrenatarts'utyan himnakhntirn aysōr. Hamahaygagan Kidazhōghōvneri Zegutsumneri Zhōghōvadzu* (2008). Available at hayrenadardz.org/eduard-melkonyan.html (accessed 15 July 2012).

Melqumyan, Armen, 'Turkagan ishkanut'yunneri k'agahak 'aganutyunĕ ew Bolsahay hamaynkĕ 1945–1947 T'T''', in S. Krikoryan et al. (eds), *Mertsavor Arevelk (VII): Badmut'yun, K'aghak'aganutyun, Mshaguyt': Hotvadzneri Joghovadzu*, RA National Academy of Sciences, Institute of Near and Middle Eastern Studies (Arevelakidutyun) (Yerevan: Lusagn Publ., 2011).

Mıntzuri, Hagop, *Istanbul Anıları*, transl. Silva Kuyumciyan (Istanbul: Tarih Vakfı Yurt Yay., 1993).

Miroğlu, Armaveni, 'Pangaltı Ermeni Mezarlığı: Surp Hagop Mezarlığı'. Available at www.hyetert.com/yazi3.asp?Id=323&DilId=1 (accessed 30 November 2012).

—— 'G. Bolsoy Azkayin Khnamadarutiwnĕ', *Handes Amsorya* 124 (2010), pp. 423–34.

Muradoğlu, Abdullah, 'Atatürk'ten Arapça radyo gazetesi', *Yarın Dergisi*. Available at yarin1ist.tripod.com/mayis/34.htm (accessed 24 April 2012).

Neyzi, Leyla, *Amele Taburu: The Military Journal of a Jewish Soldier During the War of Independence* (Istanbul: Isis Yay., 2005).

Ökten, Ali İhsan, 'Savaşın gölgesinde Hatay'da hekimlik ve sorunları'. Available at www.hekimedya.org/index.php/yazarlar/dr-ali-ihsan-okten/465-savan-goelgesinde-hatayda-hekimlik-ve-sorunlar.html (accessed 31 January 2015).

Pamukciyan, Kevork, *Ermeni Kaynaklarından Tarihe Katkılar IV: Biyografileriyle Ermeniler,* ed. by Osman Köker (Istanbul: Aras Yay., 2003).

Papkēn, Giwlēsēryan, *Badmut'iwn Giligio Gat'oghigosats'* (Antelias: Dbaran Gatoghigosut'ean Hayots' Medzi Dann Giligio, 1990).

P'oladian, Antranig L., *Badmut'iwn Hayots' Arapgiri* (New York: Hradaragut'iwn Amerigayi Arapgiri Miut'ean, 1969).

Quataert, Donald, *The Ottoman Empire 1700–1922* (New York: Cambridge University Press, 2005).

Rogan, Eugene L., 'Aşiret mektebi: Abdülhamid II's school for tribes (1892–1907)', International Journal of Middle East Studies, xxviii/1 (1996), pp. 83–107.

Sahagian, Aram, Tiwts'aznagan Urfan yev ir Hayortinerě (Beirut: Dbaran Atlas, 1955).

Sakayan, Dora (ed.), Smyrna 1922: Das Tagebuch Des Garabed Hatscherian (Klagenfurt: Kitab-Veri, 2006).

Salzmann, Ariel, Modern Devleti Yeniden Düşünmek: Osmanlı Ancien Regime'i (Tocqueville in the Ottoman Empire: Rival Paths to the Modern State), transl. Ayşe Özdemir (Istanbul: İletişim Yay., 2011).

Sarafian, A. Kevork, Armenian History of Aintab/ Badmut'iwn Antebi Hayots (Los Angeles–CA: Union of Armenians of Aintab in America, 1953).

Sarafian, Ara, 'The absorption of Armenian women and children into Muslim households as a structural component of the Armenian Genocide', in Omer Bartov and Phyllis Mack (eds), In God's Name: Genocide and Religion in the Twentieth Century (New York: Berghahn Books, 2001).

Sarukhanyan, Vahe, 'Istanbul Armenians: Diaspora's "outsiders".' Available at hetq. am/eng/articles/953/ (accessed 15 February 2013).

Sasuni, Garo, Badmut'iwn Daroni Ashkharhi (Beirut: Dbaran Sevan, 1956).

Sayadyan, Liana, 'New book sheds light on 1933 murder of Archbishop Tourian and Church split'. Available at old.hetq.am/en/culture/terry-phillips-2/ (accessed 18 March 2013).

Şengül, Hüseyin, 'Sanasaryan Han: Gaspın ve zulmün dikilitaşı', 28 January 2012. Available at www.bianet.org/biamag/azinliklar/135782-sanasaryan-han-gaspin-ve-zulmun-dikilitasi (accessed 30 November 2012).

Siserian, Misak', Badmut'iwn Zeytuni (1409–1921) (Beirut: No publisher, 1996).

Steinmetz, George, 'Bourdieu, History and Historical Sociology', Cultural Sociology v/1 (2011), pp. 45–66.

Stone, Dan, 'Holocaust testimony and the challenge to the philosophy of history', in Robert Fine and Charles Turner (eds), Social Theory After the Holocaust (Oxford: Liverpool University Press, 2000).

Suciyan, Talin, 'Dündar: İttihat ve Terakki Anadolu'da sistematik etnisite mühendisliği yaptı', interview with Fuat Dündar, Agos, 6 April 2007, No. 575.

———— 'Diaspora kim', Taraf, 20 October 2009.

———— 'Tachjian: Her üç aileden birinde böyle bir olay yaşanmış olmalı', interview with Vahé Tachjian, Agos, 4 June 2010, No. 740.

———— 'Baron Varujan İstanbul Ermenilerinin tarihini kurtardı', Agos, 29 April 2011, No. 786.

———— 'Armenian representation in Turkey', Armenian Weekly, Special Issue, April 2012, pp. 41–5. Available at www.armenianweekly.com/2012/06/12/suciyan-armenian-representation-in-turkey/ (accessed 15 February 2013).

———— 'Bir Cumhuriyet açmazı: Ermeni karşıtlığı ortamında Ermeni temsiliyeti', Toplumsal Tarih 224 (2012), pp. 76–9.

———— 'Dört nesil: Kurtarılamayan son', Toplum Bilim 132 (2015), pp. 132–49.

Tachjian, Vahé, La France en Cilicie et en Haute-Mesopotamie: Aux Confins de la Turquie, de la Syrie et de l'Irak (1919–1933) (Paris: Edition Karthala, 2004).

———— '"Repatriation": A new chapter, studded with new obstacles, in the history of AGBU's cooperation in Soviet Armenia', in Raymond H. Kevorkian and Vahé Tachjian (eds), The Armenian General Benevolent Union: A Hundred Years of History (1906–2006), Vol. 2 (1941–2006), pp. 291–309.

——— 'Gender, nationalism, exclusion: The reintegration process of female survivors of the Armenian Genocide', *Nations and Nationalisms* xv/1 (2009), pp. 60–80.

——— 'An attempt to recover Armenian properties in Turkey through the French authorities in Syria and Lebanon in the 1920s', unpublished article.

Tachjian, Vahé and Raymond H. Kévorkian, 'Reconstructing the nation with women and children kidnapped during the genocide', transl. Marjorie R. Appel, *Ararat* xlv/185 (2006), pp. 5–14.

Tekin, Gülçiçek Günel, *Kara Kefen: Müslümanlaştırılan Ermeni Kadınların Dramı* (Istanbul: Belge Yay., 2011).

Thomassian, Levon, *Summer of '42: A Study of German–Armenian Relations during the Second World War* (Aiglen, Pa.: Schiffer Publ., 2012).

Toker, Metin, *Tek Partiden Çok Partiye* (Istanbul: Milliyet Yay., 1970).

Tölölyan, Khatchig, 'Elites and institutions in the Armenian transnation', *Diaspora* 9 (2000), pp. 107–36.

Tör, Vedat Nedim, *Yıllar Böyle Geçti* (Istanbul: Milliyet Yay., 1976).

Tosun, Funda, 'Bir canavarmışım gibi subaylar beni görmeye geliyordu', interview with Garabet Demircioğlu, *Agos*, 20 May 2011, No. 789.

Türköne, Mümtazer and Tuncay Önder, *Şerif Mardin: Türkiye'de Toplum ve Siyaset Makaleler 1* (Istanbul: İletişim Yay., 1990).

Ueno, Masayuki, 'For the Fatherland and the State: Armenians negotiate the Tanzimat Reforms', *International Journal of Middle East Studies* 45 (2013), pp. 93–109.

Unbehaun, Horst, 'Sivas vilayetinde basının doğuşu'. Available at www.tubar.com. tr/TUBAR%20DOSYA/pdf/2001GUZ/1.1svas%20vlayetnde%20basinin% 20douu.pdf (accessed 7 July 2012).

Üngör, Uğur Ümit and Mehmet Polatel, *Confiscation and Destruction: The Young Turk Seizure of Armenian Property* (London: Continuum International Publ., 2011).

Üstel, Füsun, *İmparatorluktan Ulus-devlete Türk Milliyetçiliği: Türk Ocakları (1912–1931)* (Istanbul: İletişim Yay., 1997).

Vat'sunameag (1866–1926) Kalfayan Aghchgnats' Orpanots' Khaskiwghi (G. Bolis: Dbakrut'iwn H.M. Setyan, no date).

Wacquant, Loïc, 'Habitus', in Jens Beckert and Milan Zafirovski (eds), *International Encyclopedia of Economic Sociology* (London: Routledge, 2004), pp. 315–19.

Yarman, Arsen (ed.), *Sivas 1877: Boğos Natanyan* (Istanbul: Birzamanlar Yay., 2008).

Yazıcı, Nesimi, 'Sırrı Paşa ve Vilayet gazeteleri', Available at dergiler.ankara.edu.tr/ dergiler/37/781/10025.pdf (accessed 7 July 2012).

Yeghiayan, Puzant, *Jamanagagits Badmut'iwn Gat'oghigosut'ean Hayots' Giligyo 1914–1972* (Antilias: Dbaran Gat'oghigosut'ean Hayots' Medzi Dann Giligio, 1975).

Yıldız, Özgür, 'The history of Halkalı School of Agriculture', *International Journal of Social Science* v/4 (2012), pp. 293–306. Available in Turkish at www.jasstudies. com/Makaleler/11260937_yıldız_özgür_mTT.pdf.

Yılmaz, Mustafa, 'Cumhuriyet döneminde Bakanlar Kurulu kararı ile yasaklanan yayınlar 1923–45', *Kebikeç* iii/6 (1998), pp. 53–80. Available at www.ait. hacettepe.edu.tr/akademik/arsiv/ysk.htm#_ftn211 (accessed 20 April 2012).

Yılmaz, Mustafa and Yasemin Doğaner, '1961–63 yılları arasında Bakanlar Kurulu kararı ile yasaklanan yayınlar', *Atatürk Yolu* 19 (2006), pp. 247–99.

——— 'Demokrat Parti döneminde Bakanlar Kurulu ile yasaklanan yayınlar', *Kebikeç* 22 (2006), pp. 151–204.

Zarakol, Ayşe, *Yenilgiden Sonra Doğu Batı ile Yaşamayı Nasıl Öğrendi* (Istanbul, Koç Üniv. Yay., 2012).

Zohrab, Krikor, 'Pnagch'ut'iwn', *Krikor Zohrab Yergeri Zhoghovadzu*, ed. Alperd Sharuryan, Vol. 3, pp. 519–23.

Zürcher, Erik-Jan, 'The Ottoman legacy of the Turkish Republic: An attempt at a new periodization', *Die Welt des Islams* 32 (1992), pp. 237–53.

———— *Turkey: A Modern History* (London: I.B.Tauris, 2004).

———— *The Young Turk Legacy and Nation Building: From Ottoman Empire to Atatürk's Turkey* (London: I.B. Tauris, 2010).

INDEX